ROOF OF THE AMERICAS

From Alaska to Cape Horn

JOHN WARBURTON-LEE

Foreword by
H.R.H. The Prince of Wales

SWAN·HILL
PRESS

To Louie, with all my love

Copyright © 1996 John Warburton-Lee

First published in the UK in 1996
by Swan Hill Press, an imprint of Airlife Publishing Ltd

Distributed in the USA by Stackpole Books,
5067 Ritter Road, Mechanicsburg, MA 17055-6921

British Library Cataloguing in Publication Data
   A catalogue record for this book
   is available from the British Library

ISBN 1 85310 522 8

Typeset by Hewer Text Composition Services, Edinburgh
Printed in Italy.

Swan Hill Press

an imprint of Airlife Publishing Ltd
101 Longden Road, Shrewsbury, SY3 9EB, England

Acknowledgements

There are a great many individuals and organisations who contributed to the mounting and success of this expedition. First amongst these are those individuals in the Army, the Household Division and the Welsh Guards who believed in and supported the project throughout its difficult formative months and in the face of some daunting political and financial odds. I am particularly grateful to HRH The Prince of Wales for accepting the mantle of Patron and supporting us so enthusiastically and to the expeditions's two Honorary Directors, Major-General Sir Robert Corbett and Major-General Iain Mackay-Dick, whose strong and unswerving assistance kept the expedition on track.

Secondly I would like to extend the heartfelt gratitude of the team to the governments of the United States of America, Canada, Mexico, Guatemala, Honduras, El Salvador, Nicaragua, Costa Rica, Panama, Guyana, Ecuador, Peru, Bolivia, Argentina and Chile for allowing us to visit their countries and derive the tremendous benefits from exploring, adventuring and observing in such fantastic and diverse environments. At the same time I am grateful to the British Government for sanctioning each individual element of this expedition and in particular to the many desk officers at the Foreign and Commonwealth Office, together with their counterparts in the Embassies and High Commissions of all the countries that we travelled through without whose perseverance, understanding and positive approach much of our journey could all too easily have been condemned as too politically sensitive.

Thirdly, again on behalf of the team, I would like to thank all of our sponsors for their extremely generous support: British American Tobacco; Headquarters Land Command; the Dulverton Trust; The Hedley Foundation; The Trustees of the Household Division; The Gosling Foundation; JP Morgan Trust; Torco Europe; Ambrose, Appelbe & Pyke Solicitors; Dunhill Medical Trust; Maersk Company; The trustees of The Household Cavalry, Grenadier Guards, Coldstream Guards, Scots Guards, Irish Guards, Welsh Guards, Royal Electrical and Mechanical Engineers; Royal Army Medical Corps, Adjutant General's Corps; Miss M Pilcher; Peter Moores Foundation; the Joint Service Expedition Trust; Gough Charitable Trust; Prince of Wales Charities Trust; Stoneham Langton and Passmore; Severn Trent Plc; Sun Alliance Group; Arthur Anderson & Co Foundation; John Holman & Sons; Joe's Basement; Mrs A Fetherstonhaugh; Firbank Charity Trust; Saffery Champness; Mark Cannon Brookes; Roger Sant; The AES Foundation; Goldman Sachs & Co; Vandervell Foundation; LASMO Plc; Brixton Estate Charitable Trust; Edinburgh Fund Managers; EM Lloyd Charitable Trust; JA Pye's Charitable Settlement; Jonathon Dunlop; PW Ockleston; Cape Plc; Cumnock & Doon Valley District Council; NM Rothschild & Sons Ltd; HDH Wills Charitable Trust; Drapers Charitable Trust; WNM Lawrence; Proform Technology Ltd; Sertec; The Upper Hand Ltd; The Coldstream Guards Association; Laurence Keen Ltd; Western Estates; Robert Fleming Holdings; The Cray Trust; The Hon Mrs Sarah Mason; Adrian Swire Charitable Trust; The Duke of Marlborough; TORCO International; Perseverance Mills; The Park Lane Hotel; Tiffanys; Mentzendorff; Carringtons; Shrewsbury Optometry; Ciba Vision UK Ltd; Sir Charles Pickthorn; Wyeth Laboratories; Napp Laboratories; Norbrook Laboratories; Nellcor; Pfizer Limited; Bayer plc; Lilly Industries; Parke-Davis Veterinary Division; Lederle Laboratories; Rhône Poulenc Rorer Ltd.

In addition to the above I would like to thank both personally and on behalf of the team the many other individuals and organisations who gave their time, assistance, products and services so generously and who played every bit as vital a role in getting the project off the ground, each of the six teams to their start point on time with the correct equipment and helped each phase continue to a successful and safe conclusion. In particular:

In Britain:

Military: General Sir Charles Guthrie; Admiral Sir Benjamin Bathurst; Brigadier Reddy Watt; Lieutenant-Colonel Charles Stephens; Lieutenant-Colonel Huw Phillips, Headquarters Land Command; Lieutenant-Colonel John Regan, Mrs Shirley Fox and the staff of No 4 Sub-Depot Thatcham; Wing Commander Ted Vary, Ministry of Defence; Major Tony Bradborn and the Staff of the Guards Adventure Training Wing, Fremington; Brigadier Kim Ross, Brigadier Richard Heywood, Colonel Gerald Lesinski, Colonel Tom Fitzalan Howard, Colonel Jonathon Trelawny, Lieutenant-Colonel Terry Macaree, Major Lance Brett and Nigel Jolly at Headquarters Household Division; Colonel Frank Essen, Lieutenant-Colonel John Wyatt, Lieutenant-Colonel Barney Rolfe Smith, Major Stuart Hepton and Mrs Kathy Davenport at the Directorate of Army Training; Colonel World, Royal Army Medical College; Colonel David Farrant, Defence Attaché Brasilia; Colonel Terry Glenn, Defence Attaché, Panama; Brigadier Andrew Parker Bowles, Royal Army Veterinary Corps; John Wells, Army Staff Duties 3; Paul Welch, Peter Stanforth, and Adrian Wootton, Directorate of Supply Management; Charlie Lowndes, British Forces Broadcasting Service; Ben Hughes, Peter Evans and Heather Warren, Central Services Establishment; Central Services Graphics; Central Services Photography; the Defence Clothing and Textile Agency; Directorate of Medical Supplies; Major Brian Moore and Major James McIntosh, Directorate of Service Food Management; Engineer Resources, Long Marston; Andy Faulkener, HMS *Sultan*; Tina Jenkins, Infantry Film and Television Department; the Infantry Trials and Development Unit; Map and Air Chart Depot, Guildford; Mrs A Eldridge, Military Survey; WO1 Hamilton and the staff of Printing Section, BOD Donnington; Ration Supply Depot, RLC Aldershot; Derek Davies, Reprographic Section, MOD; Brian Calderick, Reprographic Section, School of Infantry; Alan Rogers and Norman Webber, Royal Naval Victualling Depot Burnetts Lane; WO1 Starbuck, School of Military Survey; Lieutenant-Colonel Andrew Fisher, Nigel Gaspar, Dr Richard Scott,

Victor Puddick and Neil Wilson, Science and Technology Division, Defence Clothing and Textiles Agency; Joan Cranston, Services Sound and Vision Corporation; Julie Jones, Technical Equipments Division, Base Ordnance Depot Donnington; Terry Dove, Union Jack Club; Yeoman Warder Patrick Nolan; and the equipment managers at Headquarters Quartermaster-General, Corrinne Allen, Len White, Ben Burnip, Andrew Howson, Liz Clift, Martyn Howard, Paul Tanswell, Julie Wyatt, David Greenwood, Richard Sheppard, John Sheen and Susan Ashby.

Civilian Agencies: The Earl of Clarendon; Sir Michael Craig-Cooper; Kenneth Rose; Christine Adlam, Automobile Association; Camping and Outdoor Leisure Association; Colonel John Blashford Snell, Discovery Expeditions; Charles Thompson, Folio Productions; Greg Forte and Andy Keeler, Joe's Basement; London Flight Centre; Peter Laidlaw, NGFK Limited; Ian Benfield, Portishead Radio; Jamie Robertson McLeod, David Taylor Smith and Lindsey Boswell, Raleigh International; Michael Holden, Advanced Textile Concepts; David Findlay and Alan Mawer, Automotive Technik; Reg Gill, EP Barrus; David Stevens, Cotswold Camping Limited; Chris Burrows, Eurocraft (GB) Limited; Brian Fox, Foxy's Suede Leather and Fur Cleaning; Jeff Ingarfield, Glenn Freight Services; Richard Chambers, Lyon Equipment; Aron Newton and Tina Revsbach, Maersk; Dorothy Watts, Mercantile (GB) Limited; Ralph Wilding, MGH Limited; Nick Davis, ML Lifeguard; National Map Centre; Clive Painter, Ni-tech Limited; Steve Laycock, Perseverance Mills Limited; Les Baynham, Printique; Louise Wigley, Quality Embroidery Designs; Rab Carrington, RAB Down Equipment; Hazel Murphy, Remploy Limited; Ralph Hepple, RH Positive; Jane Davies and Amba Hall, Sloane Hospital Travel; Richard Johnson, SMC Mountaineering; Roger Daynes and Richard Olivier, Snowsled Limited; Tom Greenley, TG Supplies; Nick Lewin, Steve Clark and Tom Perry, TORCO Europe; Zenith Data Systems; Lyn and Bruce Hall; Rick Jones and Peter Orange, Randy International (UK) Ltd.

In Alaska:

Military contacts: General Jo Ralston, Commander Alaska Command; General Hugh Cox, Adjutant,

General, Department of Military and Veteran's Affairs; Brigadier-General KM Taylor, Commander Alaska Air National Guard; the United States 11th Airforce; the 6th US Infantry Division Arctic Light; 1st and 3rd Eskimo Scout Battalions, 207th Infantry Group; Wing Commander & Mrs Phil Ledbetter RAF, Major John Stocker, US Alaska Command; the crews of the US 11th Airforce, Alaska Air National Guard and Alaska Army National Guard aircraft who flew us and our supplies to the distant outposts of the state; Colonel & Mrs John Goodman, Lieutenant-Colonel & Mrs Bo Austin, Lieutenant-Colonel Craig Christensen, Major & Mrs Steve Dewan, Captain & Mrs Lee Owen, First Sergeant Ray Calver, Captain Mike Haller, Captain Jeff Johnson, Staff Sergeant Leslie Richard, Sergeant Gazzaway and Nick Buchta of the Alaska Army National Guard in Anchorage; Lieutenant-Colonel Bethel, Sergeant Mike Kershaw, US 6th Infantry Division; Bill Strauss, Tom Skala and Sergeant Brodie, US Northern Warfare Training Centre; the staff of Elmendorff Military Hospital; LD Fleschman, Fort Richardson Range control; Steve Jacobs, 11th Air Force logistics; Staff Sergeant Dave Proehl; the staff of the Combined Support Maintenance Unit; the staff of the Alaska Army National Guard workshops, Fort Richardson.

Civilian contacts: the Department of Natural Resources; the Bureau of Land Management; the Fish & Wildlife Service; National Parks; Roy & Lesley Monk, Joe Reddington Snr, John Gourley and Duane Lambert for the use of their huskies; Dr Jim Leach; Brian Okonek, Alaska-Denali Guiding Services; Dennis Mitchell, Mitchell Customs Brokerage, Anchorage; Inspector Jewitt, United States Customs Service, Anchorage; Rick Fremling and Richard Dale, United States Postal Service; Mike Dellabonna, Alaska Commercial Company, Barrow; Gus & Geri Gillespie, Alaska Fur Exchange, Anchorage; Tim Sonnentag, Animal Food Warehouse, Wasilla; Apocalypse Design, Fairbanks; Jim Day, Arctic Recreational Distributors, Anchorage; Jim Okonek, K2 Aviation; Keith Poppert, Kema Sleds, Wasilla; Patricia Rae, Rae's Harness Shop, Anchorage; John Norris, Underdog Feed, Wasilla; the Civil Air Patrol; Randal Le May, Torco Alaska; Dee Dee Jonrowe; Linda and Trevor at Schapachka Kennel.

On the trail: The Nana, Doyon, Bering Straits and Arctic Slope Native Corporations; the communities of Nenana, Manley, Tanana, Ruby, Nulato, Kaltag, Unalakleet, Shaktoolik, Koyuk, Elim, White Mountain, Nome, Teller, Cape Prince of Wales, Shishmaref, Deering, Kotzebue, Kivalina, Point Hope, Cape Lisburne, Point Lay, Wainwright and Barrow. In particular Gopher Lord and the Senior Citizens Club, Nenana; Art Mortvedt, Steve and the Manley Roadhouse, Manley; Freddie Jordan and family, Stan Zurray, Charlie Campbell, Bill White, Tommy Krisca, Cynthia and Dale Erikson in Tanana; Emmett and Edna Peters in Ruby; Dave Colson and the staff of USAF Galena; Albert Nickoli in Nulato; Bill Solomon and Adolf McGinty in Kaltag; Ivanoff Walter Unalakleet in Unalakleet; Mike Sookiak and Saul, the Public Safety Officer in Shaktoolik; Zeke MacDonald and the ladies of Koyuk; Robert Charles in White Mountain; Major Dusty and Yvonne Finlay, Sergeant-Major John Bahnke, Sergeant Toby Reich and the men of 1st Eskimo Scout Battalion in Nome; Vernon Kugzrak and Henry Ollanna in Teller; Roy Sockpick in Shishmaref; Martin Karmen, Erik Karmen and the school at Deering; Sergeant Lonewolf, Sergeant Lem Savok, ex Regimental Sergeant-Major Wilfrid Lane in Kotzebue; Conrad Koenig in Kivalina; Warren Nashookpuk in Point Hope; Myran Bracken and the staff at Cape Lisburne Radar Station; Al Gore and the staff at Point Lay Radar site; the members of Wainwright Search and Rescue Team; Mayor George Ahmoagak, Jim Christensen, Jim and Mitsuko Wood, Frank Bozanich and Chuck Caldwell in Barrow.

The Lower 48: Lieutenant-Colonel The Lord Crofton, Major Nigel Holland and the Staff of the British Embassy Washington; Major Tandy Carter at the Office of the Secretary of Defense; The Nevada National Guard, Las Vegas; CW3 Johnny Lopez; Dick McCallum and the staff of Expeditions Incorporated, Flagstaff, Arizona; Joe Cocquyt, Eagle Products Incorporated, Indiana; Jennifer Gombas, Mountain Safety Research, Seattle; Rob Lancaster, TORCO International Corporation; Vincent Dichirico UFP Technologies, Maine; Pat Young, Young's Trailers, Texas.

Central America: Colonel Steve Daniel, Mexico City; Colonel John and Hazel Dobson, Guatemala City; the Escolar Militar, San Salvador; Simon Hart, First Secretary British Embassy, Panama City; Dr

Velasquez, La Chorerra; Paul Kay and Charles Langman of Associated Steamships, Panama.

Guyana: Mr David Johnson, British High Commissioner, Bob Webb and the staff of the British High Commission Georgetown; Brigadier Joe Singh, Chief of Staff, Guyanese Defence Force; Major Mark Phillips, Lieutenant Duane Jervis, Staff Sergeant Sanmoogan, Staff Sergeant James and Sergeant Johnson of the Guyanese Defence Force; Charles Quentin, Demerara Tobacco Company; Hayden Gonzales; Vincent de Silva; John Fernandes Limited; Michael Chan-A-Sue, Trans Guyana Aviation; Michael Correia of MC Correia; Hilli Laborde; Rafael Sweicki; Robert Alfred and the villagers of Imbaimadai; the communities of Kamarang, Enachu, Issano, Bartica and Fort Island; the staffs of Aruwai, Peaima and Enachu mining camps; Father Steven Dorman; Jerome Mendonca; Benny Choo; John, Lion, Piggy and Cai Coochi, our Mazaruni river guides.

Peru: Tim Bayley and the members and staff of the Lima Cricket and Sports Club; James Birkbeck; Arturo Bellido.

Bolivia: The Bolivian Mountainerering Regiment, Carnhuara; Colonel Milton Puerta and the Regimiento Perez, Potosi; Bolivian Army Regiment at Tarija; the Anglo-Bolivian Society, La Paz;

Argentina: Noblessa Piccardo; Brigadier Juan Llavar and the VIII Argentine Mountain Division; Colonel Santos Maria, Lieutenant Luis Maria Cabanillas and the 5th Cavalry Regiment, Salta; 17th Infantry Regiment, Catamarca; 22nd Mountain Regiment, San Juan; 8th Mountain Brigade Signal Squadron, Mendoza; Major Jose Hernandez, Captain Riccardo Juarez and the Compania de Cazadores; Lieutenant Javier Salgado; Colonel David Lawson and the Defence Staff of the British Embassy, Buenos Aires.

Chile: Patricio Bellolio, Patricio Ihnen, Douglas Munoz and the staff at Chiletabacos; The Chilean Military; The Chilean Carabineros; Captain Bob Rowley RN, Captain Richard Johns RN and the British Defence Staff, Santiago; John Rees, Honorary Consul, Punta Arenas; Jorge Sarquis; Sergio and Theresa Sarquis; David Wynne Finch and the remainder of the Brat Pack, Tamara Heber Percy, Kate Taylor, David Fergusson, David Santos, Sid Ingliss, Axel Lanoy, Sharon, Hamish, Dominic Ely, Christian Hinchcliffe; Ivan Robles; Roxanne and Claudio Paredes; the crew of MN *Beaulieu.*

My personal thanks go to all those who worked in the expedition office during the planning and execution of the expedition: Major Ben Bathurst, Major George Doughty, Major Tim Wakefield, Captain Chris Daly; to my sister Jenny Warburton-Lee and Louie Macpherson for typing my diaries, assisting with research, drawing maps and general morale boosting; to Christopher Woodhead for steering me gently along the path of authorship and to all at Swan Hill Press for producing this book. Most importantly of all, my sincerest thanks for an enormous effort, unceasing support, encouragement and commitment from the expedition permanent cadre who really made the expedition happen: Captain Richard Gaffney, Captain Mike Charlson, Captain Andrew Phasey, Colour Sergeant Charlie Mckeown, Sergeant Mark Jordan and Corporal John Steggles.

To all of the above and the many other individuals who gave their time, assistance and advice, some longterm supporters who have been there through thick and thin, a million thanks and I apologise in advance for the next time your phone rings.

ST. JAMES'S PALACE

I was delighted to be the Patron of this most ambitious expedition to reach the geographical and physical extremes of North and South America. I have followed its progress closely through regular despatches from the expedition team and was thrilled to receive a telephone call direct from them as they reached their first objective, the remote Eskimo village of Cape Prince of Wales that lies on the shores of the Bering Straits at the western point of the Americas.

This story of their adventure makes no elaborate claims of first ascents of previously unscaled mountain faces or of the team having stood where no man has trod before, but rather chronicles the trials and triumphs of six teams of soldiers as they pitted themselves against challenges that caused them to look within themselves, pose fundamental questions about their own abilities and, at times, reach for hidden inner reserves. It is told simply and honestly and shows the men behind their uniforms, revealing them as ordinary, caring and feeling people who experience the full range of elation, despair, fear and hurt.

Their journey provides an illuminating insight into a large number of remote and exotic regions, from the Alaskan arctic, the jungles of Amazonia and the wastes of Patagonia. It introduces a diverse cast of entertaining and often eccentric characters whom they encountered en route. Besides the adventurous and exploratory aspects of the expedition, it is particularly satisfying to have raised a substantial sum of money for the expedition's charitable beneficiary, The Midlands Centre for Spinal Injuries.

Each of the six adventures encapsulated within the expedition demanded resourcefulness, determination and perseverance in the face of daunting conditions. The most remarkable aspect of the venture is that it was attempted by mainly novice expeditioners - volunteers - who put themselves on the line to tackle challenges designed to push them to their limits. That they did so successfully, and without sustaining any serious casualties, is a testament to the spirit and robustness of the men of the Household Division. My congratulations to the team for attaining their goals, both personal and physical, in doing which they embodied the best traditions of our redoubtable British servicemen.

Contents

Maps

Chapter One

From Dream to Reality

Cameroon, November 1990

Thick wood smoke drifted across from the camp fire complementing the smell of the rich red African soil. All around I could hear the gentle babble of the team chatting after supper at the end of another long day. In the background the night-time chorus of frogs, cicadas and crickets echoed out of the jungle blackness. I sat staring into the embers of the fire reminiscing wistfully. It was our last night in the bush after almost a year on expedition.

Mounting the expedition had been a great challenge but more than that it had been a great freedom: the freedom to dream a dream, plan that dream and then actually live it out. Now with the end all too quickly rushing towards us, I tried to shake myself out of my rather melancholic state by reverting to the escapism of dreaming once again. I turned to Richard Gaffney, my partner and Deputy Leader of the expedition.

'I know we can't, but just suppose that we were allowed to go again, what would we do?'

We were both twenty-seven years old and serving Captains in the Welsh Guards. We had been lucky enough to be allowed to plan and lead the 'Roof of Africa Expedition' but had both been told quite categorically by our Commanding Officer that it was now time to settle down and concentrate on our military careers. It was not a prospect that either of us found particularly appealing. Richard had decided to resign his commission and go and study law. I had made no such fundamental decisions but was chasing a rather far-flung notion that I might write a book. Day dreaming was a pleasant and harmless escape.

We chatted idly around various options. At that time the Berlin Wall was still up and the Soviet Union very much a closed region, especially to British soldiers. Conflicts in many other countries in Asia meant that putting together an overland route would be a political nightmare, if not downright impossible. Neither of us had the experience to lead an expedition to either the polar ice cap or Antarctica and anyway I did not like the cold that much. Australia smacked of gap year students, bungee jumping, Ayers Rock and lager and sounded rather predictable and tame. North and South America, on the other hand, had much of the romanticism of Africa and offered all sorts of possibilities. There were great mountain ranges, huge rivers, jungles and deserts . . .

England, Spring 1991

The annual Major-General's Inspection of a Guards Battalion serving in England holds a prominent place in the calendar and is an important and much rehearsed event. We had spent a substantial proportion of the morning parading on the drill square at Elizabeth Barracks, Pirbright, whilst the Major-General first inspected us and then watched as we were put through our paces. Following tradition, we then retired to the Officers Mess where the senior officers worried whether the Battalion had put on a suitably good performance. Those of us of less exalted rank heaved a huge sigh of relief at being able to get out of our constricting tunics and bearskins and got stuck into a good lunch.

After lunch, the Major-General made his way around the room chatting to each officer. When it came to my turn he asked about the 'Roof of Africa Expedition' and how everything was going with wrapping it up. I gave him a brief rundown of the state of accounts, plans for a reception for our sponsors, a photographic exhibition and my search for a publisher. Then, seeing that the Commanding Officer was safely out of earshot and feeling the courage provided by the liquid refreshment, I said that it seemed a pity not to take advantage of all the experience we had gained in Africa. Surely we should plan an even larger expedition on behalf of the Household Division so that soldiers from every regiment in the Division could take part.

General Simon Cooper is an utterly charming Household Cavalryman and had been supportive of Roof of Africa but clearly knew of the Commanding

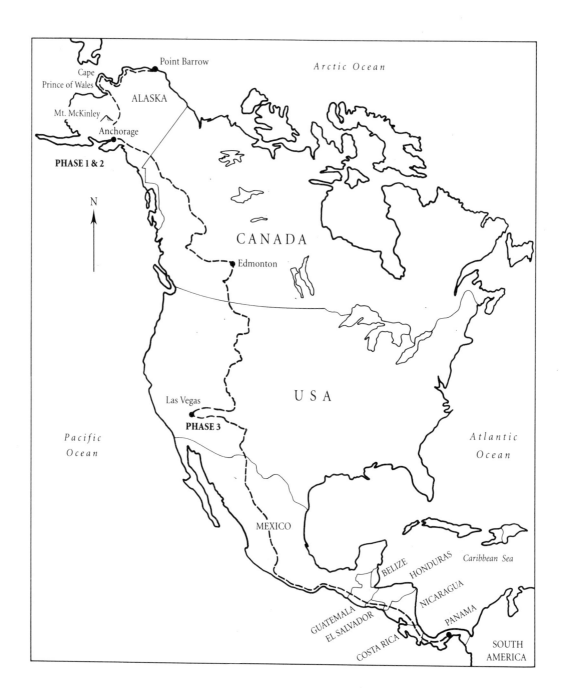

Roof of the Americas Expedition Route Phases 1–3

Roof of the Americas Expedition Route Phases 4–6

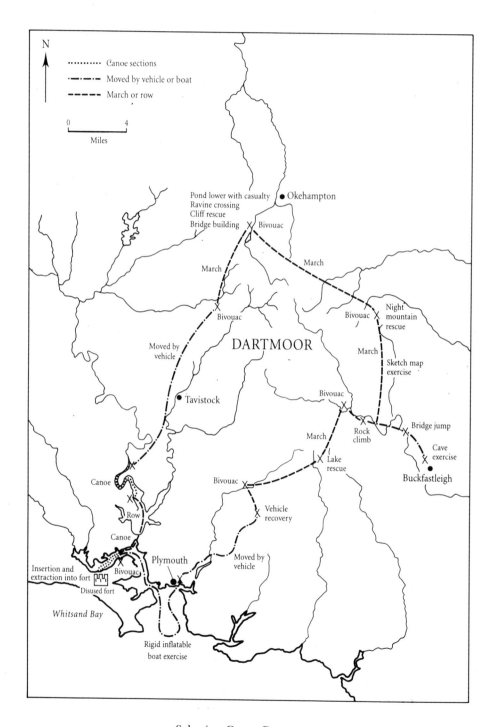

N

·········· Canoe sections

·—·—·—· Moved by vehicle or boat

———— March or row

0   4

Miles

Pond lower with casualty
Ravine crossing
Cliff rescue
Bridge building   X Bivouac   ● Okehampton

March   March

Bivouac   X   Bivouac X   Night
                              mountain
Moved by   rescue
vehicle
              DARTMOOR   March
                              Sketch map
                              exercise

                    Bivouac
              ● Tavistock   X   Bridge jump
                              X
                    March   Rock   X   Cave
                    X Lake   climb   exercise
                       rescue
        Bivouac X   ● Buckfastleigh
Canoe X
                    X
    Row   Vehicle
                     recovery
Canoe X   Moved by
        ● Plymouth   vehicle
Insertion and
extraction into fort   Bivouac
                  Disused fort

Whitsand Bay

        Rigid inflatable
        boat exercise

Selection Camp, Dartmoor

Officer's edict about no more expeditions and I received an interested but rather disapproving look which seemed to say 'Warburton-Lee, you shouldn't be bearding me with this!' The matter was dropped once again.

Several weeks later I bumped into a friend of mine, Oliver Richardson, who had just come back from Northern Ireland. On the aeroplane home he had sat next to the Commanding Officer who had talked about the idea of another expedition. Oliver said that the Commanding Officer intended to support the idea and was just waiting for me to go and see him. I did not realise that Colonel Reddy even knew about it and I was quite sure that if he did he would not approve and so expressed some scepticism. Oliver certainly was not above setting me up for a laugh. However on this occasion he was so insistent and protested the purest of motives so strongly that I, somewhat incredulously, decided to follow it up.

I accosted Colonel Reddy when he came into the Mess for lunch. His response was typically direct, 'Oh God, I have been waiting for you to ambush me. You had better come and talk to me in my office'.

When I did so, it rapidly became apparent that not only did he know of my supposedly secret scheming, but that he had considered the matter carefully and in some detail. The idea was still very much in outline and centred around an overland expedition throughout North and South America that would take large numbers of young soldiers in relays to face a variety of challenges. It was fundamental to the concept that we should involve as many soldiers as possible and that they should be largely novice expeditioners.

'The Roof of the Americas Expedition', as it came to be called, set out to take the basic principles of Adventure Training and extend them to their ultimate conclusion. At that first interview, we thrashed out some of the ground rules. I suggested a start date in 1993 with a run-up expedition to all the highest summits in Europe as a training and selection project. Fortunately, Colonel Reddy, whose feet were rather more securely anchored to the ground, saved me from these flights of fantasy and argued for a more realistic start of 1994 with a correspondingly more modest training programme.

I wandered back to the Mess rather confused and not a little dazed by all this. Suddenly life had been turned upside down, the mundaneness of ceremonial soldiering had been flung out of the window and a dream was there to be dreamt. We had a largely unrestricted mandate, just how fantastic could the dream become?

I found Richard tucking into tea and toast.

'You're not going to believe this but Roof of the Americas has got the go-ahead. I have just come from Colonel Reddy's office,' I gabbled on fairly nonsensically, filling him in on all that had been discussed. 'Are you coming?'

'Of course I am coming, people just don't get these sort of opportunities,' was the strong and unequivocal reply.

For the remainder of 1991, in amongst Army Staff Courses, writing a book and holding a photographic exhibition we set about developing the concept. Starting with an almost blank piece of paper we could let our imaginations run riot and indulge our wildest fantasies of exploration and adventure.

To involve as many people as possible, we needed to organise the expedition into phases within which fresh teams would come out from England to face their own particular challenge and complete a section of the journey, all contributing to an overall expedition aim. We wanted the phases to stand up in their own right as expeditions and to have their own character. Each must be challenging, demanding and adventurous.

After flirting with several ideas for an overall aim, we finally decided to attempt to reach the geographical and physical extremes of the Americas. This rather open-ended aim led us towards a journey to reach the four cardinal points, each one of which required an expedition to remote and interesting places, and also allowed us to put in as many other extremes as we wanted.

With wonderfully naive enthusiasm the concept began to be cobbled together. The more we read, the more we schemed. I have always believed that if you want to do something badly enough there must be a way to make it happen. In an expedition environment this comes down to extremely detailed research leading to the formulation of a credible operational and logistic plan.

Logistics are vital to the success of any plan. They may be complex and are often expensive, but there is always a solution if you look hard enough and employ a broad-minded approach to a particular problem. Once on the ground, the success of an expedition relies on having a good team with the determination and cohesion to implement the plan and pull together to overcome unexpected and often apparently insurmountable problems. I believe that firm but fair leadership keeps coherence in the conduct of a plan and there is no denying that every team needs a bit of luck if you are truly sticking your necks out.

Our way of developing the concept may have seemed fairly haphazard to an outsider, and I suppose that it was. However I suspect that it is the way of all expeditions; you rely on experience and instinct to guide you towards what is difficult but achievable and away from what is romantic but irresponsible and even suicidal. At times it can be a fine dividing line.

In 1992 planning began in earnest. We split the expedition equally in half: I took on the research and planning of the first three phases in North America and Richard took the second three in South America. We now set about collating as much information about each of the challenges as we could. This involved visits to the library and map room of the Royal Geographical Society, the Alpine Club library and the archive section of the Army's Expedition Department. There followed many hours of reading reference material, old or new; taking notes and pursuing obscure texts found in bibliographies or writing to seek advice from anyone who had ventured into the various regions, for whatever reason.

Every piece of information that we gleaned, no matter how trivial, was recorded until we began to build up a picture of each challenge. This gave us an idea of the physical difficulties involved, the equipment that would be required, rules governing access to regions at political and local levels, viable methods for getting equipment and supplies from Britain to the appropriate area – be it at a remote Eskimo village, the glacier at a base of a mountain or deep in the jungle. All aspects of safety and the implications of having to evacuate an injured team member from any place on our route no matter how difficult also had to be considered together with a general idea of cost of all of the above. There were many factors that went into each and every facet of the phase plans.

All the source information had to be evaluated for accuracy and relevance. At the turn of the century, Hudson Stuck had travelled several thousand miles each winter with only two or three malamute huskies pulling all his kit. He had walked most of the way, but now Alaskan mushers use larger teams of smaller dogs and ride on their sleds. We wondered which we should do, how much time we should allow for bad weather above the Arctic Circle and whether we would be able to cross the rivers in the Darien jungle in the rainy season.

We found documentary coverage of foot, Land-Rover and Hovercraft expeditions in Amazonia but how long a journey by powered raft would take along our route was anyone's guess. How we were going to get re-supplies to a group of skiers on the Patagonian ice cap was another problem, there are no helicopters in the south of Chile and anyway the ice cap is subject to frequent high winds and white-out conditions which can last for a week or more at a time. The list of questions was endless.

Early on in the planning I went for a meeting with the relevant desk officers at the Foreign and Commonwealth Office. Given the fact that their role is to promote British interest and protect the country from any potential political embarrassment they took a surprisingly enthusiastic and supportive position towards the expedition. However, a brief look at the countries along our intended route from their perspective revealed a large number of potential problems.

As soldiers and therefore representatives of the British Government, our status abroad is somewhat different from that of civilian nationals. We have to receive clearance from the British Government to visit any country and then secure permission from the host country for us to enter their country. This two part clearance procedure can be fraught with difficulties and produces all sorts of political delicacies about which one might normally be totally unaware.

Many countries are deeply suspicious about the motives of foreign militaries who request to visit the remote regions of their countries in the name of Adventure Training, a concept not readily understood by countries who are more concerned with real internal or external security problems and anyway could not afford such training.

The United States and Canada posed little

problem from a political perspective but as soon as we progressed further south the picture changed quickly. An internal security problem had broken out in the Chiapas region of Mexico with the indigenous Mayan Indians briefly taking control of parts of the area. Mexico's stability was to slip further with a number of assassinations of high profile political figures. Guatemala was in the process of emerging from a long period of internal strife and was still far from safe. El Salvador, Nicaragua and Honduras had all had prolonged civil wars and, although ostensibly peaceable, there was no guarantee that any one of them would remain that way.

Costa Rica was the odd one out, having such a tranquil nature that they do not have an army. Panama on the other hand, had recently experienced the dictatorial rule of General Noriega and was still feeling the reverberations of the American invasion to oust him. The geography of Central America, with each country lined up one after the other, meant that if we were unable to enter any one of these countries we would have a major problem getting around them, particularly as they are not well served by shipping lines.

In South America the situation was no better. The area of Colombia into which we intended to emerge from the Darien jungle was in the hands of drugs cartels and guerrillas. At that time, government troops could not get into the region at all and there were many reports of locals and tourists simply disappearing. An estimated 20,000 to 30,000 people had been killed in Colombia in the previous year. Needless to say, we were already being strongly advised by the Foreign Office to abandon any ideas of visiting the area.

Venezuela was peaceful, but a short time later suffered an attempted coup. There had been no British military expeditions to Brazil for many years and whilst no one at the Foreign Office was against us going there, nor could come up with any good reason why we should not be allowed to enter the country, they were sceptical over whether the Brazilians would permit it. Along the east coast, Guyana and French Guiana were friendly and stable but Surinam had a small scale internal security problem.

On the west coast, Ecuador was stable, but for a long time expeditions had been prohibited from visiting Peru due to the activities of the active Maoist terrorist organisation, the Sendero Luminoso. The level of violence, which at its worst had almost paralysed the country, had decreased and there was an outside chance that we might be allowed to transit the country along a strictly governed route.

In Bolivia the terrorist situation had also quietened down to an acceptable level and the daily bombings which had characterised La Paz a few years previously had now stopped. Both countries undoubtedly had undercurrents of political unrest remaining and both had areas which were controlled by drugs barons and were thus unsafe to visit.

The highest mountain in South America, Mt. Aconcagua, lies high in the Andes on the borders of Chile and Argentina, but the bulk of the mountain massif is undisputably in Argentina. Since the Falklands War, relations between Britain and Argentina had been, unsurprisingly, strained. Both sides were trying to restore old links and improve diplomatic relations but as yet no British military expedition had visited Argentina and in the game of diplomatic cat and mouse that was currently underway, it was far from certain whether the political climate had improved sufficiently for it to be acceptable to either side.

The Southern Patagonian ice cap and Cape Horn were within Chile, which, in itself, was one of the most stable countries of the region. However, Argentina laid territorial claim to a number of areas along the border of the two countries. The Argentinians and Chileans loathe each other and these territorial disputes were long running and deeply felt, regularly stirring up strong nationalist feelings in each country.

Trying to piece together a physically practicable route in amongst this jigsaw of political turmoil was not easy, particularly given the fluid nature of Central and South American politics. In some cases, such as that in Colombia, we had no choice but to totally change our plans. In others, we could compromise on some of the fine detail to reach an acceptable solution. We tried our hardest to maintain the character of the expedition as we had dreamt it

Overlying all of our plans was the knowledge that all the clearances from the Foreign Office were given with the rider that 'they were subject to no deterioration in the political situation within any country' and therefore could be withdrawn at any stage with almost no warning. This of course made perfect sense from their point of view as it built in a safeguard and was a positive step in trying to enable us to realise as many of our aspirations as possible. From our perspective, whilst we were grateful for this constructive approach, it meant that we had to have contingency plans for each stage of the route.

This planning was all taking place outside our normal army jobs. Richard spent the first few months of the year on a junior staff course whilst I took my part in Battalion training for Northern Ireland and then went to Ballykelly on the North Antrim coast for four months. The fact that we rarely met and that we both kept moving did not make matters any easier. In August I returned to London to take up my new position as Temporary Equerry to HRH The Prince of Wales. He had very kindly agreed to be Patron of the expedition once again and so this tied in nicely. It also meant that, at last, I could establish a permanent expedition office from which to mount our fund-raising campaign.

We had calculated that we needed a cash budget of approximately £380,000. This did not take into account the large amount of assistance and particularly equipment that we anticipated getting at no charge from the Army, nor the support in kind that we hoped to get from civilian sponsors. I tried not to think about the rather terrifying size of this sum and instead concentrated on the mechanics of trying to raise it. If we thought that the experience and contacts gained during the planning of 'Roof of Africa' would make the raising of the necessary sponsorship easier, then the onset of the recession soon put paid to that.

Our funding was to come from three main areas. First, the expedition members themselves. Each member of the team would contribute a quarter of their daily pay for the time that they were on the expedition. We estimated that this would raise us somewhere in the region of £85,000. We also planned to set each team member a personal fund-raising target to boost this cash pool although with soldiers serving everywhere from Belize to Bosnia this was no sure-fire way of raising money.

The second main area of support was from Army sources. We sought grants from every regiment that was involved and from a broad variety of Service funds which helped pay for equipment, guides,

food and basic allowances such as postage, travel within the UK and stationery.

The remainder of the funding had to come from commercial sponsorship. Securing either donations or sponsorship deals is far from easy in an increasingly competitive market place. It was a case of all hands to the pump to begin creating a database of potential sponsors or donors to be approached and then ringing people, following up with letters and brochures and subsequently keeping the application alive with further phone calls and updates.

Jenny, my sister, took on the unenviable task of going through Who's Who, which catalogues over 28,000 biographies, extracting businessmen with military backgrounds who might be sympathetic to an approach. Richard was now out in Northern Ireland, having returned from an extremely low budget recce to gather information and establish contacts in Panama, Venezuela, Brazil and Chile. In his time off he was sending applications to the reams of names that Jenny was churning out.

Trying to obtain sponsorship, you find yourself in the classic 'chicken and egg' situation. To attract major sponsors you need to be able to demonstrate large-scale media interest and guaranteed television and national newspaper coverage. However neither television production companies nor newspapers will commit themselves until they are convinced that they are dealing with a viable project. Companies often feel more comfortable signing up to a project when they see a number of other reputable companies have already done so but none like to be the first.

Many letters went unanswered and the vast majority came back with a polite refusal, however, the few early cheques that we did receive kept up our faith. There was always the hope that the next letter could produce the big one. We were trying to market sponsorship of each phase at a premium of £40,000 but were tending to receive token donations for anything from £5 to £1,000 with the majority at the lower end. There was a long way to go.

In the autumn, we received a major boost in the form of a new member of the team, Captain Andrew Phasey, who was to be our full-time Quartermaster. Andrew had joined the Army as a private soldier in the Grenadier Guards and had progressed all the way through the ranks from Guardsman to Regimental Sergeant-Major and had then been commissioned. Forty years old, he brought with him a wealth of experience and a level-headed approach to problems.

Andrew's task was huge. He was responsible for collating the vast array of equipment that we needed from both military and civilian sources. He then had to design a system to control the movement of this equipment to and from all the locations in which we would be operating, together with a fail-safe system of re-supply for those on the ground. We could give him almost no money with which to do it and thus he had to use all his considerable charm and ingenuity to cajole people into granting us favours, reductions or sponsorship and in many cases had to design or modify equipment to fulfil our often unusual requirements.

Andrew brought with him a fresh perspective. Well organised and methodical by nature, he undoubtedly found the rather unconventional approach that Richard and I were used to, difficult to work with. However, we quickly learnt to respect his opinion and method of working. The results spoke for themselves as he gained substantial support from areas of the Army that I had never heard of and established a network of contacts in all fields that were to help us through even our most difficult periods. I came to trust his well considered and constructive advice and could rely on him not to shy away from any difficult issues. It was often comforting to be able to turn to an older head for counsel.

At the end of 1992 I went to Washington DC to begin the negotiations for the provision of support from the United States Military for our plans for the first two phases. It had rapidly become apparent that our planned dog-sled and snowmobile journey to reach Cape Prince of Wales and Point Barrow was to be logistically extremely complicated and therefore expensive. Whilst it was undoubtedly possible to make the journey without outside help, it would be considerably easier if we could take advantage of some of the military facilities which existed in Alaska. They had bases that could provide accommodation, storage and food; aircraft flying regular re-supply flights to a network of outposts and radar sites through the interior and along the Arctic coast; and Eskimo guides within the ranks of the National Guard.

Despite being our closest ally, the US Military had suffered their own keenly felt Defence cuts and this support was far from certain. Obtaining it was not made any easier by the facts that firstly the US Military do not practise Adventure Training in the same way that we do, and secondly they do not let junior officers have anything like the latitude for command or decision making that we do.

In all the meetings that I went to, I was the most junior by a considerable margin and it became obvious that the Colonels with whom I was dealing were having a hard time coming to terms with negotiating with what they saw as a maverick Captain operating on an unofficial agenda. Within their system such a situation would never be allowed to happen.

The third problem was the US Military's proclivity for referring any decision involving a foreign army, that was not already governed by an established Memorandum of Understanding, to a legal review. I was to learn to dread this term which instantly sent any official request spiralling into a bureaucratic quagmire where it could become lost for months or even years. I returned to England with some very cautious offers to 'see what they could do'.

The New Year brought a fresh urgency to our planning. We had just twelve months until our intended start date. There seemed to be an impossible amount to do and yet we had little scope for slipping the start date as each of the phase plans were scheduled to take advantage of the appropriate seasons, none more so than our dog-sledding journey through Alaska for which we needed a full Arctic winter. Richard returned from Northern Ireland to work full-time on the expedition which made the co-ordination of our efforts much easier.

The political situation remained disconcertingly volatile, but it was finance and the lack of sponsorship that was rapidly becoming the largest threat to the successful launch of the expedition. Each reply seemed to bring another disappointment and our gains appeared so small set against the target figure. We went over the budget time and again, paring it down to include only absolute necessities, but there was a level beyond which it simply was not either safe or sensible to cut back any further.

Safety was not something that I was prepared to

compromise on. Sooner or later we would be out in the cold of the Arctic, high up a mountain or being blasted by the wind on the Patagonian ice cap and we would bitterly regret any decision to compromise on the quality of clothing or equipment taken from the warmth of a centrally heated London office.

On a number of occasions our hopes were raised, only to be dashed again. I spent sleepless nights praying for confirmation of the sponsorship, but each time it was back to the drawing board.

In amongst this, Andrew and I were preparing for a detailed recce to Alaska. The Phase One plan had gone about as far as it could on paper. Now we needed to carry out direct personal liaison in Alaska to start putting some substance into it. We had to find husky owners who would lease us teams of dogs; a base from which to mount the expedition and where we could carry out an initial training package; suppliers of fresh meat, straw, veterinary supplies and a myriad of items of dog mushing equipment from sleds to ganglines.

We had to work out a way to get ourselves and our equipment to the start point, a method by which we could be self-supporting for the projected three month journey and a system of re-supply to get regular packages of food, straw and fuel out to the villages through which we would be passing.

I was very aware that what we were attempting was an ambitious plan and likely to be regarded with some scepticism by local Alaskan mushers, particularly given our lack of experience. Not wanting to appear any more green than I had to, I set about tracking down the little known husky owners clubs in Great Britain. I spent weekends charging off to Wales and the Midlands to their rallies where I was kindly received by these wonderfully enthusiastic and dedicated people who taught me to harness their huskies to the small three-wheeled carts which they race and then with great forbearance allowed me to take my turn driving their highly cherished racing dogs around courses marked out along muddy forest tracks.

I flew out to Alaska at the end of February. There I was met by Roy and Lesley Monk. Roy is a retired English businessman from Burnley in Lancashire. He and his wife had been racing huskies in England for a number of years before they decided to go and compete in the long distance races in Alaska. They had come out each year since and taken part in middle and long distance races, including the 1,100 mile Iditarod Race. They fell totally in love with the Alaskan way of life and so, having sold his business, Roy had bought a cabin and was now establishing a sizeable kennel of his own. He and Lesley spent each winter in Alaska and the summer in Britain.

I had been introduced to the Monks through the British husky owners' network. Roy had shown great enthusiasm for our plans and invited me to come and stay at his cabin so that I could get some first hand experience at handling a dog team on snow and in the extreme conditions of Alaska. He also offered to introduce me to the Alaskan dog mushing community.

Once established at the cabin we pored over every aspect of our projected plans. I wanted eight members of the team to travel on dog teams, with a further eight members of the team in support on snowmobiles. Two more team members, who would be rotated within the group, would remain at our base to provide the safety back-up and logistic support. In this way, travelling in convoy with snowmobilers breaking and marking the trail, interspersed between the dog teams to assist in case of problems and bringing up the rear, I believed that we could create our own safety envelope around the mushers. We already planned to bring with us a veterinarian from the Royal Army Veterinary Corps to provide cover for the huskies and would have a doctor as part of the permanent expedition cadre.

Roy believed that given the distance that we intended to cover and the inexperience of the soldiers at handling dogs, nine huskies was the ideal size of dog team to provide power and stamina and yet be manageable for a novice musher. He offered to provide up to five of the eight teams so long as he came along on a sixth team. Indeed it already seemed to be publicly accepted that this was the way that the expedition was due to run.

Although I had some disquiet at being presented with a fait accompli, not least because I found Roy difficult and unpredictable to work with, it was undoubtedly a kind offer and one which had much to recommend it. Hiring husky teams for a full season could cost up to $10,000 per team and here we were being offered five for free, together with the experience of someone who had been involved in mushing for many years and could teach us a great deal.

As I was rapidly finding out, running husky teams is an extremely expensive business. It seemed that no longer in Alaska do huskies live on a diet of whatever meat their handler can hunt for them, nor bed down in the snow with only their tails tucked over their faces for protection. Today's highly competitive and image conscious racing has changed the Alaskan sled-dog into a valuable athlete with all of the dietary requirements and finicky living conditions of a modern sportsman.

Roy was quite naturally and correctly taking a strong line in insisting the best provision of care for his dogs. Meanwhile Andrew, who had just flown out to join me, and I, were trying to work out the practicalities of putting these various stipulations in place for a long journey in the Arctic. We were not planning to race, quite the reverse, so we were trying to moderate some of the high spec racing requirements with which Roy was used to keeping a twenty dog racing team on the move for up to one hundred miles in a day, in favour of a more modest regime applicable to our intended steady plod.

Ascertaining a reasonable level of supplies, when none of us could predict the weather that we were likely to encounter nor therefore our rate of travel or likely amount of hold-ups on any given stage, proved difficult and contentious. We studied daylight charts, weather records and sought the advice of local mushers, veterinarians and animal nutritionalists. I like to question every point in a plan, and will happily argue that black is white in order to provoke a debate to ensure that we have considered every aspect and are making a well considered decision. There was an intense and at times highly charged atmosphere as we thrashed out each detail.

Alongside these protracted discussions, we visited a number of kennels to find the remaining three teams of huskies that we needed to hire. Andrew and I also spent a considerable amount of time in meetings with the US Military at their main base in Fort Richardson, Anchorage, bearing in mind all the while, that whatever we agreed was still subject to Pentagon approval and thus had to be covered by a civilian alternative in case we did not get the ratification that we were hoping for.

By far the best part of the recce for me was the time that I spent working with Roy's huskies. They are magnificent animals with their silver grey fur, ice blue eyes and wolfish appearance. They have apparently boundless energy and an inbred desire to run. Every time you produce a harness they leap and bound, shrieking and yelping in their enthusiasm to be off. Nothing could have prepared me for the thrill of that first surge of power as you pull up the snow anchor and nine dogs in harness lunge forward at full gallop. The first few hundred yards of every run is a headlong dash and for the novice musher a hectic period of gathering your wits, clinging onto the sled and trying to guide the runners round the first few corners as you steady the team down into the brisk trot of the long-distance team.

The learning curve is undeniably steep. There are few other sports that can leave you pouring with sweat in sub-zero temperatures and weeping tears of frustration as, having failed to successfully impart your shouted directions to your lead dog, you are up to your waist in powder snow trying to untangle the resulting confusion of struggling and fighting dogs.

Sled-dog teams have a greater ability than even the most malevolent of fishing lines to tie themselves up into the tightest and most inextricable of knots which is only compounded by nine powerful huskies all struggling to pull in different directions. The strength of huskies should not be underestimated. A man can only realistically hold two medium-sized dogs on his own. When frustrated or frightened, their normally placid temperament deserts them and they reveal flashing teeth and strong jaws that can seriously wound the other dogs with whom they have become entangled. Diving in to separate fighting dogs or sort out the chaos, the musher is vulnerable to his own share of bites.

There can, conversely, be few activities that offer such utter contentment when all goes well, when musher and team harmonize and you experience that almost primaeval euphoria of working, man and dog, power harnessed, to travel across the vastness of Alaska. Every sensation is heightened by the sheer immenseness of your surroundings, the extremes of weather and temperature and the all too apparent implications of making a mistake or getting separated from your team.

Having grown up with working dogs, I found it relatively easy to get on with them as characters.

I found the huskies far more affectionate than I had imagined. They displayed none of the savagery with which they are so inaccurately characterized in the popular but sensationalist Jack London stories. Their power is exhilarating and the challenge of communicating your wishes just by shouted commands, with no reins or whip to enforce them, makes driving a sled-dog team a far more testing and satisfying experience than being behind the wheel of any sports car.

I hitched a ride aboard a United States Airforce C-130 out to Nome and Kotzebue, two of the larger Eskimo settlements on the Bering Sea coastline. Flying over hundreds of miles of tundra broken only by forests, frozen rivers and mountains I gained a feeling for the scale and emptiness of the country that we were to pass through. Conditions out on the coast, with low temperatures and high winds pushing the wind-chill down even further, served only to emphasise the seriousness of our undertaking.

One evening I was taken out by snowmobile onto the frozen sea ice. Steve Nicol, my guide, led me away from the dim lights of the village and along the coastline. We were curiously anonymous, swathed in down suits and with all other areas of flesh hidden beneath large gauntlets, face masks and thick goggles. We drove along in the flat half-light until we were brought to a halt by pressure ridges with individual blocks of ice over ten feet high.

I flew home leaving Andrew to tie up some of the details of the logistics plan before he went on down to Nevada to do the same for our Grand Canyon challenge. I left with a much clearer appreciation of the true scale of our proposed journey through Alaska and with the images of all that I had seen indelibly printed on my mind.

The practical difficulties of driving dog teams, the scale of the logistics and the very real threat posed by the huge distances that we must cross and the conditions that we would encounter had all made a both vivid and real impression. However I was firmly convinced that we had the basis of a workable plan and that with a determined but flexible approach we could overcome all of them.

On one afternoon I had taken advantage of the offer of a ride in a light aircraft up into the Denali Range. We flew all around Mt McKinley. The mountain had its own well documented history of dramas and tragedies that boded caution and demanded respect. Looking at the great sweeping glaciers that led up to the base of the mountain from every direction, the sheer rock faces, knife-edge ridges and sharp summits from which plumes of spindrift blew up even as I watched, I was under no illusion as to the amount of effort that would be required if we were to make the summit. Although posing a quite different set of difficulties, our second objective was going to be no easier to achieve than our first.

Back in England there was much to be done to put in place all that we had learnt in Alaska and Nevada. We were working flat out on every stage of the plan but none was more important than the training and selection of the six teams that would take part in the expedition. Before going to Alaska, Andrew and I had conducted a whistle-stop tour of the regiments of the Division. We had dashed between London, Windsor, Edinburgh, Northern Ireland and Germany with a slide and video presentation of our plans, calling for volunteers. Several hundred put their names forward for the phases of their choice.

In a perfect world we would have liked to have run dog sledding in Sweden, mountaineering, white-water kayaking and rafting in the Alps, jungle training at either of the Army's bases in Belize or Brunei and cross-country skiing in Norway. In reality, there was no way that we had the time, resources or money to run such an elaborate set-up.

Working on the basis that the vast majority of applicants were total novices at each of the activities, we decided instead to base the selection on a set of criteria which we felt were essential for any member of the expedition regardless of their age, experience or the position that they would hold. These included mental and physical robustness, stamina, determination, enthusiasm, an aptitude for the skills that would be involved in each phase, a sense of humour and the ability to fit into a tight-knit team. The last of these was arguably the most important of all.

The Guards Adventure Training Wing is a little known organisation based down at Fremington in Devon. For a number of years, under the command of Major Tony Bradborne, they had been conducting Adventure Training Exercises on Dartmoor and around south Devon for recruits in training, potential officers for the Household Division, adult soldiers and those preparing to attempt Special Air Service Selection.

Many of us had been through Tony's mill at one time or another and experienced the arduous, inventive and often unorthodox tests and exercises that he sets. I now rang him and asked if he would be prepared to help with the creation and running of our selection exercise. In his inimitable laconic drawl he agreed and so I went down to Fremington to form the plan taking Andrew with me, as ever, to work out the logistic bill. The idea was for all applicants to go to Fremington Camp where they would be given a four-day package of instruction in basic rock climbing, rope handling, kayaking, vehicle recovery and pulley systems to give them just enough of a grounding to be able to tackle the various elements of the test exercise.

The test exercise was to last for a week during which applicants would be placed in groups of up to eight and faced with a different task every few hours. Some of the tasks would test confidence and require individuals to overcome a natural fear, others would assess specific skills, some would be pure hard graft whilst yet others would evaluate an individual's ability to fit into and contribute towards the cohesion of a group as they worked to co-ordinate a complex rescue problem. The tasks were varied, interesting, and a number would, I hoped, surprise people. They were all intended to be physically hard and tiring. The one element that I felt was lacking however was a serious test of stamina and commitment. Tony suggested an Iron Man competition and was clearly longing to let the more Machiavellian side of his nature run riot.

We ran the exercise three times; in May, August and September. It was set up to put 100 people through the full training and selection package each time. It worked better than I had ever dared hope. The soldiers arrived to find a considerably more demanding regime than they had anticipated. After the initial shock, they settled down to the task in hand. As usual, they rose to the situation, enjoying the challenge. On the test exercise they carried their kit round Dartmoor, rock climbing on tors and crags, kayaking and rowing the Tamar River, potholing in Pridamsleigh Cavern, jumping off high bridges into the river below, winching vehicles out of slippery gullies, navigating both by sketch map and at night, building their own bridges

or aerial ropeways over ravines and carrying out every manner of stretcher-borne rescue, as they went. The latter is a time honoured way of making an activity both more complicated and arduous. We had lodged 'casualties' up rock faces, at the bottom of caves, in remote parts of the moor requiring a long man haul across some of the roughest tussock grass that we could find and one which had to be lowered down a cliff onto canoes waiting in the pond below.

We returned to Fremington for the Iron Man competition. Despite having toned down some of Tony's more extreme ideas, it was still a daunting test. Conducted in pairs, it involved crossing the Taw estuary with one of the pair swimming and the other paddling a kayak, running five miles in a circuit over the sand dunes of Braunton Burrows, re-crossing the estuary, this time exchanging roles and then running the two miles back to Fremington Camp.

Richard and I had decided to run it together each time to set an example. Standing in a group, semi-naked and shivering as we looked across the singularly uninviting half-mile wide estuary I could feel the soldiers all looking at me as if to say 'you can't be serious!' To those who are not particularly strong swimmers, as I am not, it was an intimidating prospect. It was never a pleasant experience, heaving the kayak down the beach and across the estuary, towing the apparently dead weight of your floundering partner towards a distant shoreline that never seemed to get any closer, then running over the dunes at your best pace with sand working its way into all the most uncomfortable places. All the while you dreaded the moment you had to plunge back into the ice-cold estuary and make the final dash back to camp, battling to motivate half frozen legs and heaving lungs along the teasing arrow-straight final two miles. Roughly one hour and forty minutes of continual struggle and excruciating discomfort brought the relief of being able to stop and that rather perverse satisfaction of having put yourself through something hard and unpleasant but having not given in. I was very impressed that save a couple who suffered cramp on the swim and had to be hauled in by the safety boat, everyone completed the course and interestingly it created a strong team feeling amongst everyone who had taken part. A final competition man-handling a railway sleeper over the assault course in teams of eight completed the selection.

Each of the camps provided a great relief from office life, an escape from the constant paper war that we were fighting and allowed us to concentrate on something satisfyingly practical. Most importantly it enabled us to select six teams with a balance of age, rank and experience appropriate to the phase for which we were selecting.

I had been dreading making the selections, especially having seen so many men really trying their hearts out on the test exercises but when Richard and I sat down at the end of the third camp to make the selections it was relatively straightforward. We had been able to build up a reasonably complete and fair picture of an applicant's performance in a whole range of different situations. It was then a question of grading them across the board, assessing our requirements for each phase, selecting instructors, drivers, mechanics, signallers, and medics first and then fitting in the best of the rest according to their aptitude.

Over the period of the training camps a further four permanent staff had joined the team. Captain Mike Charlson was to be our doctor. Thirty years old, Mike came to us from the 2nd Battalion The Parachute Regiment to whom he had been Regimental Medical Officer for the previous two years. He had a rather unusual outlook for a doctor in that in the long-term he no longer wanted to pursue medicine and strongly gave the impression of being a frustrated killer rather than a vocational healer, avidly reading anything that he could get his hands on about Special Forces soldiering.

However, any misgivings that I may have had regarding his short-term commitment to the healing arts were quickly dispelled as he threw himself into the medical preparations for the expedition. He was fastidious in his research of each area that we were going to and all of the associated medical problems posed by operating in those areas including the most obscure illnesses and their cures. For any further confirmation, you only had to try and pick up the enormous rucksack full of medical supplies that he carried with him wherever he went; there was certainly no mistaking his level of fitness or physical determination.

He also showed a healthy robustness in his treatment of soldiers on the selection camps,

always providing the best treatment that he could to get an individual in a position to carry on with the selection if they had the motivation to do so, but giving short shrift to any malingerers or those seeking sympathy for minor ailments. This was not an attitude displayed by all military doctors and whilst it might appear a little short on compassion it gave me confidence that I could rely on strong and supportive medical back-up once we were out on the ground.

The paper war had by this stage totally overwhelmed us. I had put up a case for two Army clerks to join the team. Lance-Sergeant Mark Jordan joined us from the Household Cavalry. A mild mannered man with a soft West Country burr, he came not only with a good recommendation as a clerk but with the added bonus of being a qualified carpenter. He was to work for Andrew on the logistics side of life and would remain in England throughout most of the expedition. Lance-Corporal John Steggles was a young, chirpy Midlander who had approached me when I went to give one of the presentations to his regiment, the Coldstream Guards. He had immediately struck me as being bright, motivated and having a certain spark about him. He was to work as my clerk and assistant both during the run up to the expedition and once out on the ground.

The last member of the permanent team made an instant impression on all of us, and anyone else who was within range. Colour Sergeant Charlie McKeown was a larger-than-life Scots Guardsman who attacked life with an invigorating ebullience. Wherever he was, his broad Glaswegian accent could be heard booming out orders, humorous insults and a seemingly endless supply of unlikely stories. As the senior non-commissioned officer on the team, he ran the camp routine, minor discipline and the local control of stores and equipment for the team on the ground.

In line with the normal role of a non-commissioned officer, he would be the interface between the leadership and the soldiers. It was vital that he and I achieved a good working relationship as we needed to be sensitive to each other's requirements and work in harmony to keep the team happy, well motivated and efficient.

When the selection camps were underway we left a skeleton crew in the office to try and keep the planning going whilst the rest of us charged around Devon. We were in overdrive in all departments. At last we were receiving some sponsorship but we were still far short of our target with costs rising all the time. We were trying every angle that we could to drum up more funds. Andrew was working flat out to get the first forty-foot container load of equipment ready to be shipped to Alaska in time to be met by the Advance Party in mid December.

Our application for assistance from the US Military in Alaska was still helplessly lost in a mire of Pentagon bureaucracy and the dreaded legal reviews and to complicate matters further our proposed route through Brazil had been turned down twice by the Brazilian Government and the strong indication that we were getting from our Defence Attaché in Buenos Aires was that the third application looked like going the same way

We needed to work on an entirely new plan for Phase Four. This was going to be easier said than done if we were not allowed to cross Brazil, a country the size of Europe. We clearly would not be able to reach the easternmost point on the Americas, Recife, which was in Brazil. However I did not see why we should abandon the nature of Phase Four as conceived. It was to be a river journey through a remote jungle area, for which we had already selected a team of soldiers.

Both Venezuela and Guyana offered a large number of possibilities. Eventually having fired off a volley of investigative faxes to contacts in both countries, read yet more books and talked to other expeditioners, Guyana began to emerge as the favourite. After agreeing on some basic principles and an agenda to pursue, Richard set off across the Atlantic bound for Guyana whilst I headed back to Alaska to continue to discuss the details of notional support with the US Military there.

Richard returned from Guyana considerably encouraged by all that he had discovered. He had confirmed the suitability of several of the rivers that we had identified on our initial study of the map and he had received both encouragement and offers of help from Brigadier Jo Singh, the charismatic head of the Guyanese Defence Force.

Guyana seemed to fulfil our criteria perfectly; it had large rivers that passed through huge tracts of remote jungle, few people, an entirely different culture and little infrastructure. My first choice

of objective, the Mazaruni River, was broken by frequent rapids and waterfalls and had all the makings of a grand adventure. The reservations of Brigadier Singh, that the country that we would be entering might prove too difficult, only made it more appealing.

The last two months of the year passed in a blur. Office life reached fever pitch. Our three telephone lines were in constant use throughout the day. Last minute ideas for sponsorship were pursued, political clearances chased, items of equipment sourced, haggled for and despatched for shipping. The eighty-one huskies that we would be using were all collected together at Roy Monk's kennel in Alaska where they began their gradual conditioning and fitness training.

The Royal Army Veterinary Corps is a very small and tightly stretched organisation. Fortunately for us, the Director-General happened to be an ex Household Cavalry Brigadier, who kindly released his personal staff officer to the expedition to provide veterinary care for the pre-training and our journey to Point Barrow. Major Dougie MacDonald had been a practising vet for fourteen years. A Lowland Scot, with a relaxed easy going manner, Dougie said goodbye to his wife and children for six months, and set off to Alaska at the beginning of November.

With the freight on the way to Alaska, the first priority was to tie up the arrangements for the documentary coverage of the expedition on television. We hoped this would lead to further sponsorship. Our second priority was the launching of a PR campaign to try and establish a profile for the expedition in the national, regional and local media, once again with a view to further sponsorship. We also set about organising our reception for Sponsors which doubled as the official launch of the expedition.

In mid-December the Advance Party of Andrew Phasey, Colour Sergeant McKeown and Sergeant Wayne Sculley, a cockney Grenadier Guardsman due to take part in the first phase, set off for Alaska. They were to receive the sea freight on its arrival, set up our training base and begin the process of preparing the re-supply packages. The remainder of us raced around trying to tie up as many loose ends as possible.

In London people were getting into the familiar trail of Christmas parties. I found myself beginning to experience a rather strange sense of unreality. The parties and the gaiety seemed to have little relevance to the world that I was going to. I wondered how many of the people that I talked to, even my good friends who were all wishing me luck, really understood what we would be facing. I wondered frequently whether even I did. I felt myself pulling back, distancing myself emotionally from friends and family and my comfortable lifestyle. It was a necessary mental gearing-up for the transition to expedition life for such a prolonged period, a period during which I knew that as a team and as individuals we were to face some stern tests.

For Christmas, I went home to North Wales where I went around all the members of my family and my old, childhood friends saying my goodbyes. I have never been good at goodbyes and frequently found myself becoming emotional. They seemed to stir up all the old self-doubts. Would the plan really work? Were we capable of achieving the ambitious aims that we had set ourselves? Would my dreaming be responsible for the serious injury, or worse, of novices who by definition might not understand the danger they were putting themselves into? Was I myself capable of meeting the challenges and decisions ahead? Did I really want to go away for fifteen months?

Some goodbyes were harder than others. It upset me considerably to leave my stepfather, stuck in his twilight existence, unable to hold a proper conversation as a result of a stroke and immobile following a heart attack. He had been very kind to me over the past twenty years and I wondered if I would ever see him again. In my heart of hearts I knew that it was unlikely. My mother was in tears. At my other home, my father tried to maintain his stiff upper lip but when it was time for me to leave we were both choked up and the look in his eyes gave away the emotions behind his rather formal handshake and 'Good luck old boy'.

Hardest of all was saying goodbye to my girlfriend, Louie. We had not known each other for all that long but over the last few months she had become a tower of strength and encouragement. We had both been on expeditions and travelled abroad for long periods in the past and so knew what was coming but as the day of my departure approached it became more difficult to discuss. She could not have been more wonderful or supportive and was far braver than I, but at times

we just hugged, both in tears, neither wanting to voice the uncertainty of such a long parting.

On Monday 3 January we got up early and Louie drove me to Broadcasting House for an interview on Radio 4's Today Programme. From there we went to Wellington Barracks where the Phase 1 team were already waiting. I emptied my lockers of all my uniforms and piled them into her car to be put into storage. Then packing the last few items of kit into my already inordinately large and overweight luggage I said farewell to the few well-wishers who had turned up at the office to see us off, issued a few rather muddled instructions to the Rear Party and boarded the coach.

At Heathrow, we were met by Jane Davis of Sloane Travel who performed her usual miracles by talking the airline officials into accepting all of our excess personal luggage, together with fifteen boxes containing three-quarters of a ton of batteries and a complete seven-foot-long dog sled, onto the aircraft for no extra charge. She further excelled herself by getting Richard and I upgraded to Club Class for the long initial flight to Seattle. For the first time in what felt like months we were able to relax for a few hours and take stock of the situation.

Phase One was a huge project and there was still an enormous amount to be done before we would be ready to begin our journey in three weeks time. Our planned ascent of McKinley was logistically relatively straightforward but I had considerable misgivings about our ability to cope with the technical side of the climb if we were hit by storms. Of more immediate concern, we still had no vehicles or any means of continuing south once the climb was complete and there was no money in our already critically under filled coffers to pay for them. Our Grand Canyon expedition was in place but fearsomely expensive. The remainder of the journey through Central and most of South America remained politically uncertain. Much work still needed to be done on the planning of our revamped Phase Four in Guyana and I would not have liked to put a bet on our chances of being allowed into Argentina to climb Mt Aconcagua or onto the Patagonian ice cap.

I sat gripped in a maelstrom of emotions. The dream had become a reality – but how much of the reality could we complete, that was the question.

Chapter Two

To Cape Prince of Wales and Point Barrow by Dog Sled and Snowmobile

We arrived at Anchorage airport after almost twenty-four hours of travelling. We were met by Andrew Phasey, Colour Sergeant McKeown, Sergeant Sculley and Wing Commander Phil Leadbetter, an RAF exchange officer working on secondment at Elmendorff Airforce Base. 'Wingco', had been instrumental in brokering many of our arrangements with the local US military and a constant source of encouragement and assistance. As we drove through the dark, snow-covered streets of Anchorage on our way to Fort Richardson we caught up on the Advance Party's news.

Next morning I got up to survey my surroundings. We were established in Camp Caroll, a small National Guard training camp, located within the much larger Fort Richardson military base. In January, Anchorage was locked into perpetual greyness. The sun rose mid-morning and was safely tucked away again by mid-afternoon. The few hours of daylight rarely lifted beyond a flat, dull gloom but when the sun did break through there were inspiring views over Arctic Valley and the surrounding Chugach Mountains. Further north, above the Arctic Circle, the sun never creeps over the horizon for most of November, December and January.

We had just three weeks to prepare ourselves for the 2,000-mile journey to Cape Prince of Wales and Point Barrow, our two objectives for this phase, the westernmost and northernmost points in the Americas. It was a journey that would take us along frozen rivers, through mountain ranges and over the tundra deep into the interior of Alaska and up the frozen coastline in the depths of an Arctic winter by dogsled and snowmobile, neither of which we were familiar with.

Camp Carroll was ideal for our purposes. We had comfortable warm accommodation, drying rooms, class rooms, stores and offices. In the woods behind the camp, there was almost unlimited space for training of every kind. We got stuck straight into our training programme. Beginning with basics, Tom Skala and Sergeant Brodie, our two instructors from the Northern Warfare Training Centre, gave us an orientation to Alaska and then took us through the fitting and wearing of our wardrobe of Arctic clothing. If we needed any further encouragement to take their advice and warnings seriously this was aptly provided by a lecture on cold weather injuries. Gory slides of self-amputating fingers and ankle stumps gained as a result of severe frostbite certainly concentrated the mind.

It was noticeable that, initially, most of the team were reluctant to leave the warmth of the buildings and go out into the rather intimidating conditions outside. Although not cold by Alaskan standards, there was undoubtedly a feeling of insecurity in this unfamiliar and threatening environment. Individuals' wariness was only increased by the careless touching of metal gates or ski bindings with bare hands which stuck to the metal and suffered searing cold burns. It was important to overcome this fear of the cold quickly.

Our first foray onto the training area incorporated an introduction to snowshoes. Strapping the outsized tennis racquets to our feet we shuffled outside and took our first tentative steps. Inevitably most people fell over, almost immediately catching one snowshoe on the other, until we began to develop the curious, penguin like waddle of the novice snowshoer. With practise you can learn to move relatively fluidly, picking your feet up carefully and adopting an unnaturally wide gait, but there is always that very special moment when you snag your snowshoe on a protruding willow stump and your 70lb pack drives you face down into the snow.

Cross-country skiing on old-fashioned US Army skis strapped to rubber Vapour Barrier boots was no less comical. We looked like a group of baby giraffes learning to walk for the first time until we got the hang of the kick and glide action that lets you skim along on the flat. Negotiating slopes was

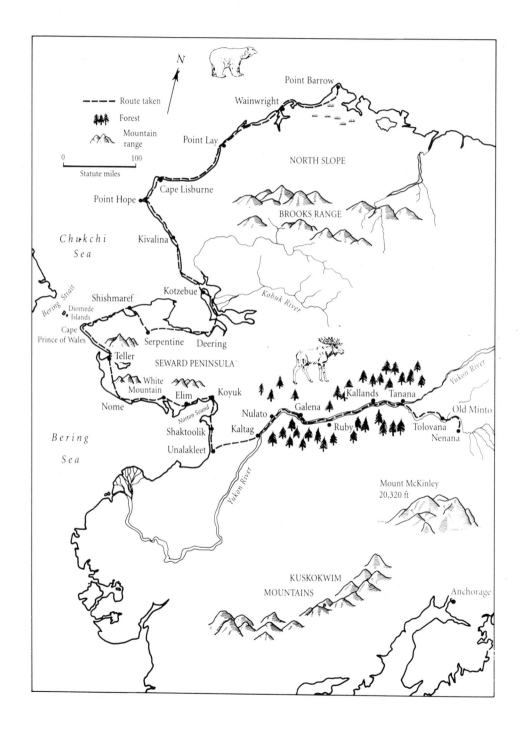

Phase 1 Route

quite another matter. We crabbed our way upwards with varying degrees of success but maintaining any form of control on a downward slope, as the skis continually popped off our flexible rubber boots, defeated many of the team. After several hours hard work, we returned to camp with tired, and in some cases bruised limbs, and ruddy faces.

We had been allocated a large fenced area to use as our dog yard. Preparations to make this ready for the imminent arrival of the dogs did not start well. The first work party to attempt to knock the solid steel posts into the ground, between which we planned to tension chains to which we would attach the dogs, broke the hafts of three out of our five sledge-hammers and bent innumerable posts with no single stake ending up secure in the ground by the end of a morning's work. Perseverance prevailed but at a not inconsiderable risk of over enthusiastic sledge-hammering within millimetres of fumbling gloved hands.

With the arrival of our eight brand-new Arctic Cat 'Cheetah' 440 horsepower long-track snowmobiles, we were able to go out onto the area behind camp and prepare training trails for the dog teams along the forested tracks. The requirement was for 4 to 5 mile circuits on broad tracks with shallow descents and wide bends on which we could learn to control our dog teams. Later we could extend these distances and attempt more difficult terrain as our confidence and ability grew.

The arrival of the dogs brought a buzz of excitement to the team. Everyone had heard so much about the huskies and the challenge of driving dog teams and now, at last, there were eighty-one dogs in our yard expressing their vocal eagerness to run. Before we could do that however, we had to learn how to handle, feed, look after and harness them.

The dogs were staked out in their teams of nine, each team to one main chain. All of us now paired off, each pair taking on the responsibility for one dog team. My intention was that once the expedition was underway each pair would be responsible for their dog team and one snowmobile, alternating the driving at appropriate intervals and assisting each other. This would have to be changed to some extent, as members of the team rotated through the Rear Party which would remain in Camp Carroll, but provided the greatest possible degree of constancy.

The dogs were fed twice a day during training. We laid out individual bowls of steaming hot, watery meat stew thickened with a commercial dog biscuit. It was a great time to get to know each of your dog's characters and an important opportunity to familiarize yourself with their habits and foibles. Some pounce on any food that is put in front of them whilst others pick choosily for their favourite morsels, spurning particular menus.

Their feeding is all-important. Not only does it provide them with their energy, for which we had allowed up to a staggering 10,000 kCalories per day when on the trail, but it is also their main means of hydration. Following feed times we would complete the dog yard chores, washing up bowls, sweeping old straw and dog excrement into bags, re-laying fresh straw and mixing with the dogs. After their evening feed they would throw their heads back and howl in concert into the darkness. Dougie MacDonald began our husky education. He started with handling and restraint techniques and then took us through the use and fitting of every piece of equipment in a mushers' inventory. We learnt the correct tightness of collars, fitting of harnesses, assembly of sled, brakes, gang lines, neck and tug lines, and how to fit bootees and coats. He continued with the treatment of minor ailments, care of dogs' feet and the diet that we would use on the trail.

Each dog has its own place within a team. The lead dogs, which may be run in single lead or as a pair, are responsible for holding the central line out straight and reacting to the mushers shouted commands of 'haw' for left, 'gee' for right and 'go ahead' for straight on. They tend to be the most experienced and intelligent of the dogs, although it is a myth that they are the strongest fighters who lead the pack through fear. Behind the leaders, in swing, dogs require a responsiveness to commands to assist the leaders in keeping the team on the correct trail. The team dogs, in the middle, contribute to the pulling power whilst at the back, the wheel dogs, generally the strongest and most robust of the huskies, are responsible for pulling the sled around corners after the team.

Dogs may be capable of running in more than one position but few have the special qualities required of a trusted leader: determination, drive, steadiness and ability to withstand the stress of continually interpreting commands and making decisions.

Legion are the stories of mushers who have been lead to safety through violent storms or around patches of weak ice by intuitive lead dogs.

Driving a sled-dog team is not about just shouting instructions to an instantly reactive and obedient line of huskies whilst resting casually on the back of the sled. The musher must steer by shifting his weight on the runners and by judicious application of pressure on the brake to flip the sled around corners. On broad, open trails this is not difficult but in tight woodland it can be intensely physical. As the team weaves between trees the musher is constantly wrestling with the sled, heaving it over first onto one side and then the other to present the base of the runners to pivotal trees.

Few husky teams show any reaction to cries of 'whoa'. Certainly at the beginning of a run with nine powerful dogs in harness the musher needs all his strength to stop them. He has a choice of three brakes: firstly, a rubber pad with metal cleats screwed into it which he can stand on to gain friction with the ground; secondly, a spring-loaded set of serrated metal teeth; and finally a savage metal anchor which can be stamped into the ground or used to snag a passing tree.

There is one golden rule: whatever you do, you must never, ever let go of your team. Even if the sled is thrown completely over onto its side and both sled and musher are bouncing off trees, the musher must cling on until either the team stops or he can fight his way back onto the runners and right the sled. The implications of losing sled and team are almost unthinkable. Driverless, the team may run on for many miles leaving the musher to flounder along in their wake through deep snow, without snowshoes or any of the equipment essential for survival.

Before entrusting us with driving the huskies, Roy and his team of handlers dragged each of us on a sled around a tight circuit towed behind a snowmobile. Only once everyone had completed this successfully were we allowed to harness four dogs for our first run with the huskies. In turn, escorted by snowmobiles, we set off on the prepared trail between snow-laden birch and spruce trees, each person returning breathless and euphoric, converted mushers all.

Over the next few days we continued to take our teams on training runs, gradually increasing the number of dogs and the length of the runs. In the evenings I had arranged for a number of old Alaskan hands to come and share some of their experience with us. Joe Reddington, the revered patriarch of the mushing community, had been born in a covered wagon on the Chisholm Trail in Oklahoma. He talked of Alaska in the old days and his life of subsistence hunting and fishing. He had driven his huskies in rescues to save crashed pilots, or to drag back entire aircraft in sections and on one occasion even to the top of Mt McKinley.

He had founded the annual Iditarod Race to commemorate the 1925 emergency relief operation during which desperately needed supplies of diphtheria serum had been carried by relays of dog teams to the stricken community of Nome. Since its inception, he had competed in the race eighteen times. Two of our husky teams were leased from Joe's kennel.

Dr Jim Leech, the Chief Veterinarian of the Iditarod and accepted authority on huskies came to talk to us about care of dogs on the trail. He took a robust line espousing the importance of recognising symptoms of illness or strain early to prevent rather than cure problems. He talked at length of the remarkable healing capacity of huskies.

Lieutenant-Colonel Bo Austin, a native Tlingit Indian from South-east Alaska, had lived and worked in many areas. His last job had been as Commander of the Eskimo Scout Battalion based in Kotzebue on the Bering Sea coast. Apart from stories about Tlingit customs and way of life, a nation that he said was still at war with the government of the United States, he had a lot of hints about survival in the extreme cold. The basis of his advice was to be patient, not to try and move in conditions of high wind-chill, to put a great emphasis on keeping everyone hydrated in what is essentially a cold desert environment and to pay rigid attention to the buddy buddy system of regularly checking each other for signs of frostbite or hypothermia.

All these people were mines of information and fascinating to listen to but in some ways only served to emphasise how little we knew.

Our training continued. There were lessons in snowmobile maintenance, the use of our cookers, tent routine and the construction of snow shelters. While this was going on, we had to prepare all the re-supply packages for the time that we would be out on the trail. We had calculated that we needed 660lbs of supplies per day including dog food, human rations, straw, batteries, snowmobile oil and various sundry items.

By far the largest element of this was the dog food. This comprised bags of commercial dog biscuit, fresh lamb, beef, chicken and fish, tubs of animal fat and various mineral and vitamin supplements. All the frozen meat had to be sliced and wrapped, nine slices to a package, and then boxed and refrigerated with the remainder of the re-supply. We were relying on US military air assets to move the bulk of these re-supplies out to a few main hubs and from there to the villages that we would be passing through. The remainder would be sent out by By-Pass Mail, the heavily subsidised system by which remote communities receive large parcels of provisions or equipment.

The culmination of our training period was a 24-hour exercise during which I wanted to bring together every aspect of our plan, trying out each piece of equipment and testing our intended method of travel and routine. We set off with full nine-dog teams and snowmobile outriders on a glorious 26-mile run. The trees were starched with hoar frost and underfoot the snow was crisp. Patches of overflow on the rivers steamed due to the temperature inversion. Away in the distance I could see Mt McKinley rising above the other mountains. I had a tremendous sense of well-being watching everything coming together.

Having arrived at our planned overnight stop we unclipped the tug lines which run from the back of each dog's harness to the main gang line, removed their harnesses, gave them a snack of a slice of frozen meat and then spread them out along the gang line which we had already tethered securely between the anchored sled and a tree. We then set about melting snow. Once we had adequate water for the evening feed we added frozen meat and left the broth to heat whilst we went to cut spruce boughs for the dogs' bedding.

Later, once the dogs were fed, we set up tents, lit lanterns and prepared our own food. No sooner had we settled down for the night than the dogs became restless. At the slightest imagined sound one of them would get up with raised hackles and start barking which then set others off. Time and again throughout the night we dived out of our tents to catch dogs that had somehow managed to wriggle free and were stirring all the others up or starting fights. Eventually I took my sleeping bag and went and lay down by my team in the snow.

Much of the problem was caused by the freshness of the dogs, who had been built up to a peak of training over the previous three months and were rather under-exercised within the constraints of our training programme. As a result they took off next morning with a renewed vigour. Running downhill on smooth trails I found myself bracing my arms up against the top bar of the sled to force extra pressure to my already full weight on the brakes. At one point when I lost control I had to throw the sled over onto its side until I could bring the team to a halt. Most of the others were suffering similar problems. As the morning progressed the dogs settled down and we had a good run back to camp.

Once we had got all the dogs securely back into the dog yard, settled and fed, we ran over the lessons learnt form the exercise. These included precautions against tent fires that could potentially be caused by stoves and lanterns, wet clothing that would lead to cold injuries and the importance of individuals looking after themselves and not taking short cuts with their own hydration and feeding in amongst all the other things that they had to worry about. On the dog side Roy talked about the techniques of controlling a team, use of the brakes, not issuing excessive and confusing voice commands and developing a rigid system for the night-time routine.

Despite the various problems that we had experienced he was pleased with the way that the training was going and the attitude that the soldiers had developed towards the dogs. They had taken on board all of the lessons of dog care and notified even the tiniest concerns to Dougie. Most were really enjoying working with the dogs and had become fiercely protective and affectionate towards their team.

Whilst the second half of the team set out on their 24-hour exercise I tried to tie up as many of the loose ends as possible. We needed to organise the out-load of our supplies from Nome, where they had been delivered by USAF Hercules, to the villages hopefully using National Guard Twin Otter aircraft and Blackhawk helicopters. I was also keen to co-ordinate a series of Eskimo scouts to guide us from village to village. Their local knowledge of routes through the mountains and safe routes across river and sea ice would be a great reassurance. Both areas of support were under threat due to funding limitations but Major Dusty Finlay, my contact at the Eskimo Scout Battalion in Nome, was trying everything that he could to overcome this.

The other chief area of concern was our ability to produce the re-supply packages fast enough to tie-in with the availability of freight space on Hercules flights once the team had set off. This production line was to continue for several weeks and it was becoming rapidly apparent that the small rear party was going to be stretched to keep up with demand. I was slowly and extremely reluctantly coming to the conclusion that I was going to have to leave Richard behind for the first leg of the journey to drive this programme and co-ordinate the out-load.

The Americans gave a small party to mark our departure, all of these people had done so much for us. Many had stuck their necks out professionally to provide us with the support that we needed. Several of them had invited us into their homes and later, I learned that it was they who came into camp to help the Rear Party once we had gone, rolled their sleeves up, manned the bandsaw and helped get the re-supply packages ready. We owed them a great deal.

Sergeant Brodie urged us to be careful and not to take a single short cut in our precautions against cold injuries. Bo Austin privately cautioned me not to be impatient in my decisions and to be prepared to wait for bad weather to pass. He gave me a pair of sheepskin gauntlets which he had made himself to go under my cotton outer mitts. When it was time to say goodbye I noticed a definite look of concern in people's eyes as they wished us good luck and a safe journey. Further north, as we all knew, conditions would be a lot less benign.

Our out-load from Camp Carroll 300 miles north to our start point at Nenana had to be staggered for the simple reason that we did not have enough vehicles to lift eighty-one huskies, nineteen of us, eight snowmobiles and all of the sleds, tents, general equipment and first three days of supplies at once. As it was we were using two specially designed dog transporters, a forty-seater coach, a flat-bed artic lorry and a four-tonne truck. The

initial move of the first load of dogs had not gone well. They had arrived at Nenana to find the ground so solid that they could not set up a temporary dog lot to secure the dogs whilst the vehicles went back to pick up the second load. After this false start we had gained permission from Gopher Lord, a local musher, to use his dog yard a few miles outside Nenana which was currently vacant.

The remainder of us, bringing the majority of the equipment, left Camp Carroll early next day whilst it was still dark. Richard, Colour Sergeant McKeown, Andrew Phasey and Wingco waved us off. Although he never once complained, the look on Richard's face gave away his disappointment at not coming with us. I felt extremely guilty that it was I who had researched and planned this phase and yet it was he who had to stay behind and sort out the shortcomings of that plan. Such is the lot of a Second-in-Command but I was glad that he would join us at the first team changeover.

Most of the team slept for the first part of the journey. The further north we drove the deeper the snow became. The boughs of the trees were heavily laden with ice-encrusted snow and the air seemed to crackle with the cold. After a dull start the day cleared and we had fine views over McKinley and the Denali Range to our west. Gopher Lord's yard turned out to be ideal. There were fixed stakes for all the dogs and we could all squeeze into the tiny cabin which saved us putting up tents and engendered a better team atmosphere.

Next morning we were treated to a slap-up breakfast by Nenana's Senior Citizens Club who plied us with coffee, moose steak, eggs, bacon, muffins and lashings of maple syrup. We then set about our final checks and preparations. Sleds, gang lines, neck and tug lines were all laid out and checked over. Screws and lashings were tightened and sled bags firmly tied onto the sleds. Snowmobiles had gear and engine oils topped up and their engines started. Citizens Band radios were fitted into brackets on the snowmobiles and tested. Each individual's load of human and dog food, feeding bowls, cookers, oil, axes, shovels, skis, snowshoes, cookers, portable kennels, tow ropes, together with all their personal kit and other general paraphernalia were laid out and packed.

In the afternoon Lieutenant Andrew Holman, Corporal Shaw and I went off on snowmobiles to

Each dog in the
team has its
particular role as
they work together
to haul a heavy load.

A snowmobile passes along the tight overgrown old mail trail towards Manley.

A dog team climbs up off the Yukon River near Kaltag.

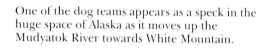

One of the dog teams appears as a speck in the huge space of Alaska as it moves up the Mudyatok River towards White Mountain.

Having fed his dog team, Guardsman Nick Perry
snatches the opportunity for something to eat.

Andrew Holman marks the trail ahead
of the dog teams in strong winds on the
way to Topkok.

The snowmobiles keep to the shore of the
Bering Sea coast to avoid rough sea ice and
pressure ridges.

Corporal Paul Martin says goodbye
to his lead dog in Nome.

Climbing a steep hill, the mushers will run beside the sled to take the weight off the dogs.

Travelling in convoy overland between Teller and Cape Prince of Wales, 1,000 miles still to go.

Justin Owen mushing his dog team along the Bering Sea coast.

Opposite: Gus Nelson and his brother fishing for Shee-fish through the ice of Kotzebue Sound.

Nick Perry on the high ground overlooking Cape Prince of Wales. In the background are the frozen Bering Straits and the islands of Little Diomede (USA) and Big Diomede (CIS).

Andrew Holman, happy at reaching Point Barrow, the northernmost point in the Americas.

Mike Charlson goes to discuss the next stage of the route with Justin Owen at a snack break for the huskies.

Crossing the Bonanza Flats in a ground blizzard on the way to safety.

recce a route from the cabin to a suitable crossing place over the Nenana River. We needed to link up with the Old Mail Trail to Manley. Out on the middle of the river ice we came across the rather disconcerting scene of a group of Indians drilling holes with augers to try and locate the body of a snowmobile rider who had recently fallen through a section of rotten shelf ice and drowned. Despite the current cold spell much of the river was incompletely frozen and dangerous. They pointed out a safe route across but I still felt a nervous shiver go down my spine as we gunned our engines and headed across the creaking ice.

On the far side we met a local musher, Mary Kassler, who showed us the trail. We followed it for several miles before turning back to Gopher's cabin. Roy had arrived with the remainder of the dogs. All was now set for the journey.

The 25th of January dawned cold but clear. As usual, it was still dark when we went out to check the dogs and give them their morning feed. As the sharpness of the cold gradually seeped out of the air we packed our sleeping bags and the last few items of dog sledding equipment into the large cordura sled bags. At the back, up near the handle bar, there is a much smaller pouch which we filled with spare gloves, goggles, hand warmers and a supply of sweets and snacks to grab during the day.

As soon as the harnesses were produced the whole yard turned into a furore as eighty-one frenzied huskies yelped, screamed and leapt against their leashes all wanting to be the first into harness and to start running. You could neither hear nor think amidst the din as we wrestled the dogs into their positions on the gang lines and clipped them in.

More experienced than the rest of us, Roy had his team harnessed first. Unable to hold them any longer, he pulled up his snow hook and took off after the first two snowmobiles with Andrew Holman and Corporal Shaw on board to show him the way. The effect was to send an already hysterical pack of huskies totally demented. I flew off after him holding on for all I was worth. Despite standing with most of my weight on the brakes my team headed out at a full gallop. I felt awkward and unsettled as I manoeuvred the heavy sled around the first few corners until they slowed down first to a lope and then into a brisk trot. Looking over

my shoulder I could see other teams pulling out behind me, their drivers clinging on to their sleds with a vice-like grip.

The nearest point of the Bering Sea coast lay 600 miles to our west. Our highways through the interior were to be the great frozen rivers, the Tanana and the Yukon. From the point where we hit the coast we had a further 400 miles to reach Cape Prince of Wales. Looking forward at my dog team, Point Barrow seemed an unimaginable distance away.

Andrew led us for nine miles in a large loop that took us from Gopher's cabin along a network of wooded trails around the back of Nenana's small airport to a point just outside the town where we could cross the main highway before moving down to the river. Lesley, Roy's wife, and Duane, his chief handler, were there to stop the traffic. As I saw them waving to us I felt very emotional. At long last we had finally started.

My euphoria was short-lived. One of the dog teams was missing. With great difficulty we stopped our teams and sent snowmobiles back to look for it. The wait seemed to last for ages as we fought to hold our fresh huskies. Dougie had missed one of the turnings in the woods and been unable to relocate the trail. As soon as the snowmobiles guided him back to us we set off again.

The dogs leapt forward once more. We raced down towards the river trying to steady them. Crossing the river all you could hear was the panting of the dogs, the rattling of the sled runners and the eerie creaking and cracking of the ice. There was a tangible feeling of relief as we pulled up the far bank. Beyond, the narrow, rather finicky trail passed alongside the highway, crossing mounds of snow at the entranceways to a number of cabins, many of which had their own dogs. Their barking only made the control of our teams more difficult and a number tried to bolt into the gateways. Having anticipated these teething difficulties the snowmobilers were on hand to help drag our lead dogs back onto the trail.

Soon we turned to the west, out into the country and away from civilisation. We headed along wooded trails packed with deep, soft snow. With teams that naturally travelled at different speeds and the concertinaing effect of travelling in convoy there was a lot of stopping and starting. This was not assisted by the snow conditions which did not make for smooth or easy travel with both snowmobiles and sleds regularly getting bogged down if they slipped off the loose packed trail.

Warm, wet snow provides another problem, balls of snow build up in the pads of the dogs feet which in turn cause abrasions and soreness. We had to stop after approximately every half hour of running in these conditions to check the dogs feet. This involved securing the sled by driving the snow hook firmly into the ground or better still, hooking it around a tree and then going along the team from husky to husky checking each paw in turn for sore spots. Any snow balls had to be melted off with the warmth from your bare hands. With thirty-six paws to check in a team of boisterous huskies this was a lengthy and at times frustrating process leading to painfully cold fingers. Every two to three hours, normally at one of these foot-checking stops, we would give the dogs a snack of a slice of frozen meat or a whole frozen, white fish.

Aside of the intended benefits of re-hydrating the dogs, these stops gave me the opportunity of getting to know my team a bit better. They had been leased as a single team from John Gourley who owned a small kennel at one of the coldest and most bleak spots I had ever been to. John normally ran one of the long distance races each year but this year he had planned to take a break whilst he built a house. I had met him on the recce the previous year and liked him immediately. Open, friendly and down to earth, with a ready sense of humour, he had a robust and realistic attitude to life. His dogs were much larger than Roy's and not as fine looking but individually they could bowl you over and as a team they pulled like a freight train.

Up at the front my two main leaders were Morgan and White Dan. Morgan was black haired and rather wild-looking. He did not like much attention and tended to shy away holding his head low whenever I approached him. White Dan was quite the opposite, white with dark patches and weighing 75lbs, he was extremely bouncy and affectionate. Both were strong and highly experienced having taken part in several of the long distance races.

In swing, I had Partner, a friendly medium-sized black dog and Bow, a black dog with brown speckling on his throat and chest who had lots of attitude. In the team positions, I had Arrow a small dark dog, Charlie a highly affectionate

and playful two year old and Yettna a slightly fat, lemon-coloured bitch.

You could not help liking Charlie and laughing at his more ridiculous antics but he was a constant distraction to the others on the team when they were running, constantly looking over his shoulder, sniffing at any strange aroma and often totally missing turns. He wanted to be friends with everyone all the time and to him life was just one big game. Yettna was a rather different case with few likeable traits. Her most annoying one was chewing both her own neck line and that of any other dog run in a pair with her which meant that before you knew it you had a loose dog on your hands and general pandemonium. Steel neck lines soon put paid to that trick but she remained a problem case.

In wheel, I had Tex, another huge, white dog with immense energy and friendliness who could run in any position from lead to wheel, and Gabe. Gabe, quite unwittingly, was rapidly turning my life into a nightmare. A young bitch, she had just come into season. No matter where I put her in the team all the dogs were trying to get at her. I could not put her in lead, as I would have liked, as she did not have the experience for it. Any dog that I put behind her fought to get loose or move up to her until they dragged the snow hook whenever we stopped, and those in front simply turned around and came back down the line blithely ignoring my shouts of protest to hold the gang line out straight.

The result each time was a massive tangle of snarling, rutting dogs which normally dissolved into a fight. Quite how I was supposed to prevent this I had not figured out, especially as the combined weight and power of the dogs in the team was several times that of my own. By the middle of the afternoon I had received several bites and rips to my clothing. I was hot, frustrated and in a less than benevolent mood.

With all the stops we made slow progress. Time went on and we seemed to be getting nowhere. Darkness fell so we drove on by the light of our head torches. We carried on and on, at last finding a decent broad trail. Snow blew in flurries into our faces. The batteries on my head torch were dying but I had not yet got the hang of holding onto the team and sorting myself out at the same time. We arrived at the deserted hamlet of Old Minto at 10 p.m. after what had certainly felt a long first day. We staked out the teams and set up a rather haphazard camp.

As we cut spruce boughs and prepared the dogs' food I reflected on the day's events. There was clearly a great deal to learn. I had always known that this would be so and had every confidence that in a relatively short period we would develop a good working routine and much more self-assurance in our ability to handle our teams. However, right at that moment, I felt our shortcomings keenly. Looking around I was not sure whether to be reassured or despondent that most of the others looked just as tired and hassled as I felt. It was almost the last straw when Roy came racing over to where I was briefing the snowmobilers to tell me that he had just found Morgan, who had broken free, tied with Gabe. As he aptly pointed out, all we needed was puppies on the trail. We had a long way to go.

Next morning the dogs were as fresh as if they had never run before and were eager to get going. In places no more than a metre wide, the trail led off into some tight woodland. Once the main trail for husky teams of the postal service to carry mail to the villages along the Yukon River and beyond to the coast, it had clearly not been used for a long time.

Behind an energised dog team it was a wild ride. I clung on for dear life as we hurtled along, bouncing off trees and ducking to avoid overhanging branches. If anything, it only became more overgrown and before long we found ourselves driving crouched low on the back runners. The lead snowmobiles had packed the trail but they had neither the time nor the means to cut back all of the encroaching undergrowth. Although much lower than us, even they were having some problems with branches whipping down and cracking their windshields.

There was no time to establish a rhythm as I worked the sled around corner after corner leaning it first one way and then the other, constantly shifting my weight to keep it exactly in the wake of the wheel dogs and trying not to cannon into the last tree that they had pivoted around. The trail switched back and forth mostly in the woods but emerging for short periods into areas of scrub willow beside the Tanana River.

I was desperately trying to protect my sled. Due to my height it had been specially built for me by a company in Britain but, whilst beautifully crafted, it was designed for more open country. I was already concerned at the way that the finely moulded wooden frame was bowing under the weight of the load. Sure enough, in one particularly overgrown section a protruding branch smacked down onto the main rail that ran the length of the sled holding the side stanchions in place and providing the rigidity. I saw a whole section of this rail fly off and the sled take on a misshapen twist. With the team still running and not wanting to exert too much pressure on it by forcing them to a sudden halt, I reached forward and snapped a spare neck line across the gap until at the next stop I could bind on a piece of willow branch to try and give it some strength.

The trail continued in similar vein until we pulled up for the night at a small clearing just short of the Tolovana River. The convoy had split up to try and minimise the concertina effect with snowmobiles accompanying each trio of dog teams. At the back some of the mushers had made heavy going of the difficult conditions. It was a cold night even wrapped up in down sleeping bags inside our pyramid tents. Andrew Holman went out on his snowmobile to pack the first few miles of the trail so that it could freeze overnight. We quickly saw the benefits of this when we headed on in the morning. The packed and frozen trail gave us good going whilst beyond, when we came to deep soft snow it was a slow, hard grind.

Part of the problem was not with the dog teams but with the snowmobiles. We were rapidly finding that there was more to driving a snowmobile than there looked. If you slipped off the track, which was easily done where it was hidden beneath a fresh layer of snow, the hugely overladen sleds tipped over or bogged down which caused the snowmobiles to dig themselves down into the snow. This then required two or more people to push, pull, drag and heave it back onto the trail again. With a couple of feet of fresh snow, forcing the trail onwards became a lengthy and arduous ordeal for the front snowmobiles.

After several hours of this we came upon the training trails of the mushers in the next village that we were heading for, Manley. These afforded better going enabling each team to travel at their own pace and we spread out over a considerable distance. I travelled the last few miles on my own. It was blissfully peaceful as we glided along well groomed trails alongside the Tanana River in the soft afternoon light.

My team had settled down into a steady trot and had become slightly less manic in their attempts to get at Gabe. They were even responding fairly well to my commands. The sled was not so good. The brush bow at the front was broken and I had boughs bound to both sides of the main frame. It looked decidedly Heath Robinson and needed some major repairs. As I pulled into the village a small, wild-looking white guy in some of the filthiest clothes imaginable, flew past on a racing sled pulled by a fast team.

Andrew Holman helped me tether my team. He had found the truck with our supplies that Corporal Pearce and Corporal Painter had driven up the ice road from the highway. Stuck to the windscreen was a sketch map indicating where we should stake out the dogs and telling us that they had gone off in a Civil Air Patrol plane to deliver the supplies ahead to Ruby and Kaltag. We collected each team as it came in and staked them out in a small paddock in front of the Road-house.

As we began the evening routine of laying out straw for the dogs, checking their feet and pre-paring food, villagers began to appear and came over to chat to us. They were soon offering help and hospitality of all sorts. The wild-looking Steve reappeared and took me off to see his mate Jack who agreed to fix all the broken sleds. Someone else opened up the natural hot spring baths and the owners of the Road-house kindly offered open house to all and an impromptu party began. We could not have been made more at home.

I spent the evening shuttling between the tall stories that were being told in the Road-house bar and the hive of activity in Jack's workshop with re-supplies of beer, driven by an increasingly drunk and high Steve. I finally crashed out under a table in the Road-house at about 1.30 a.m. absolutely shattered, but at least all the sleds were repaired.

After a long, hard ponder I had come to the realisation that certainly at my level of experience it was not possible to run a dog team and lead the expedition. The dog team required total dedication 24 hours per day. You could never relax or drop your concentration on the trail and once stopped, the chores took up nearly every other waking moment. Even at night you had to be constantly watchful in case a dog slipped its collar or the team pulled the snow hook free. Gabe being in season only exacerbated this.

I did not have the flexibility to move up and down the convoy checking on problems or the ability to reach a night stop first to co-ordinate the arrival of the dog teams and the allocation of supplies. I certainly was not getting the time to go around the other members of the team to see how they were coping and help, advise or encourage individuals as I should be. I knew that the only solution was to hand my dog team over to one of the snowmobilers and drive their machine.

I was bitterly disappointed as the dog sledding had always been my dream and I longed to take my team all the way. It captured every element of true old fashioned adventure as I saw it. I had every confidence that as we got into the journey the teams would all settle into a much more mellow routine but for now there was still a lot of co-ordination required to generate the confidence in people that would create this atmosphere.

I decided to go with the recce party to see for myself the difficulties that they were facing. Andrew Holman and Corporal Shaw had taken on this mantle and both were proving their worth. Andrew had come to the expedition under slightly unusual circumstances. I had been working in the office in London before the second of our selection camps when the telephone had rung. It was the Adjutant of the Household Cavalry Mounted Regiment at Knightsbridge Barracks who happened to be a friend of mine. He had a problem and was seeking my help. Andrew Holman, one of the subalterns, had fallen foul of the Commanding Officer. Andrew had been in fairly regular trouble for a variety of reasons. As a result of some fresh misdemeanour, the new Commanding Officer was attempting to get him posted anywhere that he could away from the regiment.

Andrew had applied to come on the first phase of the expedition in any event but the Adjutant asked whether I would take him on immediately and employ him until we set off. I had never met Andrew, although I knew that our parents were friends, but I had already heard of his reputation for unruly behaviour. We had enough on our plates without looking after delinquent young officers but

I agreed to take him on the stipulation that he passed the selection and that if I had any trouble at all I would send him straight back to face his Commanding Officer's wrath.

When I first met Andrew, he turned up to the training camp in an open-topped sports car. I laid down the rules in as stern a manner as I could muster and then left him to it. As I had suspected, away from the restrictive regimen of ceremonial soldiering, against which he rebelled, he came into his own. He quickly proved himself to be tough, resourceful and popular with the soldiers, finishing off a good performance on the camp by coming first in the Iron Man Competition. Although he had not cared much for the office work associated with the organisation of the expedition he had reluctantly settled down to it and produced some detailed research. The unconventional aspects of life on expedition suited his character and he revelled in the practical difficulties that confronted us.

Corporal Shaw had also stood out on the training camp. He was solid both in build and character with a calm unflappable air. I enjoyed his gentle, wry sense of humour and was sure that he would be dependable in a crisis.

All three of us now set out together with a local guide from the village who had offered to show us the way to our intended camp at Fish Lake. The first fifteen miles were straightforward along a broad graded road that led out to some disused mine buildings. As we drove along, it was wonderful to have the space to think and plan.

We moved onto narrow, winding trails that took us across scrub-covered tundra. We began to have a lot of problems with the snowmobiles slipping off the narrow trail that was concealed beneath the surface snow. I noticed that our guide drove his machine far more aggressively than we did, throwing his weight around and rocking the machine violently to help gain traction if he got stuck. We had to cross frequent creeks. In a number of places these were not completely frozen and pools of overflow lay on the surface. Each time that we passed through one the mushers would have to stop and dry off their dogs' feet.

Three miles short of Fish Lake we came to American Creek. It was wider than the others that we had crossed and when we got to it, we saw to our dismay, that the trail disappeared into a large pool of open water. Although only about five metres wide, it would be far too deep for either snowmobiles or dog sleds to cross. A cursory look revealed no patches of better ice nearby. This was a serious problem. The creek extended for many miles in either direction and there were no bridges.

Our guide shook his head, sucked his teeth and pronounced that there was no chance of us finding a way around, we might as well turn back. We could not do that, to do so would be to give up on the whole venture. Somehow we had to find a way over it. Seeing that we weren't going to leave he said that it was late, he was planning to take his wife out to dinner and turning his machine around, he sped off back to the civilisation and warmth of Manley leaving us to survey our predicament.

Andrew reacted first and strapping on his snow-shoes set off downstream. I dug around in my sled for my snowshoes but in the time that I had taken to unearth them, chip the ice off the buckles and attach them to my boots he was back saying that he thought he might have found a possible crossing site. I followed him for a couple of hundred yards through some brush alongside the creek until we came to a spot where four trees were leaning over the creek. Andrew suggested that if we dropped them and then bound them together we would have the basis for a bridge. The plan relied on the trees falling the right way and being strong enough. I wasn't overly optimistic but in the absence of a better idea we went back to brief Corporal Shaw. Leaving him to greet the on-coming dog teams and show them where to camp, as I could see this was going to be no quick job, Andrew and I grabbed axes and a rope and went back.

Taking it in turns we chopped down the first couple of trees which fell roughly the right way. Encouraged by this we dropped another. Inevitably they had not fallen neatly together or straight across the creek, so with me belaying him on the end of a rope Andrew made his way rather tentatively across, balancing his weight on two of the trunks. Teetering along snow-covered logs in clomping great snowshoes in the dark he cut a comic figure and I grinned at the thought of what our fathers would say if they could see us now. We managed to pull the three trees together and lashed them both to each other and securely to the far bank. Very pleased with ourselves we went back to recruit some extra help.

We found the others settling into the overnight routine. As soon as feeding was over, having left a small group to watch the dogs, we got everyone else armed with axes, machetes and shovels. We then set people to work, some blazing a route from the main trail to the crossing site, chopping back the brush and stamping down the snow, whilst others chopped down further trees for the base of the bridge and then branches to lay crosswise over the trunks.

Working by the lights of head torches and lanterns, trying not to injure each other or get wet, the bridge slowly began to take shape. It was great to see officers, NCOs and soldiers all working shoulder to shoulder. Some people really came to the fore. Despite his volatile nature Guardsman Miller was a useful guy to have in a tight spot. Strong, practically minded and handy with an axe he contributed much more than his share with both physical effort and ideas.

It was after midnight before Andrew and I were able to drive our snowmobiles along the prepared track, down onto the bridge and across to the far side. But for the odd heart-stopping creak and lurch it was sound. Leaving everyone else to follow in the morning we pushed on. With the moon nearly full we could see remarkably clearly in the light reflected off the snow. We stopped to camp when we reached the edge of Fish Lake. We both dug trenches in the snow next to our snowmobiles to protect us from the wind and having laid out sleeping bags and bivi bags settled down to a peaceful night's sleep, or what was left of it. I felt a quiet satisfaction that we had beaten the sceptics and overcome our first major hurdle.

I woke up at 7 a.m. Sticking my head out of my sleeping bag I found freezing cold air and pitch darkness, so hastily withdrew for a few more minutes warmth. Two hours later I woke again. I yelled to Andrew to get up, we needed to get moving or the dog teams would catch us still in bed. We were due to meet a guide the far side of the lake but how we were to link up with him was not clear. We set off rather nervously across the glare ice as a snowstorm blew up around us. We drove about five miles across the ice to what we took to be the far shore, but when we got there we found that it was an island behind which were a series of lagoons.

We dropped our sleds and began following the shore in an attempt to find our guide or some sign of a trail. After a broad sweep to the west we turned back. Just as we did so we saw the headlight of a snowmobile flicker out of the grey half-light. Our guide turned out to be an Indian called Ronnie. As we went back to pick up our sleds I could just make out the head torches of the dog teams in close convoy at the far side of the lake.

With Ronnie leading we followed an old trail through some woodland for about thirty-five miles. We stopped frequently to place out orange painted stakes or tie plastic tape to trees to mark the route. It snowed for much of the way. I felt for the mushers standing unprotected on the back of their sleds. Finally we emerged at the junction of the Tanana and Yukon Rivers. The Yukon was a broad expanse of open, windswept ice. Heavy snow-filled clouds and a howling wind only served to make it appear even more unfriendly and intimidating. We cut across the river to the north side, passed by a small wooden church and then climbed up the steep bank and stopped outside a small cabin where Ronnie's brother-in-law Freddie Jordan was waiting for us.

Freddie's heavily jowled face creased into smiles as he greeted us. A huge man in both girth and character, he was one of the few Indians to run a competitive dog-team. He told us in his low, gravelly voice that he had planned to come and meet us himself but had been drinking all night at a party to raise money for his next race. Inside, the cabin was chaotic but a pleasant relief from the biting wind. Bits of ramshackle furniture were laden with old clothes, parts of engines and tools. All around were strewn strips of raw meat and the hooves of a moose. A tousled mop of black hair emerged from under the covers of a bed in the corner revealing the presence of his wife.

Freddie offered us a beer in the expectant way of a man who is rarely without one. After we had shared a few stories, mainly about his mushing exploits, over another couple of beers and had a chance to warm up, Freddie sent his son with us into the town to find our supplies.

Tanana is one of the main trading centres on the Yukon River. Most of its occupants are either engaged in subsistence fishing during the summer or the provision of supplies or services for those that are. We found our re-supplies in the care of another Indian, Bill White. The town policeman, a pony-tailed white man called Stan Zurray, appeared and offered to help us find a place to stake out the dogs and to open up the wooden Lion's Club cabin for us to sleep in.

By the time that we had carried all the supplies to the dog lot and prepared trails for each of the teams it was dark. I was worried how they would have fared in the storm and so drove back out to Freddie's cabin. Just as I was about to set off back up the trail to search for them, their headlamps appeared, bobbing across the river ice with the movement of their sleds. We guided the teams through the town to their allocated place where we had piles of straw, food and jerrycans of water ready. Later, in the Lion's Club, Indians kept appearing and either just stood staring or chatted to us as we cooked our food and sorted our kit out.

The next village along the Yukon is Ruby, over 120 miles downstream. We hoped to make the journey in two to three days depending on the trail conditions. The natives told us that no one had been that way so far that winter and so there was no trail. However a snowmobile racer, Tommy Krisca, offered to put it in for us. Tommy told us that he had done the journey in an astonishing hour and three quarters. Crouched low over his powerful racing machine next morning, he streaked off downriver.

The dog teams set off next keeping in his tracks and we followed when we were ready, having cleaned up the dog yard and loaded up our sleds with the remainder of the supplies. The early part of the trail was relatively easy going, even with sleds piled high, but further on it was canted at the side of the river and the sleds repeatedly slipped off into the deep soft snow beside.

After a long, exasperating afternoon we caught up with the dog teams preparing to camp. Having driven twenty-five miles, they were still ten miles short of the planned night layover but the soft snow had tired the dogs out. We now planned to push on with the Recce Party to pack the trail and give it a chance to freeze overnight.

I wanted to try and establish a routine whereby those of us in the Recce Party would always travel twenty-four hours ahead of the team so that they would have continually good trails and we would have plenty of time to prepare village layovers. The other snowmobilers would remain with the dog teams; a couple running in front to clear any fresh snow or moose from the trail and the remainder at the back to help any stragglers.

As we were making our plans, a rather shaken Tommy reappeared. He had gone about forty miles when one of his front skis had hit a concealed block of ice and he had been launched up into the air. The machine had flipped pinning him beneath it. It had taken him fifteen minutes to wriggle free. Having hurt his leg and damaged the machine he had turned around. This was just before a point where the trail should have turned away from the river over a portage section to avoid an area of bad river ice. He drew a diagram in the snow to show us the trail that we should follow but the confusion of lines representing trap lines and fire breaks did little to foster much confidence in our chances of finding it.

We had a hot meal and set off, Andrew and I with considerably lightened sleds and the Doctor, Sergeant Sculley and Corporal Shaw following behind. Even with lightened sleds we bogged down frequently and it was 11 pm before we reached the summer fishing camp at Kallands, our intended night stop. We now started trying to interpret Tommy's instructions but all of the trails we followed kept leading us away in the wrong direction or petering out.

We found one that we were convinced must be right and followed it for a good distance up a steep hillside into the woods. Time and again we bogged down. Each recovery became more difficult until on the last occasion it took us forty-five minutes of cursing and sweating to get the machines free. We decided to turn back and rather dispiritedly returned to Kallands where we found the other three. With heavy sleds it had taken them seven hours to cover just ten miles. We all crashed out in a fish drying shed. It was 2 a.m.

We got up at first light and went back up the previous night's route to see if we could find the trail that we were looking for but to no avail. Despite Tommy's warning about the roughness of the river ice I could not see that we had any alternative but to try and find a route through that way. We met the dog teams at Kallands and explained to them what we were doing.

We followed Tommy's tracks along the river until we came to the spot where he had flipped. Just further on we hit a patch of surface overflow. My machine ground to a halt in the grey, glutinous mush. Both Andrew and I got wet pushing it out. We dropped our sleds and went gently on. As the river came to a large, sweeping bend the current in the water had forced up a series of ridges, steps and blocks of clear rock-hard ice. We carried on a short way into this tortured icescape, our skids bouncing sharply off the unavoidable protrusions and throwing the machines around violently. The pace was impossibly slow and the ice appeared to be getting worse. Standing on our machines we tried to see where it ended but the broken ice stretched all the way to the horizon and it was impossible to judge how far away that was. For all we knew it might extend all the way to Ruby.

We clearly had neither the experience nor the driving skills to put a route through ice like this. I decided to leave Andrew to continue to try to find the overland route whilst I set off immediately with Sergeant Sculley back to Tanana to see if we could enlist some local help. I was all too aware that we were only carrying limited supplies and the dogs were fast eating their way through them. I needed to get the expedition moving. At Tanana no one was prepared to help us but just as I was beginning to get desperate a message arrived to say that two Indians had just come into town having travelled along the river from Ruby.

Tommy Krisca had rung ahead to ask his friends there to look out for us and when we had not turned up, they had come out to look for us. They had bumped into the remainder of the team at Kallands and had shown them the route.

In the morning we filled up our jerrycans with fuel and bought extra snowmobile oil to replace that which had been burnt up trail breaking and some extra supplies for the team.

The journey back was unremarkable. We found just Corporal Martin and Guardsman Thomas waiting for us. Andrew Holman had set off the previous night along the trail made by the Indians and the remainder had followed at first light. We collected the equipment that we had left at Kallands and set off after them. For the first part of the journey, the trail wound its way like a snake between the formations of solid riverine ice.

It was slow, heavy going, hard on both machines and sleds, banging and crashing over the ice. We had to go through a number of patches of overflow with little option but to gun our engines and try and use momentum to force a way through the sugary

morass. We passed fairly frequent open leads which made me feel decidedly uneasy but after a while we emerged from the area of rough ice and the trail became flat and straight along the Yukon.

We caught the tail end of the convoy after a couple of hours. Guardsman Justin Owen was driving the rearmost team as usual. He seemed quite unperturbed by the fact that he was always at the back often finishing several hours after the front runners. A quietly spoken Welshman, he enjoyed working with the huskies at his own unhurried pace and attached a strong fondness to each of them. We forged on, passing Sergeant Dyer, Guardsman Miller, Dougie MacDonald and Corporal Ordish, all of whom were in good form. Corporal Steggles was clearly struggling with his dog team so I made a mental note that he might need a change.

We found the front group halted at an exposed and bitterly cold bend in the river. Andrew Holman, Corporal Shaw and Guardsman Manassie had driven all night to put the trail in thus far and had stopped and made camp at 7 a.m. They were now preparing to go on again. Roy had left the remainder of the dog teams and come on alone, travelling much faster with his well drilled team.

I asked Andrew to hold on whilst Sergeant Sculley and I had something to eat and so that I could see most of the dog teams arrive. We then set off in front once again. It took three hours to cover the remaining fifty miles to Ruby with just one bad patch as we tried to traverse a slope upon which a great bank of fresh snow had built up. We arrived shortly before midnight and found our way to the cabin of our contact there, Emmet Peters. He greeted us and apologised for not having come to meet us as previously arranged. With the dog teams not due to arrive until the next day he showed us to another cabin and gave us coffee, doughnuts and salmon. We fell on the food and collapsed into our sleeping bags.

Ruby turned out to be a pretty village of brightly painted wooden cabins perched on a hillside overlooking the broad Yukon River. All of the villages are raised well above the river as in winter the river basin maybe as much as ten degrees colder than the surrounding country.

Nicknamed 'The Yukon Fox', Emmet had been a successful long distance musher and was a respected figure throughout all of the native communities.

He soon had a small army of helpers to assist us get ready for the arrival of the dog teams. The people of Ruby could not have been more welcoming. The village elders approved his proposal that we should stay in the Community Centre. Edna, his wife, set about rounding up the local women and preparing a large meal for the team which had all the makings of a full community party. The winters are long in Ruby and I got the impression that any distraction was welcome.

In summer the village split between subsistence fishing and fire-fighting. Most of the men went away for months at a time to join the State fire-fighting teams. Whole villages would sometimes form their own crew. They used highly sophisticated techniques to fight fires sometimes even parachuting with their equipment just ahead of a fire. It was hard and dangerous work fighting the huge forest fires throughout Alaska and sometimes further south in the northern United States.

Reluctantly, I decided that the Recce team should press on to Galena, where we planned a major layover. We dragged ourselves away from the festivities and carried on downriver. For the majority of the way it was flat and even and we were able to open the throttles on our snowmobiles and travel at up to 40mph, faster than we had travelled at any other time.

There were a number of portages to avoid patches of overflow and again we saw frequent open leads. The half-mile wide river was flanked by cliffs and rolling pine-forested hills. An ice road led up off the river to the town of Galena, a much larger settlement, on the outskirts of which we located the Airforce Base.

After a good night's rest we began to sort ourselves out. This was the end of the first leg of the journey. We planned to spend three days here whilst we changed over the Rear Party in Anchorage, swapped dog team and snowmobile drivers, reprovisioned and serviced and repaired all of the equipment. We went over to a large, heated hangar where we emptied the contents of our sledges, strung tents and clothing up to dry, identified items of equipment that needed repair and swept out the clutter of spilt dog food, fuel, twigs and snow that had become a permanent mush in the bottom of the sleds.

We could not have asked for better facilities or more help as Dave Colson, the base manager,

and his team offered the use of workshops with mechanics, electricians and radio specialists to help. With the end of the Cold War and the break up of the Soviet Union as a serious threat to mainland USA the F-15 crews had left and the base was now manned by civilian contract staff.

Andrew Holman went with Guardsman Manassie to mark the route into town and to go and meet the teams further up the trail. I went with Dave Colson out to the runway to meet the incoming C12 aircraft which brought Richard, Corporal Pearse, Corporal Painter and two visitors, our Honorary Expedition Director, Major-General Robert Corbett and his aide-de-camp. It was great to see them and to catch up with all the news from Anchorage.

They had lots to tell. The two Corporals had been all over the interior delivering supplies and were full of stories of hazardous flights into remote bush strips. They had had a hard time of keeping up with the production of supplies to meet the outload schedule but the majority of the task was now done. Richard brought me up to speed with the remainder of the expedition news and progress in England.

After lunch we went out on snowmobiles to meet the dog teams and help guide them in. We met Roy about six miles from town going fast and then the rest of the team spaced out over the next twenty miles. It was great for the General to be able to see the team in action and talk to each of the soldiers as they went past. The tail-enders looked tired with an exhausted but happy Guardsman Owen at the back. It was 6 p.m. before he made it to the camp.

For the next couple of days we carried out an intensive programme of repairs. It was good to be able to sort ourselves out and get everything ready for a fresh start. I spent time reorganising the team and talking to everyone individually to see that they were all happy. Corporal Shaw, Corporal Ordish and Trooper Canning were to go back to Anchorage. I did not want to send any of them back, particularly Corporal Shaw, but everyone had to take their turn and he had hurt his back when a tree had fallen on him in the dark as we had been building our bridge across American Creek. I suspected that it was troubling him more than he was admitting.

I also spent time briefing General Corbett over a glass or two of the excellent malt whisky that he had brought with him. Since agreeing to take on the role of Expedition Director, for which he was the obvious choice as the current Major-General Commanding the Household Division, he had been nothing but totally supportive and encouraging. He now brought news of more sponsorship that he had raised through his own contacts.

The highlight of this period was the arrival of mail for the team. I had letters from my parents, some friends, a distant cousin offering to help find some sponsorship and best of all from Louie. Nothing has such a beneficial impact on morale as mail from home.

There were concerning reports of poor trail conditions further down the river. The locals were saying that there was a lot more overflow and open leads and were questioning whether we would get through. Andrew Holman went off ahead to the next village, Nulato with a guide from the Fish and Wildlife Service and the General. Leaving Andrew at Nulato they returned reporting reasonable conditions but saying that they had spotted a lot of fresh moose tracks. Adult moose had been known to get amongst a dog team and kill or maim several of the dogs with their lethal hooves. It was all too easy to surprise them as you came around a corner silently with a dog team. We carried a variety of shotguns, rifles and handguns to defend the teams against just such an eventuality.

The morning of our departure was predictably chaotic with fresh husky teams practically jumping out of their skins with energy and enthusiasm and some slippery ice roads to negotiate on the way out of the town before dropping back down onto the Yukon. The trail for the most part was an highway down the broad Yukon River crossing from one bank to the other to avoid overflow and weak ice. The dog teams covered the fifty miles to Nulato on the first day and the remaining thirty-five miles to Kaltag by mid morning on the second.

I watched as each team climbed the steep bank up into the village. It seemed sad to be leaving the Yukon so soon. Bisecting Alaska from east to west, it had been the artery along which the early fur trappers and gold prospectors had penetrated the interior, creeping steadily westwards from the Canadian Yukon Territories. It was inextricably linked to the commercial, historical and spiritual life of Alaska. Its place enshrined in folklore, rich with stories of triumphs and tragedies and hardy, resolute people driven by desperation, determination or greed to carry out heroic and unlikely feats with little but their native wit to assist them in the face of appalling odds.

Now our route took us overland, away from the Yukon and across the mountains to the Bering Sea. We halted the teams and staked them out along a line of fir trees at the edge of the village. Groups of children gathered round each team to look at the dogs and watch the strange foreigners that were looking after them.

Having seen everyone safely settled with the correct supplies I was keen to get on again with the Recce Party. We had two Indian guides from the National Guard, Bill Soloman and another man with the rather unlikely name of Adolf McGinty. They led off along a narrow, twisting trail through a pine forest. Although mercifully not overhung, the trail was founded on deep soft snow with a fragile crust that was just strong enough to support a snowmobile but if you took one pace either side you plunged straight up to your waist. We climbed steadily up into some bare-topped hills. It was open, uncluttered scenery not unlike much of northern Scotland. We ground along slowly, burning up a worrying amount of fuel.

We stopped at 22 mile cabin for some coffee and to refuel and also to leave Corporal Pearse to prepare for the arrival of the dogs at what was planned to be their night stop. We carried on for another twenty miles to Old Woman cabin. Although it was the main route between the Yukon and the Bering coast town of Unalakleet, Bill seemed less than sure of the way. Each time he strayed off the trail we found ourselves ploughing into deep powder snow with much bogging of vehicles and cursing as we cast around to find the trail once more. As we carried on into the darkness I could hear Andrew Holman muttering that we would have been better if left to navigate by ourselves.

We left a message pinned to the door of the cabin before pressing on. Gradually we dropped out of the hills. As we did so the vegetation thinned and trees diminished in favour of low scrub. We were now entering the coastal tundra. The tussocky grass was covered by a shallow scattering of snow and sheathed in ice in many places, evidence of the strong, coastal winds and bitterly cold temperatures that we had been warned to expect. After another couple of hours we came to the Unalakleet River. In the distance, under the orange glow of the town we could see lights on a radio mast and what looked like a lighthouse.

We skittered and slithered along the bare ice as the snowmobiles fought to gain traction, pirouetting uncontrollably when our heavy sleds slewed around and began to overtake us. We passed frequent patches of open water. It had been dark for hours. We all wanted to get to the warmth and safety of the town. Five miles out, we had to stop to refuel.

The closer to the mouth of the river we got, the worse the open leads became. By the time that we could see the lights of the buildings we were in a broad estuary. The surface of the ice glistened evilly. It was hard to tell in the dark what was solid and what was just a thin crust concealing overflow. We narrowly avoided one large section and then I suddenly found myself following Bill straight into trouble. I could see the sugary ice crust rippling under the weight of his machine and then he had cut through. We were moving between two sand spits. Hard ground lay only fifteen yards further ahead.

Travelling right behind him I was committed to taking the same line. I could see him fighting to keep his machine going. With each yard he was sinking lower but his momentum just carried him through and he gained the gravel the far side. However, with the crust broken I lost that extra bit of traction which had got him through. In slow motion I watched my machine drop into the water, choke and then cut out.

My initial reaction was shock and panic. I tried to re-start the engine but it was flooded. I was standing in icy water up to my thighs. Below the surface ice I could feel the current tugging at my ankles. The sled rapidly filled with water but still managed to float and was beginning to drag the machine downstream. I tried to pull the snowmobile forward, grasping onto the front crash bar but slipped on the glare ice on the bottom of the river. My feet were freezing. It felt like an age as Bill unwound a rope that he had in his sled and threw it to me. With rapidly numbing fingers I tied it to the front skis of my snowmobile. As he towed me out with his machine the others behind me took off to find another way around the overflow.

From the direction of the town three snowmobile headlights were weaving their way towards us and shortly after three locals arrived. They had been watching us making our way down the river and when they saw us stop they had guessed what had happened.

It was a bad year for dangerous ice and there had been a number of accidents. To my great relief they guided us through the maze of overflow into the town but even that short distance was fairly hair-raising. Each time we went onto the ice I could feel my heart-beat racing. I did not want to fall in again and kept thinking of the Indian who had drowned under the ice at Nenana. Once below the surface you would have no chance against the current.

It took about half an hour to reach the National Guard Armoury. Inside it was blessedly warm. I stripped off my wet clothes and put on some borrowed dry ones in their place then unloaded my sled. Everything had been thoroughly soaked and was now beginning to freeze solid. The congealing mass of dog food, bags containing several hundred dog booties, ropes, clothes and all of the hardware was a sorry sight.

I hung up all the clothing and my sleeping bag, thanking my lucky stars that it had not happened when I was on my own, far from a village. What had been frightening and unpleasant would have become a serious survival situation under those circumstances. It was after midnight. We cooked a meal and sorted ourselves out whilst talking to the guides. They said that there was more warm weather on the way and we could expect to encounter a lot more overflow. My heart sank. I could not write my diary completely, I felt too tired. I re-read Louie's last letter and sank gratefully into a borrowed US Army sleeping bag.

Next day, after a morning spent trying to dry out dog coats and bootees, we headed back up the trail to meet up with the dog teams and guide them through the overflow. We had gone twenty-five miles before we met Roy at the head of the convoy. They had had a hard time on the soft snow and had spent the night at the first cabin, continuing on in the morning once the trails had frozen. It took until after dark to shepherd the teams safely down the river, avoiding the weak ice and into the town.

Still with Bill Solomon as our guide, together with another native National Guardsman, Ivanoff Walter Unalakleet, we turned north up the coast. It was strangely beautiful landscape with the frozen sea on one side and sparsely wooded hills on the other. We came to a steep slope with a smattering of fresh snow concealing a glass like sheet of ice running all the way to the top. Despite taking a run at it with the throttle full open the lead snowmobile ground to a halt and then slithered back down again. When we tried to find a way around the flanks of the hill we found ourselves tackling a succession of small snow filled gullies. We emerged into more open country. Here, there was almost no snow covering and we bounced over bare, frozen tussocks. I winced as I felt the punishment that this unforgiving ground was meting out to our fibreglass sleds.

We approached a small deserted settlement and as we did so a herd of about sixty caribou broke across our front. The buildings were all in good condition and there was glass in the windows which suggested that it was used as a regular summer fishing camp. We climbed up into another series of hills, this time more thickly vegetated. The higher we drove, the colder it became. At the top the bushes were heavy with a thick coating of frost. Despite low cloud which gave a dull monochromatic grey light we had glimpses of views over the surrounding hills and valleys and away to the sea. Having been used to the forested trails of the interior it was invigorating scenery.

Corporal Pearse halted saying that his sled had a gash all the way along one runner. We filled up our machines from the jerrycans on his sled to lighten his load but it worried me that all the sleds were taking a battering. Down out of the hills, we crossed flat tundra, shadowing the coastline and for the most part driving along a frozen lagoon. We passed a fox with a beautiful luxuriant amber coat. It was curled up under a bush and seemed quite unmoved by us.

As we approached Shaktoolik we climbed up onto a causeway. An old abandoned truck gazed sightlessly out to sea. We passed the deserted village of Old Shaktoolik. The shattered planks and supports of rotten buildings stuck out like the bones of a skeleton. Many of the cabins had no roofs. The remains of four snowmobiles and older redundant machinery were frozen into the ice as if suspended in time. A bicycle wheel spun in the wind. Outside one building two dogs barked and a wizened old man with crazed eyes was sawing up wood. It was a macabre scene and we drove quickly on.

Shaktoolik means 'the place of the wind'. In the dusk it looked an isolated, bleak place on the edge of the frozen Bering Sea. The new village is a double line of buildings either side of a single road. We found the small Armoury and our pile of supplies. As the dog teams arrived we staked them on the only available open ground which was on the seaward side of the building. We put coats onto the dogs to protect them from the wind.

I was about to send Andrew Holman back to check on the last teams when Guardsman Manassie came in with his team. He was visibly shaking. He said that the tide had come up and as he crossed the lagoon he had felt the ice cracking. He had gone through a couple of times and been badly frightened. Andrew shot off to look for Guardsman Owen who was a few miles behind.

The wind picked up to 25mph during the night. I went to speak to Saul, the Public Safety Officer who was going to guide us on the next leg across Norton Sound. This very exposed and dangerous section took us thirty miles straight across the sea ice. It was often unsafe to travel, either due to storms or the condition of the ice. He now advised that we should wait a day to give the wind a chance to drop. He also said that being a north wind it should drain the overflow. I was quite happy with this suggestion as we had a lot of repairs to make to the sleds. Having fed and checked the dogs we unloaded all the sleds, carried them inside to dry out and then began applying fibreglass resin and matting to weak spots.

I went out in the afternoon with Saul and Sergeant Sculley to mark the first section of the trail. The icy wind cut straight through our face masks. Of more concern, the route was not a trail at all and took us straight over an area of bare, rough tundra for fourteen miles that would wreak further havoc with our sleds. We staked the trail every couple of hundred metres until we reached the shelter cabin from where we would head out across the sea ice.

In the morning the wind had dropped although a telephone call to the Public Safety Officer in Koyuk, on the far side of the sea ice, reported strong winds and poor visibility. As it was, there was considerable apprehension amongst the team about crossing Norton Sound. We had been warned of large areas of overflow and open water and we had all heard the stories of Iditarod mushers getting stranded on the ice in storms, lost in white-out or unable to make any headway against the wind. Everyone was looking to me for a decision as to whether we should go or not. I could not see that there was any merit in not doing so unless conditions absolutely precluded it, so with no further ado we hitched up the snowmobile sleds, harnessed the dog teams and set off.

The first fourteen miles were predictably punishing on the sleds, quickly opening up the old cracks, but it was good to get going. We reached the shelter cabin having had little wind, clear skies and even some sunshine which afforded great views over the distant hills. The dog teams had spread out as usual. The front runners wanted to press on but I would not allow them to. I wanted to keep the convoy as tight as possible once we moved out onto the sea ice. The two rear teams were making hard going of it so I decided to split them down, adding a couple of dogs to each of the other teams which I hoped would add power all round and even out the pace.

As soon as we got out onto the ice the wind picked up savagely. We moved from patches of relative clearness to almost total white-out. As we went on, the conditions worsened until we were travelling into the face of a ground blizzard. The driving snow and sleet caused the huskies' eyes to weep and their eyelids to freeze. The mushers had to keep getting off their sleds to wipe the dogs eyes and change over the leaders when they refused to lead into the wind. They continually veered off the line and the mushers would have to get off again, make their way up to the head of the team and drag them back onto the route. Each person was locked into their own private battle. Most people wore their down parkas with hoods up and the ruffs of wolf and wolverine fur drawn into a tight tunnel around their faces and yet still the wind pierced our neoprene face masks.

The lights of Koyuk appeared like a mirage out of the murk. Everyone made it safely with no mishaps due to overflow. Each person had their stories to tell of the thirty mile crossing. Two snowmobiles had missed the trail and been lost for a while. Several of the mushers had great

difficulty coaxing their team forward. Everyone was slightly shaken and experiencing the mildly euphoric high from being exposed to danger. Groups of Eskimo children huddled around our braziers as we prepared steaming bowls of food for the dogs. We were treated to mountainous plates of moose stew by the women of the small town and bunked down in the library.

For the next couple of days we drove ninety miles west, along the southern coast of the Seward Peninsula, to reach the villages of Elim and then White Mountain. We travelled over sea ice, mountain portages and along inland lagoons and rivers. Andrew and I rode several hours ahead locating and marking the trail. On the whole conditions were bright and clear, with an ambient temperature around 0° Fahrenheit although the equivalent wind-chill was significantly lower due to a constant stiff wind. White Mountain is located sixteen miles inland, beside the Mudyatok River. We located our National Guard contact and our supplies and were shown a place to stake the dogs out for the night amongst some willows at the side of the river. I then drove my snowmobile up to the top of the hill behind the village to watch for the dog teams approaching. The sun was setting, picking out the twists and turns of the Mudyatok River as it snaked its way between the pine forests that separated the tributaries of the river leading out to Golovin lagoon.

The dog teams appeared as tiny specks in the distance, the mushers' down jackets a flash of red against the otherwise sombre background. I reached for my camera. The fingertips of my gloves had long ago worn through and within a couple of minutes of handling the metal camera body I had totally lost feeling in the ends of my fingers. The index finger on my right hand, which I used to operate the shutter, became as hard as wood. It all happened so quickly but my hands were now useless. Luckily I had my overmitts with Bo Austin's sheepskin liners tucked behind the windscreen of my machine and I was able to shrug my gloves off and plunge my hands into them where they warmed up quickly.

Next day, although bright, it was much colder with a steady 20 knot wind that pushed the wind-chill down towards -30° Fahrenheit. Up until then I had been trying to put off wearing my down overjacket, saving it for the really cold temperatures that we expected further north. Now, despite driving in thermal underwear, fibre pile suit, aircraft technician's cold-weather oversuit with face mask, neck warmer, fibre pile cap, ski gloves and glasses, the wind's icy fingers penetrated the minutest gaps, chilling even the well covered parts.

As we drove up onto the exposed hills that lead towards Topkok the wind strengthened and I began to feel truly cold. I put on my down jacket, overmitts with chemical handwarmers inside the liners and goggles to protect the small area of cheek that was unprotected in the gap between glasses and face mask. With this degree of wind-chill any exposed flesh would quickly take on the waxy translucent appearance that signalled the onset of frostnip. If not caught at this stage full frostbite could set in.

We drove for several hours stopping literally hundreds of times to pick up the line of fallen route markers left by the Iditarod Race, chipping them out of the ice crust and resetting them. We reached a small shelter cabin in a relatively windless spot and stopped for a cup of hot chocolate from the flasks which we kept strapped inside our engine cowlings to prevent them freezing. I had become a snack fiend, craving the daily supplement to our rations of chocolate, nuts and raisins, Granola bars and my favourite, McVities finest butter shortbread.

We drove on another few miles continually staking the trail until we met a posse of National Guardsmen led by Major Dusty Finlay and Sergeant Toby Reich who had come out on snowmobiles from Nome to meet us. As we were talking to them, the lead dog teams caught up with us. Dusty told us that they had crossed a section of the trail several miles further back which was strafed by 30-40mph winds with poor visibility. The Topkok shelter cabin was just a couple of miles ahead so I decided to congregate everyone there before pushing on. The drive over the final hills to Topkok was sensational with fantastic views along the shore to Nome and the Kigluak Mountains beyond. Out on the ocean I could make out the dividing line between ice and water.

As the teams arrived outside the small, green cabin they brought news of others further back. Apparently one of the snowmobiles had broken down ten miles out of White Mountain. Dougie MacDonald had taken over Corporal Martin's dog team and he had gone back by snowmobile to see

if he could repair the broken machine. Toby Reich took a couple of the National Guardsmen with a freight sled to go and see if they could help. I also heard that Sergeant Sculley was having major problems with his team who had been fighting and were refusing to run.

Roy would not wait any longer and set off towards Safety, our planned night stop, but I insisted that the others wait for Sculley. After a couple of hours had passed with no sign of him we had no option but to press on. I left a couple of snowmobilers to wait for him. I knew that there were others out on the route involved in the recovery of the broken snowmobile so I was not worried for his safety and anyway he was one of the more sensible and calm members of the team.

It was a further sixteen miles to Safety. We drove buried as deep in our down jackets as we could get. Crossing the Bonanza Flats, the wind howled blowing any loose snow in a moving layer just above the ground. The Safety Road-house was boarded up and the surrounding area was barren and inhospitable. With Sergeant Sculley and his dog team still out on the trail there was no question of pressing on the remaining twenty-five miles to Nome. We made the dogs as comfortable as possible and put up tents. Guardsman Manassie arrived at 7 p.m. to tell us that Sergeant Sculley had arrived at Topkok cabin and planned to spend the night there.

At 10 p.m. the three National Guardsmen arrived having driven all the way to White Mountain and back. They said that the engine of the broken machine had seized. Corporal Martin had taken the engine out and brought it with him leaving Corporal Steggles and Corporal Painter at White Mountain. He was now at Topkok and would come on with the party there in the morning. The vehicle problems could all be sorted out in good time.

With no overnight gear, the National Guard team were now all keen to get back to Nome. I decided to go with them to prepare for the full team's arrival. I briefed those at Safety to wait for Sculley's party before starting out and set off for Nome. My escorts took a rather more no-prisoners approach to driving snowmobiles than we were used to. We flew off into the dark with me praying that I would not damage machine or sled.

Nome was built up around the discovery of gold first in the Snake River in 1898 and then on its own beaches a year later. At its height, the resultant gold rush brought 15,000 prospectors in a season all hoping to make their fortunes. Three years later there was no more gold on the beaches. Destitute and starving, the dreams of the majority of the Klondikers were shattered and the rush was over, leaving those who remained to continue working the modest claims that were still in operation.

Nome is still the largest town on the west coast of Alaska and dredgers still work the sea shore for gold in the four months of the year when the town is not ice-bound. The wind whips around the town incessantly and there is not a tree in sight to provide any cover. Floodlit streets and centrally heated buildings have replaced the dingy, insanitary alleys and tightly packed shanty town of spartan wooden shacks of an hundred years ago. Yet still Nome retains the feel of a frontier town.

In the centre of Front Street is the wooden arch that welcomes home the Iditarod racers for it was Nome that was the town in 1925, ravaged by diphtheria, for which the rescue operation was mounted. Nome features large in Alaskan folklore and it had been the focus of our efforts so far.

I went down to Front Street to watch as each team made their way along the sea ice and up a steep ice ramp that leads into the town. At the top of the ramp they passed under an arch with a banner proclaiming 'Welcome home to Nome's Iron Dog Racers' which marked the turn around point for the annual snowmobile race from Anchorage to Nome and back again. They may not have been snowmobiles but they were definitely iron in their own way. I felt very proud as I watched each of the soldiers drive his team up into the town. They had done a great job over the last 850 miles and whilst there was still an even greater distance ahead of us I felt that we had earned a small sense of achievement.

Over the last few days I had been mulling over an extremely difficult decision: whether to continue with the dogs or not. There was no doubt in my mind that to mush up the coast to Cape Prince of Wales and Point Barrow was physically possible. But there was no denying that running the dogs was draining the financial life blood out of the expedition. The costs went on and on. We had already expended a staggering £18,000 on dog food alone.

Whilst most of the logistics were now in place, my greatest fear was that we might get pinned down by storms at some remote location on the North Slope and have no choice but to evacuate the entire expedition by air, assuming that we could get an aircraft to us through storms which often lasted for one or two weeks at a time. Having spoken to Wingco on the telephone, he had told me that the US Airforce could provide a Hercules to lift the dogs out either now or in three weeks time at Barrow, but in the meantime they were all committed to a major exercise. The implication of an aerial rescue by chartering relays of small commercial aircraft would bankrupt the expedition and deny the other five teams of soldiers the chance of attempting their challenges.

I had a number of other concerns. The first, also related to the likelihood of storms further north, was whether we had pre-positioned enough supplies to last us if we became stormbound. We had worked on the most pessimistic rate of travel, adding a further 30 per cent for delays due to bad weather, but this was evened out over the journey. What if we got holed up in one spot for a long time? An Eskimo village might be able to help out a stranded musher with one team but there was no way that they would be able to provide the prodigious quantity of food that our nine teams ate and anyway it would be morally indefensible to take their hard earned winter's supplies.

There was also the state of relations with Roy Monk which had never been easy but during the expedition had deteriorated to an almost unworkable level. Whilst I respected his experience and remained grateful for his advice and the provision of his dogs, I felt that his influence on the team had become divisive and destructive and was seriously affecting the morale of the soldiers.

On the other hand, I was worried whether our snowmobiles would stand up to carrying two full grown men each and pulling a heavy sled for at least another 1200 miles over terrain which was only likely to get harder. Although theoretically designed to carry two people, this prolonged strain would be a severe test of their construction and we would be a long way from anywhere if they failed.

During the hours of riding my snowmobile I had turned the matter over and over in my mind. Talking it through with Richard and Andrew Holman, both urged me strongly to send the dogs back. Neither of them were any keener on the idea than I, but they were well versed in the arguments and I respected their advice.

I called the team together with a heavy heart. The response was predictably muted. No one wanted the dogs to go home but they understood the reasons for it and afterwards got on with making the arrangements. I felt a deep sense of frustration and disappointment at not being able to attempt the challenge in the way that we had dreamt it, but now practical considerations took over.

Dusty Finlay sent out a helicopter to deliver Corporal Martin to White Mountain so that he could fit a new engine to the broken snowmobile. Having done so, they loaded the sleds aboard leaving Corporal Steggles and Corporal Painter to drive unladen machines to Nome. We began to prepare the huskies and all the sledding equipment for the flight back to Anchorage. The Rear Party started ringing around all of the airlines in a bid to borrow enough sky kennels to contain each of the dogs in the aircraft.

The snowmobiles were taken to the local Arctic Cat dealer where they were serviced and all warranty repair work was carried out. The sleds were emptied and taken indoors to dry out and be sanded down. They were a sorry sight with great gashes running the length of most sleds alongside the runners. We planned to overhaul and strengthen them coating the inside of each sled with a thick layer of fibreglass resin and matting and rivetting on sheets of reinforced plastic to build up the runners and protect the belly.

After several delays for bad weather, the Hercules landed two days later bringing with it Wingco, Colour Sergeant McKeown and the three soldiers who had gone back from Galena. It was good to see them all. Loading the huskies into the sky kennels on the other hand was a depressing experience. They did not want to go into the kennels and we did not want them to go. Everyone had grown attached to their teams. They had shared our adventures and trials and many canine characters had emerged as strongly as their human counterparts. Some were boisterous, others irascible, but all had served us well and were regarded with affection.

The loading was long and complicated. The Loadmaster took a generous interpretation of the regulations as he piled equipment up to the ceiling of the fuselage securing each layer in turn. When the last piece of equipment was on board I shook Roy's hand and bade farewell to those who were going back to Nome. Wingco shouted a final good luck for the next stage of the journey as he climbed into the aircraft and then in a blast of spindrift they took off leaving us to continue making our preparations for our onward journey.

It took another two full days of fairly frenetic activity to get all our equipment into a serviceable state. On the third day, on a sharply cold morning we set off once more, ten snowmobiles in file, our eight led by two National Guard machines driven by our two new guides Roy Sockpick and Henry Ollanna. Dusty Finlay and all the National Guard personnel who had done so much to help us over the past few days turned out to wave us off.

As we left Nome we passed a succession of mines and workings. There is a well graded road which we followed for seventy miles to Teller. Except where snow had drifted over the road, we made good progress. We crossed the bottom of the Stewart River valley down which a fierce side wind howled, blasting us with spindrift. I had to hang on tight to the handle bars so as not to be blown physically off my machine, trying at the same time to cover every gap in my clothing to keep out the invading cold. I had paired myself off with Guardsman Perry who was the smallest member of the team and so had become a partner on Scouse's sled. Perry had worked hard throughout the expedition with a cheerful positive manner. Despite his lack of size I found sharing the snowmobile very uncomfortable particularly when it was my turn to ride pillion. It did however provide the opportunity to totally switch off to the present and either daydream or wonder at the passing scenery. I missed the isolation and excitement of being out in front with just one or two other people and was very conscious of all the other snowmobiles following along. The lasting memories of the day however, were the fantastic vistas. The best was saved until last as we dropped down towards Teller with the frozen waters of Port Clarence and Grantley Harbour either side of us, the sea away to our west and the snow-covered mountains in the distance.

Teller turned out to be a small, compact village of around 300 inhabitants. We quickly found the standard prefabricated Armoury building. A small crowd gathered around us as we unloaded our gear.

An old, rather correct Eskimo identified himself as Vernon Kugzrak, the Deputy Mayor. I asked if it was possible to make a telephone call to our office in Camp Carroll. He took me to the City Hall. I got the answering machine and whilst we waited to see if Andrew Holman, who had flown back from Nome to take his turn on the Rear Party, would go into the office Vernon told me something of the Eskimo way of life in Teller. The people who lived there were mainly inland Eskimos. Traditionally they lived by fishing the inland rivers, hunting for moose and collecting berries. Now they supplemented this by herding reindeer.

When he was young they used to trade with the coastal Eskimos of Cape Prince of Wales and Little Diomede, exchanging dried fish and moose meat for seal oil and blubber and whale meat. Now, people travelled far less due to the cost of fuel and the trade had largely died. In the old days every family had its own dog team for winter travel but now few families could afford one. The only employers in the village were the Government, for the posts of Public Safety Officer and school teachers; the City office and the Native Organisation's office. I had grown used to hearing every village, no matter how small, being referred to as a City. Teller had been established in its present location as a re-supply point for the gold workings but these were now defunct. The Eskimos had given up their hard, semi-nomadic lifestyle and had moved into the trading centre, drawn in by missionaries and the prospect of jobs and a more comfortable way of life. Now the jobs had gone but they had lost many of their traditional skills and values. Brought up with modern expectations through education and the false promises of glamorous television advertising, they were unable or unwilling to return to the old ways. It was a perennial problem that I was to hear mourned by the older generation time and again.

We crossed the entrance to Grantley Harbour following a causeway to Brevig Mission another village on the far side. There we stopped to collect Henry Ollanna who had gone across to spend the night with his family. Henry's beaming face appeared along with several others of the village menfolk. A debate ensued over which river we should follow through the York Mountains. I could see Henry looking increasingly vacant and confused as the argument progressed. He admitted that it had been four years since he had been that way.

We drove for twelve miles along the inside of Brevig Lagoon before turning north. Henry was looking less than confident and repeatedly asked to look at my map which he then could not relate to the ground. I switched on my Global Positioning System and began to monitor our progress carefully. We had GPS units mounted on two of the snowmobiles. They could confirm our position to within a hundred yards so long as they could get a fix on any three satellites passing overhead.

The sun rose behind us casting long shadows on the ice. Now as we climbed up into the hills it crept up the sky. The hills and mountains were clad in hard packed shallow snow which provided near perfect driving conditions. The wind of the previous day had died away leaving a beautiful clear sky as we made our way up the Don River through the York Mountains until we were able to skirt them to the north.

We saw a group of musk oxen in the distance but they were skittish and galloped away to the safety of the high ground. Further on we came across a herd of reindeer. We turned west, crossing several tributaries of the Mint River as we passed the York Mountains to our south and the rounded hills surrounding Potato Mountain to our north. I stopped frequently to verify our position and guide Henry back on course.

Suddenly we crested a rise and before us lay a view that surpassed anything that we had seen so far. Past Cape Mountain, still fifteen miles in front of us, was the shoreline. Beyond, the sea ice stretched away towards the horizon, broken in patches. Rising out of it were the seemingly vertical cliffs of the islands of Little Diomede and Big Diomede, American and Russian respectively. Hidden by Cape Mountain, at the tip of the Seward Peninsula, lay Cape Prince of Wales, the westernmost point in the Americas and the expedition's first objective. I felt as though I could almost reach out and touch it.

We stopped to take photographs and savour the view and then pressed on. As we approached Cape Mountain we could make out the antennas and large satellite dishes of Tin City, the radar station based on its southern side. It was one of the few listening posts out of the necklace of radar sites around the Alaskan coast that was still operative.

Locating the Armoury in the small village of 200 Eskimos was not difficult. There were no longer any National Guardsmen in Cape Prince of Wales and so the building was unused. The doors were buried deep under mounds of drifted snow and when we dug them free the locks were frozen. Once inside it was dark and damp but we fired up the oil heaters and soon it warmed up. As soon as we had seen everyone settled in Richard and I took off on our snowmobiles to explore the village and the mountain behind. There was not much to the village, merely a line of wooden cabins half buried in snow. The path through the village scaled high ridges of drifted snow which had blown through the gaps between buildings. The only buildings of any size were the school and the Community Hall, a large domed building.

We drove on up the side of the mountain behind the village until we reached a shale plateau from which we could see over the village and lagoon below us and far out across the pack ice of the Bering Sea to the Diomede Islands. Open leads glistened and steamed in the sunlight. It was an inspiring, mind-bending place. We were sat at the end of a continent, looking out over the slender separation between two cultures, the focal point of mistrust between two great nations. It was made all the more momentous by its remoteness and the 1,000 miles of travel over land, river and sea ice that it had taken us to get there. I was in awe of the setting and rather overcome by what I saw as our small triumph.

We remained for a long time staring, absorbing the atmosphere, talking and trying rather ineffec-tually to capture the scene on film. As the sun slid down the horizon, turning the sea ice an orange gold, the temperature plummeted. We remounted our snowmobiles and headed down to the village.

After supper I went over to the Community Cen-tre to pass our news back via Andrew Holman to the London office and from there on to The Prince of Wales, the Major-General and The Explorers Club, an American society dedicated to exploration, who had bestowed on us the honour of carrying their flag. On the way to the Dome the Northern Lights had been flickering across the night sky. By the time I made my way back they were dancing, mushrooming and exploding in soft waves of green and white light. A huge crescent of colour

arced across the sky over the village appearing to emanate from Cape Mountain. As I watched, it billowed and died, strengthened again and then faded, appearing sometimes as a single line or at others as a series of lines, curtains, strange twists or organ pipes. A fitting end to a very special day.

I decided to spend the next day at the village. There seemed no point having worked so hard to get there, only to rush on again. Richard took a group to Tin City to get more fuel whilst I went back to the Community Hall to try and ring the London office direct. They had already received my message and passed it to the relevant parties. I was told to be by the telephone that evening to receive a call from The Prince of Wales. I decided to write a full account of our adventures to him anyway.

From the top floor of the Dome I could see some of the soldiers grouped around a few Eskimos who were fishing with crude rods through a hole they had cut in the ice of the bay. Colour Sergeant McKeown and Corporal Steggles had gone to the school at the invitation of the Headmaster to talk to the children.

In the afternoon the whole team went up onto the mountain for a photograph with the Union Jack, Household Division and Explorers Club flags. Afterwards I took some photographs for local newspapers whilst Corporal Steggles did some video interviews. Even in the short time that people had to unmask in front of the cameras their cheeks and noses began to take on the white waxy pallor of frostnip.

Once again I was struck by the momentousness of our location. Tens of thousands of years previously the first primitive people had crossed the land bridge that had extended from the Asian coast. Now it is cut off by the Bering Sea. The migration of these primitive people southwards and their adaptation to the various localities in which they settled led to the formation of the vast majority of indigenous cultures throughout North and South America. Eskimos, North American Indians, Mayans, Incas, Yanomami and the Yaghans of Patagonia, amongst many others, all owed their existence to that first crossing which had taken place within just a few miles of the windswept mountain on which we were standing.

When I went back to the Community Hall for my call to come through I found, rather to my horror, that it was packed with most of the adults from the village playing bingo. A squat Eskimo was calling the numbers in a loud continuous monotone. Richard and Corporal Steggles watched, laughing at my discomfort as I sat waiting for the call. When it came through, The Prince of Wales's voice was clear and unmistakeable. He asked about the journey and I told him something of our adventures. It felt extraordinary to be talking to him from this tiny Eskimo village that was his namesake at the furthest extremity of the Americas. He repeatedly offered his congratulations to the team on reaching our first objective and wished us good luck and a safe onward journey to Point Barrow.

Next morning, as we mounted our machines to leave, an Eskimo ran up to me clutching what looked like a long, carved bone. He asked me to pass it on as a gift to The Prince of Wales. The previous night's telephone conversation had created considerable excitement in this remote outpost. When I asked our guides what it was, their eyes twinkled and they said an oosik, a prestigious gift suitable for an honoured or esteemed person. Not much the wiser, I pressed for further details and was told that it was a carved walrus's penis bone.

We followed the coast north-east, wherever possible travelling on the flat, inland lagoons. The sun rose at 10 a.m., poking its head over the mountains, painting the sea ice a delicate pink hue and warming the day up. Our second guide Roy Sockpick had now taken over leading the team. Unlike Henry, Roy was a coastal Eskimo and was visibly much happier now that we had reached the coastline and the sea. Both of them had disliked the bustle of Nome and had been keen to get away and on with the journey. That said, Henry had been quite pessimistic about our chances of coping with the trail conditions and the weather but had soon warmed up once we got going. He has a fairly cheeky sense of humour and an impish grin. Standing astride his machine with his dark, almost Mongoloid features and the claws of the wolverine ruff on his parka hanging around his neck he looked every inch the Eskimo.

Roy Sockpick had always been totally positive about our chances but was more reserved and formal in his manner. A rather shy man, he too had warmed up considerably once he had got to know us. Now leading us along the Bering Sea coastline he drove faster and faster the nearer we got to Shishmaref. He was looking forward to seeing his family and had told me several times that he missed them when he was away from home.

We passed numerous shelter cabins and fishing huts. Outside one a polar bear skin had been hung up to cure. We covered the seventy-five miles fairly quickly arriving at the village in daylight. Roy showed us to the Armoury before shooting off to see his wife and children. He returned bearing an enormous bowl full of black and orange salmon berries that they had picked in the summer. The iced fruit were quite delicious.

Later, he took me over to a small co-operative to see the whalebone and walrus-ivory carvers for which Shishmaref is known. They created ingenious and attractive sculptures using the vertebrae, jaw bones and ribs of whales inlaid with walrus ivory and baleen. Most depict whales, land mammals or the Eskimos themselves and many incorporate traditional scenes of hunting. Back at the Armoury we had been invaded by children with whom the soldiers were trading pocket knives, and I suspected a good measure of expedition supplies, for beaver skin hats.

The pack ice in Kotzebue Sound was not safe to cross. Strong currents threw up huge pressure ridges and ripped open gashes in the ice. To reach the town of Kotzebue we had to follow the edge of the Sound. We took a short cut inland via Serpentine Hot Springs to the tiny village of Deering on the southern shore of Kotzebue Sound. The route to Serpentine was relatively straightforward, following the course of the Serpentine River for much of the way. Before long it became apparent that Roy had reached the limit of his geographical knowledge. As we approached the Hot Springs, some sixty miles from Shishmaref, the trail took us up into some low mountains. In the foreground, spires of rock rose up in clusters like fairyland castles, obscured by a band of low drifting cloud.

We continued up a small gully between rock strewn hillsides and pulled up beside two small huts. The first was slightly larger containing a few iron beds, lanterns, wood stove, benches and tables. The second was placed over the bubbling spring. Inside, a six foot square tub was brimming with water almost too hot to put your hand in. The walls were coated in pure white fluted ice formed as a result of the constant condensation.

Having sorted our kit out, I went off for a walk up into the hills. From the side, my fairyland castles changed into the slumbering carcasses of great granite mastadons. I was tempted to try and climb the highest of them but alone in the cold, swaddled in down clothing and galumphing along in clumsy overboots it did not appear such a good idea. I sat down in the sun to enjoy the peace and solitude. The mountains seemed to sing with silence. Time passed but I did not notice.

The sun slid gradually down the sky bringing a fresh chill to the air. I headed back to the hut where I found Richard getting soundly beaten at cards by Roy and Henry, whose grin was spreading with each passing hand, creasing his slightly Neanderthal features. Guardsman Miller had been for a bath and nearly seared his skin off.

We had some difficulty getting a couple of the machines started in the morning. The low temperatures froze any water that had contaminated the fuel, causing blockages in the fuel lines. We climbed up over the mountains and then descended northwards to a broad plain. Drifted snow filled the frequent gullies that cut across the tundra slowing our progress dramatically.

Eventually we reached the shore and sped eastwards towards Deering. We stopped at a reindeer herders slaughter cabin where we found reindeer antlers, entrails and skins all piled high in separate heaps. A hunter appeared on his snowmobile. He told us that there was a herd of 70,000 caribou about fifty miles to our east. He hunted fox, wolves, wolverine, lynx, caribou and seals, all of which were plentiful.

Deering turned out to be a strip of houses raised up along the shore. The Mayor and School Principal came out to greet us. We had written to each community asking permission both to cross and camp on their land. They had decided that we should stay at the School and told us that they had arranged a Pot Latch. A Pot Latch is an Eskimo feast to which each person in the village brings some food. Luckily someone had given us half a reindeer carcass as we left Shishmaref and we were able to pass this on as our contribution.

The Pot Latch held in the School Hall that evening was a very dignified affair. All the village women arrived bearing pots containing all sorts of local delicacies. The village elders arrived last of all wearing their long parkas, fur trimmed top and bottom and in the case of the women, elaborately embroidered. Many were bent and bow legged from years of hardship and nutritional deficiencies. The children sang some Inupiaq songs and then the Mayor made a speech of welcome on behalf of the elders and the village.

I replied rather haltingly, introducing each member of the team. The Mayor then presented each one of us with either a baseball cap or T-shirt bearing Deering's name. It was an extremely generous gesture and must have been very costly for a village of only 175 people. After these presentations one of the elders said a long grace in Inupiaq and then the elders led us into the line for the food. There is great respect bordering on reverence paid to the elders who decide the affairs of the village.

The tables were covered in dishes of turkey, cranberry sauce, caribou ribs, reindeer stew, sheefish, berries and a horrid gelatinous mess that was seal's flipper cooked in seal oil. It was all delicious with the exception of the seal's flipper which I could not bring myself to try. Afterwards there was a basketball match at which we suffered the humiliation of being decisively beaten by children half our height. Basketball is played with a commitment and enthusiasm bordering on religious fervour by the Eskimos. At each village that we went to the School gym was used every night by children and adults alike often into the small hours.

The last 100 miles to Kotzebue was a long, drawn out crawl along the edge of the sea ice around the Sound. Our twin-cylinder engines guzzled fuel as we drove slowly to protect them from the worst of the cracks and pressure ridges. I was concerned that we might run out and was planning to leave some people at the shelter cabin at the bottom of Baldwin Peninsula whilst sending others on ahead with fuel pooled from all the vehicles, but Henry in his usual happy-go-lucky manner said 'It'll be alright, we got plenty gas I guess.' No one wanted to stay in that cold, deserted place in any event so we decided to go for it. We made it on fumes at 7.30 p.m. having crossed the Arctic Circle halfway up the Baldwin Peninsula. Our arrival at Kotzebue signalled the end of another leg of the journey and a change of both guides and Rear Party.

As we settled into the Armoury the long awaited cold weather finally arrived. On the radio we listened to weather forecasts reporting wind-chill temperatures of -70F on the North Slope and as low as -110F at Anaktuvuk Pass in the Brooks Range. We began our usual programme of re-provisioning and repair. The sleds had held up well so far but the snowmobiles were showing increasing signs of strain. One needed a new clutch. Roy and Henry flew back to their villages. I was sorry to see them go. Andrew Holman, Sergeant Sculley and Guardsman Thomas returned from their spell on the Rear Party.

On the second day storms hit the north of Alaska. The radio warned of wind-chill of -50F in Kotzebue. Both Kivalina and Point Hope, the next two villages to our north were stormbound. In Kivalina they could barely see from one house to the next. I talked to several of the locals all of whom urged us not to try and drive into the storm. Two natives had been killed in a storm the previous year and one man said that he had turned back on his way to Kivalina when he saw a log heavier than himself being hurled through the air.

The storms went on for several days as February passed into March. For the first couple of days it was grey, bleak and bitterly cold but after that the storm hung farther to our north and we could enjoy relatively bright, clear days. One of the Eskimo Sergeants, Gus Nelson, and his brother took us out onto the lagoon ice to check on their fishing nets. We stopped at two logs sticking out of the ice twenty-five yards apart. They chipped away the ice around each of the logs which turned out to be plugs securing the ends of the net. They then attached a rope that they had brought with them to one end of the net and pulled on the other end. As the net emerged three sheefish each weighing about five pounds were caught in the mesh. Gus said that they sometimes caught up to fifty fish in one haul.

For the most part we spent the time checking and repairing kit, writing letters and exploring the small town. It is the second largest Eskimo community with a population of around 3,000. Along the shoreline ships and boats were frozen into the ice. A number of mushers kept their dog kennels out on the ice. The streets are a tight mesh of largely wooden homes. Along the shore there are a few simple cafes which afford views across the Sound if the weather permits. The Arctic Dragon Restaurant bears testimony to the omnipresence of Chinese restaurants. Hunters on snowmobiles hurtled along towing freight sleds behind them, apparently oblivious to the roughness of the sea ice.

I spent one evening talking to a young married couple in their two-roomed home which they shared with their two children. Chip had by his own description something of a mongrel background incorporating Prussian, Scottish, Welsh and native American. He had met Agnes, a very pretty Inupiaq from the village of Noorvik, when they were both on a mechanics course. To make ends meet they turned their hand to whatever was profitable at the time: if the price of gold was good Chip would work as casual labourer at the local mine in summer, otherwise they hunted and fished year round moving out in summer to a tented camp alongside one of the rivers. The hunting was done on a share basis with all expenses paid for by the elders who could not go out to hunt for themselves any longer. In the winter they sewed skins into mukluks, hats and parkas, carved walrus ivory, mended guns, carpentered or welded. Chip was very proud of their life and their ability to be self-sufficient. They clearly doted on each other. Agnes's face lit up when she spoke of sleeping on skins and fishing together at their summer camp. Her laugh had a musical quality.

On the fifth day after arriving in Kotzebue it was still storming further up the coast. When I rang the State Weather Service first thing in the morning it was -20F in Point Hope with a 50mph wind that drove the windchill down to -85F. But a couple of hours later a telephone call to Kivalina revealed that the wind had died there and we could be on our way once again.

After a few days of cold temperatures and inactivity it took some time to coax the snowmobile engines into life. We drove out of the town and across the sea ice on a well-used trail that led to Sheshalik and the mainland beyond. From there we followed the coast northwards, taking advantage of the smooth ice of lagoons where we could find them and otherwise hugging the shore to avoid the pressure ridges and rough, ocean ice. Each time we stopped we checked each other carefully for signs of frostbite. We were driving wearing goggles and face masks, with our parka hoods pulled up over our heads and yet still some people where showing signs of frostnip particularly on their cheeks. I tried driving with over mitts on but my thumbs froze. In the end I found it better to drive in thinner gloves with handwarmers inside and the snowmobile's heated handgrips switched on. The constant jarring over iron hard tundra and rough sea ice became excruciatingly uncomfortable on legs, groin and back.

Just before Kivalina we saw a white arctic fox which took off as we approached. The village was small and compact with huge drifts of snow half burying the houses and forming great ridges that blocked the roads. Our next guide, Conrad Koenig, was waiting for us and showed us to the Armoury. Next day we woke up to a ground blizzard. With strong winds and horizontal driving snow where we were and reports of even worse conditions at Point Hope there was no point in trying to move. We covered the snowmobiles and sleds as best we could and sat out the storm.

The next day dawned fine. We went into the now regular battle to get the machines started. Each morning this seemed to take longer as we unfroze fuel pumps and changed spark plugs. Sometimes a squirt of oil into the air intake helped fire them up but often they would sullenly refuse to start. We continued on up the coast much as before, alternating between lagoons, tundra and ocean ice. Long sections of the beach were steeply inclined and littered with large boulders, forcing us down onto the ice. There was normally a narrow strip of ice between the beach and the pressure ridges but even this was broken and rough. We skirted rocks, bounced over slabs and cracks and skidded along glare ice.

Whilst crossing one of the tundra sections, the A-frame on my sled sheared. Fortunately we could load it onto one of the large freight sleds towed by the National Guard Alpines. We made slow, hard progress. It was already 4 p.m. by the time that we reached the deserted radar station at Cape Thompson, only a little over half way to Point Hope. We turned inland to avoid a particularly bad area of ice below a line of sea cliffs. Another A-frame sheared on one of the other sleds but we managed to repair it temporarily by binding the broken arm with rope. Conrad then led us a merry dance up into the hills. I cursed myself for assuming that he knew where he was going. I should have learnt to suspect

the native finger blithely sweeping across the map. By the time that we followed the Kunuk Creek down out of the hills it was already dark. We drove towards the lights of the town for what felt like hours before we eventually arrived. A four-wheeler bearing our second guide, Warren Nashookpuk, had come out to meet us. He led us to the Armoury. It had been a long day and we were glad to get off the machines and into the warmth.

Warren told me that he was sixty-five years old and Conrad chimed in that he was forty-five. Toothless, wizened and decidedly eccentric in appearance, both looked at least twenty years older. They cut unlikely figures for guides in the Arctic and I could see a number of eyebrows being raised amongst the team. Warren drew me off to one side, announcing that he had something important to ask me and then said that they wanted a medal from Britain for their services. I replied that if he got us to Point Barrow safely and showed me a polar bear I would get one for them.

Meanwhile, we clearly could not go anywhere until we had fixed our sleds and for that we needed welding gear. The next day was a Sunday so we faced another frustrating delay. I was worried about the state of our vehicles and sleds and that we were losing valuable good travelling conditions.

Two days later, with reinforced sleds, we set out for Cape Lisburne, a manned radar station sixty miles further up the coast to the north of the Lisburne Hills. The weather was marginal with a stiff wind blowing but we made good speed for twelve miles along a lagoon before following a creek into the tundra. As we carried on up into the Lisburne Hills the conditions deteriorated and we found ourselves driving into the face of a ground blizzard. The wind steadily increased in speed and although we caught glimpses of clear blue sky overhead, at ground level there was driven snow and white-out.

Initially it was unpleasant but bearable, but before long we could barely stand if we got off the machines and we were having to gun the engines to make any progress. We were each wearing two layers of face masks. In a very brief period of time it changed from being merely unpleasant to a survival situation. We stopped one last time when I realised that Warren was taking us the wrong way. He refused to accept what the GPS said and insisted that he knew where he was going but at the same time said that he thought we should turn back.

I walked back to Colour Sergeant McKeown where, shouting to make ourselves heard above the wind, we both agreed to turn back given the time, the distance that we still had to cover, the danger of trying to travel deeper into the mountains where the wind would be further channelled and also the approaching darkness. As soon as we turned around and our faces were no longer exposed to the headwind it became more bearable. My body was tolerably warm but at one stage I lost the feeling in all of my fingers. Guardsman Perry saw that I was getting into trouble and ripped off my gloves, put his own handwarmers into my hands and put my overmitts on for me. It was frightening to feel so helpless.

We tried to make the best speed possible to get back to the safety of the town but the wind conditions and terrain were against us. We had to stay closed up to avoid losing each other. At one point we came to a short but steep shale slope. I followed the guides up it and stopped a couple of hundred yards further on to see the others all safely with us. No one appeared. Guardsman Perry and I left our machine where it was and leaning hard into the wind began to follow our tracks back. Warren started to come with us but he was blown back by the wind and gave up. We found the others at the foot of the slope. Several of the machines were stuck and one was refusing to start. The cold numbed our minds as well as our bodies. Harried by the conditions people were beginning to draw back into themselves hiding in the warm cocoon of their down suits. With all of their protective clothing on, each individual became anonymous and isolated which made co-ordinating any action difficult. There was a danger of people allowing themselves to become frozen into inactivity.

I saw Colour Sergeant McKeown going from person to person, shouting into their hoods and physically pulling them around the next machine and sled to be pushed. The cold began to get to the machines and several more stalled. I grimaced as I watched Corporal Martin going to each in turn, taking his gloves off to thaw sections of frozen pipe with the warmth from his hands and sucking the fuel through. With my hands buried deep into my sheepskin gauntlets I was grateful that I was not a mechanic. Several people's goggles had shattered

in the cold. At one point I saw Guardsmen Miller helping Corporal Shaw who was bent over trying to prise apart his eyelids which had frozen together. His eyes were red and swollen and Miller had to lead him back to his machine.

After what seemed like an eternity each machine was started and pushed up the slope. On top, our tracks had already been obliterated. Once we were all reunited we drove slowly back to Point Hope with the wind howling around us, checking constantly to ensure that the next machine was following. Back at the Armoury it took time to unwind. There was a feeling of shock at such a naked demonstration of the power of the storm and our impotence in the face of it. We had never totally lost control but we had certainly been near the borderline. Our complacency, which had built up around the assumption that we could achieve whatever we set out to, was rudely shattered.

The storm raged for a further five days during which time we hunkered down in the Armoury and explored what we could of the town in the brief periods when the local conditions abated sufficiently. It was located on the tip of a point of land sticking out into the Chukchi Sea. It had been inhabited first by Eskimos who had migrated across the Bering land bridge and settled in this incredibly harsh place for its whale hunting. Foreigners had come by sea to the area also to hunt whales but initially they had been driven away. Later, once trade was established, the foreigners built their own village a few miles to the east called Jabbertown. By all account it had been a wild, lawless place and was responsible for bringing disease and alcohol both of which decimated the Eskimo population. Jabbertown has long since been deserted but many of the old folk in the community could remember when the Eskimos had lived in sod houses, single roomed dwellings, lit and warmed by seal-oil lanterns.

Warren took us out on snowmobiles one day to see the site of the old town before it was moved slightly further from the sea's edge and away from the danger of flooding during storms. He pointed out the old sod houses, now either collapsed or full of snow. Outside each turf and stone building arrangements of old blanched whale bones were buried in the frozen earth. In other places, pairs of whale jaw bones were stuck into the ground, trophies of successful hunts. One pair rose a full ten feet above the ground and were reputed to come from a sixty-five foot whale. At the end of the land there was a crude wooden pyramid which had been the base of a lighthouse. Behind that, pressure ridges disappeared into the bank of fog.

Nearby, he showed us the shells of disused driftwood and plywood houses. He pointed out the one that he had been brought up in. It had been a hard way of life with none of what would be regarded as the most basic of modern facilities. Money was scarce but largely irrelevant in their subsistence life-style. Many of the elders bemoaned the loss of the traditional values and respect, a word that they used with nostalgia.

Behind the houses lay the graveyard, penned in by a fence of whale bones. Each grave was marked out with either a cross at its head or a whale jaw bone bearing an inscription. It was a strangely moving place and even in that bitter cold I wanted to stand and feel the spirit of it, trying somehow to absorb something of the people who laid buried there, the lives that they must have led and the almost unimaginable hardships that they must have faced.

The town, by comparison, was incongruously modern, funded by the huge dividends produced for the native corporations by the exploitation of oil on the North Slope. The school had facilities that would outdo the most expensive of European private schools. Yet it was a strange soulless place, caught in an uncomfortable chasm between the ancient and modern worlds. Outside a number of the houses we saw the intact carcasses of seals stood upright in the snow, in natural storage for the oncoming whaling season and the fragile wooden frameworks of the whaling boats which were waiting for a fresh set of Leopard seal skins to be stretched across them. These boats were no more than 12 feet long and 3 feet deep, shaped like a canoe. In April or May, whenever the sea ice broke up, they would be carried to the edge of the ice and set into the sea. Families would camp out at the seaward edge of the ice watching for whales and when one was spotted the crews would launch, eight men to a boat, and hunt the whale using harpoons. It was a dangerous enterprise in these tiny, frail craft. The Captains of the whaling boats tended to be community leaders, carrying with them the hopes and self respect of the community.

Eating whale meat is a deeply seated part of Eskimo culture. Each kill is celebrated throughout the entire village and the meat shared out to all. Failure to hunt a whale successfully during the short season is keenly felt not just for the loss of its meat but it is also taken as a slur on the hunting ability of that community. The International Whaling Commission had imposed tight restrictions governing the hunting methods and a quota for the number of whales that each village could harvest.

The requirement to pursue the subsistence hunting was being removed by handouts from the welfare state and oil dividends. The results however, far from improving the lot of the Eskimos in all but token material ways, was to destroy their self-respect, values and traditional skills. The younger generation, driven to despair by false hopes for which they were culturally and educationally ill prepared, turned to alcohol, drugs and a frighteningly high suicide rate.

During the periods that it was too evil to go outside we talked, read, wrote letters or played cards in the Armoury. Despite almost a week of inactivity the soldiers' morale remained surprisingly high and the usual banter flowed fast and furiously. At times I felt almost overwhelmed by frustration as I watched our precious travelling time slip away from us. Point Barrow was still 400 miles away and there was every likelihood of the bad weather that was gripping the North Slope continuing. I could not come to terms with the idea of the early sailors who, on expeditions seeking a route through the Northwest Passage, had spent entire winters locked into the ice.

At last the wind dropped and we could get going again. Corporal Martin and Corporal Painter, who had become his assistant and travelling partner, had worked long and hard to get each machine ready to carry on the journey but once the time came it took an hour and a half to get them going. I found it hard to contain my impatience as each fresh problem appeared. It was as though some hidden force was conspiring to stop us making any headway. Eventually we formed up in convoy, drove out of town onto the lagoon and began the journey once again. I felt incredibly tense just waiting for the next problem to manifest itself.

In the sunlight the Lisburne Hills appeared far

more benign. For the most part we followed a series of creeks sticking to the low ground until we dropped back down to the coast and followed it along to Cape Lisburne. On the way, various parts began to drop off the suspension system of Warren's Alpine.

At Cape Lisburne we found our way into a complex of large modern buildings sited beside an airstrip. It was manned by civilian contractors who welcomed us warmly and helped us repair the broken machine using spares from one of their own machines. They offered us every hospitality and told us of their lives manning this remote outpost. They spent three to four months at a time at the station, operating and maintaining the electronic surveillance equipment and the runway and then flew back to civilisation for a period of normality before returning once again to their solitary vigil.

They were, not surprisingly, very highly paid. Each had a different story for why they lived this unusual life separated from their families for months on end. For some it provided the money with which to build a new house or maintain a better standard of living, others relished the escape from so called civilisation whilst others enjoyed the camaraderie that such isolation engenders. They said that polar bears often walked into the complex and in summer they could see up to five grizzly bears at a time feeding on the shore.

During the night the wind blew up again to gale force, physically shaking the large warehouse building that we were camping in and shrieking like a demented banshee. In the morning, I went up to the observation tower to see walls of spindrift obliterating the surrounding hills. Just in case reports of better weather further on up the coast tempted me to set off, two of the contractors took me out onto the runway in one of their maintenance vehicles. The pick-up truck was rocked and buffeted and visibility went down to ten yards in the stronger gusts. With a wind-chill of -50F they were hardly suitable conditions for snowmobile travel with 120 miles to the next village.

Next day the wind had dropped to 25mph and with clear visibility we pushed on. The pressure ridges on the ocean ice were bigger than anything we had seen to date. Some rose to over fifty feet with blocks the size of trucks. We made our way on, sometimes overland, sometimes threading our way amongst the pressure ridges. We reached a patch of flat, crystalline sea ice and were able to open up the throttles and speed along at 40mph. It was great to make some progress and give the engines a good blow through after the hours of slow grind.

By mid-afternoon we reached another deserted radar station, roughly halfway to Point Lay. The doors of the buildings blew in the wind and old bits of machinery lay rusting outside. A raven had built its nest up the stairs leading up to the radar and I saw a wolverine loping away into the distance. We stopped for a snack and some coffee after a unanimous decision to press on.

We continued along the sea ice for a while and then cut inland to the end of a thirty mile lagoon which lead all the way to Point Lay. It should have been a simple matter of speeding the rest of the way but things began to go wrong. Andrew Holman's GPS flicked onto a different map series and before I could stop him he had directed the guides back out onto a particularly broken area of sea ice. Due to the ridges and rough ice it took some time to work my way up to the head of the convoy and stop them.

Once we got back onto the lagoon however, we found that a thin smattering of powder snow concealed glare ice. The tracks of our machines could get no purchase on the mirrored surface and spun ineffectually. If you stopped on anything but a down hill slope the machine had to be pushed to get some forward momentum and then as other crews stopped to help they in turn became stuck. It was hard to keep our footing and the whole exercise began to turn into a series of slapstick sketches which would have been funny had we not been tired and keen to reach the safety of the village.

The sun went down at 8.30 p.m., a perfect red orb setting on the surface of the ocean. Half an hour later it was dark. We continued for another two hours drawn to the distant lights like moths. We pulled up at the radar station after fourteen hours on the machines and not before three idler wheels had fallen off the Alpines and an A-frame had snapped.

A detailed inspection in daylight revealed that not only was the suspension on Warren's Alpine shot to pieces but once the ice had thawed off the underside of the machine, a gaping hole in the fuel tank was exposed. After a quick phone call to Dusty Finlay in Nome to get his authority,

I decided to abandon the Alpine where it was and told Corporal Martin to cannibalize the parts that he needed to repair the other one.

The 105 mile journey on up the coast to the next village, Wainwright, was again plagued by problems. We were continually changing spark plugs and working to re-start stalled machines. The two Eskimo guides were not strong enough to manage the remaining Alpine with them both riding on it. In fairness, with its single front ski the Alpine was less stable than our twin-ski Arctic Cats and reared sharply whenever they hit a block of ice. They were thrown off several times. Their already stretched patience, for which neither of them was renowned, was further tested by their inability to maintain a constant direction and our frequent corrections.

Several times Warren got off and stormed about in an Eskimo tantrum kicking the side of the machine. On the final occasion they both got off to look under it. A bolt securing one of the shock absorbers had sheared rendering it useless. It took an hour of puffing, blowing, scrabbling with spanners and cold fingers to remove it. We carried on with Warren now travelling with Andrew Holman.

The tundra was frozen solid and totally unforgiving as we bounced along crunching time and again into solid ice formations. With fifty miles still to go Corporal Steggles and Corporal Ordish's machine broke down. This time it was more serious, a front shock absorber had sheared. To continue driving it risked major damage and possibly destroying the machine.

With no spares left we had little choice but to leave them where they were and go on to Wainwright and try and get a spare. They set up a tent beside the machine and waved us off with a poor attempt at bravado. It was much colder this far north, to the extent that it was uncomfortable to stop anywhere for very long. We were also in polar bear country and the many stories of hungry polar bears turning the tables on hunters had led to a constant wariness amongst the team.

We had another ten miles of tundra to cross before we made it to the relief of a flat lagoon. Once again we drove alongside a perfect Arctic sunset and on into the twilight. There was a great group of people on snowmobiles gathered at the outskirts of the village to meet us and much excitement when we materialised out of the darkness. They led us to their small disused Armoury and helped fire up the gas heaters.

The Mayor appeared to greet us and as soon as he heard that there were two people still out on the tundra, he called for the village Search and Rescue team. We went over to the Fire Station where they gathered. They were well used to going out to rescue hunters who had got lost or whose machines had broken down and were not in the slightest bit put out at the idea of driving a round trip of an hundred miles in the cold and darkness. We offered to go with them but they declined. Families drifted in to talk to us. The women brought parcels of cake and doughnuts which we fell on ravenously and hot drinks.

The Search and Rescue Party returned at 6 a.m. They had driven out fast following our tracks until they came upon the pyramid tent. Having taken a tent heater with them, as well as some food and coffee, they got the two corporals properly warm before starting back. They loaded the stricken snowmobile onto a freight sled and hitched our sled to another machine and drove back at their normal breakneck speed.

When they walked into the Armoury, Steggles and Ordish were cold and tired but relieved to be off the tundra and with us again so soon. Despite wearing their down suits inside both sleeping bags and bivi bags they had been very cold. They said that the journey had been fairly harrowing as they found themselves clinging on for all they were worth.

Corporal Martin was able to weld the broken shock absorber and refit it. It was not a perfect repair but should have been adequate for what was reputed to be a flat, easy trail to Barrow. There was also considerable work to be done on the National Guard Alpine as the suspension had collapsed once again. It was mid-afternoon by the time that all the machines were ready. I had overheard the locals giving Warren a fairly clear description of the route which they described as a highway taking three to four hours. Even allowing for our much slower rate of travel, with usable light now lasting until 9 p.m., I thought that we could make it. We had another planned changeover of team members scheduled for the following day. It had taken considerable negotiation to get a Civil

Air Patrol aircraft to make the journey and I did not want to undo the plans that had been made.

We got everyone packed up, found Warren and Conrad in the house of some relatives of theirs, every Eskimo seemed to be able to claim relatives wherever they went, and got ready to take off. Three machines refused to start. Eventually two were coaxed onto action but no amount of spraying oil into intakes, changing plugs or fiddling with fuel lines could get the third started. Corporal Martin took it back to the workshop where having stripped and reassembled the carburettor the engine fired up. I decided despite the lateness of the hour to go. If we remained another night we would only go through the same charade again in the morning.

There were several halts whilst we changed the spark plugs of machines that were not running on both cylinders but once we got going we made good progress until fourteen miles out my engine died. We went through the rigmarole of changing spark plugs but one had burnt out. Corporal Martin did a rudimentary compression test and announced to my horror that the pistons had blown and the machine could not be driven. I was now faced by a quandary. Clearly we could not all go on and I was loathe to split the team, however if we turned back we would miss the flight.

No solution was perfect but in the event I decided to leave three crews with two working machines to return to Wainwright with the broken-down one. Within the six people that I left behind were Corporal Martin to make the repairs and Andrew Holman to navigate once they were fit to travel again using the GPS on my machine when it was fixed. I would take the remainder on to Barrow, including those who had to catch the flight, using Andrew's GPS to check the navigation of our two guides. I would then be in position to arrange for spares to be sent on the mail flight to Wainwright and to plan the final leg of the journey.

It was already 6 p.m. but I still believed that we could make it in reasonable time if the trail was as good as it had been described. Warren seemed less confident which should have rung warning bells but I overrode him thinking that he just wanted to take the easy option of another night in Wainwright. We carried on over the sea ice missing the obvious turning onto Peard Bay. I thought that this must have been intentional but when I stopped Warren several miles later it was

clear that he did not know where he was. Visibility was poor and the light fading fast but fortunately we had not gone far out of our way and I was able to direct us across Peard Bay to link back up with our planned trail.

Once back on route we sped on as fast as the ice conditions allowed until we came to the radio tower and collection of buildings at Nalimiut Point that we had been told to look out for. It was pitch dark and intensely cold. We stopped to stretch our legs and have some coffee but it was so cold that we could not bear to stay still and had to run around and stamp our feet so as not to freeze.

I was sure that from the description of the route that I had overheard we should have gone down onto the sea ice again at that point but Warren insisted that it carried on overland. As he had been given the description and not me I did not press the point. We followed the coastline for several more miles before I stopped the group once again. I was now positive that we had gone the wrong way. Unfortunately there were several tiered cliffs between us and the sea ice and try as we did we could not get down them.

Warren did not trust the GPS and became angry if ever his judgement was questioned. He now lost his temper, said that he knew what he was doing and jumping onto his machine set off at a tangent. I could not let the team get split up, nor could I abandon him to his own devices in these conditions, much as I was tempted to and so I followed on. Over the next hour he quite unconsciously led us around in a huge circle. I realised that all he was doing was looking for old snowmobile tracks to follow.

Finally I managed to stop him and reassume control. We were critically short of fuel after the hours of jinking around and negotiating the rough tundra. I then made another error of judgement. Instead of turning the team around, heading back to the radio tower and picking the trail up from the last point that we knew was correct I decided to press on in a direct line for Barrow across the tundra. It would mean travelling a shorter distance and I hoped that we might be able to get down onto the sea ice further on.

For hour after hour we bounced across rock-hard tundra. The prevailing winds had packed down sharp edged snow drifts directly across our line of travel. Every few yards we had to climb, lurch and crash down over these unforgiving obstacles.

I tried directing Warren but he was incapable of holding a straight course and veered all over the place until I could stand it no longer and took over myself regardless of his hurt pride.

It was awkward trying to watch the dimly lit GPS, relate our position to the map, pick a line and negotiate the incessant drifts all at the same time. Many times the snowmobiles and sleds became stuck or tipped over. We became more and more tired as we followed an unending routine of pitching over ridges and stopping to help push stuck vehicles, change drive belts which kept stripping and check the navigation.

The cold was savage. I was particularly worried by Colour Sergeant McKeown's snowmobile which was developing a major fault. Each time he stopped, the drive belt and clutch seized so that he could not crank the engine over to start it. It became progressively worse, on each occasion requiring more time, effort and cussing to get it going. With a certain inevitability it stopped for a last time and despite forty minutes of concentrated effort by Corporal Painter, our mechanic designate, and Guardsman Miller who was also fairly handy with the vehicles, it refused to start. I did not dare risk stopping and resting everyone, even though it was now 3 a.m. and we were exhausted, in case we could not get the engines to start again once they had been switched off.

I took the rather hard decision to change Colour Sergeant McKeown and Guardsman Miller over with Corporal Shaw and Trooper Canning as the former pair were needed for the flight. We left the others setting up a tent and pressed on. The remaining hours of darkness passed slowly. We saw lights in the distance which Warren assured me was the inland village of Atqasak but when we got up to them turned out to be unmanned buildings along the oil pipeline. Then in the far distance, still twenty miles away according to the map, we saw the lights of Barrow.

In the middle of the night there had been an impressive display of Northern Lights, white curtains of light billowing across the sky, but now, as dawn began to break, it was cold and damp and the murk provided a flat, one-dimensional light through which it was hard to make out the ridges and obstacles. The beckoning lights also disappeared in the half light so we ploughed on along a compass bearing in the rough direction of Barrow, hammering into the ice crusted ridges and falling off when we were too tired to avoid them or care.

Eventually, at 7.30 a.m., we came to an ice road which led towards a large town by arctic standards. I did not feel so much elated at having reached our goal as relieved that the nightmare of the tundra and the endless jarring ridges was over. The urban sprawl which lay in front of us lacked the charm of the small villages that we had stayed in along the coast and detracted from my more romantic notions of reaching the northernmost tip of the Americas.

A police vehicle drove towards us. Just as it pulled up Warren's Alpine stopped. It had run out of fuel and none of us had any to give him. The policeman lead us through the silent streets to the Armoury and then disappeared to find a key. He reappeared shortly after with two members of the National Guard, Frank Bozanich and Jim Wood, who let us in. In a haze of tiredness we unloaded our kit and set about cooking some hot food.

We rang Chuck Caldwell at the Search and Rescue Center who kindly said that he would go out by helicopter and pick up Shaw, Canning and the broken machine. I had some breakfast and was just about to grab a quick sleep when he rang back to say that the helicopter was ready. Jim Wood took me up to the Search and Rescue hangar. A lavishly equipped command and co-ordination centre overlooked four gleaming modern helicopters and a couple of aeroplanes. All were fitted with every form of location and rescue device and funded from the North Slope Borough's $100 million annual oil revenue.

We took off in a Bell 210, a massive powerful beast of a helicopter. From the air the tundra looked flat and innocent. Although we could clearly make out the fingers of the myriad snowdrifts, they appeared harmless, like a dusting of spiders webs. We quickly picked up our trail and followed it down to the almost imperceptible indentation of a frozen lake and just beyond there was the snowmobile and the distinctive orange pyramid tent. We hovered and then landed a short distance away to prevent the down draught blowing the tent over.

As it descended the helicopter blasted all the snow in the immediate vicinity into the air with hurricane force. Amongst this, Corporal Shaw's head poked out of the tent opening and then they both climbed out. They were very cold and Trooper Canning was having trouble getting his hands to function. We unrolled a cargo net and lifted the dead snowmobile and its sled into the centre of it before hooking it up to the helicopter. After a couple of hastily snatched photographs we lifted off and, with the load underslung, flew back to Barrow.

The whole operation took just over an hour. Chuck could reach any part of the North Slope with his aircraft and by education, technology and providing hunters with the free loan of Personal Locator Beacons when they went off into the interior, had saved many lives.

Jim Wood took Colour Sergeant McKeown and I back to his house to make some telephone calls. We were instantly fed, watered and generally pampered by his Japanese wife, Mitsuko. The co-ordination of the changeover flight and movement of snowmobile spares to Wainwright took until the early evening. By that stage I was feeling decidedly second best having been thirty-six hours without sleep. I lay down for a nap and woke twelve hours later.

Over the next few days I based myself between the Armoury and Jim and Mitsuko's house where they kindly let me have the use of their telephone and some peace and quiet to write and plan. Mitsuko appointed herself as surrogate mother to the team and would regularly despatch Jim to go to the Armoury and fetch another load of 'the Kids', as she referred to us, so that she could lavish yet more huge meals upon us.

I had gradually come to the conclusion that we should stop the journey at that point and not continue back into the interior, re-crossing the tundra and taking the Anaktuvuk Pass through the Brooks Range to finish at Bettles, as we had planned. We had already achieved our two objectives and if we carried on, the terrain ahead threatened to be even tougher on the vehicles than that which we had experienced to date: we would have to cross several hundred miles of tundra and then face the deep snows and fiercely cold temperatures of the Brooks Range.

I longed to go on to see the Anaktuvuk Pass which was meant to be very beautiful and it went against every grain of my instinct not to complete what we had said that we would do but the harsh realities were that we still had a group stuck at Wainwright,

the snowmobiles needed a long programme of major repairs before they would be fit for such a journey, we were fast running out of money and we had little time left if we ran into impassable snow or more breakdowns. To press on regardless would have been irresponsible when looking at the management of the expedition as a whole.

Barrow was a strange place, a modern town perched on the edge of the Arctic Ocean, virtually ice bound for ten months of the year. In winter there was unbroken darkness for sixty-seven days. In summer the tundra became a mosquito ridden quagmire trodden by migrating herds of up to 100,000 caribou. It was an uncomfortable rather soulless place with the inhabitants prisoners trapped both physically between the ice and the unending flatness of the tundra and culturally in the juxtaposition between a traditional native lifestyle and the modern commercial existence provided by being the hub of the oil producing region.

Although it was the capital of the region, governed by the native members of the North Slope Borough Council, Barrow was an administrative centre. The oil was drilled several hundred miles further east, which only made its location all the more incongruous. They still hunted seals and whales and celebrated their long period of midnight sun but somehow it did not all fit together.

Before we left we had one important mission and that was to go out to Point Barrow, the true northernmost point of land. With all of the snowmobiles either in workshops or in the process of being sold, Jim Wood and Jim Christensen, another National Guard friend, drove us out of the town along a graded ice road that followed the shoreline. After five miles we came to a small shanty town of snow-covered wooden shacks. It was currently unoccupied but, located under the flight line of the migrating ducks and geese, many of the townspeople had second homes here and moved out for the summer.

Three miles further on the road ended, still a couple of miles short of the Point. We got out of the vehicles and continued on foot following a shingle causeway to the distant radio mast that marked the end of the land. We scanned the shoreline carefully for polar bears as there was reputed to be a den nearby with a mother and cubs.

The town council maintained a bear patrol throughout the winter months. Only the night before they had driven one out of the town where it was scavenging for food. The *Tundra Times* carried the story of a man in Prudhoe Bay who had tried to shoo one away from the window of his sitting room by swatting the inside of the window with a rolled up newspaper. The bear had come through the window and killed him. We carried our shotguns and rifles with us.

On the way out the sun and wind were behind us which gave us some protection from the wind-chill. The snow was not deep enough to warrant snowshoes but made walking awkward and hot in our protective clothing. At the end of the causeway the beach curved round in a broad sweep. On three sides the sea ice stretched away to the horizon. There was no more land, just ice, water, seals and polar bears between us and the North Pole. I had mixed emotions; satisfaction at having reached the expedition's second major objective, sadness at coming to the end of an amazing journey and a longing to carry on and explore more of this vast land of extremes.

We stopped to reflect and take photographs against the backdrop of the frozen Arctic Ocean. With no more to do and the temperature dropping swiftly as the afternoon sun slid lower in the sky, we turned around and headed back. Walking with the wind in our faces we felt the cutting effect of the wind-chill. We walked in goggles and facemasks until they became too claustrophobic. By the time that we reached the vehicles our beards were frozen solid with the condensation from our breath. I longed to shave mine off. As the ambient temperature had dropped to -45F with wind-chill even lower it was no time to be walking around with a freshly shaved face. As it was my face

and nose was peeling quite heavily from where I had been frostnipped through my neoprene face mask during our night crossing of the tundra.

Two days later a Hercules aircraft flew in to carry us back to Anchorage. Barrow would still be locked in by ice for several months to come and the seal hunting and whaling seasons had not started yet so we stood a much greater chance of selling our snowmobiles there than further south where the ice was already beginning to break up. We formed a chain gang and loaded on all the equipment that we were not leaving behind to sell.

Once on board we sat down on the netting backed benches, isolated by the din of the aircraft. Looking down the body of the plane I could see people passing around copies of *Playboy* that a member of the crew had thoughtfully provided or reading their mail. Two and a half hours later we banked sharply before landing at Elmendorff Airforce Base, right back where we had started. As we walked down the tail gate I noticed members of the ground crew staring at us. With our beards, long hair, bulky, grime encrusted clothing and motley collection of fur hats we must have looked like a load of primitive hill-billies compared to them with their crew cuts and smartly pressed uniforms.

There was still snow at the side of the runway and on the hills but it was melting in temperatures that felt positively tropical to us. In the bright sunshine our training base appeared far more benign than when we had left it more than two months previously. They had been two busy months, full of excitement and new experiences but now we had to put them behind us and concentrate on the challenges that lay ahead.

Chapter Three
Mount McKinley

I was beginning to have considerable misgivings about our second objective. Mount McKinley rises to a height of 20,320 feet, towering above the surrounding peaks of the Alaska Range and dominating the skyline for many miles. On one of the rare days when the mountain is not enshrouded in cloud, it is clearly visible from the dining rooms of the expensive Anchorage restaurants that look north across the Cook Inlet and up the Sustina Valley. However for those planning to try to reach the highest peak in North America it is not the gastronomic delights available 120 miles to the south that give cause for concern, although these may occupy an increasing amount of your thoughts as you spend yet another day on unappetizing mountain rations, but Mt McKinley's proximity to the Arctic Circle just 200 miles to the north.

McKinley has a reputation for being the coldest mountain on earth. Undoubtedly there are those that are colder, but few feature on a climber's itinerary. The Alaska Range is subject to the full range of Arctic weather. For much of the year McKinley remains locked in cloud, ravaged by storms that last for days or weeks at a time. Ambient temperatures of -40° Fahrenheit and below are common on the mountain and it is frequently swept by high winds that have been recorded at well over 100 miles per hour.

To add to this unprepossessing prospect, McKinley's summit is over 18,000 feet above the surrounding plains. The vertical interval between base camp and summit is greater than that for Mount Everest. Easy access to the mountain, and therefore escape, is denied by the surrounding peaks whose virtually unscalable faces are linked by high, jagged, knife-edged ridges. In between lie huge glaciers, great swathes of ice flowing inexorably down from the mountain, riven by deep crevasses.

Denali National Park's *Guide for Mountaineers* makes sobering reading. In between sections itemising the special equipment required to combat McKinley's ferocious conditions, recommended quantities of supplies and Park regulations, are extracts from the diaries of top International climbers, warning of the dangers of McKinley's weather system. The guide contains descriptions of storms that have raged for days on end, destroying tents, overwhelming individuals physically and mentally and inflicting many casualties. During the previous year the worst storms recorded for fifty years had gripped the mountain, catching climbers at various stages of their ascents. Those that had ignored the warnings to retreat or prepare a safe camp in which to sit out the storm had paid a heavy price. Twelve people had died in a month.

The guide highlights the need for each item of equipment to be capable of withstanding the severest Arctic conditions. At the bottom of one section which explains that top of the range, high-altitude mountaineering boots as normally only deemed necessary by climbers going to the high Himalayas, were insufficient and should be complemented by a thick overboot, there is an italicised warning: *'this advice should not be taken lightly'*.

Another section deals with the need to know how to dig snow caves and build snow shelters as protection against storm-force winds which could destroy even the best tents. The guide goes on to explain the difficulty of effecting rescues when the conditions are bad, the times at which rescues are most likely to be needed.

Helicopters and aeroplanes are unable to get near the mountain during storms let alone pluck an injured climber from a high exposed face. Rescue teams on foot could take several days to reach a casualty under normal conditions and might not be able to move at all in high winds or white-out conditions. The strong, clear message that comes across is that teams of climbers should come prepared for the worst conditions imaginable, retreat or batten down in the face of bad weather and expect to tend to and recover their own casualties which might involve carrying one or more injured people down the mountain

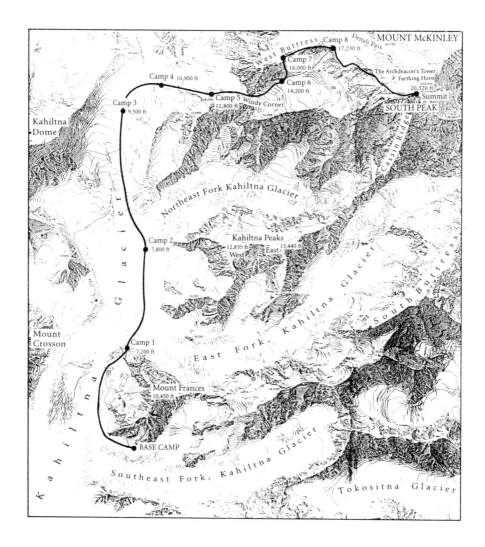

Route taken by Phase 2 Team up Mt McKinley

Phase 2 Vehicle Journey

until conditions improve and an aerial recovery becomes possible.

I was confident that we had taken every step that we could to give ourselves the best chance of success and to minimise the dangers. We had obtained all the special equipment: high-altitude tents and cookers, double-layered boots with overboots, cane wands to mark the route, pulks, skis and snowshoes, down clothing, radios and even a satellite telephone with which to communicate to Anchorage if radio conditions on the mountains were unworkable.

We had recruited two mountaineering instructors; Colour Sergeant Craig Offless, a full-time mountaineering instructor with eight Alpine seasons behind him and experience of cold weather and high-altitude climbing on expeditions in Norway and the Himalayas, and Sergeant Taff Mason, also a military mountain guide who had climbed McKinley two years before on a previous expedition.

Amongst the rest of the team Colour Sergeant Pete Richardson had worked as one of Tony Bradborn's instructors for the last few years at Fremington and had expedition experience of technical rock and ice climbing; Corporal of Horse Andy Wells was a tough physical training instructor and had experience of winter mountaineering; Corporal Andy Howard, our mechanic, had shared some testing moments on Mount Stanley in the Ruwenzoris during Roof of Africa where he had shown himself to be resilient, determined and capable of operating under some fairly adverse conditions.

Most of the others had been amongst the strongest performers on the selection camps although a couple of the youngest members of the team were replacements for others who had dropped out. However, no matter how well they had performed, there is no way that even the most rigorous of test exercises on Dartmoor could be compared to the conditions that we would face on McKinley.

The team emerged from the airport terminal in the dazed, rather disorientated way of long haul passengers. It was good to see a number of familiar faces. Leading the way was the beaming face of Lance-Sergeant Andy Brown. In the way of the Welsh Guards, as someone with a common surname, he was known by the last two digits of his Army Number, in his case, 16. From the valleys

of South Wales, he was a keen rugby player and had played prop forward for the regiment for a number of years. We had known each other for a long time, serving in the same Company in Northern Ireland and Germany. Subsequently we had been on expedition together, climbing volcanos in Mexico and driving across the central African jungle where we had climbed a number of mountains en route.

A hugely strong man with the heart of a lion and an enormous zest for life, 16 is a Welsh Guardsman down to the last stitch in his socks, volunteers for everything out of principle and is the most loyal man I know. It was always good to have him on a team; with his bubbling enthusiasm, zany humour and repertoire of songs, he could lift even the most depressed of spirits.

Also from the Welsh Guards was Lance-Sergeant Anthony Brown 80. We had also known each other for a long time and he was another member of the team I knew to be strong and dependable. With the exception of the two instructors, the remainder had taken part in one of the three selection camps so I knew them all to some degree. Colour Sergeant Craig Offless came up and introduced himself. On first meeting he came over as well spoken, easy going and enthusiastic for the task ahead but Anchorage Airport Car park was hardly the place for a long introduction so we loaded up the kit, less the almost mandatory set of luggage which had got lost en route and drove to Camp Carroll.

The next two days were a hectic period of fitting and issuing equipment, practising rope techniques and packing for the mountain. All items of clothing had been carefully sized to ensure that none would be too tight and restrict the flow of blood to limbs thereby increasing the risk of frostbite. Crampons and snowshoes had to be adjusted to fit each individual's boots, skins stuck to the bottom of our skis and each item of equipment checked and tested. It was important to agree and practise uniform techniques for tying into harnesses, crevasse rescues and belaying. In that way when people were tired and under pressure there would be less danger of a mistake and someone undoing a vital knot or karabiner.

Looking at the vast pile of equipment lying on the floor beside my bed I wondered how I would ever pack it into my rucksack let alone carry it, and we had not been issued with our rations yet. I went through the familiar routine of packing, unpacking and re-packing in an attempt to remove unnecessary kit and reduce the overall weight. There were some hard compromises to make and yet much of the equipment and clothing was vital. Did the weight gain from leaving behind a heavy set of overmitts justify the risk of not having them if we got caught out away from camp in cold conditions?

I always dislike the period of preparation immediately before any expedition. All the underlying uncertainties come springing to the surface and by the time that I had eventually packed for the last time I felt hot, flustered and uncomfortable with each decision over the items of equipment that I would take or leave. All around the crowded Barrack Room the other members of the team were going through the same procedure and I suspect feeling the same disquiet. People walked up and down comparing notes on their packing, envying those tidy, efficient individuals whose rucksacks lay neatly packed at the foot of their beds or coveting the luxury items of personal kit that the more experienced mountaineers displayed proudly.

The morning news on the 26th April made depressing listening: two climbers had died in an accident on a mountain near McKinley. The newsreader went on to describe the growing death toll on McKinley in recent years. I fought to control my feelings. For some reason this mountain had begun to psyche me out. Never before had I experienced such negative feelings about any expedition that I was about to embark on and it was totally against my nature.

In another world, I knew that back in Wales my stepfather was becoming increasingly ill. I had spoken to my mother who was trying to put a brave front on a rapidly worsening situation. I wished that I was in a position to be more supportive not disappearing into the nethermost reaches of an ice-bound mountain range where I would be to all intents and purposes out of contact for the next three weeks. I sat in the office numbly waiting for the bus to take us to Bryant Airfield.

The American Army had provided three Chinook helicopters to fly us first to Talkeetna, a small town to the south of the mountains, where we had to go to the Park Headquarters for a mandatory briefing and then up to the Base Camp on the Kahiltna Glacier. The flight to Talkeetna took

forty minutes. We landed in broad sunshine and had clear views of the mountain as we walked the half mile to the Headquarters, sweating in our thick mountain clothing.

Three Park Rangers took us through the various Park rules. The meat of their briefing was a description of the route and the current conditions on the mountain. We were attempting to climb the mountain early, before the beginning of the normal climbing season. Few teams were on the mountain, none had made it above 14,000 feet and each of the five teams that had come down so far had had cases of serious frostbite.

At 14,000 feet the temperature was dropping to -40° Fahrenheit at night and there had been strong winds high on the mountain for several days. They stressed the need to protect ourselves against the cold, warning us never to move from camp without spare socks, gloves, goggles, down jackets, sleeping bags and cookers. Looking around the room I could see that this description of the conditions that lay just a short flight ahead of us had shocked many of the team. Any reverie had been shattered by a dose of stark realities.

It was an introspective team that strapped in for the last lap of the flight, each one of us was reflecting on what we had just heard and tentatively mulling over unspoken questions about our own abilities. They were questions which danced around my mind probing delicately for answers that as yet were not there and were posed gently so as not to unearth too many doubts or shatter already unsteady confidence.

The flight was sensational. We flew north-east out over the broad Sustina Valley. Two thousand feet below us fir trees flanked the river and its tributaries. The rivers were in the process of melting but either side the ground was still covered in snow. We flew over the foothills and into the beginning of the Alaska Range. Saw-toothed peaks and sheer rock walls flashed past as we rose over high ridges and squeezed between the tightly packed peaks.

Below us the haunting shadows of deep crevasses formed an impassable lattice work, unrelieved for kilometres at a stretch. It would be near impossible to use these glaciers as a means of escape and yet they filled the only channels between the mountain sentinels. Climbers do approach the mountain on foot from the north if they are attempting the northern and eastern routes on the mountain but for those aiming for the West Buttress flying is the only viable way in.

Having clambered over One Shot Pass, the helicopters flew low up the Kahiltna Glacier leaving Mounts Foraker and Hunter to left and right and turning right just before Mount Frances to land on a raised plateau of ice a short way up the South-East Fork of the Kahiltna Glacier. We touched down in line amidst a tremendous blast of driven snow. No sooner were the skids down and the rotor blades stopped than the loadmasters were yelling at us to drag the kit off. Human chains formed at the back of each helicopter as we passed rucksacks, skis, pulks and boxed rations out to be piled into the snow.

As soon as the aircraft were empty the rotors began to turn in preparation for lift off. We lay across the piles of kit and buried our faces in our coats to protect our skin against the hurricane-force down draught from the twin rotors. With a great roar the helicopters lifted up, slowly turned in unison and flew back down the glacier, heading left along the main Kahiltna Valley and away out of sight. We all watched as they grew smaller, conscious that with them lay our means of extraction from the mountain that was not scheduled for another three weeks.

Snow had been blasted into my eyes, ears, nose and inside most of my clothing. With the silence came the opportunity to look around and survey our surroundings. McKinley Base Camp is a rather humbling place. You are all at once conscious of being very small. All around rise sheer-walled mountains, their impossibly steep faces heavy with snow. We were at the lower end of an enclosed valley imprisoned by ridges running south from Mount Frances, west from Mount Huntington and north from Mount Hunter, at whose North Face we gazed. The open end of the valley led down to the main Kahiltna Glacier which would provide our route to Mount McKinley.

Nine miles north-east and 13,000 feet above us, the South summit of McKinley was clearly visible. Spindrift was blowing off the summit ridge but that aside it did not look impossibly far away. I was all too aware that we were enjoying some of the best weather that year and it was not likely to last long.

Having checked for crevasses, we selected an area for our tents, marked out a track plan and began to dig pits for the tents. Each tent had to be protected from the wind. That either meant digging a pit deep enough for the tent to be set up inside without even the top protruding above the surface of the snow, or building walls with blocks of ice around the tent to achieve the same end. Whilst the snow was deep lower on the mountain we would dig pits.

Once the tent was erected and anchored securely with heavy-duty pegs and alloy stakes driven deep into the snow, we dug recesses into the sides of the ice walls to house our rucksacks, which we sealed with upturned sleds, and covered shelves on which to cook. We had experienced a number of flare-ups with our field cookers and could not risk a fire in the confined space of a tent.

I was sharing a tent with the two other members of my rope team, Corporal Howard and Guardsman Brown, and with Colour Sergeant Offless. The Colour Sergeant and I dug the pit whilst the other two went to help Colour Sergeant McKeown. It was hot work and we began to burn in the sun. I felt weak and light-headed although we were only at a little over 7,000 feet. It took us about three hours to dig the tent pits by which time we were all dehydrated.

We spent the evening sorting out our kit, adapting to the routine of living in the tight confines of the tent hole and drinking us much as we could to redress our dehydration. Staying hydrated would be a constant battle as our only source of water was the snow and ice around us and the higher we progressed up the mountain the less efficient our cookers would become in the rarefied air. Having had several large drinks I began to feel a lot better. Now that we were on the mountain it did not seem so daunting and anyway we were too busy dealing with immediate practical concerns to dwell on any worries.

I woke up several times during the night to the sound of snow falling on our tent. At 7 a.m. I was driven out of my warm sleeping bag by the painful desire for a pee. I had been too shy to use my pee bottle in the close confines of the tent but seeing that Colour Sergeant Offless had used his, I resolved not to have the same qualms in future. It was not possible to get up in the night without disturbing at least one of the others. We were laid out head to toe, with Corporal Howard and Guardsman Brown, the two smallest amongst us, on the outsides.

We had to shovel snow away from the tents and dig out our rucksacks in the morning. Surprisingly it was not particularly cold but it was still snowing. We began the long, slow procedure of melting snow, brewing up, cooking breakfast and filling flasks and water bottles. I felt sick and could not force my breakfast down.

We decided to wait and see if the weather would improve and so spent the morning sorting out our rations for the climb. Each man was issued twenty-one days of boxed rations together with a supplement of extra drinks, chocolates, biscuits and nuts. We had debated at some length the best way to get the huge weight of supplies up the mountain. One suggestion was to carry food up in bulk, stocking camps in a sort of Himalayan siege. I was convinced that this would mean a great deal more work than each man simply carrying his own rations.

We needed to break the Army ration packs down to reduce the bulky packaging in any event, but I believed that each man should be able to decide for himself what to take up the mountain. The question of how much to take was a difficult compromise between weight and the requirement for calories to give you strength, energy and warmth during the climb.

Fortunately for me, I do not eat a great deal at the best of times and therefore I was able to cut down dramatically the huge pile of food that lay in the snow at my feet. I ended up with an American Army kit bag two thirds full of food having thrown out a roughly similar amount. I hoped that I had not cut back too far. Some of the larger men needed a complete ration pack each day. I could barely lift their loads.

The weather cleared and we were rewarded with fine views of the surrounding peaks which served to emphasise our dramatic location. Having paused for more brews and a snack lunch, we harnessed up, put on skis and went a short distance to a slope of deep snow. There we practised all the forms of snow and ice belays using skis, ice axes, deadmen and rucksacks sunk into the snow for anchors. We took turns in our rope teams to dig a huge trench some 10 feet deep and 3 feet wide which we used for crevasse rescue training.

I noticed that there was beginning to emerge a marked difference in style between the two instructors. Colour Sergeant Offless was inclined to teach complicated rope handling techniques which, although technically correct, involved intricate knots and rope systems that were not always easy to follow. I was also surprised by how impatient he was with some of the novices. Taff took a much quieter, less hurried approach always opting for the simplest solution to any problem on the basis that it would be easiest to carry out and less prone to a mistake when we were tired or in a tight situation. The two men both came from the Parachute Regiment and therefore should have had much in common but they almost always produced different solutions to any problem. Although there had not been any difficulties so far, I could see that their very different styles might lead to friction later on.

It was a productive afternoon, reinforcing in people's minds the techniques that we would each rely on for our safety as soon as we got going. I began to adapt to the altitude and felt much better. Back at the camp we had a meal and issued fuel and group safety equipment for our planned first load carry the next day. A clear sky sent the temperatures plummeting as we retired into our tents.

It was a cold night, even in a goose-down sleeping bag I shivered. After a poor night's sleep getting up in the morning was a lethargic, unmotivated operation. In the limited space of the tent, we had to take it in turns to clamber into layers of thermal underwear, pile suits and Goretex oversuits. Socks, gloves and boot inners came into our sleeping bags with us to prevent them from freezing, woollen hats were worn in bed if it was cold.

You could not put your head down inside your sleeping bag or the moisture in your breath would soak it by morning and there was no way of drying anything save by body heat if the conditions were bad. As it was, when we woke up there would be a layer of ice around the top of our sleeping bags where our breath had condensed and frozen. We kept our plastic outerboots between the inner tent and the fly sheet.

Having battled your way into all the gear the first of each pair had to go out into the cold, dig around in the snow to find the half-buried cooker and, with much pumping and adjusting, fire it up and begin preparing brews. We boiled water each evening and stored it in flasks which we kept either in or beside our sleeping bags overnight so that when we woke up we could use the water to make the first brew of the day relatively quickly. The first brew not only gave that wonderful inner suffusion of warmth but also something around which to warm chilled fingers.

I was very fortunate to be partnered with Corporal Howard. Not only did we know each other well, but he was both practical and efficient and remarkably tolerant of my uselessness in the mornings for which I was eternally grateful. We packed our pulks for the load carry. We had a few proper pulks fully equipped with material covers, aluminium traces and padded towing harnesses which we were trying out in preparation for the planned crossing of the Patagonian ice cap on Phase Six and some plastic children's toboggans.

The proper pulks were capable of carrying a much larger load and tracked better in the snow. The metal traces held them comfortably in line but on an incline they forced the skier awkwardly onto one side. The sleds were much cruder and more awkward to pack and secure. They had an infuriating habit of tipping over but could be allowed to trail below you on inclines and were lighter if you needed to carry them strapped to your rucksack when empty.

Having sorted out our loads we harnessed and roped up in our teams of three. The expedition was split into two halves with one instructor responsible for each. I noted Taff carefully looking over each man in his group, checking that knots were tied correctly, karabiners fastened, jumars and prussik loops attached ready for a crevasse rescue and testing the signal of the avalanche locators.

We all wore small electronic devices strapped under our clothing which emitted a permanent signal. If you were caught by an avalanche, any of the others in the party or any rescue party could switch their device to Receive and by carrying out a sweep search locate where you were buried and hopefully dig you out before you suffocated or froze to death. We had carried out a couple of trial exercises, burying emitters in the snow and setting the team to finding them. The exercises worked well, proving the theory, but I was in no hurry to test it for real when a casualty may be buried many feet below the surface under tons of snow. For all that, it was comforting to have them.

It took a long time to get everyone sorted out into their teams, checked over and ready to go. I was very conscious that the unfamiliarity with the equipment that was causing this would mean that we would freeze on a really cold day. We needed to become much quicker but without compromising any safety. We set off slowly, getting used to moving on skis whilst roped to each other and with the added hindrance of our pulks dragging behind us. The basic pulks tipped over many times requiring loads to be repacked, but gradually we settled down to a steady, if not very fast, pace.

With Colour Sergeant Offless at the front breaking trail, we descended slowly along the Southeast Fork to the main Kahiltna Glacier. We passed large crevasses a couple of hundred yards from our campsite. The main glacier was criss-crossed with regular, large slashes. Many more were covered over with snow and except where there were indentations or shadows in the snow we crossed them oblivious to their existence. Late in the summer, once the surface covering had melted, the full extent of these crevasses would be exposed and the trail would have to pick an intricate route weaving amidst the crevasses as climbers moved up the glacier.

The sky was azure blue setting off the pristine white mountain sides. As the sun rose, the temperature increased dramatically. With the reflection of the sun off the surface of the snow we began to burn despite frequent smothering with total blocking cream. Some of the more fair skinned members of the team had to wear cold weather masks to protect their faces.

The pulks glided relatively effortlessly on the way down to the glacier but as we started to climb their full weight came onto our harnesses. However it was still a great deal better than trying to carry everything in a rucksack. Frustratingly there was a significant amount of safety equipment that we had to carry with us at all times and which therefore ended up getting carried up and down every section of the route several times, all the while adding to the weight.

We threaded our way through some large open crevasses and climbed a short, steep slope before stopping between ridges running down from Mount Crosson on our left and Mount Frances on our right. Colour Sergeant Offless dropped his pack and unhitched his pulk and then skied around in a circle at the end of his rope checking for crevasses before declaring the area safe for our cache and subsequent Camp One. The ice on the major glaciers could be up to 1,000 feet deep and the larger crevasses disappeared down several hundred feet. McKinley's crevasses had claimed many climbers' lives.

We unroped and then dug caches in which we buried our food, spare fuel and spare equipment. Having covered the caches back over to prevent them being raided by ravens, we marked the spot with pyramids of bamboo wands so that we could find it again after heavy snowfall. Three feet of snow in a night was not unheard of.

Having drunk most of the contents of our flasks and water bottles we roped up once again and set off back towards our camp. On the way down we passed a man and a woman toiling up towards Camp One in a single push, bearing enormous loads. Another group of three climbers were heading off towards the East Face of Mount Crosson. Light aircraft had been buzzing overhead all day, taking advantage of the good weather to land groups of climbers at Base Camp and take tourists on flightseeing tours of the mountain. Doubtless we were a special interest feature – the climbers who came to pit themselves against the mountain and by the way have you heard the death statistics? I wondered whether the tourists felt envy or pity as they watched us plodding along the glacier.

It was 4.30 p.m. by the time we hauled ourselves back up the long hill to Base Camp. We guzzled brews as fast as we could make them until we began to feel less dehydrated. At the top end of the ice landing strip is a small hut manned throughout each climbing season by Annie. Fount of all knowledge and dispenser of endless hot drinks, kind words, encouragement, consolation or general bonhomie, Annie was paid by the consortium of flight operators to man the Base Camp Radio, report on the local weather conditions and co-ordinate all flights on and off the glacier. She sets up home for four months in her hut on the ice. Several groups had arrived during the afternoon including a five-man RAF team who set off immediately using neither skis nor snowshoes, a very proficient looking six-man Korean team bound for the West Rib and two American climbing dudes who had come to spend time 'attuning' to the mountain. Annie told me that the weather forecast was for three days of snow.

Next day we packed up camp, leaving just two tents erected containing spare rations and equipment in case of an emergency retreat. The fabric of the tents had frozen to the ground where the warmth from our bodies had melted the snow under us. The joints of the collapsible tent poles had also frozen up and we had to warm them with bare hands or by breathing on them before we could dismantle them.

Once again it took a long time to get everyone loaded, roped and ready to go. Our loads were larger and more awkward than on the previous day and so we had correspondingly more problems with pulks repeatedly tipping over. This was largely avoidable if they were very carefully packed and strapped down but most of us experienced some difficulties. It was frustrating both for the person whose pulk turned over, as it instantly became a dead weight snagging in the snow and dragging you backwards, for the others in the same rope team and for those behind who had to continually stop and wait whilst the pulk was righted or repacked.

Manoeuvring on skis whilst attached to each other only made the whole process more time consuming and cumbersome. Pulks had the ability to exasperate even the most patient person. The Doctor was struggling with a huge load which refused to tow properly. Corporal Steggles fell over several times, on one occasion yanking back on his rope so sharply that Colour Sergeant Richardson in front was ripped straight off his feet. Trooper Roskell had not secured his pulk properly and bits of kit kept falling off. I could see him beginning to lose his temper. Gradually we began to sort ourselves out and establish a rhythm.

Once underway, you just put your head down and tried to maintain a steady pace. We passed the RAF team who were labouring along on foot carrying all their kit and making extremely slow progress. To be walking in boots in the soft surface snow seemed to me to be insane but I was not sure whether we might not have been better on snowshoes. Given our lack of confidence in skis they might have proved easier.

Plodding along in the wake of the lead team I had plenty of time to think. I was already beginning to identify members of the team that I just could not see getting to the summit. Clearly the most important thing was to place someone from the expedition onto the summit and the more the better. That said, I was determined that the climb should not be mounted as a group of prima donna summitteers supported by all the novices. I hoped to get all of the team to 14,000 feet at the base of the true climbing and take a fresh look at everyone there.

To reach even that level in the conditions prevalent on this mountain would be a major achievement for a novice mountaineer. How realistic that goal was would remain to be seen. I was equally clear that if someone had to take those who could go no further or anyone who was injured down the mountain then it should be me. There were only three members of the team qualified to lead people on the glaciers, the two main instructors and me. They had both come out specifically for this mountain and both were more highly qualified than I was. Richard was quite capable of taking decisions from an expedition perspective in conjunction with them if I went down. Added to that, he and Colour Sergeant McKeown had both stood down for substantial parts of the first phase to organise our re-supply and support from Anchorage.

Having reached the cache we dug it up and then carried on digging, creating new pits for the tents. This was to be our routine as we progressed up the mountain – carry a load to a cache, return to sleep at our previous camp and then move the camp up the next day. In that way we kept to the old mountaineering adage climb high, sleep low. This, combined with regular rest days, was the best way to aid acclimatisation.

The Korean team came past us moving fluidly in two rope teams of three. Another pair of climbers came past us in the other direction. Although they did not stop to talk we gathered that they had turned back from 15,000 feet. They walked with a fixed stare and looked pretty rough.

It snowed hard for most of the night. We got up at 7 a.m. keen to press on, only to find driving snow, ice-cold wind and almost zero visibility. It would have been feasible to make a load carry but if we had more of the hold-ups that we had been having over the last two days we would risk people getting cold injuries. Avoiding crevasses would have been fairly hazardous too.

We checked the weather every half hour but it did not improve. The cloud shifted partially at times but for the most part it was driving snow. We sheltered in the tents, only emerging to shovel away the snow accumulating inside our icy hollows,

prepare brews or to go to the loo. For most of the day we lay in the tents grateful for the protection afforded by the walls of the pits that we had dug. The time passed slowly as we slept, day dreamed, read and wrote letters. In the evening the weather finally cleared. Everyone emerged from the tents and there was almost a party atmosphere.

When elsewhere in the World people were enjoying May Day celebrations, we got up to a cool, overcast morning. The conditions were good enough to move in, so we began to pack. The night before we had discussed doing a double carry to make up for the day that we had lost. Taff now suggested that instead of pounding up and down the route three times in a day, we try to load up everything and move it in one lift, taking our time. After a quick consensus of opinion we decided to go for it. It took a bit over an hour to pack up but with pulks and rucksacks loaded to the gunwales we set off. Despite the usual hassles with the pulks and being rather unsteady under our huge loads, we made fairly good progress along the glacier.

Moving between the prescribed campsites was not taking as long as I had anticipated, instead it was achieved in relatively short periods of intensely hard physical graft. All the preparations for each move and the construction of each new camp however filled most of the rest of the usable day. Before the sun rose and after it had sunk behind the ridge of Mount Crosson it was bitterly cold.

We stopped for a break overlooking our intended campsite which lay before a long steep hill. Taff came forward from the head of his team to chat as we drank our brews. He said that he thought that we should camp on the near side of the small bowl in front of us to provide better protection from avalanches particularly in view of the recent snowfall. This made good sense to me but he said it in his quiet, rather staccato way of talking and I could see that Colour Sergeant Offless had not taken it in. After lunch he set off and ignoring Taff's advice headed straight for the bottom of the bowl. This caused a minor contretemps between the two of them. They began sniping at each other, Offless getting on his high horse about having the higher qualification and Taff letting fly that he might not read a lot of fancy books but any idiot could see that his was the better and more safe place. I intervened and then later in the day once camp was established sent for both of them, ostensibly to discuss the following day's plans but I took advantage of the opportunity to take them to task and tell them to sort out their differences in private.

A couple of other groups of climbers arrived including an extremely boisterous Slavic solo climber called Adrian who was on his ninth trip up McKinley and specialised in skiing its extreme faces. Conversely three groups came down from 14,000 feet. None had made it higher than that. They said that it was very cold higher on the mountain and that the headwall above their last camp looked dangerously icy with an overhanging cornice on top. One further group who were still up there, had got to 17,000 feet but encountered 60 mph winds and turned back.

To avoid the concertinaing and continual hold-ups of a great 22-man crocodile we introduced an hour's interval between the start time of each group. The lead was to be alternated each day. Our group had a deliciously relaxing 8 a.m. reveille. I got up and took photographs of the other group as they geared up and then again as they snaked their way up the hill in front of us. We followed an hour later.

Moving straight onto the steep slope made a savage start to the day. We raised the heel supports on our touring skis to give us an easier base to push against. The hairs on the skins that we had stuck to the undersides of our skis gained traction against the snow but the weight of our pulks dragged us backwards. Having got the pulk moving upwards we worked to maintain momentum. When our thighs and calves were burning and we paused to rest, we angled the pulks sideways or got the person behind to let the pulk rest against their ski poles driven into the ground, to take the weight off our harnesses.

We climbed steadily up, sweating hard despite the cold morning. The slope was broken by a couple of flattish sections. We passed a cache marked with flagged wands with Chinese characters on them that must have belonged to the Koreans. The weather began to close in around us. After a while, driving snow sent us back into the Goretex oversuits that we had stripped off earlier.

We climbed on slowly but our rate of advance was getting less and less. I was unsure how much further we had to go. I knew from the map that sooner or later it would flatten out. At the far end of a plateau we planned to make our cache but I was beginning to get mildly concerned by the continued deterioration in the weather. At that moment I heard voices above and in a few more minutes we pulled up to the other half of the team. They had already cached their gear and were preparing to descend. They were on the beginning of the plateau at around 9,700 feet.

We dug in our cache as quickly as we could. The weather was growing steadily worse. A cold, strengthening wind was driving snow into our faces and there was almost no visibility. We locked down the heels of our boots, strapped our empty pulks to our rucksacks and headed downhill after the others. I stopped my rope team almost immediately to get them to put overmitts on. We were already skiing with our hoods up to protect our faces from the spindrift.

Predictably the descent was fairly chaotic. We had begun to master skiing roped together on the level or uphill, but now shooting downwards with our rucksacks on, wearing mountaineering boots attached to touring skis and roped to each other it was a recipe for disaster. When I could risk looking up from my own skis, I saw people falling over all the way down the slope. Those that were not falling over themselves were being repeatedly pulled down by the others on their rope. Most of the team treated it as a good crack but I saw one or two getting stressed and banging their poles into the snow or taking their skis off and walking down in frustration.

Back at Camp Two it was significantly warmer. I went around from tent to tent to check that everyone was alright. There had been a certain amount of chuntering up on the hill but now there was just excited chatter and the usual leg-pulling. Annie came on the radio at 8 p.m. with the weather forecast which was for more bad weather with strengthening winds for at least another two days.

It was our turn to lead in the morning so we got motivated and set about packing up. I noticed how much quicker we had become at organising ourselves. Despite a cold start which did nothing to help the packing or harnessing process we were ready to set off just after 9 a.m. The snow overnight had obliterated our tracks and now as we headed up in near white-out conditions we regretted not having put out more wands to mark the route. We peered through the gloom, searching for the next wand and, when we could not see one, feeling our way forward until we could. I had organised my load better and found the going easier. My pulk did not seem such a dead weight although it was still painful around my hips.

The wind grew stronger and colder and the white-out intensified. We went some distance without being able to find a wand. By the time that we reached the cache, conditions were pretty dismal. We decided not to try to go any further and wasted no time digging in. Once we had dug down a couple of feet and built up a snow wall on the windward side we were much more protected and the feeling of being threatened by the conditions subsided. Even so we worked hard and fast to get the pit dug and the tent erected.

The second group appeared as we were about halfway through this. I was relieved to see them. They too had had trouble finding the route. Our tracks from just an hour before had been covered over and Taff said that he had practically been on his hands and knees looking for them.

Having dug in and put our tents up we prepared hot drinks and took shelter. Around 4.30 p.m. the cloud lifted revealing a number of other groups of tents not far away including the Koreans and Adrian. Our slower traditional method of advance by carrying loads and making caches did not seem to be holding us back. They had not moved that day. We had great views of the Kahiltna Dome, a towering white face streaked by crevasses that rose 3,000 feet above us, and away down the valley to some of the lower peaks. Another pair of climbers came down from 14,000 feet having got no higher.

Taff popped his head through the tent in the morning to say that the weather was too bad for us to move. It was blowing a gale and driving snow. I lay in my sleeping bag grateful for being warm and daydreamed for most of the morning until I could stand being in the tent no longer. I struggled into my clothes and went outside. Our tent hole had filled with deep powder snow which had buried all of our kit. I shovelled it away and fired up the cooker once I found it. I then went around the tents chatting to each group.

It was important not to let people sink into lethargy or start to feel isolated from the rest of the team during long periods stuck in the tents.

The boredom and constant shrieking of the wind could play on people's nerves and tent visiting was a good way to relieve the monotony and share the conditions. It also gave me a chance to check on how everyone was feeling and to ensure that they were looking after themselves properly, digging out the tent holes and getting adequate food and brews.

Two pairs of climbers passed us going up with their heads down and faces buried deep in their hoods. One further pair appeared through the snow flurries from above. They were the ones who had reached 17,000 feet and turned back. They had spent nine nights at 14,000 feet but with no signs of the weather improving they were heading down. I called the two instructors, Richard and Colour Sergeant McKeown to my tent to discuss the tactics that we should adopt.

I felt that we needed to try and move in the bad weather and that so long as we wanded the route carefully we could always retreat if the conditions became too bad. At least we would be making progress and it would be better for morale than festering in the tents. As we talked, the weather cleared and although it was late in the afternoon we decided to make a quick carry for a kilometre to the base of another steep hill. As soon as the word to move was passed everyone leapt into action.

The weather began to deteriorate again but we pressed on anyway, glad to be out of the tents. Going gently uphill with the wind behind us we reached the intended cache quickly. We turned back into some fairly unpleasant weather. We put on facemasks and peered through iced-up goggles as we skied back down to the tents. There we dived inside for cover emerging only to take turns at the cooker until we could stand the cold no longer. We spent the evening playing word games to the sound of howling wind and blowing snow on the thin tent walls.

Next day we established Camp Four at 10,900 feet with a double carry. The weight and altitude were now beginning to take their toll. Mike Charlson had been battling his way up the mountain with a fearsome load. That day he had to make three loads to get up the sharp climb to the camp. By the end of the third ascent he looked grey with the effort. He took his role as Expedition Doctor extremely seriously and his rucksack was far heavier than anyone else's, packed with medical supplies and the equipment for his research project. If he tried to continue forcing his way up by sheer brute force, his dogged refusal to give in would make him the first casualty. Aside of a natural concern for his welfare we needed him to provide our medical cover higher on the mountain. I persuaded him to thin down his supplies and share out the surplus amongst the team.

It was cold the next morning as we packed up a load carry. We wore down jackets and I had to work my fingers in my gloves to prevent them freezing. I packed my sheepskin overmitts in case it became much colder higher up. We made our way up several hundred feet to where a few other groups were camped at the base of the steepest slope that we had encountered so far. As we took a breather, Corporal of Horse Wells called me over to look at Corporal McCauley. He was sitting hunched over on his pulk and complained of feeling sick. He clearly was not fit to make the load carry and so I told Wells to take him back down to camp and keep an eye on him. Richard also sent Guardsman Davidson down whose hands had lost all feeling and taken on a rather suspicious colour.

The slope was steep and increasingly icy. I felt uncomfortable with two ski poles and changed one for my ice axe. At least I would now be able to hold a fall if any of us on my rope slipped. I was aware that the angle would begin to intimidate the less experienced members of the team. Our pulks hung down below us as dead weights. There were a couple of delicate moments towards the top as we stepped over cracks on some bare ice that afforded little purchase to our crampons. The rope teams had spread out, each moving at their own pace. We pulled up onto a dramatic ridge which fell away sharply on the far side. 2,500 feet below lay Peter's Glacier. Taff stayed at the top belaying those teams that were having difficulties hauling their loads up the steep, bare ice. The wind was blowing strongly making us bitterly cold.

Moving slightly further along the ridge we came to a sheltered hollow where we decided to make our cache. We dug a shallow hole just before some rocks at the edge of the vertical drop to the north. The great rock wall of the West Buttress swept up to the sky above us. Turning back I found Taff belaying the last couple of teams up. He was stoically helping each group in turn but the slight edge to his voice gave away his urgency to get off his very cold and exposed stance.

An American man and his Canadian girlfriend passed us heading upwards. She looked absolutely exhausted. We had seen them several times as we had moved up the mountain. They were a friendly couple and had stopped to chat whenever we saw them. Neither appeared to be very experienced and we had formed the impression that the man was pushing hard, possibly too hard, to get to the top. Adrian also came past. He had made his cache a few hundred feet higher up and said that it was blowing hard and much colder up there. Moving alone, without the encumbrance of ropes and comfortable with his own technique, he covered the ground a lot quicker than us.

Back at camp, Corporal McCauley was no better. He was not seriously ill but had not slept for a couple of days and was showing mild symptoms of Acute Mountain Sickness; headaches and nausea. I hoped that after a day and further night of rest at this altitude he might have become sufficiently acclimatised to go on. As it was, a day of bad weather provided a further rest but still his condition did not totally improve. In fact, by the time that we were able to go on, two more members of the team, Corporal Steggles and Trooper Roskell complained of similar symptoms. We were only just at the lowest height at which cases of serious altitude sickness might be expected but the RAF team who were camped nearby were experiencing similar problems. I suspected that the problems were as much mental as physical and that some of them were simply becoming overwhelmed by their environment and the scale and seriousness of the undertaking.

There was no question of anyone who did not feel up to it going any higher on the mountain. To do so might risk serious altitude sickness developing into Pulmonary or Cerebral Oedema, literally the flooding of lungs or the brain which in turn could lead to a state of coma and then death. I was sure that more people would have problems by the time that we reached Camp Six at 14,000 feet and intended to re-appraise everyone's condition at that stage. I was anticipating having to bring other members of the team down from there and so wanted to carry on at least that far myself.

The condition of the three who were already suffering mild symptoms of Acute Mountain Sickness did not warrant taking them back to Base Camp but it did require someone sensible to stay with them and to be able to take decisions or react in an emergency if for some reason any one of them suddenly deteriorated. Having gathered the whole team together and explained my plan for the rest of the climb I called for volunteers from the officers and non-commissioned officers to stay behind. As I had anticipated none came forward. I had been dreading this as it meant that I would have to appoint someone and that would mean the end of their hopes to reach the summit.

I had run through the team several times in my head. No one stood out as being particularly weak. Almost by definition this group were the most motivated and capable members of the team however I had to assess each individuals chances of success. Reluctantly I decided upon 16. The disappointment was written all over his face but true to form he accepted my decision. I left him a radio and arranged a schedule of calls between us and then briefed him that I would probably be back with those who were not going to attempt the headwall in about four days time and then we would make our way back down the mountain together. As he waved us off I felt as if I had betrayed his effort and support.

The route up to our cache was no easier than it had been two days previously although the weather was better and the views to the south across the Alaska Range spectacular. We carried on past the cache up an ascending ridge line until we came to a plateau of hard wind-packed ice beneath the rock wall of the West Buttress. Rocks up to sizeable boulders were strewn over the snow and ice, their tell-tale trails leading from the direction of the shattered buttress. We set up camp on a shelf of rather exposed ice as far from the base of the rock wall as we could safely get, away from the danger of rockfall.

The packed snow and ice was iron hard which made digging down more than a few inches impossible. Instead we chopped out blocks with our shovels and ice axes which we built up into disconcertingly insubstantial walls around the tents. I did not have much confidence for the protection that they would afford and paid more attention than usual to anchoring the tents to the ground. A bad storm threatened to blow us straight off our precarious perch and down to Peter's Glacier. Several groups passed us on their way down from making a cache further up towards

the 14,000 foot camp. They all looked shattered and reported glare ice on the awkward traverse around Windy Corner.

It was cold enough to warrant putting on our thick, padded overboots for the first time. Leaving the tents in situ, we roped up and headed back down the ridge to collect our cache. The wind tugged at us but I was warm in my down jacket. I felt comfortable and strong until the bale on one of my crampons snapped. I could not repair it so I had to teeter down the steep ice on one crampon holding my ice axe ready to self-arrest in case I slipped. Fortunately I had a spare set of crampons at the cache. We collected the gear and headed back up the ridge. We stopped at the tents to pack up camp and have something to eat and drink and then headed on with all our kit. We planned to carry everything to a cache in the rocks at Windy Corner and then continue on with the camp equipment to Camp Six.

The route rose gradually as we followed the wall of the West Buttress avoiding the worst areas of stone-fall. The wind was bitingly cold. Pulks were overladen and tipped over frequently. We stopped twice for Guardsman Brown to totally repack his pulk, each time stamping while we waited to ward off the cold. Our progress was frustratingly slow. About halfway up the 1,000ft slope one of my replacement crampons broke. The remainder of the slope was sheer agony with the pulk dragging on my hips as it rolled time after time on the side incline, Guardsman Brown constantly dragging back on the rope as he fought with his pulk and all the while trying to hop forward on one crampon without losing my footing. By the time that we made it to the windswept rocks I felt exhausted. We cached the surplus food and equipment, covering them with stones, and then carried on. It was about a mile to the camp climbing a further 1,200ft.

We moved gingerly around the corner concentrating on forcing all our crampon points into the hard ice. We climbed steeply up on a rising traverse. The ground fell away sharply to our right. A slip here would have been difficult to hold and a fall would almost certainly have been fatal. Once round the corner we were shielded from the wind by the West Buttress rising sheer above us and the temperature rose accordingly. The ground flattened out but there were now large crevasses to negotiate. We trod carefully across snowbridges, testing every part before committing ourselves to them and jumped over those that were narrow enough.

The route continued up a series of seemingly endless snow slopes. On our right were open snowfields with some truly enormous crevasses to which we could see no bottom. The camp was perched the far side of a large depression cut by more of the giant crevasses and at the bottom of the headwall that lead up onto the West Buttress.

We stopped to rest more and more often, longing for the relief of unhitching our loads. It was after 7 p.m. by the time that we hauled our pulks up the last slope to the plateau and selected ourselves an area to camp. The weather cleared leaving the headwall bathed in sunlight above us as we began once again to dig the tents in. Tired and parched after a hard day of load carrying, it took longer than usual to set up camp but I was glad to have us finally established at this strategically important point, the jumping-off point for the true climbing.

A number of the team had found the going hard and several were now complaining of headaches and nausea but that was to be expected. Once we had eventually got the tents up, eaten and had successive brews to re-hydrate ourselves we collapsed gratefully onto our ground mats. I lay in my sleeping bag turning plans for the next stage over in my mind. Now was the decision time to select who was to go on and attempt the summit and who was to turn back.

The 14,200ft camp, our Camp Six, was in a spectacular setting. The views south over the Alaska Range to Mounts Hunter and Foraker were sensational. In the early morning banks of mist and cloud boiled over the peaks and ridges. From just a few hundred yards away our camp, peeking above the surface of the snow on the broad plateau, looked so insignificant against the panorama of peaks and valleys. Away in the far distance, a darkening beneath the haze marked the surrounding plains below the snowline. It was a world apart.

Above us rose the headwall that lead up to the next camp at 16,000 feet. This was the crux of the climb. It provided an intimidating barrier and a committing step between our current position and the remainder of the route to the summit. Once above it, a team was considerably more vulnerable to bad weather and any rescue

was correspondingly more difficult. Although no problem for experienced technical climbers, its icy, upper slope demanded respect and had taken its toll of accidents. Later in the season new ropes would be fixed up the severest part for climbers to be able to jumar their way up safely.

I called the planning group together. I had already decided that Cardwell, Elms, Davies and Davidson were not for the summit. They had all found themselves fully stretched on the more difficult parts of the route so far. Question marks were also placed over Colour Sergeant Richardson, Corporal of Horse Wells and Guardsman Brown, all of whom had been feeling under the weather since arriving at this camp although all three were well motivated and should be okay with a day's rest.

Taff stated very strongly that the Doctor should remain at this height. We had all seen Mike struggle into camp the previous night under a third load, clearly very tired. Taff argued that if there was a casualty they would bring whoever it was down to this level for treatment, both he and Offless were well experienced in emergency First Aid, but he thought that there was a danger of Mike becoming a casualty himself if he pushed on.

Usually during the climbing season the Park Rangers established an emergency First Aid Post at this level manned by a doctor and a Park Ranger. They had started up the mountain and were expected imminently but had not yet arrived. I knew how disappointed Mike would be as he had told me only the night before how determined he was to reach the summit. The argument for him staying was however a strong one and all of the others supported it.

The remainder would split into two summit parties of six under Taff and Colour Sergeant Offless. I would lead the four who were not to attempt the summit down to Camp Three, collect the others and make for Base Camp clearing as many camps as possible of our cached rubbish.

I felt extremely uncomfortable about going down. Never before on any expedition that I had organised had I not led the team to the summit of each of our objectives. I was fit and strong enough to go on but someone had to take the others down and that someone had to be qualified. Taff made a comment about my eagerness to get down the mountain which rather touched a nerve. In fact we were already concerned about our dwindling fuel supply and it was important to leave what was left for those who were going on to give them the ability to wait-out a storm if necessary.

I called the team together and explained the plan. Then I spoke to Mike on his own. When I asked him to remain at Camp Six he gulped hard but was extremely good and took it well. He acknowledged that he was tired and although he felt that he would be strong enough to go on with some rest, he understood the requirement for guaranteed medical back-up. I was very grateful for his lack of complaint and self sacrifice and although I did not know it at the time, it was to prove a crucial decision.

The remainder of the day was spent re-allocating equipment amongst the new rope teams. A large lenticular cloud sat over the summit which did not bode well. We could not raise Base Camp on the radio but cloud of that type indicated high winds and very low temperatures higher up the mountain. I longed for us to place a group on the summit. As yet no one had made it although several teams had tried and many more were poised to move up for a summit bid. I had watched three people struggling to put in a cache at the next camp. It had taken them eight hours to get up the headwall. More than anything else I prayed that each team would return safely.

The following day the whole team went back down to the cache at Windy Corner. There we split. I wished each person good luck and a safe climb as they collected their equipment and turned back to the mountain. Once they were gone the five of us headed down. It took two days to reach Base Camp, stopping at each camp on the way to collect the caches of rubbish and spare equipment until we could carry no more.

With large loads and full pulks skiing downhill was not easy and the steep sections in particular became a test of patience and perseverance. On inclined slopes our pulks rolled over and over. If you skied with your pulk in front of you, it veered off the track unless the slope was straight down and if you tried keeping it behind you, it savaged your calves and ankles like an aggressive terrier. Having tried each technique in turn, with varying lack of success, I finally managed to let it slide down in front of me like a dog on a tight leash.

We collected 16 and his crew on our way past. He was in his usual irrepressible form, waiting for

us with brews ready and a catalogue of stories about the other climbers that had passed by. The loud behaviour of a German group had particularly incensed him. It was amusing to hear the level of his indignation overlying his rich Welsh accent. We spent the night at Camp Three and continued on next morning in similar vein.

Skiing down the lower part of the Kahiltna Glacier a low distinctive rumble, building in volume, caused me to look round. I saw a large powder avalanche mushrooming down to the Northeast Fork from the seracs beneath Windy Corner. My thoughts went to the rest of the team and I wondered how they were getting on.

The final pull up the appropriately nicknamed Heartbreak Hill to Base Camp was a long hard slog. Annie later told me that she frequently got radio calls from exhausted climbers at the bottom of it saying that they could not manage a load any further and were abandoning their kit.

Next morning, after several false starts and some extremely hair-raising aborted attempts at lifting off the glacier by a disconcertingly myopic and unconfident pilot, Corporal Steggles and I flew off the mountain in a light aircraft. The little Cessna clambered reluctantly into the air, gained almost imperceptible lift and to the audible relief of the passengers, including an Austrian tourist who had been marooned at Base Camp overnight by bad weather, we flew down the valley.

Having gained some height the tension eased and the remainder of the flight was stunning. As we flew between the walls of Mounts Hunter and Foraker and over One Shot Pass, the snow was bathed a deep, rich gold by the dawn sunlight. The morning cloud lifted revealing the full Alaska Range in all its glory. In front of us, as we headed for Talkeetna, I could see that most of the snow had melted. The rivers were running freely, great glistening snakes transecting the wooded tundra. Snowmobile tracks still scarred the ground leaving trails across the mushy surface of the partially unfrozen lakes.

We landed at Talkeetna to the sounds of birds singing. It seemed a warm, green haven compared to the icy embrace of the mountain. We booked onto the morning bus to Anchorage and then gorged ourselves on a vast breakfast, revelling in the fresh food whilst sparing guilty thoughts for those still on the mountain. Unable to affect events from Base Camp, I had decided to leave

Richard to it and go back to Camp Carroll where there was a great deal of preparation to be made to get everything ready so that we could leave as soon as the team came off McKinley.

We drove out of Talkeetna, gazing up at the mountains through the back window of the bus, not wanting to break our link with the others still up there. The journey was so different from the last time that we had driven this road on the way to start our dog sledding journey four months previously. The heavy cloak of snow and hoar frost which had carpeted the ground and burdened the trees had gone, taking with it the atmosphere of oppressive gloom. In place were bright blue skies and the warm colours of spring; yellows, russets and verdant green.

Having parted from us at Windy Corner, the remainder of the team had slogged back up to Camp Six. There they spent the rest of the day sorting out kit, rations and fuel for their ascent and making their plans. Several groups made load carries further up the mountain during the day. The traditional route took the headwall to a camp at 16,000 feet but further to the right a steeper line climbed Rescue Gully direct to the 17,200 feet camp.

Taff watched a large Italian team set off and split with groups following both routes. Those that took Rescue Gully made just as good progress as the others and did not appear to encounter any major difficulties. Weighing up the benefits of each, he decided to take his team up Rescue Gully. He had descended that way on his previous climb and did not remember it being too steep. It had the added attractions of avoiding the exposed ridge line that ran between the two camps and cutting a day off the climb. Colour Sergeant Offless was less sure and resolved to make his final decision when he reached the point where the two routes diverged.

It was the coldest night that they had spent on the mountain so far, an estimated -35° Fahrenheit at 14,000ft. There was heavy snowfall but still they set off in the morning. Taff's group led as planned. They were down to five men as Guardsman Brown had begun to experience symptoms of altitude sickness and had been left behind with the doctor.

It took them two hours to reach 15,000 feet. Despite hard going through soft snow, they still had not warmed up properly. The route had

already steepened considerably and they took a twenty minute rest. At the junction of the two routes they peeled off right, zigzagging as the angle became more severe. Their first major obstacle was the bergschrund, a wide crevasse that had formed where the glacier split off the steep ice of the mountain face. Taff probed carefully, sweeping aside the fresh loose snow and protecting their crossing of the snow bridge with a belay.

The ground now rose sharply as they moved slowly up to the base of the gully. Initially they all moved together, Taff kicking steps at the front and the reminder splaying their feet to get as many points of their crampons into the ice as possible. The further they went the more difficult it became. The snow covering was thin and slipped off under their weight. The ice offered little purchase and they were carrying heavy loads including tents, sleeping bags and food and fuel sufficient for four to five days.

Each time they stopped, Taff had to carve out a shelf in the side of the slope for them to rest on. Corporal of Horse Wells began to feel twinges of the headaches and altitude sickness that he had suffered lower down. An extremely fit man, he was more used to leading than holding others up. He forced some drink and chocolate down at the next break to try and give himself more energy and shake off his lethargy.

Seeing that several of the group were not comfortable on such a steep slope, Taff started leading in pitches, fixing a belay each time by stamping his ice axe into the snow and winding the rope around it and then getting the others to jumar up to him, climbing on the front points of their crampons. Just before 16,000 feet Corporal of Horse Wells was three-quarters of the way up a pitch when he found that his body simply refused to respond to the commands that his head was sending to it. He was also finding it increasingly difficult to breathe. After a long pause he managed to clamber up to the belay ledge where he flopped down. He felt overwhelmed by light-headedness and found it difficult to balance on the ledge. He was clearly in trouble and needed to go down.

Outwardly he had shown little sign of any problem up to this point and when Taff asked him if he felt okay to make his own way back to camp he said yes. However, as soon as he stood up he began to sway, teetering on the limit of his balance and he stumbled in the first few steps. Taff stopped him and then asked for a volunteer from the other three for one of them to accompany him down. After two or three minutes of awkward silence whilst each of them studiously examined their boots and checked knots they knew to be perfectly secure, Corporal Allison said that he would go down.

They reorganised the rope teams. Corporal Allison, who up to that point had partnered Taff, joined Corporal of Horse Wells and Taff moved to the second rope in front of Richard and Lieutenant Sandy Carrick Buchanan. Although tired and finding the steepness testing both their resolve and confidence, they were fit to carry on. They watched as Wells and Allison sorted themselves out and started down the slope.

The weather had closed in and the two Corporals soon disappeared from sight. Turning back to the slope the other three pushed on upwards entering the actual gully. The ice steepened to between 60 and 65 degrees. Belaying pitch after pitch, they clawed their way upwards. They kept hoping for a resting place on the bare ice but the ice only appeared to become steeper making it impossible to stop and relax their burning calf muscles.

Sandy was determined not to be beaten but for the first time since his basic training began to feel murmurings of self-doubt. At the steepest part of the gully, the slope was concave and he found himself gripping the blade of his ice axe and shoving the adze into the ice for support. He wished that he had a second ice axe to give him better grip and help allay the sensation of exposure. Eventually they emerged from the gully, climbing a final six foot bank of vertical snow, to arrive shattered at a small, flat area on top of the ridge where they put up their tent.

Corporal of Horse Wells' and Corporal Allison's descent was to turn into something of a nightmare. Wells led initially. They both fell numerous times. On one occasion one of Allison's crampons slipped off and in horrendous conditions of blowing snow it took them fifteen minutes of combined effort to get it back on. The cold was penetrating even the down jackets that they wore. Allison's hands became so cold that he found it hard to hold his ice axe as he belayed Wells down. Where the ice dropped down short steep walls they had to turn and face it, going down on their front points. Wells found it increasingly difficult to concentrate and make rational decisions.

They made it down to the bergschrund and then realised that the blowing snow had covered up their original tracks and in the white-out they could not see the snow bridge. Luckily two other climbers, the American and his girlfriend, appeared from below and began shouting a warning that they were heading for a cornice. Wells tried to follow their shouted directions but his fuzzy oxygen-starved brain refused to interpret their instructions and he began to get disorientated.

Aware that there would be an accident if they did not do something about it, the other pair shouted at them to stop where they were and climbed the snow bridge towards them. They asked Wells and Allison if they were okay or needed assistance to get down to the camp but they said that they would be able to follow the fresh tracks down.

After some tense moments they made it across the snow bridge and carried on down. By the time that they reached the junction of the tracks Wells was finding it very difficult to breathe. Allison kept talking to him and tried to prop him up but it became progressively more difficult. Although losing lucidity Wells realised the seriousness of their situation and had it fixed in his mind that he must keep going at all costs. He tried to go quicker than his tired legs and dulled senses could cope with and fell every few yards. Allison kept telling him to slow down and take his time as they stumbled down the slope.

A brief window in the cloud gave them a glimpse of camp and Allison was able to point his partner in the right direction supporting him all the way. As they got to within shouting distance of the tents Allison screamed at Guardsman Brown to come and help him. Between them they took Wells' rucksack off him and then, quite suddenly, he collapsed unconscious in the snow. Allison quickly undid his harness belt and loosened his clothing and told Brown to run for the doctor and more help.

Mike sprinted over to find Wells lapsing in and out of consciousness and having great difficulty getting air into his lungs. He tried to stick a plastic airway down Wells' throat but he kept rejecting it. By a stroke of luck the Park Ranger and doctor had arrived and their medical post was in the process of being set up. Several other climbers had arrived to help and now they loaded Wells' prostrate body onto an unrolled Karrimat and

McKinley basecamp on the Southeast fork of the Kahiltna Glacier at 7,200 feet.

Digging our tent pits at basecamp, Sandy Carrick-Buchanan
and Pete Richardson.

Load carrying up the Kahiltna Glacier, hauling pulks whilst roped together on skis.

Opposite:
Camp 2 under the Kahiltna Dome.

Richard Gaffney, the deputy expedition leader, tapes his feet up ready for another load carry.

Moving up to our cache at the proposed site of Camp 3 at 9,700 feet.

Danny Brown and Andy Howard sort out their kit in the tent pit.

Richard Gaffney leads his rope team up a steep section at around 12,000 feet.

Craig Offless and Charlie McKeown break trail en route to the cache above Camp 4.

Offless and McKeown approaching Camp 6.

Dawn at Camp 6, 14,200 feet.

Sandy Carrick-Buchanan and Richard Gaffney
on the summit of Mt McKinley,
at 20,320 feet, the highest point in North America.
(Richard Gaffney)

Looking up at the headwall from Camp 6. Half-way up the
slope, tiny figures return from making a load carry.

Taff Mason and Sandy Carrick-Buchanan
make their way carefully back down the summit ridge.
(Richard Gaffney)

began to drag him towards the emergency post. As they were doing so he momentarily regained consciousness. Not understanding where he was or what was going on and frightened by being unable to breathe he struck out and tried to fight his way free. They restrained him until he lapsed into unconsciousness again when they carried him bodily to the makeshift medical post.

He woke up to find a doctor slapping him and a nurse taking his pulse. He had been stripped but was warm in a large down sleeping bag and had an oxygen mask over his face linked to a large machine in the corner of the tent. The medical team monitored his condition for the next few hours and then having transferred him back to his own tent kept him on oxygen all night.

Had they not stopped and turned back when they did, there is every likelihood that Corporal of Horse Wells might have died, and as we were later to discover, Corporal Allison may well have lost all his fingers. As it was, Wells had advanced Pulmonary Oedema and had it not been for this oxygen supply they would have been unable to bring him back to consciousness and Mike would have had to instigate a major rescue to get him down to at least 10,000 feet where the air was more oxygen rich.

Wells and Allison were not the only people in trouble on the mountain that afternoon. Colour Sergeant Offless's group had set off about half an hour after Taff's and followed them up towards the point of divergence of the two routes. At that stage Offless was still undecided as to which route to take. Looking up to his right he could see Taff's group some way in front making slow progress on the steep ground ahead.

Snow was blowing into the other group's tracks filling them up quickly and he was concerned at getting stuck in deep fresh snow on the steeper route. They managed to shout to each other above the wind and he heard Taff shout back that they were finding the going more difficult than they had anticipated. Having taken a quick poll of opinion and chatted the matter over with Colour Sergeant Richardson, the other rope leader in his half of the group, Offless decided to revert to the original route and turned off to the left.

They walked on slowly through the deep snow. The ground began to rise sharply as they climbed up towards the base of the headwall. Maintaining a steady pace they made their way up to the bergschrund at around 15,000 feet. There they took a break and sorted themselves out for the more technical climb above. One or two of the novices had been having problems with their crampons slipping off their padded overboots and now looking up the steep ice face they began to get slightly intimidated by it. There were old fixed ropes running to the top of the headwall but Offless did not like the look of them at the lower end and decided to lead the first 300 feet on two joined ropes and then bring each climber up to him in turn. They could then attach themselves to the fixed line and jumar up to the top of the wall.

He set off with Colour Sergeant Richardson belaying him from below. He was climbing well within his ability and moving comfortably up the ice when, halfway to his intended stance, he noticed a large group of climbers coming down the fixed lines manouevring a body on a makeshift stretcher. Seeing that there was a rescue in progress, he cut himself a shelf in the ice to stand on and attached himself to the ice with an ice-axe belay. The group above were members of an Italian expedition who had come not only to climb the mountain but to recover the body of a colleague who had died and been left frozen into the ice the previous year. They had climbed extremely fast, reaching 17,000 feet in just a week, but now this rapid gain in altitude had taken its toll and their expedition doctor had collapsed with Cerebral Oedema. He was critically ill and if he was to be saved he had to be taken down as quickly as possible.

The Italian team only had one 9mm rope with them and were having difficulty lowering the inert casualty down the ice face. Offless and his team were kept shivering on their stances for two hours as the rescue operation progressed. By the time that they had seen the casualty, wrapped in a sleeping bag with a Karrimat bound around the outside, lowered past them, they were all deeply chilled. Offless shouted down for the first man to climb up to him. Colour Sergeant McKeown started up but after a few feet one of his crampons slipped around on his boot and he had to be lowered back down to the stance.

Corporal Howard went next, climbing strongly despite feeling cold and stiff. He climbed up to Colour Sergeant Offless, showing the others that it could be done and attached himself to the fixed line above. It was the turn of Lance-Sergeant Brown 80 next. Another strong and determined individual, he was going well until one of his crampons slipped. He tried to struggle on up but the added pressure was too much and the other crampon came off too. As his feet shot from under him he lurched forward banging his head on the ice and concussing himself.

Cold, late in the day and now with one member of the group who could not go on and needed assistance to get back to camp there was little option but to turn around. Offless lowered Corporal Howard back down the ice and climbed down himself. They trudged disconsolately back down to the camp cutting steps for 80 on steep, icy sections. Three quarters of a mile away, they could make out Taff and the remaining two members of his team still struggling up Rescue Gully.

They arrived back at the tents tired and demoralised to find the Doctor embroiled in the treatment of Corporal of Horse Wells and the place abuzz with stories of the day's dramas. Each man in his own mind was facing the question of whether he wanted to go back to the headwall and try again.

Most of the group, having had a hot meal and several brews, threw their hats in the ring for another try. Meanwhile it was becoming apparent that at least two people would be needed to help Wells down the mountain when he was strong enough to move. That evening as they retired to bed still mulling over their plans, Corporal Allison approached Colour Sergeant Offless. Since getting Wells back to camp he had not stopped. He had put up their tent, made himself some food and then gone to talk to Wells in the medical tent where they had a rather emotional chat. His hands had been cold all day and his finger tips had refused to warm up or lose their numbness. Now that he finally removed his mitts and inner gloves he saw that the tips of his fingers were discoloured and swollen. He had not seen frostbite before but was now concerned by what he saw before him.

Colour Sergeant Offless had no such doubts. He depressed the flesh on each of Allison's fingers and could see straight away that the blood was not flowing back as it should have been. They called the Doctor who confirmed it as frostbite. Mike dressed Allison's fingers and told him to keep them warm overnight in his sleeping bag. He was very conscious of the danger to Allison's fingers if they were frozen again. He needed to get him to hospital where they could be treated properly as quickly as possible. Now there were two people who needed to be taken down to Base Camp.

Up at 17,000 feet Taff, Richard and Sandy took advantage of the last rays of daylight on the high ridge to set up their tent. The cold and lack of oxygen affected the performance of their cooker and they had to make do with cold food and lukewarm brews. It was well after midnight by the time that they turned in.

Getting going the next morning was equally slow as they continued to have problems heating water. Taff woke with a headache but put that down more to dehydration than the altitude. The air was so dry that it stripped the moisture out of their lungs.

A broad, steep slope of hard-packed neve led up a thousand feet to Denali Pass. They made a long, rising traverse, taking nearly three hours to arrive at the col between McKinley's North and South summits. They were happy to take their time, stopping to rest when they felt the need to and as a result they all felt reasonably strong up at 18,200 feet. In February 1967, during the first winter ascent of the mountain, several climbers were trapped in a storm for six days at Denali Pass. By digging a snow cave they survived wind-chill recorded at -148° Fahrenheit.

From there, another long ridge led on for a mile rising a further 1,500 feet to a broad plateau known as The Playing Fields. Near vertical, snow-packed cliffs fell sheer away to their right. It took several more hours of head-down trudging to reach the plateau. Even from here, as they stopped to rest, they could not see the summit. Rather to their dismay another severe slope led up out of sight.

Taff was beginning to feel the altitude badly. He was staggering and lurching as though drunk but insisted on carrying on. They left their rucksacks in a small cache and set off up the summit ridge carrying just their ice axes and cameras. They zigzagged up the slope and then came up to a series of false summits. Each time they hoped that they had reached the true summit, but each time the ridge rose up again. Taff's condition continued to deteriorate and he became more and more tottery. He had experienced similar problems on his previous ascent and knew that if he could only get to the summit and get down quickly he would be okay but he could not stop himself becoming increasingly agitated.

Finally at 7 p.m. they hauled themselves over the last crest. The ridge rose no more and at their feet lay the entire Alaska Range. In front of them, the South Face dropped 8,000 feet to the Kahiltna Glacier. All around lay a carpet of jagged peaks. Mount Hunter and Mount Foraker, both of which had towered above us for so much of the way, were now well below them.

Although a breeze was beginning to pick up, it had been a warm day and was still above freezing. With no higher ground, there was nothing to cast a shadow upon them and they could enjoy the evening sun. The air was crystal clear and they could see full 150 miles across the surrounding plains. Alaska lay spread out beneath them but any feeling of elation was for the time being overridden by concern for Taff. They snapped off a couple of photographs and then turned back down.

With the summit achieved they now had to concentrate on getting down the mountain safely. Each of them was well aware that the majority of mountaineering accidents happen during descents when bodies are tired, concentration slips and a careless trip or failing to check that a karabiner is fastened securely leads to a fatal fall. As they began to make their way down, watchful in case Taff should slip, Sandy also began to feel unsteady. It was as if he was detached from what was going on and he had to rein in his wandering concentration and remind himself that everything was happening for real. At the back of the rope team Richard became increasingly concerned and poised himself ready to arrest any signs of a fall.

Back at their rucksacks Taff was close to collapse and had to stop and get some fluids into himself before he was fit to carry on. After an half hour break and a good drink he began to come out of his sun drunk state and felt much better. They went back along the ridge to Denali Pass. The final slope leading down to their tent had had the sun on it for most of the day making the snow looser and more avalanche prone. They had to be careful as they picked their way down the steep traverse which in descent was a lot more awkward than it had been on the way up.

Sandy slipped and fell but caught himself with an ice axe arrest. It gave him a sharp reminder

to concentrate and stop daydreaming. The track that they had made in the morning fell apart as they stepped along it, so Taff cut across to an older and more firm track further down the slope. In many ways the snow conditions made this the most hazardous part of the entire climb.

They reached the safety of the tent some time between 10 and 11 p.m. Physically they were deadbeat. As they prepared their brews and settled down for the night, the success of the climb began to sink in. Now that they had stopped and were no longer worrying about each other's condition they could reflect. The overriding emotion was that it was all downhill from there but although they did not know that the expedition's hopes of a summit bid had relied on them, they felt a quiet satisfaction that they had not let the rest of the team down.

In the morning they took their time getting ready to leave, ensuring that they got plenty of drinks and food. They decided, rather than trying to fight their way back down Rescue Gully, to follow the West Buttress Ridge and descend the fixed ropes down the headwall. Just as they were preparing to leave they were surprised to see Colour Sergeant Offless and Charlie Morgan approaching unroped up the ridge. They had climbed the headwall the day before and camped part way along the ridge. They now planned to attempt the summit that day and return to their camp. They were travelling light and had left their tent, sleeping bags, cooker and all their heavy equipment at 16,400 feet.

Taff, Richard and Sandy all remonstrated as forcefully as they could that in the light of their experiences the previous day, this was to attempt a fiercely long summit day of around 5,000 feet of ascent. It was already late to be starting out and they would certainly find themselves returning in the dark. If they ran into difficulties high on the mountain they had no equipment with them to survive a night out. Offless reacted crossly and felt that the others were being simply doom and gloom merchants. Richard drew Charlie off to one side and urged him to see the danger that they were putting themselves into. To illustrate his point he pointed to a couple who had set out that morning for the summit and after two hours still had a long way to go just to reach Denali Pass let alone the summit.

Once the seeds of doubt were sown in their minds both Charlie and Colour Sergeant Offless accepted the others advice not to attempt to reach the summit that day. Instead they arranged that they would keep Taff's groups' tent and gear and the others would pick up their gear on the way down the ridge and carry it down to Camp Six with them.

Taff suggested that they could press on as far as Denali Pass, camp there and then have a short summit day the following day. But in the event, once Colour Sergeant Offless had returned from collecting some personal things from his tent, it was beginning to grow cold and they decided stay where they were and make their bid from the conventional start point.

Back at Camp Carroll, I was unaware of all these goings-on. I tried to immerse myself in the arrangements for our journey south but all the while I was fretting about the team on the mountain. It was intensely frustrating to be out of touch, unable to take part in the decision-making or share the problems and I hated feeling so helpless to assist.

I only became aware of difficulties amongst our own team when I received a telephone call from Jim Okonek at K2 Aviation to say that one of our party was at Base Camp with serious frostbite. He had sent a plane and two people were flying out. He was getting another plane ready at Talkeetna to fly the casualty straight down to Anchorage. Meanwhile, he was having difficulty getting permission to land on the Airforce Base at Elmendorff and asked if I could try to do something. As soon as he rang off, I rang Wingco. If anyone could cut through the red tape, he could.

Shortly after the telephone rang again. This time it was Colour Sergeant McKeown ringing from Talkeetna saying that they were about to fly on and giving me the details of Corporal Allison's injuries. Once they were airborne, K2 Aviation rang again to say that the plane had been given permission to land at Elmendorff over the radio. Wingco had clearly done his stuff. Their other news sent my stomach into instant knots of trepidation. There was a major rescue in progress high on the mountain. Two people were involved. The Search and Rescue team had been deployed by helicopter and the National Guard had launched a Hercules aircraft which was circling the mountain acting as an aerial communications link. All civilian aircraft had been ordered to stay away from the mountain. As yet no further details had been given out.

I knew from the brief conversation that I had with McKeown that we had two summit teams somewhere up above the headwall, Taff's group and Colour Sergeant Offless with Charlie Morgan. Either could be involved but the day's interval between them pointed towards the latter party. I prayed and prayed that it was not our people. I feared for Offless and Morgan, they were the right number at about the right height. There was nothing that I could do bar wait. Any more brooding had to be set aside as we rushed to the airstrip in time to meet the K2 aircraft landing. To my relief Corporal Allison was able to walk off the plane unaided to a waiting ambulance. He was his usual reserved self and said that he felt fine. His fingers were covered but tingling.

We all went to the hospital. There the medical staff unbandaged his hands. The finger tips of three fingers on one hand and two fingers on the other were swollen and blistering, classic examples of frostbite. The ends of the remainder were red. The affected areas were thankfully small, down to the first joint on each finger. They warmed his hands and arms gradually in a special whirlpool bath. We left him being pampered by the nurses having heard from the doctor that any tissue loss should be relatively minor.

I took Colour Sergeant McKeown for a large meal after which he announced that he could eat the whole thing again. It had taken them two days to get back to Base Camp with Colour Sergeant Richardson and Guardsman Brown to assist. Wells had been unable to carry a load for most of the way and Allison's bandaged hands had meant that he needed assistance to rope up and put on or take off clothing. They had got on reasonably well until they reached the skis, but after that they had fallen over a lot. Having caught up on all the news that he could tell me from the mountain, I dropped him at the barrack room to sort out his kit. I went back to see Corporal Allison and take him his mail. He was in good spirits and looking forward to talking to his wife.

After supper I went back to the office. I had rung K2 Aviation and the Park Rangers several times through the afternoon, trying to get more information on the rescue but with little result. I sat, unable to concentrate on my paperwork, thinking all the while of the men on the mountain. If one of them was badly hurt or worse it would be my fault for having taken them there. I wished myself back on the mountain although I knew that practically there would have been little more that I could have done from Base Camp than I was doing now.

At 7.30 p.m. the telephone rang. It was Richard ringing direct from Camp Six on the satellite telephone. He told me briefly that he, Taff and Sandy had reached the summit the day before. Offless and Morgan had attempted to summit today but had become involved in the mountain rescue. Neither of them were hurt and they were now safely back down at Camp Six. Everyone was rather shocked as the rescue had involved the American guy and his Canadian girlfriend that we had got to know on the way up, she was dead and he was very seriously injured.

He could not talk for long or the batteries would be drained. We arranged that I would try to get the Chinooks to pick them up from Base Camp in three days time. I stammered out my congratulations. When he had gone I sat staring at the phone, half in tears and gulping for air, trying to take in all that he had said. They were all safe – thank God. More than that they had made it, all our hard work had been worthwhile. I could not have been more delighted that Richard himself had summitted and I felt desperately relieved that he was okay. We had shared so much that I felt a special responsibility for him.

I sat trembling at my desk turning it all over in my mind. It had been a close call but we had made it and they were safe! The phone rang again, this time it was Tammy the wife of the Camp Carroll Commandant. She was driving down to Whittier with her friend Beth to pick up some engine parts and asked if I would like to join them. When they arrived I wanted to run out and dance and sing and tell them that we had done it, but I could barely get the words out and my eyes filled with tears. The poor girls did not really understand what was happening. It was a warm sunny evening. As we drove alongside Turnagain Arm there were beautiful views across Cook Inlet and over the mountains of the Kenai Peninsula. Slowly the tension went out of me and I began to unwind. They were safe.

Colour Sergeant Offless and Charlie Morgan had passed a poor night at 17,000 feet once Taff and his team had left. They had gone to bed early and lain awake for most of the night. They looked at their watches at 5.30 a.m. and decided to get up and get going. It was bitingly cold. When they breathed the air outside the tent they felt their bodies slow down. Offless tried to get the cooker going but lost his temper with it when he could not get it started. Charlie took over.

All of a sudden, Offless said that he could see two or three blobs that looked like rocks in the snow at the base of Denali Pass about a mile away. He was sure that they had not been there the night before and to add to his suspicions he thought that he could see one of them moving. They went to check the tent of the American and Canadian girl but it was still empty. Now deeply concerned, they went to another tent and borrowed a camera with a telefocus lens from a climber there. On looking through it they confirmed that it was not rocks but two people. They geared up as quickly as they could and having collected the sleeping bags from the empty tent, started across to the bodies in the snow. Charlie had problems with his crampons so Offless went on ahead.

As he made his way carefully across the crusty ice, avoiding the crevasses, the tragic scene began to unfold in front of him. Two parallel trails were scored into the long, steep ice face leading up to Denali Pass. Items of clothing and equipment were scattered down the trails; an ice axe, some gloves, a hat. At the bottom lay the body of the girl, face up in the snow. Flakes of snow had settled on her hair and face. Her right hand was clenched as if deformed and frozen snow filled the crevices between her fingers. Her sightless, staring eyes, twisted poise and total absence of any colour in her skin gave her the unmistakable countenance of death. A quick check of her pulse confirmed what was already obvious.

Ten feet away, her boyfriend was on his knees rocking backwards and forwards, mumbling incoherently. He had heavy bruising around his forehead which suggested concussion. He was clearly deeply hypothermic. One hand was bent unnaturally backwards, both fingers and hand were frozen solid and had taken on a blueish hue.

The first priority was to try and stabilise the man until a rescue could be organised. The greatest threat was that he would die of hypothermia. There was no way of telling how long it was since they had fallen but he was in a critical state. Working as quickly as he could, Colour Sergeant

Offless put him into one of the sleeping bags that he had brought from their tent.

By the time that Charlie Morgan caught up, Offless had begun to dig a shallow trench across the line of the slope so that he could lie the man down comfortably and securely. Together they finished this and manoeuvred the man into it once they had cut him free from the rope which was still attached him to his dead partner. It was 7 a.m. and around -40° Fahrenheit. They gently fed him warm sugared water that they had brought in their flasks. With that he gained some lucidity and managed to tell them that his name was Rick. Leaving Charlie to look after him, Colour Sergeant Offless went to alert the other climbers to the need for a helicopter rescue which he did by a pre-arranged series of signals waving a sleeping bag in the air.

For the next three hours, as the others radioed for help and prepared for the arrival of the helicopter, Charlie stayed with Rick. He kept talking to him determined not to let him drift off to sleep in case he should slip into unconsciousness. He complained of pain in his ribs, back and legs and lapsed in and out of lucidity. Charlie managed to piece together that they had made the summit and were on their way down the steep ice face from Denali Pass when Rick had stumbled. He believed that he had fallen and pulled his partner with him. They had fallen roughly 700 feet and he estimated the time of the accident to be around midnight which meant that they had been lying where they were found for almost seven hours.

On several occasions he became more alert and began asking about his girlfriend and worrying that she was very cold. They had built a small snow wall around her so that her body was hidden. Charlie found himself in an impossible moral position. He was not medically qualified to proclaim her dead, although he was in no doubt that she was. What concerned him much more was Rick's own well-being if he confirmed to him what he may well have suspected. Rick needed every bit of fight that he could muster to keep himself alive. Charlie decided to make out that she was still alive but in a very serious condition.

As they waited for the helicopter to arrive they became very cold. They kept Rick as warm as they could, putting him in a bivi bag as well as his sleeping bag and lying him on rubber mats. Charlie lay down beside him to try and impart some of his own body warmth. At one point he had to physically shake Rick to keep him conscious.

Eventually the high-altitude Alouette helicopter arrived but due to the steepness of the slope it could not land nearby. Instead, the pilot had to fly back over to the tents where he dropped off a Park Ranger and a doctor and then flew off while they assessed the situation. It took another forty minutes for them to reach the casualty, the doctor to carry out some on-the-spot checks and the Park Ranger to locate a safe landing site. In turn, they carried first Rick and then the girl to the helicopter. After it had flown away for the last time, Offless and Charlie headed back to their tent to warm up and get themselves some food. Without needing to discuss it, they made the mutual decision to go down.

As they made their way back along the ridge and down the fixed ropes on the headwall they had to wait to take their turn amidst countless rope teams establishing caches or moving up ready for their summit bids. Camp Six had swollen to three times the size that it had been only two days before. Further on down the route as they made their way back to Base Camp over the next two days, they passed endless swarms of guided parties, great crocodiles of adventure tourists paying to be led to the top of the continent.

Without doubt anyone who makes the summit of McKinley does so only after a great deal of their own hard graft and concentrated effort but with the onset of the main climbing season the special feeling of pushing out the route in isolation, breaking trail and digging in each camp in the face of intimidating and threatening conditions is lost. Where we had established something of a pioneer spirit amongst the few teams that were trying to forge their way up a mountain that had spurned all attempts so far that year, now there was more of a cocktail party atmosphere as groups stopped to gossip and exchange news whilst they queued up and down the route.

However McKinley continued to exact its due respect. On arrival back at Base Camp, another storm set in. Cloud covered the mountain and two feet of snow fell in a night. It was a further two days before the weather cleared sufficiently for the helicopters to sneak up the Kahiltna Glacier through a window in the cloud and round the corner of the Southeast Fork. They touched down on the ice and with the rotors still turning the team loaded the kit on board, jumped on themselves and with no pause for ceremony they lifted off and away.

When the helicopters touched down at Bryant Airfield on Fort Richardson, those of us who had already got back from the mountain were there to greet the returning team. They were hugely relieved to get back to civilisation and were set on fresh food, cold beer and the bright lights of Anchorage. As we drove back to Camp Carroll there was much excited telling of stories.

The next four days were a mad rush to get ready for our journey south. At the ninety-ninth hour, in response to a plea for help from General Corbett, the American Army had allowed us to purchase some of their cast vehicles. As a result we were the proud owners of two Ford Broncos and two Ford Clubwagons. Hardly spring chickens, they all had between fifty and sixty thousand miles on the clock. They had been used, amongst other times, during the clear-up operation after a volcano eruption in the Philippines and bore the scars of having been left standing in water, covered in a thick layer of volcanic ash, for a considerable period. They were not exactly smart but they were our means of transport south and without them we would have been faced by a long bicycle ride!

We now had to look after them and coax them all the way down to Patagonia. The National Guard had come to our aid once again and were working on the vehicles in their workshops servicing them, replacing faulty parts and fitting roof-racks, ladders, second spare wheels and Citizens Band radios.

While Colour Sergeant McKeown organised the loading of a sea freight container to go back to Britain and sorted out our equipment for the journey south, I caught up with the planning on the remainder of the expedition. Routes had to be finalised through Central America, aims confirmed in Guyana and the political side of the last two phases was still in the balance.

We said goodbye to the many people who had done so much to look after us during our time in Alaska and then, almost five months into the expedition, we began our vehicle journey. We drove out of Anchorage heading east through the Matanuska Valley. It seemed strange to see cultivated land after all this time. The roadside farms looked compact and yet lush and open compared to the surrounding forests and mountains that hemmed them in and horses cantered free in railed paddocks outside neat wooden farmsteads. As we drove up towards the head of the valley, we passed the Matanuska Glacier whose massive crevassed snout reaches down from the Chugach Mountains. Beyond, the country became far more wild and remote as we moved towards the Canadian border.

For the next week we travelled south through the Yukon Territories and along the Rocky Mountains as we passed through Canada. The early part of the journey took us through some spectacularly desolate country with endless willow, fir and aspen trees surrounding a myriad of small, crystal-clear, moss-lined tarns.

Further south, in British Columbia, the scrub bush disappeared in favour of tightly packed forests of tall straight spruce trees. For mile after mile, the only colours visible were shades of green broken here and there by silver trails of rivers leading into black lakes which reflected distant mountains.

The highlights of this journey were the repeated sightings of black bears. We met the first ambling alongside the road. As we approached he retreated into the woods where he stood up on his hind legs watching us, steadying himself with his front paws against a tree trunk. The smallest of the bears found in North America, they had very fine black coats with brown muzzles and rather intelligent, almost cheeky faces.

Entering Alberta, we drove along the spine of the Rockies passing beneath the impressive and intimidating south face of Mount Robson. We continued along the Icefields Parkway driving between towering rock spires, sweeping glaciers and turquoise lakes. We drank in the scenery and wildlife during long days on the road as we sped south. Having re-entered the United States we spent a second week travelling rather more slowly as we followed the Continental Divide down through Montana and Wyoming, before turning off into the deserts of Utah, Arizona and Nevada. We marvelled at the 1,000-foot deep pink and yellow rock walls of the Grand Canyon of the Yellowstone; rolling, wild pastures filled with herds of bison and elk; Old Faithful shooting its column of boiling water up into the sky; Utah's wind-sculpted red sandstone arches and the pillars, buttresses and plinths of rock in Monument Valley.

Turning west we drove through the Navajo Indian Reserve to reach the lip of the Grand Canyon. As we watched the sun set over the Canyon, the impossibly twisted and convoluted ridges of rock merged in the soft light, colours gently harmonised and a mile below us the Colorado River thundered through the Inner Canyon.

The final leg of this stage of the journey took us across the Hoover Dam and out into the Nevada desert to the neon oasis of Las Vegas. where we spent a couple of days sorting out all of the equipment and servicing the vehicles prior to the team flying home.

Returning from a final night out on the town we had certainly come a long way from Alaska: a 20,000 foot mountain and 4,000 mile journey from the remotest Eskimo village to the brightest lights in America. At the Armoury I found Colour Sergeant Richardson sitting with his head in his hands staring at the floor in vacant disbelief. Starting with $20 he had built up $2,000 on the blackjack tables and then lost the whole lot on a single turn of the cards. I was secretly glad that after all of the events of the previous few weeks, this was our greatest loss.

Chapter Four

Grand Canyon to the Panama Canal

Driving out into the Arizona desert I felt as though I were returning to reality, escaping from the bizarre fantasy existence of Las Vegas. The peace and space of the desert seemed welcoming after the non-stop gaudiness of the outlandish hotels and casinos.

Louie had come out on impulse for the weekend. She was not enjoying her job, endlessly touring the country trying to sell jetskis and power boats, and for me the journey south from Alaska had been heavily tinged with sadness due to the death of my stepfather and, subsequently, one of my oldest and closest friends. In our way we joined the ranks of those seeking to escape life's realities. Our three short days flashed by and then she was gone and the new team had arrived.

Ahead of us, we had sixteen days to explore the Grand Canyon and face the white-waters of the Colorado River before travelling the whole way across Central America to Panama. The vehicle journey began inauspiciously when, only thirty-one miles from Las Vegas, one of the Broncos ground to a juddering halt as a result of a broken transmission. Out in the desert there was nowhere to get it repaired so we towed it all the way to Flagstaff, Arizona where we were to meet up with our Grand Canyon guides.

Dick McCallum was waiting for us at the Expeditions Inc. office. Tall, thin and grizzled with a long beard and a slightly offbeat manner, Dick is one of the old school Grand Canyon rafters. He ran the Canyon for the first time in 1951, aged seventeen, and has been running it more or less ever since. He showed us all the kit which was laid out ready for us and we began to sort out kayaks, spraydecks, paddles and personal gear.

From the Glen Canyon Dam, at the bottom of Lake Powell, the Colorado river drops 1,700 feet over 279 miles until it reaches Lake Mead, which was in turn formed by the building of the Hoover Dam. In between these two man-made lakes, the Colorado River is channelled through the faulted and convoluted rock walls and canyons that make up the Grand Canyon. The river's course is varied, spectacular and punctuated by many violent rapids.

In the American system of categorisation rapids are graded from one to ten. The Grand Canyon contains the full spectrum within this categorisation with a significant number of rapids towards the upper end of the grading, including two of Grade Ten. Within the Grand Canyon, the Colorado is characterised by its high volume which even since the building of the Glen Canyon Dam in 1963 has seen recorded flow rates of up to 92,000 cubic feet per second.

The Grand Canyon was first successfully traversed by boat by Major John Wesley Powell in 1869. Powell was a retired officer of the Union who had lost one arm at the Battle of Shiloh. Together with nine other men he attempted to navigate the unknown waters of the Colorado. They started their journey with four large wooden boats. Unable to work the oars, Powell directed operations from a wooden armchair lashed to the top of one of the boats. It was an adventure of the utmost bravery and faith as they were entering country that, for the most part, had never been seen by white men. They had no means of knowing what they would encounter within the inner canyon.

Powell's account makes harrowing reading. They experienced many upsets, losing the majority of their rations early in the expedition. Half starving, they had to portage and line their boats through the larger rapids. Faced by what they took to be an impossible rapid which must surely kill them and was unavoidable due to the sheerness of the canyon walls, the party split and three of the men attempted to walk out to safety. They were never seen again and were believed to have been killed by Indians. The remainder abandoned most of their equipment but did successfully shoot the rapid and went on to complete their journey.

Powell made a second expedition through the Grand Canyon and then went on to be appointed director of the US Geological Survey. Such were the difficulties and dangers faced by Powell and his men

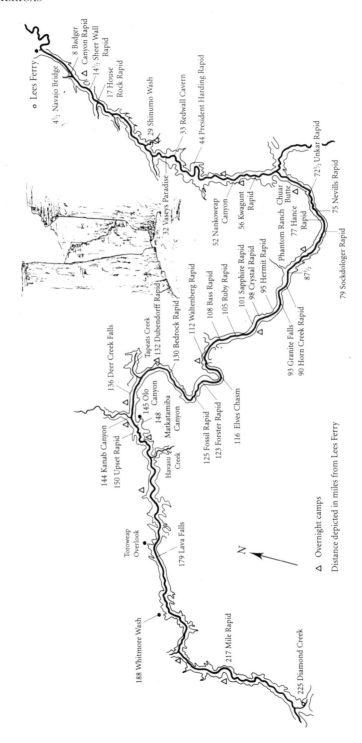

Phase 3 – The Grand Canyon

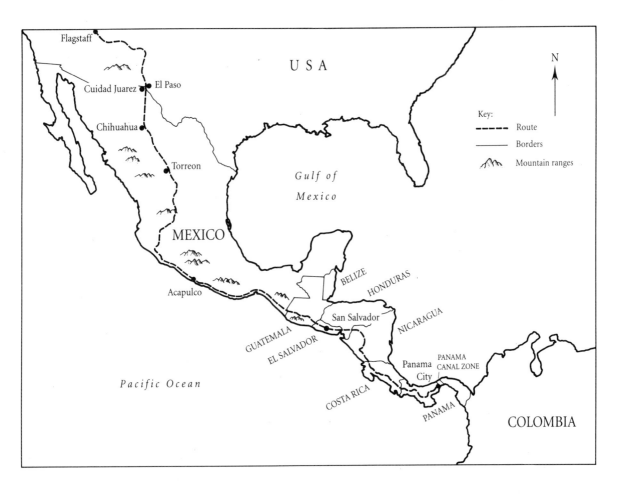

Phase 3 Vehicle Journey

that no further attempt was made to pass through the Grand Canyon until 1889 when Frank Brown and Robert Brewster Stanton, a railroad engineer, sought to survey a rail route through the Canyon to carry coal to the West coast. The journey was abandoned when Brown and two other members of the survey party where drowned in two separate incidents at rapids within the first twenty-five miles of the Canyon.

The survey expedition was later completed by Stanton but the railroad was never built. Grand Canyon river lore is rich with stories of the early trappers, prospectors and other adventurers who explored the Canyon by foot, mule and boat but it was a relatively slow process due to the harshness of the desert terrain and the severity of the rapids blocking the river. Settlements on the Canyon Rim began to attract and cater for tourists from as early as the 1880s but it was not until 1938 that the first commercial river journeys were made through the Canyon.

There are a number of accepted methods of navigating the Colorado: the majority of tourists are taken through on huge motorised pontoons. Whilst these can provide exhilarating runs through the larger rapids, their sheer size intentionally forms a stable and safe viewing platform from which to enjoy the scenery. The next level of excitement can be found in oar-powered inflatable rafts or dories rowed by a professional guide. Much smaller than the pontoons, these provide a far wilder ride and require the active participation of the crew throwing their body weight around the craft as ballast to force the boats through stoppers and try to prevent them overturning. There are also paddle boats: inflatable rafts in which seven crew members, each armed with a single-bladed paddle, power their way down the river and through the rapids. It is a skilled operation requiring hard physical effort and tight co-ordination. You are right amongst the action and it is all too easy for individuals to fall out, or for the whole boat to flip, scattering all the paddlers into the river. Finally there are the white-water aficionados who take on the huge rapids single-handed in their small kayaks.

We planned to paddle 225 miles from Lees Ferry to Diamond Creek in six kayaks and two paddle rafts, supported by five oar rafts through the entire length of the Grand Canyon. Any river journey is much more than just a voyage by boat. A river has a life, a soul and many facets of its own story to tell. We wanted to explore as much of the Grand Canyon, its side canyons and the surrounding country as our time would allow and discover for ourselves the history of the land and its peoples, the wildlife and the inter-relationship of all the forces that had shaped this small inaccessible area.

Having spent the night sleeping on the small patch of grass outside the Expedition Inc. office, we got up with the sun, packed our few remaining articles of kit and boarded a bus. A large lorry carried all the boats. As we drove across the flat wasteland of the Arizona desert we breakfasted on doughnuts, bagels and cream cheese; there was no doubting that we were in the hands of Americans!

After three hours of driving, the red plateau dipped down and suddenly, there before us lay the Colorado River. We drove across a metal span bridge and then down to the bank of the river at the site of Lee's Ferry. Reflecting off the bare sand, the sun was blindingly bright and the heat oppressive.

It took some time to prepare the equipment ready for departure. All the rafts had to be unrolled and inflated, large metal frames were fitted into the oar rafts and all our personal equipment and stores lashed securely into place. We had to carry sufficient food and equipment for the entirety of our planned sixteen-day journey. That left precious little room for personal equipment. We were each given an allocation of two small waterproof bags into which we put a sleeping bag, change of clothes, trekking boots, sun block, spare glasses and hat, diary and a book. Our lifestyle in the Canyon was, of necessity, going to be simple.

Our plan was for individuals to take turns in the paddle rafts and kayaks so that each person could build up their confidence and practise their techniques on the smaller rapids in preparation for the huge water that we expected to encounter further into the canyon. Having selected six kayakers and given a short brief to those paddling a raft for the first time, we set off down river.

There was a strong upstream wind creating white backed waves on the vivid green water and we had to lean into our paddle strokes to make any headway. The water was surprisingly cold and the spray chilled us quickly. Coming out of the bottom of the Glen Canyon Dam, just fifteen miles upstream of us, the water emerges at around 46° Fahrenheit. By the time that it reaches Lake Mead, 270 miles later, it would have risen to 60° Fahrenheit.

I had put myself into a raft initially so that I could watch how everyone was getting on. There had been a certain amount of scepticism about our ability to kayak the Colorado with such a novice group and I was keen to make sure that we gave ourselves the best possible chance of success whilst ensuring that no one was overstretched. I knew that if I went into a kayak I would be concentrating on self-preservation rather than looking out for everyone else.

We concentrated on perfecting the paddle strokes and building the co-ordination of the raft teams. Each boat had seven paddlers, three on each side to provide the power and one, the guide, at the back to steer the craft.

Successful rafting relies on instant, co-ordinated response to the paddle Captain's shouted instructions to provide the power that he needs to manoeuvre the boat across currents and down rapids avoiding rocks, stoppers and any dangerous obstructions. You sit leaning out over the outside edge of the inflated tube that runs around the edge of the raft, paddling with firm vertical strokes of the single-bladed paddle. Grasping the paddle with both hands, you are unable to hold onto the raft. There are cups attached to the floor of the raft into which you can slide your feet. The only way to stay aboard is to brace yourself against the side of the tube and use the pressure of the paddle on the water to stop yourself falling out. Your attachment to the boat feels extremely tenuous as indeed it is, but it is vital that you are not secured to the raft by any means or you would almost certainly be drowned if the raft flips over.

Around the outside of the raft is a line of rope which you can cling onto if you are thrown out in a violent rapid or if the raft flips. We practised our reactions to commands: 'All forwards!', 'Back left!', 'Back right!', 'All backwards!', 'High side left!' at which those on the right of the boat would hurl themselves over to the left to prevent it rearing up so far that it then topples over backwards, or 'Down!' – the final desperate cry when the raft is going into something so large that people are surely going to be thrown out unless they duck

below the level of the tube and hang on to the rigging lines or anything else they can find.

An inflatable raft gives a wild ride through high standing waves and individual crew members are often involuntarily jettisoned from their precarious perch. In the Grand Canyon it was not unknown for even the large motorised pontoons to flip and they were many times the size and weight of our small rafts.

We quickly entered the beginning of the canyon. Red sandstone walls rose vertically above us on either side. Swallows dived overhead, flying in and out of small holes bored into the walls. For the most part the water was fairly flat. We paddled a few small rapids which provided little risk to the rafts but gave the kayakers an opportunity to begin to sort out their strokes and balance. We had two highly skilled kayaking instructors of our own, Corporal Ivan Key and Corporal of Horse Simon Knowles, both of whom were confident of paddling and leading teams on high-grade white-water. In addition, we had one of the Expeditions Inc. guides, Carol Fritzinger, or Fritz as she preferred to be known, who had paddled the Canyon many times and knew the safest lines to take through the major rapids.

The first rapid of any significance that we came to was Badger Rapid. Although not graded higher than Grade Five at the volume of water that was running, the river's fifteen-foot drop in height provided some large standing waves and a couple of nasty black holes. Sergeant Everett, one of the two mechanic's on the phase, got his line wrong and dropped into one of the holes. He capsized and was held underwater for some time before being spat out of his kayak. He emerged wide-eyed and shaken, coughing up water.

Seeing that he was in trouble Corporal Key paddled out to him and having got him to grab onto the stern of his kayak, towed him to the shore. Two of the other kayakers recovered his boat and paddle. The sensation of being held helpless by the power of the water had frightened him badly and he asked not to be put back into a kayak.

We stopped to camp on a sandbank a short distance below the rapid. It had been a relatively gentle introduction to the Colorado although Sergeant Everett's experience acted as a timely warning of what was to follow. After a relaxed evening, we retired early. It was wonderful to sleep under the stars and to be warm, even if the windblown sand was irritating.

We got up at dawn rubbing sleepy, sand-filled eyes and tucked into a welcome extravaganza of scrambled eggs, bacon and bagels, washed down with ground coffee. It was a relief to be able to let someone else worry about the logistics and although the guides considered that they were giving us a rather more spartan diet than usual, to us it was the height of luxury. We stuffed our few belongings back into our waterproof bags, repacked the rafts and set off once again.

We began to move deeper into Marble Canyon. The scenery became more dramatic with every passing moment. Our path down the river took us on a journey through geological time. As the river dropped in elevation, we encountered each successive band of rock: Kaibab and Toroweap limestone, Coconino sandstone, Hermit shale and continuing down, further limestone layers. These were the younger, surface layers of rock, laid down by an overlying sea a mere two to three hundred million years ago. From our water-level viewpoint, the vertical cliff walls rose up tier after tier in bands of white, cream, grey, coral pink and ochre red. Areas of black marbled rock stood out in harsh contrast. Where the moving water reflected off the lower riverside rocks it formed a wondrous kaleidoscopic image, at times resembling a Medusa's head of writhing snakes.

We ran a succession of well spaced rapids and riffles; the deceptively diminutive term for rapids that did not warrant their own name but could quite easily bring an unwary kayaker to grief. At Mile Twelve we passed an inscription to the unfortunate Frank Brown, leader of the 1889 railroad survey expedition, whose life had been claimed in one of these riffles. At each of the larger rapids both rafters and kayakers would stop in an eddy above the rapid and then, having secured the boats, we would walk down to study the rapid before attempting to run it. These recces were vital to identify the safest line avoiding stoppers and pour-overs and to check for any recent obstructions such as fresh rockfalls or fallen trees that had become lodged across the river forming a lethal barrier.

We pulled in above Houserock Rapid for just such a recce. The kayakers had gone on ahead and had been studying the line for some time. For them it was even more important to get it right. The power

and weight of a raft could carry it through a hole or reversing wave that would trap a small kayak.

There was a period of psyching up before a rapid and whilst the rafters might re-embark with a sinking feeling in the pit of their stomachs having gazed into the mesmerising depths of some particularly evil-looking hole, for the kayakers who had to face the rapid alone without the reassuring bulk of a raft and six solid crew members who could stick out an arm and hoick you back in if you fell out, this was a much more concentrated emotional steadying. Houserock Rapid swept around a gradual right-handed bend with the main force of the water pushing up tight against the left rock wall.

We went first, crashing through a series of massive standing waves. It was the job of the men at the front to lean out over the bows of the raft using their body weight to keep the nose down and their paddles to pull the raft forward through each standing wave. Such was the size of the larger waves that the front of the boat reared up high in the air, immersed in a wreath of spume and hurling us all to the slippery floor. We fought to regain our places and paddle on.

At a couple of stages we teetered at the point of balance. I found Geoff, our guide, high-siding beside me and yelling at the others to do likewise. The action was fast and furious and then we were through. We pulled in immediately below the rapid and got ourselves in position to be ready to rescue any swimmers either from the other raft or from amongst the kayakers.

The second raft had an even wilder ride. At one point the entire boat was submerged leaving just a couple of heads, hands and paddles showing from the enveloping whiteness. The weight of water that poured over the front of the boat pummelled the paddlers to the floor. They emerged jubilant but shaken. When they joined us, Colour Sergeant McKeown said that it had taken conscious determination on his part to pick himself off the floor and get back into action. The term 'respect' kept creeping into conversations whenever the river was discussed.

The kayakers were paddling well despite frequent swims from the less experienced paddlers. None of them had seen water of this volume before let alone paddled it. Corporal Key and Corporal of Horse Knowles were both still well within their ability and already Guardsman Andrew Jamieson was showing that he was a stylish and confident paddler but for others the learning curve was somewhat steeper. Trooper Clive Spencer had become self-appointed team clown. From the moment that he bounced out of bed in the morning, which he did with an obscene amount of energy, he romped through the day acting the goat, singing, engaging anyone and everyone in water fights and generally larking about. He was neither an experienced nor skilful canoeist but was gutsy as hell and no matter how many times he capsized and endured another cold swim he clambered back into his boat eager for more.

We paddled on through Eighteen-Mile Wash and Boulder Narrows which was formed by a boulder the size of a warehouse that had tumbled down from the cliffs into the centre of the river. After a break for some lunch, I had a go at rowing one of the oar boats. Although physically the same size as one of the paddle boats, it felt much more stable due to the weight of the tightly packed cargo and the heavy steel frame.

Sat on a cool box and braced against the frame, manhandling the long wooden oars was reasonably straightforward on the flat water. For the rapids however, the oarsmen stood up and rowed facing downstream which was a lot trickier than it looked. The oars felt awkward and clumsy and it was much more difficult to wield them in the way that I wanted them to go. If they caught against a wave, the force of the water could rip them from your grasp. They then became a flailing menace that risked seriously wounding the oarsman or snapping against a rock as the raft flew, out of control, down river.

We rowed and paddled through the Roaring Twenties, a series of twelve rapids spaced over eight miles before stopping on a sandbank at the end of Shinumo Wash. Leaving the boats, we walked a short way up the side canyon before making a delicate scramble up into a narrow gorge. The rock walls were sheer and smooth. At the back of the gorge we swam, slithered and crawled our way from one slippery rock pool to the next until we were able to clamber up into a natural amphitheatre higher up. There was little available light inside, but the keyhole view out from the cool silver-walled grotto to the bright sunlit Canyon wall beyond was most impressive. We camped where we had beached with the sound of the river running past and the waves lapping against the sand.

We spent a gentle morning drifting down river with Geoff telling us more of his inexhaustible supply of Grand Canyon history and lore. We stopped at various points to explore and take photographs. The first of these was at Vasey's Paradise, named after the botanist on Powell's first expedition. Water poured out of a circular hole in the rock, 200 feet above the river. It flowed down the inclined wall of the canyon, splitting into a series of fine rivulets like the tresses of a girl's hair. Below, the fresh water nourished a small green oasis of mesquite and tamarisk trees, columbine bushes and beds of watercress, which made a welcome relief from the arid surrounds.

Slightly further down river we pulled over again. This time we scrambled up to a small ledge 100 feet up the side of the right Canyon wall. We filmed and photographed as the rest of the team came past. They made a fine sight as they made their way in procession down the river between the great red walls. The Canyon had narrowed noticeably making the height and steepness of the walls all the more apparent. Looking up the canyon, the sides are convoluted in an endless chain of walls, buttresses and spires that reach to the sky. There are fantastic formations and deformities in the rock; caves, gouges, amphitheatres, slots and high up, the dry chutes of waterfalls that would cascade into the canyon at the first hint of rain. The rafts appeared as a flotilla of water beetles, with the kayaks no more than fleas buzzing around them.

Everything in the Grand Canyon is extreme: the scale is totally overpowering, the canyon walls indescribably beautiful and yet oppressive and domineering. The surrounding desert is so dry that it supports only the hardiest cacti and after only a short time away from one of the few life-giving rivers or streams you find yourself searching for the next, threatened by the aridity. Where there is life, the colours are so vibrant that your eyes can barely comprehend them; the contrast between rock, vegetation and sky almost a physical barrier. At the heart of all this, the Colorado roars its warning.

We approached a low cave at the side of the river. From a distance it looked unremarkable, a long lozenge-shaped cavity at the base of the canyon wall. Once we paddled closer, its true size became apparent, revealing a vast elliptical cavern eroded by the flow of the water. We stopped again at the foot of a faint path which climbed steeply up the side of the canyon to the top of the Redwall limestone, one of the mid layers of rock. We scrambled up, picking our way past barrel cactuses and prickly pears, Mormon Tea and a variety of other low, spiky bushes. Several were in flower and surprisingly colourful.

From our elevated position we could see that the canyon that we were paddling through was only an inner layer within a much larger canyon. Further tiers of rock formed successive plateaux all the way back to the rim. Immediately opposite, we looked across to a natural rock arch known as the Bridge of Sighs. Seven hundred feet below us, a group of motorised pontoons passed down the river, an insignificant intrusion in the life of the Canyon.

In the afternoon I took to a kayak for the first time. Although only two feet lower than you are in a raft, as a kayaker your perspective and appreciation of scale is totally different. Down at water level, without the reassurance of others around you, you are conscious of being very small and vulnerable. The rock walls seem to tower above you even more menacingly. Every movement of the water has a much more dramatic effect and you have to be constantly on your guard even on the flat stretches against boils, whorls, whirlpools and eddy lines that appear as if out of nowhere and can snatch your kayak and tip you over.

Fortunately, most of the afternoon was spent on a reasonably flat stretch of water and I could take my time getting used to the feel of the boat, settling my balance and practising my defensive strokes. The Schlegl Extreme paddle felt reassuringly solid in my hands and the kayak responded well to each movement of the blades.

Having spent the night camped on a beach at the mouth of Saddle Canyon we continued downstream for another five miles to Nankoweap Canyon. Moving quietly in our kayaks, we startled two mule deer feeding at the river's edge. Nearby, we saw one of the ungainly wild turkeys that had moved into the canyon. A peregrine falcon landed beside us on a beach and another larger falcon flew overhead carrying a small bird in its talons.

Our plan was to leave the boats with some of the guides at Nankoweap Canyon and walk up the canyon. From there we would climb up onto the Mesa and camp the night on top, descending

next day by a different route to rejoin the boats which the guides would have floated four miles down river to the next side canyon, Kwagunt. The limited amount of space in the rafts had allowed for little more than a pair of trekking boots each and a small rucksack between two men. Away from the river, water was the priority and aside of that we packed a few sandwiches and biscuits each and some extra clothes for the night.

We followed a steep, dusty trail that clung precariously to the wall of the Mesa until, several hundred feet above the level of the river, we came to some old Anasazi granaries carved into the rock. The Anasazi occupied the North Rim of the Grand Canyon from roughly AD 600 until AD 1150 when a prolonged period of drought forced them to abandon their land. Their descendants, the Hopi, live in the Kaibab Reservation one hundred miles to the east and still maintain sacred salt mines within the Canyon. Over the last 1,000 years various other Indian tribes competed for the fragile hunting and farming grounds within the Grand Canyon. Today, the Navajo, Havasupai and Hualapai all have reserved land bordering the south rim and to the north the Paiute live in the Kaibab Reservation.

Traversing around the mesa we dropped into Nankoweap Canyon which we followed upstream for a couple of miles. We filled our water bottles for the last time and then branched off on a side canyon that led directly up to the north face of the Mesa. For two hours we scrambled up through consecutive bands of rock, picking out the best line that we could up the face. We shuffled along narrow flaky traverses and clambered up steep rock pitches. The top section was a nightmare of loose rock and scree which had us ducking frequently to avoid rockfall from those above.

Once on top we collapsed under whatever shade we could find until we regained our breath. When there was cloud cover the heat was bearable but as we had moved onto the most strenuous part of the climb, the clouds had parted leaving the sun boring down onto us.

A mesa is a flat table of rock with sheer sides standing free from the surrounding country. Nankoweap Mesa is roughly a third of a mile wide and just over a mile long. At the same height as the Canyon rim, it afforded spectacular views in all directions. To the east it dropped 3,500 feet straight down to the

The kayakers follow in line through one of the smaller rapids.

Previous page: The cool shade of Silver Gorge.

Bursting through a standing wave the spray blinds you and the world turns white.

Led by Scott Wilson, Ivan Key and Peter Rylands, the kayakers head into Marble Canyon.

One of the paddle rafts hits a standing wave.

Redwall Cavern.

The scale of the Grand Canyon can only be fully appreciated from a view-point high on the outer rim.

Below: Simon Knowles, one of our two kayaking instructors.

Andrew Jamieson fights his way through some large whitewater.

The learning curve was steep and for those who couldn't roll, swims were frequent.

Simon Gammell adds weight to the front of one of the oar rafts.

Alone in a kayak there is a tremendous sensation of isolation.

The crew of a paddle raft is submersed.

Opposite: Deep in the Inner Canyon, over a mile below the surface of the surrounding country.

Away from the river the side canyons offer beautiful trekking.

A stream provides relief from the arid desert.

The end of the journey at Diamond Creek, Mile 225.

Colorado. Beyond, we could see out across the flat lands of the Navajo Reserve. To the south it looked along the line of Marble Canyon and to the west out over a vista of buttes, mesas, valleys and ridges all folded and twisted as they reached out towards the Canyon's North Rim ten miles away. Once again the scale was hard to comprehend.

From an airy promontory jutting out into Marble Canyon we watched a spectacular sunset paint the undersides of the clouds a shimmering red then as it grew dark we made our way to a rather less exposed patch of ground to spend the night. The realities of our rather spartan equipment quickly made themselves apparent as we sipped our precious supply of water, attempted to chew hot, congealing sandwiches and lay down on the hard rock.

The temperature dropped sharply. Despite putting on all the clothing that we had, without sleeping bags we passed a cold, uncomfortable and sleepless night. We woke, or more accurately stirred, as it grew light. There was another stunning dawn, the first rays of the sun highlighting every contour and fold in the convoluted landscape. It took some time as we reversed our awkward climb down the mesa wall amidst even more falling rock and then cut over the back of a dry saddle into an equally dry gully beyond. We followed the gully for a further mile until we came to the musical sound of running water. We drank our fill and then lay prone in the stream letting the water run over us as we regained our senses. Within just a couple of hours the direct sun could leave you weak and groggy.

We followed the stream down through Kwagunt Canyon and back to the main river where the boats were waiting. Each person in turn arrived looking dehydrated and worn out. It seemed ridiculous that such a short time should have had such a profound effect on a group of fit men but it had and that in itself was a salutary lesson not to take any hike into the desert lightly.

Once we had sorted ourselves out, we got back into the boats once more. We were into a sizeable rapid almost immediately. No one felt particularly strong or geared up for a difficult rapid. I adopted my usual maxim of 'If in doubt, paddle like hell and don't stop until you are safely out the far end'. Unlike Corporal Key, who seemed to glide effortlessly through rapids putting in a few deft strokes, I am not a good technical paddler. In place of his more elegant style, I adopted an all-guns-blazing flail of arms and paddle to bludgeon my way through rapids. I slipped down the smooth tongue in his wake and switched to manic mode as I dropped into the first trough. On this occasion the brute force and ignorance philosophy worked and having corrected one major wobble I burst through each wave emerging at the far end exhilarated and considerably more awake.

We paddled several more small rapids and riffles and then drifted down to the mouth of the Little Colorado River. Its clear aquamarine water pouring over white sand and glittering, mineral-rich rock made a startling comparison to the dark water of the main river. Better still, having flowed for over an hundred miles along a shallow river bed through the Painted Desert it was the temperature of the Caribbean, unlike the icy Colorado. We spent the remainder of the afternoon practising kayak rolls, body surfing and chatting to the other river users.

That night a strong, hot wind blew up the Canyon. The pages of my diary filled with sand and the end of my pen became a sand-encrusted inky blob. Heavy clouds threatened rain but aside of a few spots, nothing came.

The next day saw the start of the big rapids. Time and days had lost their meaning and began to blur into each other. The only thing that existed for us was the Canyon and the progress of our little party moving through it. We had established a fixed routine: we got up when it became light, stopped to eat lunch when we were more than just a bit hungry, took a short siesta and then paddled on until the sun lost its power. We then piled into a huge meal before collapsing onto the sand to sleep ready for the next cycle. The events of the outside world had no relevance.

We put our A team into the kayaks: Corporal Key, Corporal of Horse Knowles, Corporal Woodward, Guardsman Wilson, Guardsman Jamieson and Guardsman McIlvogue. Setting off from Cape Solitude, we passed the sacred Hopi salt mines and continued into the Great Unconformity, which marked the beginning of another whole bracket of rock layers known as the Grand Canyon Supergroup which were raised by up to two miles during a period of massive geologic upheaval. As we entered the Furnace Flats, the canyon walls dropped away leaving both rims, thirteen miles apart, visible from river level for the first time. I had tried desperately hard to be interested in the geology to match the avid fascination of our guides who greeted each new rock layer as a long-lost friend, but I could not. Mesozoic, Palaeozoic, Devonian, Silurian or Cambrian, sandstone, limestone, shale or granite, they were all the same to me. Whilst wonderful to look at, I was far more interested in the animals and plants to be found living in the Canyon. I became resigned to being a geological pagan.

That night, the team was buzzing with stories of the day's adventures. We had paddled some big rapids including two of Grade Nine, Hance and Sockdologer, the latter named after a knockout punch. It had certainly lived up to its name. Both rafts and kayaks had been in the thick of the action and several people had taken long swims. Dale, the novice amongst the oarsmen, had lost an oar at Nevill Rapid and then let go of one in Hance. He was being run ragged by the other guides.

Mid-afternoon, the Canyon had closed right in as we entered Granite Gorge. Looking down river the black walls of the gorge appeared to almost touch. We had reached the base layers of rock, the Vischnu schist and Zoroaster granite, laid down some 1.7 billion years ago. I felt as if we were disappearing into a cleft deep in the earth's core from which there was no means of escape, a sensation that was heightened by dark brooding clouds which seemed to put a lid on the gorge and added to the foreboding air. As the evening wore on and tongues loosened, the stories grew taller as each rapid was re-lived again and again.

Next morning, after a watery hike up Bear Creek to a crystal clear pool into which powerful jets of water spouted from around a huge chockstone that blocked the stream above, we continued downstream. A large wave train in Zoroaster shook out any cobwebs and got everyone back on their toes. Now eighty-eight miles into the canyon, we came to the first and only point at which a re-supply would be practicable. We passed under the Kaibab suspension bridge built in 1920 to take mule trains coming down from the South Rim. Just beyond was Phantom Ranch established in 1903 as a rest place for tourists and hunters on their way to the North Rim.

Huge rapids now began to appear thick and fast.

Bright Angel Rapid and Pipe Spring Rapid both came and went without posing any major problems but then there was Horncreek Rapid with two large rocks protruding from the water in the middle of the river. The oar boats 'split the horns', running between the two rocks. Even they were engulfed by the standing waves. The kayakers bravely sallied forth, fighting their way down with mixed success. Both James McBrien and Guardsman McIlvogue wiped out and took long swims.

Lunch gave everyone a breather but it was a tense affair as there were even bigger rapids to come. Granite Rapid, graded 9+, dropped seventeen feet over a couple of hundred yards of massive standing waves. The rafts careered through, punching their way through each wave in turn. Fritz and Corporal Key both had clean runs in their kayaks but Corporal of Horse Knowles was quickly in trouble. Halfway down the wave train his boat was knocked around and he was carried on into the next waves backwards. He was trying to maintain his composure but real alarm showed through the fixed expression on his face and his desperate paddle strokes.

Simon Gammell made it through by the skin of his teeth but Rylands and Spencer were both eaten by giant standing waves. Spencer was taken out at the top of the rapid and had a long uncomfortable swim. Both of them appeared fairly shaken by the time that they were fished out; Spencer was unusually quiet and just kept saying that he had learnt to respect the river, Rylands looked totally white, his face drained of any expression and his eyes a vacant stare.

A mile downstream we came to Hermit Rapid, another Grade Nine extravaganza of massive, irregularly spaced standing waves. The rafts practically took off as they hurtled through them. The kayaks were totally overwhelmed by waves of 12-15 feet from trough to crest. Simon Gammell and Rylands both wiped out. I was concentrating on photographing the action and had two cameras with motor drives churning through frame after frame as I followed each boat's progress.

When I returned to the oar boat that I was using as a photographic platform I found Corporal Woodward and Guardsman McIlvogue waiting for me. One of the guides had told them that it was safe to swim the rapid; did I want to come too? It seemed madness to cast yourself bodily into that huge water but the question was put in that quiet teasing way that implied not to do so would be to lose face and as both of them were fellow Welsh Guardsmen it was one of those male bonding things.

In for a penny, in for a pound. I handed my glasses to Corporal Steggles who gave me one of his old-fashioned looks as if to say: 'Is this really wise? – and don't even think of asking me to come too!'

Dick rowed out into the main stream and as we entered the tongue at the top of the rapid, we all three jumped into the water. The current snatched us up straightaway and carried us forward. We had planned to stay together but Woodward was dragged away immediately. McIlvogue had hold of my shoulder and such was his desperation not to be separated that he kept forcing me underwater. The waves loomed impossibly high above us and crashed over us pushing us down under the surface. The white aerated water offered little support. Wave followed wave as we soared up and through each crest before plunging down the far side. At times it was hard to know if you were above the surface or not, such was the confusion of bubbles and spray. I gulped for air whenever I thought that my face was clear and choked on water as I did so.

It was frightening to feel so utterly powerless against the force of the current. For a short while I became desperate to get a breath as I was being thrown and spun through the waves like a rag doll. I came up finally, spluttering at the side of Dick's boat. I clung on to the safety line coughing up water and catching my breath before I could summon up the energy to heave myself back in. The others had fared no better. We all felt rather shaken but on a total high. Our plight in the rapid and rather bedraggled reappearance had provided much amusement for the rest of the team so we set about making as much capital out of it as we could, joshing the others that they had not had the courage to come too. Joining in the barracking with the best of them, I made a small mental note not to take on a Grade Nine rapid without a boat again.

By the end of each day the sun, frenetic exercise, adrenalin and frequent dousing in cold water all combined to make you both ravenous and exhausted. We ate like men offered their last ever meal and then collapsed on the sand with the wonderful satisfying feeling of having lived a full day. The evenings were mellow, we spent the time telling stories and later, lying back and watching the moon tint the canyon walls silver to the sound of the river rushing by.

Crystal Rapid had loomed large in our imaginations since the beginning of the journey. The first of the Grade Ten rapids, its reputation had been built up to giant proportions. In the past it had been even bigger until it had been partly washed out by a flash flood. Despite this, it was still an intimidating prospect looking from the bank at the huge train of massive, standing waves and three giant stoppers that were large enough to hold even a raft. The consequences of a swim were not pleasant; there was a broad sweep of shallow water flowing over an area of rocks on one side of the river and immediately below lay another rapid.

A number of motorised pontoons had stopped and there was a great crowd of tourists waiting to see the live entertainment that we promised to provide. Somehow all the kayakers got through unscathed despite Corporal of Horse Knowles being bowled over and having to roll back up and Simon Gammell unintentionally flirting with the largest of the stoppers which had those of us watching quailing on his behalf. We paddled on through Tuna and Lower Tuna Creek Rapid and the jewels: Agate, Sapphire, Turquoise, Ruby and Serpentine. Spencer swam four times and had lost most of his usual chirp. Wilson had also taken a couple of swims.

I had been itching to take my turn in a kayak and try my luck in some of the bigger water and now in the afternoon I got my chance. As I squeezed into the tight cockpit of my kayak I felt half excited and half apprehensive. The first rapid that we came to was bigger than anything I had kayaked so far. I felt unsteady and compensated by putting my head down and paddling hard. The front of my boat was thrown to left and right by the crests of huge converging waves and I fought to get back on line with powerful sweep strokes. I was determined not to be turned by the water or cast off into one of the side eddies. By the time that I reached the bottom the adrenalin was pumping freely. Shinumo, 110 Mile Rapid, Hakatoi and Waltenberg all followed in a similar vein.

We stopped at Royal Arch Creek where we scrambled up tier after tier of rock bypassing streams, pools and small waterfalls to reach Elves Chasm, a great rock amphitheatre with walls draped in green moss and ferns and a trickle of water seeping 200 feet down one side. It was a cool, peaceful place, a welcome respite from the burning sun, bouts of violent exercise and gnawing fears of the rapids.

It was after 6 p.m. when we took to the water again. Still half asleep from my siesta, I nearly wiped out in a series of holes in a small rapid. We paddled on for three more miles and stopped to camp on a broad beach. The full moon seemed to have a strange effect on the team sending most of them crazy. For no apparent reason what started as a quiet evening turned into high jinks. There was a lot of laughter and rebel rousing with home-made fireworks firing in all directions.

If I harboured any concerns that I had missed out on my share of the white-water action, the 23rd of June soon put paid to them, with interest. We set off late after a slow, relaxing start taking advantage of the location of our camp which stayed hidden from the direct rays of the sun until it was well up in the sky. We ran straight through Blacktail, 122 Mile and Forster Rapids, bouncing along the wave trains. You had to be careful at the bottom of every rapid to avoid whirlpools and swirling eddy lines that materialised out of nowhere and could catch or spin the front of your kayak without warning.

The adrenalin surged as we charged through each rapid. Apart from the two instructors, the other kayakers that day were Steggles, Jamieson and McIlvogue. Steggles was finding himself more in his element during this phase. Up in Alaska he had been overwhelmed both by the conditions and some fairly dominant and aggressive members of the first two teams. Although not a good kayaker, he felt more at ease on the water.

Up till now he had been concentrating on videoing the expedition but having got white water action footage from every conceivable angle he now had the chance to have a go at kayaking. He tended to sit still in his kayak as he bounced through the rapids, reacting to the water rather than controlling the movement of his boat through it. That is fine for the experienced paddlers such as Corporal Key whose balance and accurate strokes got him through, but not for a novice on water of that size. He appeared at the bottom of every rapid, grinning from ear to ear, saying, 'Cor, that one nearly got me!'

Fossil came next, a beautiful long sweeping rapid that curved first left and then to the right in a great S bend. It was much longer than the other rapids we had paddled and enormous fun. You had to work all the way through, powering forward, slapping for support if you began to tip, keeping the kayak in the centre of the wave train, watching for boils and stoppers and above all else keeping on paddling. Everyone got through although Corporal of Horse Knowles had to roll. We were all flying.

We paddled over to the oar boats for a snack raid and drifted downstream holding onto their safety lines munching apples and coming down from the adrenalin high. As we were chatting I could hear the roar of a rapid growing steadily nearer. Martha gave a deceptively cool appreciation: 'It's no problem, just a riffle, a little bitsy at the bottom'.

We each broke off from the raft. I stuffed my half-eaten apple down inside my buoyancy aid and paddled forward. I entered the rapid on line and rode the first few waves okay but then suddenly a transverse wave caught me and spun the boat round. Careering along backwards I felt distinctly out of control. A swirl flipped me sideways, I slapped for support but as I did so I hit another shear line and flipped the other way and was thrown over. In a shock of cold water, I found myself hanging upside down in my cockpit with water boiling all around me. I tried to roll but failed and, taking discretion as the better part of valour, I baled out. I managed to hang onto my boat and paddle as I bounced on down the rapid. Jamieson came out to me and once I had grabbed the toggle on the stern of his boat, towed me to shore. The others needless to say found it highly amusing, particularly Steggles who was counting his swims against mine.

Randy's Rock, 127 Mile and 128 Mile rapids were not too large, just the familiar battering in the waves which served to get my confidence back and help reassert balance and strong positive strokes. I was surprised how unsettling just one capsize in that water was. There was little time for self-congratulation as Spector loomed in front of us. It was one of the larger rapids so we got out and recced it. Looking from the left bank, we could see a series of enormous standing waves pushing up towards the left rock wall. There were holes everywhere but they were unpredictable and seemed to come and go. Fritz's less than reassuring advice was that it was impossible to read, you just had to run it and hope for the best.

Getting back into my boat I felt like the jockey in Surtees' painting of the Grand National: 'Oh murther! The dhrink dried out of me and the wrong side of Bechers!' I could not see how we could avoid going for a swim. I tightened the straps of my buoyancy aid and secured my helmet and then followed Fritz, Corporal Key and Corporal of Horse Knowles out into the current. We let the water take us slowly towards the rapid, angling ourselves slightly left of the centre of the main tongue. Everything seemed to go into slow motion as we glided down the velvet smooth tongue and then suddenly each person dropped out of sight and all I could see was glimpses of their blades flashing above the waves.

As I came to the end of the tongue, I took a deep breath and powered forward. The next couple of minutes was a blur of confusion as I fought my way through the white wilderness. Massive waves appeared from every side launching me up into the air, dropping me into deep troughs or breaking in a rolling wall of foam over me. I was thrown around as though I did not exist. I was turned sideways and almost backwards but managed to maintain some semblance of control. The boiling water offered little support or purchase to the paddle so it was difficult to resist the current or react to the waves. I emerged the far end somewhat dazed with my heart pounding. With a great whoop of delight I realised that more by good luck than good judgement I had got through.

Lunch came as a blessed relief and a chance to calm down and unwind. For the first time we could relax and appreciate the magnificent high walls and polished black rock of the Middle Granite Gorge through whose depths we were travelling. From where we had stopped we could see the next rapid, Bedrock. A huge section of the bedrock had been forced up in the centre of the river giving the rapid its name. The main chute led straight to the centre of the rock and piled up against it. There were runs either to the left or the right. The right had some massive waves and required an awkward traverse to avoid the bedrock but the left disappeared behind the rock in a seething mass of white water which looked like a whole world of hurt. There was a lot of talk amongst the oarsmen as to the best line and angle for them to take. One of them had flipped his raft there the last time he had attempted it. The kayakers sat apart,

eating with little appetite and fighting back waves of butterflies.

The seven rafts all went first pulling hard over to the right before eddying out at the base of the bedrock in the middle of the river. The paddle crews climbed up onto the rock to watch us come down leaving the oarsmen in their boats ready with throw lines to catch any swimmers. We set off in the same order as before, although at the back Guardsman Wilson had taken over Jamieson's boat.

The three in front of me all followed the line that we had picked out making it look easy. I drifted down the tongue putting in a few small strokes to hold my line. As I careered into the waves I felt myself drifting uncomfortably close to the looming rock face and threw in a few big powerful strokes pulling hard to my right. My momentum carried me past a rather evil-looking pour-over and then into the right channel and over to the eddy. It had been surprisingly easy and I experienced a sense of anticlimax that felt like a physical pressure relaxing.

The others did not fare as well: Steggles hadn't appreciated the need to work to keep his line and was swept towards the bedrock. I saw the alarm spread across his face as he realised that he could not make it to the right channel and was dragged helplessly to the left. He saw himself heading for the wall and stuck out an arm but as he did so, his boat was swallowed bodily by a huge stopper and he was spun around and around, first upright and then back underwater again, as if caught in the fast cycle of a gigantic washing machine. At one point he appeared above the surface and was propped up on a cushion of water by his outstretched arm and then he was taken by another stopper and dragged underwater.

The raft crews watching from the rock only a few feet above him, said that they had seen naked fear in his eyes as he was taken down once more. He bobbed up fifty yards further downstream out of his boat. Guardsman Wilson had been paddling behind Steggles and had taken a line even further left. He had no chance of getting back to the right and disappeared into the left abyss and wiped out. At the back, McIlvogue saw the other two heading for trouble and powered right. He just avoided the rock but had left his move too late and came down the pour-over a foot or two to the right of the rock and capsized. There were bodies, boats and paddles everywhere in the water. Those of us in the eddy headed out to help as the paddle rafts launched and began collecting stray kit.

Having got ourselves back together and taken a brief pause to give everyone a chance to collect ourselves, we carried on. Just a mile downstream was Deubendorff Rapid. Looking at it from the rocks above, enormous stacks of water surged in every direction with huge standing waves, deep, dark holes and cross waves that could slam you sideways. If Specter and Bedrock had been intimidating, this was more so. There was nothing for it but to tighten all the straps once again and paddle for your life.

As always, the calm glide down the tongue seemed to be in slow motion and then as the water quickened and the kayak lurched down into the trough at the foot of the first wave my resolve hardened and it was all or nothing. I was tossed in all directions. The waves were breaking over my head blinding me. I was throwing out support strokes every which way in an attempt to correct the sudden lurches to either side. I reached the bottom still upright and panting, on a massive adrenalin high. Some of the others were not as lucky; the same three that capsized at Bedrock Rapid, did so again.

The rescue boats went out. I caught a couple of paddles floating past. As I ferried them over to the shore, I saw Corporal Key towing Steggles to the far bank. Someone else was dragging his boat over to him, but instead of getting in it he was towed all the way back across the river. As they got to the shore Corporal Key shouted for help. Several of the raft crews ran forward and carried Steggles up onto the beach. He was grey with pain and also clearly in shock. His leg appeared to be injured and he was shaking all over. Mike checked him over. Luckily nothing was broken but his lower leg was badly scraped and bruised and he was fairly shaken up.

He said that he had dropped into a massive hole right at the top of the rapid. He had tried to roll but could not in the wild water and so ejected from the boat. He kept hold of his boat for buoyancy as we had been taught, but then dropped into another hole and it was ripped from his grasp. He had been taken down under the water and raced along in the undercurrent banging along the rocks on the river bed.

Fortunately, we had reached the point where we had planned to stop for the night. Mike packed Steggles' leg with some ice from one of the cool boxes and settled him in the shade with plenty of fluids. Those with any energy headed off on a hike up Stone Creek. We stuck close to the stream passing several waterfalls, some more Anasazi granaries and wonderful desert vegetation; flowering barrel cactus, yucca, bear grass and some lush green trees. We hiked on for a couple of miles climbing gradually between sheer rock walls as the gorge twisted and turned with frequent side canyons breaking off it.

At the far end of the valley, on the skyline, a solid massif of rock sat dominating the scene. Bands of strongly coloured ochre and yellow rock contrasted against the deep even blue of the sky and the bright streamside vegetation. We came to a halt at the foot of a dark, rock wall with a high waterfall pouring down it.

By the time that I got back to camp I was dog tired. I bolted supper and then crawled away to my bed on the sand. As I lay looking up at the stars, I could hear Colour Sergeant McKeown's distinctive Glaswegian accent calling out to the guides the orders for a demonstration of The Ceremony of the Keys. The Tower of London and ceremonial soldiering seemed a million miles away.

For the next four days we carried on down river stopping frequently to explore the various side canyons along the way. The rapids were, on the whole, amongst the more modest of those that we encountered in the Canyon although our criteria for judging rapids had totally changed. What we would have considered as monstrous and terrifying just ten days previously was no more than an unnamed riffle further down the Canyon. The one exception was Upset Rapid which claimed both Simon Gammell and Trooper Spencer. Simon took a particularly bad swim having capsized in a large hole and had been held underwater for a long time. Having been winded on rocks at the bottom of the river and swallowed more than his fair share of the Colorado, Simon's confidence had taken a heavy knock.

A hike in Grand Canyon parlance involves rather more than such a simple term suggests and should be taken as a euphemism for trekking, scrambling, rock climbing, wading up rivers and clambering

over waterfalls. The bare rock is extremely unforgiving and by the time that we had got halfway
through the canyon, our clothes were in tatters and
our boots falling off our feet. Having completed
the usual natural assault course for three miles
up Tapeats Creek we came to the head of the
Thunder River where it poured out of a hole high
in the rock face at the valley head, cascading down
a couple of hundred feet, first sheer and then in a
blur of spray as it tumbled from pool to pool. The
water was ecstatically cold as we stood underneath
it, letting it beat down on our heads and shoulders.
The narrow gorge was enclosed by leafy, knarled
trees and yet bright and cheerful: the white foaming
water and green of the trees set off by bright red
monkeyflowers.

As we drifted on down an eight-mile flat stretch
of river to Kanab Creek, Martha entertained us
with stories of the Canyon's exploration and some
of the adventures of the first people to run the
Colorado. One of the best of these regarded Bessie
and Glen Hyde. Glen Hyde had built his own boat,
a wooden sweepscow, which employed fore and aft
oars, and persuaded his tiny 4ft 10in bride, Bessie, to
accompany him on a journey through the Canyon
for their honeymoon in November of 1928. Having
reached Phantom Ranch after a fairly hair-raising
journey through the first part of the Canyon, they
hiked up the mule trail to the South Rim to get fresh
supplies. There they met and befriended Emery and
Ellsworth Kolb, two brothers who had established
a photographic studio in Grand Canyon Village
sometime around 1902. The Kolbs gave them a
place to rest and helped them carry their supplies
back down to the river.

It was rumoured that, frightened by their experiences so far, Bessie did not want to continue with
the expedition but that her domineering husband
had forced her to. It was further rumoured that
she had an affair with Ellsworth Kolb. In the event,
they continued on their way but they never reached
their planned pick-up. A large search was mounted
and their boat was found floating upright in an eddy
below 237 Mile Rapid. Curiously, Bessie's diary was
found open on the top of the boat which caused
people to doubt the official story that they had both
drowned. The fate of 'the Honeymoon Couple' was
the centre of considerable conjecture. There were
many theories; one that Bessie, with or without the
help of Ellsworth Kolb, had done away with her
husband and hiked out of the Canyon to begin
a new life elsewhere. A woman exactly matching
Bessie in age and description had gone along on
an expedition that Martha had guided many years
later and Martha firmly believed from the way that
this woman behaved, that it was Bessie.

Kanab Creek flowed through a tight, high-walled
canyon. We followed the stream up, splashing our
way through deep pools, oozing mud flats and over
huge boulders that blocked the dark gorge. After
a last couple of steep scrambles, we shuffled along
a narrow ledge that brought us out at the foot of
Whispering Falls. The Grand Canyon is so full of
contrasts. For most of the time the heat is searing,
boring into your head and frying your brains and
then you enter the cool, relaxing shade of one of
the quiet side canyons or on other occasions half
freeze from the chilling rain or spray.

It is just the same with the water: in places the
rivers and creeks become raging torrents, threatening your very existence and elsewhere they are
calm and serene, lazily drifting downstream or
cheerfully gurgling down the rocky side streams.
At Whispering Falls, the water sings as it trickles
down a smooth slide of rock. Large shiny droplets
patter down like softly falling rain onto the surface
of a beautiful deep, clear pool. A shallow cave
with shaded rock ledges encloses the pool. Even
the hardiest of the soldiers were swept up by the
mood of the place and we passed the hottest part
of the day reading, writing letters, sleeping or
swimming quietly so as not to shatter the general
air of tranquillity.

On another day, Olo Canyon proved rather
more challenging. The entrance to the canyon
was guarded by an overhanging rock face that in
winter turns into a powerful cascade. We climbed
twenty feet up a free-hanging rope before hauling
ourselves over the lip. From there the canyon
wound its way up smooth shelves of rock and
through deep swirling passages, gouged out by
the flow of water. We crossed the bare stage of a
Romanesque amphitheatre, the baking rock floor
dominated by two tall pillars. Giant boulders and
chockstones filled the tapering gully. We pressed
on, scrabbling up short rock walls, bridging gaps,
swinging out over overhangs and shimmying up
chimneys until we were brought to a halt by an
impassable dry waterfall.

We finished each day totally worn out. Having helped unpack the boats, prepare dinner and set up my small sleeping area, it was fantastic to bathe naked in the river and let the flow of the current wash off all the sweat and grime. Later, after a large dinner, I would sit back with a glass of whisky and write my diary or look up at the moonlight playing on the canyon walls and the trails of satellites passing overhead. We went to sleep to the sound of flowing water and the chorus of chirruping crickets.

The largest of all the side canyons that we explored was Havasu: a broad creek, punctuated by frequent waterfalls of all sizes, that leads back into the Havasupai Indian Reserve. The water is pure turquoise, dammed at regular intervals into fantastic swimming pools by barriers of porous rock. Large cottonwood, acacia and Arizona grape trees provide welcome shade and dense undergrowth adds to a feeling of lushness that is not to be found anywhere else in the Grand Canyon. The trail wends its way up beside the creek, crossing from bank to bank in search of the least obstructed path.

After three and a half miles we came to Beaver Falls. The stream cascades from one perfect pool to the next down the tiered falls. Led by McIlvogue, the more fearless members of the team began hurling themselves off higher and higher terraces into the pools below.

I left them and carried on up the creek. Birds sang overhead and banded lizards scurried away into the undergrowth as I continued for the next two miles up towards the beckoning roar of Mooney Falls. A vast spout of water plunged two hundred feet vertically over a cliff that blocked the gorge. Beside the waterfall an elaborate mudstained cascade of travertine was frozen into mushrooms and sculptured terraces. I tried swimming out under the main curtain of water but I was forced back by the ferocious down draught of falling water and compressed air.

That night there was an anxious buzz in the camp. Next day we were due to tackle Lava Falls, the largest rapid on the river with a drop of thirty-seven feet over a couple of hundred yards. Although by no means the last, it was the culmination of the white-water and there had been considerable soul searching on each person's behalf about whether they were going to attempt to shoot it in a kayak. There was a period of intense psyching up before each of the big rapids.

Standing on the rocks at the riverside and staring into the mesmerising mêlée of thrashing water, huge wave trains and ominous holes, all but the most professional kayakers experienced a hollow, slightly fluttering feeling in the pit of their stomach and fought to overcome their nerves. But for one or two of the largest rapids, those whose reputations preceded them and whose names were whispered up and down the river in anxious anticipation, the build-up was a far more fundamental spell of gnawing self-doubt. Over half of the team had already said that they would not attempt Lava Falls in a kayak and several more were wavering.

When we got up in the morning, I noticed that each of the guides was a lot more particular than usual about the way that the boats were packed and rigged. The pressure in each of the inflatable rafts' air chambers was checked and pumped up. Every piece of equipment was lashed securely and all the rigging straps were tightened and their ends tucked away. The obvious concern of the guides did nothing to buoy up the confidence of the rest of us. We had roughly fifteen miles of mainly flat water, with just a few minor rapids to negotiate, before reaching Lava Falls. Amongst the kayakers there was noticeably less of the usual banter.

Hummingbirds zipped across the river in a whirr of small wings, an osprey looked down at us from his eyrie high in the Redwall limestone and the morning passed slowly with the heat increasing and the sense of anticipation building. A mile before the falls we came to Vulcan's Anvil, a great black volcanic plug protruding over fifty feet out of the centre of the river. Below, we could hear the menacing thunder of the falls.

Lava Falls was formed where the outwash from Prospect Canyon had brought boulders down into the canyon constricting the river. Where it narrowed, the Colorado rose up into a series of truly massive standing waves with the king of all, a huge V wave at the top end of the rapid. After that came a succession of huge haystack and transverse waves whose troughs were lost somewhere beneath the surrounding peaks. Enormous holes appeared at various stages and towards the bottom of the rapid an arm of rock stuck out into the river from the right bank. The water boiled up against it before raging on past.

Tubes were re-checked and topped up from a foot pump, all extraneous equipment removed or secured, buoyancy aids and helmet straps tightened, hats and glasses either put safely away or tied on with stout cord. In Geoff's boat, we were to go first of the paddle rafts and before the kayaks so that we could film and photograph the others coming through. In front of us, I saw Dick and Dirk's oar rafts drop down the tongue and out of sight reappearing momentarily on top of the V wave before disappearing again. Having settled ourselves down, we paddled with pounding hearts steadily out into the current. Geoff called out the commands calmly but with an edge to his voice. He stopped us, angled the raft slightly right and told everyone to be ready to give him full power the moment he called for it. We each adjusted our position on the tube, kicked our feet under the lip of the stay in front to give us what little security we could get and gripped our paddles firmly.

'All forward! Hard forward! Come on, give it all you've got!'

We leant out and dug in our paddles with all of the strength that we could muster. The raft lurched down into the first trough and then reared up against the wall of water in front. We were through and plunging down again, then came the V wave. The rubber raft bent almost in half as we cannoned into it and then we were careering on down the wave train. The raft was submerged; arms, heads and paddles protruded from the whiteness, people were on the floor fighting to get back up onto the tube. I heard Corporal Steggles scream as we lurched straight towards the rock and then at the last moment we veered past, caught up by the current. We emerged at the bottom full to the brim with water. Those at the back bailed furiously whilst the rest of us paddled hard to break out of the current and into the first eddy. Exhilaration mixed with anticlimax; it had all happened so fast.

We tied the raft to a rock on the bank and climbed out. The black basalt rock had been baking in the sun all morning and was too hot to touch. We scrambled forward over the rocks until we found the best vantage point from which to watch the action. Geoff and Steggles went and perched on the protruding rock with the video camera and I set up close to the water's edge. As each kayaker broke out of the top eddy and committed themselves to the current, I concentrated on keeping them in

the frame of the camera. Poised above the rapid, they looked small and vulnerable. Each dropped down into the maelstrom with flashing paddles.

Fritz went first, battling her way through with a few quick support strokes. Corporal Key went next. He was the best of us by far and paddled each rapid with a fluid unpanicked grace but at this rapid he was unable to stop his hands shaking as he paddled out of the top eddy. He had a smooth professional run. Corporal of Horse Knowles followed and nearly capsized twice. I could see the entire bottom of his kayak but each time he managed to push himself back up again. Wilson went next and despite a fairly hairy ride through the larger waves made it intact. Corporal Woodward and Guardsman McIlvogue both wiped out at the V wave. McIlvogue had a fairly nasty swim and was under the water for a long time. At the back, Jamieson made it through in one piece.

There was then a lull in the action as we waited for the other rafts to come down. Lava had claimed plenty of raft flips in its time and I knew that Dale, the novice oarsman, and Fred were both fairly anxious. Fred had not been with Expeditions Inc. for all that long and was rowing his own boat for only the second time. He was a full blood Hopi Indian with a mane of waist length, jet black hair. He and his boat partner, Robin, another Hopi, were popular members of the team. Both were young and great fun and the first to join in any horseplay.

Despite their rather unlikely names, they took their Hopi beliefs seriously. I had seen them draw themselves to one side on several occasions when we stopped at important Hopi sites in the Canyon. Fred was the elder and appeared to be teaching Robin the Hopi ways and traditions. There were always great cheers when they came flying through a rapid with Fred's huge arms pulling on the oars and Robin perched at the front of boat like a diminutive figurehead.

While we were waiting Woodward, McIlvogue and Corporal Key got back in their kayaks. The first two had decided to have another go and see if they could beat the rapid. Corporal Key went with them to show them the line once again. He was a most impressive man, shy, unassuming and ever attentive to the needs of others. He took his role as guide and instructor very seriously and coached, encouraged and counselled each of us in his quiet, unhurried way, instilling confidence in even the most faint-hearted.

I admired the courage and determination of the other two to put themselves into the rapid again. They ferry-glided across the river and paddled up the eddy to the far side before climbing back out of their boats and carrying them on their shoulders across the beach and up through the bulrushes on the left bank to the top of the rapid. Corporal Key had another clean run but both of the others were again knocked over in the huge waves at the beginning of the rapid and had long swims. The remaining oar boats and the other paddle raft followed. Each made it through one way or another with varying degrees of ease or drama. The frozen expressions on the faces of the paddlers summed it all up.

As I was packing up my cameras, I found Corporal Key standing beside me. Did I want to have a go at paddling the rapid? Watching the others go down, I had been wrestling with my conscience. I was severely intimidated by the size of the water but I knew that if I did not give it a go I would bitterly regret not doing so and I would not forgive myself for being so weak. There was really no choice and with more conviction than I felt, I said that I would. To my surprise, and much to his credit considering the hammering that he had taken in Bedrock and Deubendorff Rapids, Corporal Steggles said that he would give it a go as well. Corporal Woodward with commendable fortitude, said that he was not prepared to give up without getting down the rapid upright and would show us the line.

We sorted out boats and spraydecks. I realised that there were no left-handed paddles but Corporal Key quickly prevented an honourable discharge by producing a split paddle which he carried in his boat and assembled it for a left hander. With a distinct feeling of heading for impending doom I got into the boat, ferry-glided across the river and paddled up the eddy to the beach. We were a silent group as we trudged along carrying our boats, the tension building inside us. Having reached the top of the rapid, Steggles and I both stopped for a nervous pee. As we walked back to where we had put down our boats he turned to me and said, 'I don't think this is a very good idea, Sir'. A master of the understatement.

I replied with some feeling that I was not much

more enthusiastic than he was, but that it was too late for regrets now. We helped each other fit our tight neoprene spraydecks over the cockpit rim with fumbling fingers. Having tightened every strap that could be tightened and ensured that Steggles had done the same, I nodded to Corporal Woodward.

For some reason in my mental deliberations over the past few days as to whether I would kayak Lava Falls or not, I had decided to do it for Dai, my step father, and for James Griffith. I had not been able to go to either of their funerals and in a slightly sentimental way I felt that this would be my personal tribute to them. It was the type of activity of which they would both have fully approved; Dai had seen service in the Second World War and had ridden to hounds all his life and James, also an accomplished horseman, had ridden many races as an amateur jockey including twice attempting the daunting fences of Aintree. As I pulled out into the current after Corporal Woodward, I gave them a quiet mental salute and then set my mind to the rapid in front.

We drifted steadily down towards the tongue, the sound of the water beating louder and louder in our ears. I saw Corporal Woodward drop down into the trough, burst through the first wave and then he was gone. There was no more time to think. I dug in my paddle and pulled like hell. If I was going to get wiped out, I was going to go down fighting and anyway paddling like fury helped give me confidence. I hurtled down into the pit of the wave and then stopped, knocked backwards by the wall of water in front of me. I reached forward and pulled hard on my paddle and then I was falling into the next trough. The V wave towered way over my head straight in front of me. I felt the nose of the boat lift up and I was launched over the crest of the wave. Feeling myself turning over, I lashed out with a desperate support stroke and managed to push myself back up. I flew on, being knocked from side to side by each wave, blinded by the flying spray.

I found myself shouting out loud a self-rallying mantra. 'Keep paddling! Don't stop! Keep paddling! Don't stop! Come on, keep going!'

My heart was beating so hard I thought it would burst out of my chest. The spectre of the protruding rock flashed past and gradually the waves began to get smaller. I was through. Realising that I had made it, I gave out a great roar of suppressed nervous energy. I could see other kayakers out in the mainstream rescuing Corporal Woodward in front. I headed towards them and picked his paddle out of the water and paddled on clenching it together with my own. Further back Corporal Steggles was being rescued by one of the paddle boats. I was in a hazy world of my own, totally elated, I had never thought that I would get through. Adrenalin coursed through my veins and every nerve-ending in my body tingled. It was an high like no other.

As we were getting everyone sorted out, Trooper Spencer announced that he too wanted to have a go at kayaking the rapid. No-one else wanted to join him but not wishing him to be denied his chance, Corporal Key offered to show him the line and run it himself once again. Having been involved in rescuing poor Woody and Steggles, Corporal Key took a few minutes to get himself ready and set off after Spencer, back up to the top of the rapid. To the horror of all those of us watching, instead of waiting for Corporal Key to get to him, Spencer got into his boat and pulled out into the current on his own. There was nothing that we could do to stop him. Having started without getting a signal to go from the bottom of the rapid, we were not even in position at the top of the eddy where we would be ready to help him if he capsized. We watched as he came uncertainly down the tongue. He narrowly missed a large hole on the left, only spotting it at the last moment and just managing to pull away from it.

He was off line when he went into the first wave and capsized immediately. He was swept through the rapid, carried by the current into some of the worst holes and disappeared under the surface. Starting from further down than we would normally have been, it took us longer than we would have liked to reach him. Jamieson got to him first: he was coughing up water and gasping for breath. His eyes were wide and he looked both frightened and shocked. Once we had got him to the bank and he could finally talk, he kept saying how terrified he had been and that he would not take on anything like that again. He sat in the shallows, with his head in his hands, shaking.

Immediately below us was a long, sweeping right-handed rapid in which the current pushed up against the left wall in a series of large waves and boiling water. The oar boats had gone ahead and broken out of the current into a tight eddy. To do so they had to make a sharp move. If you missed the break-out move, you would be swept on downstream by the current and unable to stop for a considerable distance. As they were setting up for lunch the incentive to get it right was high. Fritz warned us that it could be a tricky run and that we needed to watch out for holes and cross currents. Spencer looked around imploringly for someone to take his kayak. I decided that I might as well stay in mine and change back after lunch.

We set off in line but were all rather bunched when we got into the rapid. There was a large standing wave at the entry point and then a series of waves forcing us towards the left wall with some nasty holes appearing in amongst them. I was going along fine, although further left than I wanted to be, when suddenly I felt my boat stop and start surfing backwards. I was held in a stopper.

I realised what was going on and started trying to pull my way out but as I did so I heard a shout of alarm above me. I looked up just in time to see McIlvogue's boat dropping down onto me. We were both knocked over. The swirling water knocked me this way and that. I stayed in the boat until I felt the buffeting slacken which signalled that I had come out of the stopper – I certainly did not want to come out of the boat any earlier and risk letting go of it in case I was held, trapped in the stopper without the volume or buoyancy to break free. Being rescued right in front of the rest of the team was a slightly ignominious end to the morning but I did not care, if I capsized at every other rapid that I ever paddled, I had kayaked Lava Falls and I felt unconscionably pleased with myself.

That afternoon heavy cloud amassed overhead and fast moving convection air currents rising from off the black basalt rocks combined to create strong upstream winds. At times these intensified to an alarming degree, whipping the sand up off the beaches and blasting it into our faces. Whilst these winds were at their strongest we could make little headway even with seven men in each raft pulling hard on our paddles. The winds died away as quickly as they blew up.

For the last two days we paddled on down the widening canyon. We were no longer enclosed by continuous vertical cliffs. In their place were sections of canyon interspersed with open plateaux and bare-rock mountains set back at various distances from the river's edge. It was a wonderful period of reflection, with the splendour of the volcanic scenery and with enough rapids to keep up the whitewater excitement.

On the 30th June the conical Diamond Peak hove into view signalling the end of our journey. For the final few miles, as we paddled steadily towards Diamond Creek, I relished our last moments of peaceful isolation. The Colorado trundled on for another fifty miles to Lake Mead but the backed-up waters of the lake made the river sluggish and washed out the rapids that had once been along the lower sections of the river. For us, Diamond Creek signalled not only the end of our river journey but our return from the timeless tranquillity of the Grand Canyon to the hectic bustle of the modern world beyond its protective embrace.

Looking around the team, as we deflated the rafts and loaded all of the kit back onto the lorry, they had changed from the people who had entered the Canyon. Superficially we were all fit and bronzed but underneath there was a more subtle change. Each person carried within them a quiet confidence. The many faces of the Canyon had left their mark on us, giving us both humility through an appreciation of the scale and power of nature and our insignificance and vulnerability within it, and yet the strength to face it.

The realities of the ongoing expedition planning were waiting for me back at Flagstaff in the form of a fifty-page fax from London which had at its foot a note asking me to ring the office at 9 a.m. their time, 2 a.m. Arizona time, with answers to all the questions contained within it. Welcome back to reality. On the positive side, British American Tobacco had undertaken to sponsor our in-country costs in Guyana and were considering the same for Argentina and Chile also. Our cash flow situation was dire but this sponsorship provided a glimmer of hope. There were various other sponsorship bids out with companies in London, I just hoped that some of them would be successful. Finance aside, there were a thousand details to be resolved for the next three stages of the expedition not to mention the immediate problem of negotiating our way across the whole of Central America.

Having collected the vehicles and bought fresh supplies for the journey, we drove down through Arizona and into New Mexico where we camped just short of the Mexican border at a dusty, characterless town. Next day we crossed into Mexico at El Paso. It had lost any of the romantic appeal that its name might once have suggested and is now a featureless urban sprawl characterised by roadside brothels and mock saloons.

For the next week we drove hard, stopping only to camp once the sun was down each night, as we made our way south through the largely empty northern desert. Flat, wind-blown plains, bare of vegetation save small bramble thickets and tumbleweed, were relieved by similarly uninspiring, dust-covered towns and villages. They combined to form a bland, depressing landscape.

After the arid wastes and languid pace of the peasant villages, Guadalajara seemed almost incongruous with its smartly-dressed business people walking purposefully through avenues of both baroque and ultra-modern architecture. Further south the country became more green and stimulating. We passed through many more towns but they still appeared tired and run down, filled with the small shops and stores redolent of third world countries the world over.

The southern coast road wound its way tortuously in and out of every cove, passing through banana groves and wild, jungle-covered hillsides. Hundreds of scarlet crabs raised themselves on tiptoe and scurried off the road in a clatter of claws as we drove by.

Acapulco brought the first respite from the endless days of driving. We camped on a beach just to the west of the city. The campsite was shaded by tall palm trees and dominated by the surf booming in the background. The team lost no time in taking off for the promised land of bright lights, beaches and Mexican women.

After a 36-hour break we set off more or less intact save a few hearts left behind and every member of the team pledging their intention to return on their next leave. Two more days of dodging death at the hands of maniacal Mexican drivers took us to the Guatemalan border.

Driving into Guatemala, the countryside instantly became more attractive. Healthy livestock grazed in fields of lush grass alongside well tended plantations of maize, sugar cane and fruit trees. Mature deciduous trees, not unlike British hardwoods, were interspersed with tall palms. Exuberant red and yellow flowers joined the riot of orange flame trees in breaking up the prevalent rich green of the vegetation. The people appeared to be largely Mayan: small, squat Indians with jet black hair. Many wore the straw hats so favoured by Central Americans and all the men carried long machetes. I saw a number of women bearing huge loads of logs strapped to their heads by crude headbands.

We were stopped at frequent military checkpoints. On each occasion having asked a couple of basic questions and shown our papers we were allowed to proceed. We drove on for several hours through increasingly beautiful scenery. The sweeping cones of volcanos dominated the skyline. We crossed many small rivers in which people were bathing and women washing clothes as egrets waded in the shallows. Both towns and country appeared much cleaner and more organised than their Mexican equivalent.

Negotiating our four-vehicle convoy through the centre of Guatemala City was an experience not easily forgotten. Having got lost and separated on several occasions, we persuaded a man on a moped to lead us through the maze of one-way streets to the address that Colonel John Dobson, the Defence Attaché, had given us. We pulled up in a smart residential street and having talked our way past armed guards both on the street and at the house, we were welcomed by his wife, Hazel, the epitome of an English lady abroad. Over tea and cake, we heard that life in Guatemala was not as tranquil and well ordered as our pleasant drive had suggested. Murders, assassinations, kidnappings and rape were all commonplace.

Although previously widespread, the guerrilla organisations had been brought under control but attacks against the security forces still occurred and there was a high level of lawlessness and violence. Within Guatemala City, all the expatriates lived in well guarded enclaves. Movement outside the city was considered dangerous to many areas. An American schoolgirl had been kidnapped recently and another American woman had been hacked to death by a machete-wielding mob for taking a photograph of a child in a rural village. The American Embassy were strongly discouraging tourists from visiting the country.

All this underlined what we had already been told by the Foreign Office in London and further explained Colonel John's insistence that we should enter Guatemala and drive direct to his house. Having spent the night there, we were to leave the next day and drive directly to the El Salvadorian border.

With great hospitality, the Dobson's threw their house open to us. That evening they hosted a party in our honour, inviting the Embassy officials and their spouses and a Guatemalan Army Major. It was a good-natured evening over a delicious dinner. The Colour Sergeant seized on the opportunity to give his kilt an outing and was holding court with a book of poems by Robert Burns.

After a two day enforced delay whilst we made some vehicle repairs and sorted out a couple of local difficulties we found the road for El Salvador fairly easily and drove out through the city into the countryside beyond.

The road was badly potholed so it was late afternoon by the time that we reached the Salvadorian border. We were instantly besieged by touts offering their services to get us through the border formalities. A small boy grabbed our papers and dashed from desk to desk, ducking under barriers and waving them under the nose of each official in turn.

It was a lengthy trail from Customs, to Immigration, police, fumigation and other apparently spurious functionaries all of whom had to stamp our form but not, of course, without the payment of the requisite 'tax'. This procedure had to be repeated on each side of every one of the seven borders that we had to cross en route to Panama, rarely taking less than three or four hours. It was a process, the corruption and illogicalities of which, would have tested the patience of a saint.

Eventually we passed through the final barrier into El Salvador. For the first hour or so, we drove along narrow twisting country lanes. Keenly aware of El Salvador's recent troubled past, a particularly vicious civil war which had witnessed widespread torture and murders committed by right-wing death squads, massacres of civilians, blanket bombings and a torched-earth policy against villages suspected of collaboration, I imagined FMLN guerrillas waiting in ambush behind every tree but to my relief we reached the outskirts of San Salvador without incident. We met up with our Embassy contact who led us to the Salvadorean Army's Officers School where he had arranged that we could spend the night. We were shown a place to camp at the side of the football pitch.

We were woken at 4.30 a.m. by a barrage of martial music emitted by some massive speakers on the balcony of the nearest building. For the next two hours we were physically shaken by the blasting music, chanted marching songs and the stamping of feet as the cadets went through their morning drill and physical fitness regime outside our tents.

San Salvador turned out to be an even more difficult maze than Guatemala City as we crawled through endless suburbs and shanty towns. Street markets filled the narrow unmarked alleys. Stalls were piled high with watermelons, papaya, mangoes and pineapples. Pigs, donkeys and goats roamed free amongst barefooted children and gauchos on horseback.

Getting out of El Salvador was even worse than getting into it. We were physically mobbed by would-be guides all waving dubious identity cards at us and trying to wrestle us away from their competitors. Even when we had engaged the services of one for the Salvadorian formalities and another for the Honduran side, we were still constantly pestered by other guides who would not accept that they had missed their chance and by money changers waving wads of notes in our faces, shouting 'cambio'. Somehow it took almost all day to travel just over 100 miles from San Salvador to the border and then get through the formalities and into Honduras.

In the evening light the Honduran countryside looked pretty and untroubled. There were few towns or villages and the land was green and rolling with tall conical hills presided over by clusters of mudbrick buildings with hammocks swinging under the porches. Crudely fenced paddocks held cattle, horses and donkeys whilst elsewhere there were small fields of maize. A gaucho rode past with a live pig strapped across his horse's flanks and peasant farmers pushed handcarts with solid wooden wheels, laden with produce. It appeared a quiet rural scene.

The Pan American Highway dissolved into a badly rutted and potholed track until we crossed into Nicaragua where it underwent an instant transformation. We entered Nicaragua on a Sunday. Gauchos in all their finery rode by on high-stepping horses decorated with ornate saddles, large leather stirrups and an arrangement of leather tassels. I had fully anticipated towns in a state of decay with bullet-scarred buildings and bands of wandering Contras. In fact, everything looked well-ordered and in good condition. The agriculture was on a much more elaborate scale than we had seen elsewhere, the estancias appeared prosperous and the villages clean and colourful. Sadly the time constraints of our journey to Panama did not allow the opportunity to stay long enough to discover whether this was a veneer or reality.

We had decided to spend what little spare time that we had exploring some of the wildlife reserves on our way through Costa Rica. We started in Santa Rosa where we walked in a forest alive with birdsong. Flocks of green parrots flew overhead and troops of chattering white-faced monkeys moved through the jungle canopy. White-tailed deer grazed peacefully alongside huge iguanas and a whole range of exotic birds. Enormous surf, rolling in from the Pacific Ocean, pounded a beautiful beach several miles long but we were too early in the year to find the olive Ridley turtles which nest there. We camped under some huge old trees and woke to a wonderful cacophony of birds whooping, singing, trilling and warbling.

Further south we stopped again at the Quaker settlement of Monteverde located high in the cloud forest of the Cordillera Tilaran. We walked through the dimly lit, tropical forest. Cloud hung in dense pockets, wreathing the trees and luxuriant vegetation in a cool damp gloom and obscuring the view out towards Arenal volcano. Both birds and mammals remained out of sight in the forest but at night our torches picked out the implausibly large beaks of toucans at roost in the canopy and the striped fur of a coati-mundi scuttling about his business. By looking carefully under the vegetation we found all sorts of plants, insects, amphibians and reptiles: stick insects swaying on the bottom of leaves, cockroaches of all colours and sizes; great, hairy-legged orange tarantulas; minute frogs; darting glow-worms and some fascinating mushrooms that radiated a hazy, blue almost supernatural light.

We drove on through the Central Highlands to the southern Pacific coast. Coffee, sisal and banana plantations gave way to dense but attractive jungle with swaying palms and huge, vibrant tropical flowers. We spent our last night in Costa Rica in the charmingly rundown and decaying port of Golfito. The small town is squeezed into a narrow strip of land between the sea and steep, jungle-covered hillsides. A line of ancient gantries stands idle on a long, rotting pier that had once served a thriving banana industry. Wooden shacks line the single road and the centrepiece of the town is an old, rusting steam engine, a relic of the abandoned railway that had carried loads of bananas from the plantations to the port. I half expected to see Ernest Hemingway drinking at one of the street bars.

Our arrival in Panama signalled the end of our journey through Central America. It was not safe to trek through the Darien jungle into Colombia, as we had originally hoped to do, due to the presence of drugs cartels located on the Colombian side and so our road journey ended at the Panama Canal.

We consigned our vehicles to a shipping agent who had arranged to store them under guard before shipping them to Ecuador ready for the beginning of the fifth phase of the expedition which was due to start there three months later. On 29th July, at the end of our first seven months on expedition we flew via Colombia, Venezuela and Trinidad to Guyana ready to brief the Phase Four recce party.

Chapter Five

Guyana and the Mazaruni River (from Teef Men to Pork Knockers)

Richard, Mike and I stepped off the BWIA flight feeling distinctly second-hand and walked out into the bright morning sunlight at Timehri International Airport, a deceptively grand term for Guyana's main airport. Our journey from Panama had been a trail of short flights broken by delays designed to irritate and discomfort the traveller. I had spent several of the small hours of the night laid out on the floor of Trinidad airport with my kit piled in a defensive corral around me, as cleaners swept and mopped away the debris of the preceding day.

Having steered ourselves and our equipment through Customs and Immigration, we selected a taxi driver from amongst the waiting throng. We somehow forced all the kit into the taxi and jammed ourselves in amongst it, before setting off at an alarming rate in the direction of Georgetown. Our taxi driver proudly told us that the road between the airport and the capital had been improved for the visit of The Queen just six months previously, but it showed little signs of it as we veered from side to side, swerving to avoid frequent potholes and playing 'chicken' with heavily overladen minibuses.

To the left of the road we caught glimpses of the smooth brown waters of the Demerara River and to the right, fields of sugar cane, sustained by an antiquated system of irrigation ditches, stretched away into the distance. Children played outside wooden buildings, some of which were raised up on stilts.

After a knuckle-clenching half hour, we sped into the outskirts of Georgetown, a bustling mayhem of street markets, wandering animals and hooting taxis. Old ladies in plastic hats shopped from stalls piled high with pineapples, coconuts, mangoes and other tropical produce. Other stalls sold pirated cassettes, clothing, electrical appliances and all manner of kitsch ornaments. There was a blend of cultures: Rastafarians mingled with negroes and a large number of East Indians who appeared to have a monopoly on the commerce if the names

on the shop fronts, hoardings and the sides of passing lorries were anything to go by.

The scene was rich in colour, sound and smell; at times overpoweringly so, when we passed a dead dog floating in the open sewers. The town had a general air of decrepitude. Paint flaked off rotting wooden buildings which at their best looked rundown and at their worst, were downright dangerous.

By a series of misadventures we found our way to the humble but welcoming Rockies Hotel in one of the less salubrious parts of Georgetown. Our Afro-Caribbean hosts were Jennifer, who beamed a brilliant white smile beneath her wreath of yellow plastic curlers, and Stretch, her lumbering giant of a husband. Having settled us into our rooms and provided beers from a small fridge that worked whenever there were not power cuts, Jennifer warned us about 'Teef men' and 'choke'n rob gangs' that operated after dark in the area around the town towards Stabroek Market.

After a much needed siesta we went for a walk to get our bearings. Tree-lined avenues, by turn dry and dusty or steaming and humid after the short but violent tropical downpours, lead towards the centre. Loud music emanated from busy cafes in the main street. Large ornamental gardens adorned with palm trees, Victorian pavilions and lily-covered ponds that once were the pride of the town, still provide a blaze of colour and a welcome respite from the hustling street sellers and suicidal taxi drivers.

The façades of many of the fine old colonial buildings are now crumbling but stand as a testament to Georgetown's former glory. In front of the Courthouse building is a statue of Queen Victoria, or Jin Jin as she was known in the patois of the slaves. She stands proudly, crowned and bearing a sceptre, but in a poor state of repair and with one hand missing she seems to epitomise the decay of this Commonwealth country.

As it was a Sunday, people were flocking to the sea wall. Some promenaded in their Sunday best, others

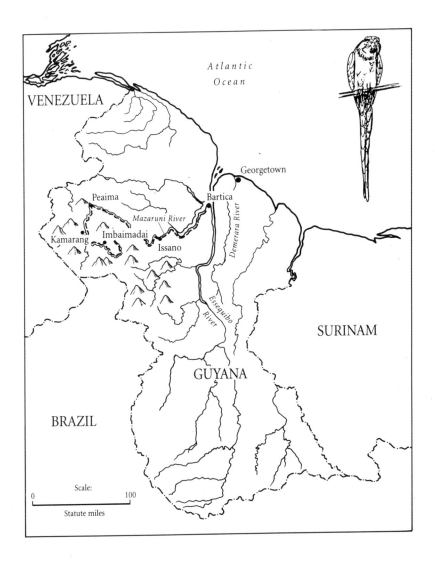

Phase 4 – Guyana

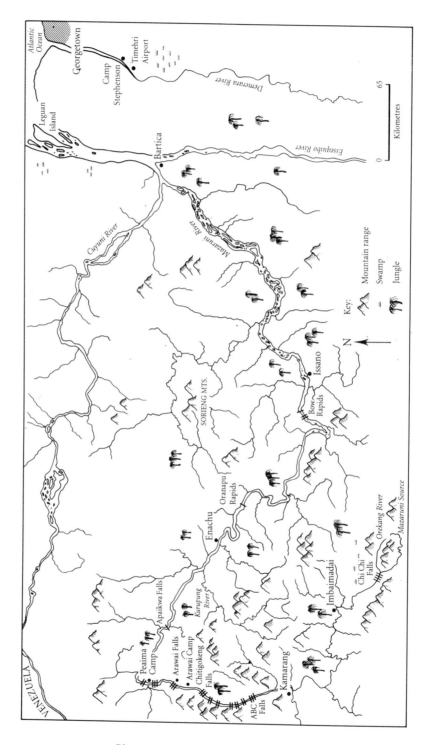

Phase 4 – Mazaruni River, Guyana

stood chatting in groups, whilst many sat in couples looking out over the sea. Although dilapidated, Georgetown has a happy, characterful soul.

Marginally smaller than Great Britain, Guyana has a population of under one million people, the vast majority of whom live either in Georgetown or along the coastal strip. Less than half of one percent of the country is cultivated. The remainder is either savannah or dense jungle. We had elected to try and find the source of the Mazaruni River which was located deep in the Pakaraima Mountains in the west of the country and to trace the river, 380 miles through the jungle until it joined the Essequibo River. From there we would continue on down to the sea and around the coast to Georgetown. By design, this journey was to take us to one of the remotest and most inaccessible regions of the country. Everything that we had read about Guyana and the Mazaruni region in particular, promised a true old-fashioned adventure.

Although researching the Mazaruni had not proved to be at all easy, we had managed to piece together enough information to give us a rough idea of the problems associated with each stage of our proposed journey. Access to the region was only practicable by flying into one of the Amerindian villages towards the upper end of the river, each of which had bush strips. From there on, all progress into the interior would be by boat or on foot. Above the top village, Imbaimadai, the river was interrupted by the huge Chi Chi Falls. We would have to portage all our kit around this substantial barrier continuing on towards the source as far as possible by boat and completing the journey on foot, or follow one of the other small rivers that led off into the jungle to their head and then cut over land to the head of the Mazaruni.

Information on this ground was almost non-existent but all the indications were that it would be extremely difficult. Opinion on how much time we should allow to reach the source varied greatly. This had a considerable impact on the logistics required to support us: more time required more rations and fuel, but they in turn required bigger boats and more effort during portages.

Further downstream from Imbaimadai, the river is flat for a stage and then disappears for roughly twenty miles into a narrow gorge where it tumbles down a succession of waterfalls. No-one knew whether it was possible either to shoot these falls or to portage around them within the gorge. Below the Chutes, the river becomes calm again before being split into a maze of channels by large numbers of islands. Many of these channels are unsafe due to rapids and waterfalls and navigation through them requires detailed local knowledge. Even when we finally reached the Essequibo our troubles would not be over as the mouth of the Essequibo had a nasty reputation for strong currents and rip tides which could make rough going and the coast around to Georgetown was also susceptible to storms and high waves.

For the previous three months Lieutenant David Avis had been beavering away in the London office trying to put together a viable operational plan which would in turn produce an equally detailed logistic requirement for Andrew Phasey to fulfil. However, despite poring over all of the limited information that he had managed to amass, there were a large number of fundamental questions that still needed to be answered before we would be ready to start.

Answers to some of the questions, such as flow rates on the river, strengths of currents, grading of rapids and so on, simply were not available. As a result they had had to take some best-guess decisions regarding the equipment and rations that we would need. Taking all these difficulties into consideration, I had decided, that we must allow adequate time in Guyana for a proper recce. Both of the officers who were due to take part in the phase, David Avis and Lieutenant James Geddes were to come out for the recce, as was Andrew Phasey bringing with him Sergeant Mark Jordan, his clerk from the office in London.

One of the biggest areas of concern for David and Andrew had been the type and design of boats that we required. We expected to have to negotiate smooth and fast running water, both upstream and down, shoot rapids and have craft that we could portage around large waterfalls. This was a demanding set of requirements that vexed them for some time, particularly in the absence of the data on water conditions that the manufacturers kept asking for or an accurate idea of the weights that the boats needed to be capable of carrying.

Due to the length of time required to ship all the equipment from England to get it in place ready for the arrival of the team, it was not possible to wait until after the recce and so they had done their best with the information that they had. Sizeable safety margins had been incorporated where possible and they had purchased two rubber workboats powered by 25-horsepower outboard engines, and four inflatable canoes. They worked with Chris Burrows of Eurocraft, the manufacturers of the canoes, to design a frame to fit over two of the canoes and support an outboard engine, thereby turning them into a powered catamaran. The frame had to be capable of being dismantled and used as a stretcher to carry the heavy outboard.

On arrival, we set about meeting the key agencies with whom we were to work. The first of these was the British High Commission where we established an expedition office. We were accorded every possible assistance by David Johnson, the High Commissioner and all his staff. Secondly, we went to see Brigadier Jo Singh, the head of the Guyanese Defence Force. A keen supporter of expeditions, having taken part in many himself and a great advocate of cross-national ventures, Jo Singh welcomed us to his office. He offered whatever help he, or the GDF, could provide. He is an extremely well respected man with influence far beyond the confines of the country's Defence Force.

It rapidly became apparent that his name carried enormous weight and that he had almost instant access to any government minister. He was very keen that members of the GDF should take part in the expedition and, to that end, we agreed that we would be accompanied by an officer and two non-commissioned officers from their Special Forces Squadron and one more Staff Sergeant who was a qualified and experienced medic.

Brigadier Singh had also offered the use of one of the GDF's barracks as a training and logistic support base for the expedition which we had accepted with alacrity. There were many more aspects of their support such as radio frequencies and access to their manned radio nets which we discussed. He questioned us on our plan in detail and expressed his concern that we should carry snake anti-venom with us.

Having obtained all the information that we could from the GDF, we set about tracing other organisations that might have local knowledge of the Mazaruni. Besides the Army and some missionary and Aid agencies working in the Amerindian villages, the only other organisations with an interest in this remote region were the mining corporations.

The Mazaruni had relatively rich gold deposits. These were tapped on a small scale by illegal gold miners or 'pork knockers' who set up on the rivers edge with shovels and sluices, and by larger organisations operating both dredges and land-based operations. The biggest of these companies was MC Correia. We found their colourful head mining surveyor, Rafael Swiecki, in the bar of the Tower Hotel.

Amidst a host of unlikely stories, Rafael had a lot of useful tips and local knowledge. He warned us that the ground surrounding the headwaters of the Mazaruni, and particularly that to the north which we were proposing to cross from the Upper Partang River, was a nightmare of broken ground carved up by deep gashes in the earth. These looked like larval crevasses and would make our progress terribly slow, if not impossible. We went to his office the next day to look at one of the very few sets of 1:50,000 maps of the region in existence. Through Rafael's accounts of his explorations searching for minerals and scrutinising a series of jealously-guarded aerial photographs through a stereoscope, we were able to build up a better idea of the terrain. It was not a particularly prepossessing picture, but forewarned was forearmed.

Richard and I went for meetings with several of the Government Ministers, accompanied either by the High Commissioner or Brigadier Singh, to get the requisite permits to enter the interior and pass through regions and villages inhabited by Amerindians. Meanwhile, Mike was visiting Georgetown's two hospitals and a number of the civilian air charter companies trying to piece together a workable Casualty Evacuation Procedure in case anyone became seriously ill or was injured when we were in the jungle. It had become clear that the GDF had no workable aircraft in operation to help us. Their two helicopters, long since obsolete Russian models, were rusting, abandoned up at Timehri and otherwise all their air movement was done by charter. This and the fact that there were no other helicopters operating in the country made CASEVAC a serious concern.

The time programmed for the recce also meant that after seven months of being constantly on the go, those of us on the permanent cadre could take a break. Colour Sergeant McKeown had flown back to England from Panama to spend a short leave with his wife and child before coming back out to Guyana to help us get ready. Corporal Steggles had also flown back for some leave with his fiancée and would then replace Sergeant Jordan in the London office for this phase. By the time that I had completed all the initial round of meetings and talked at length with David and Andrew, we had built up the basis of a workable plan. Using this as a framework, I briefed the recce team on their tasks and how I wanted things organised and then left them to it. Louie had flown out to Guyana to join me and now together with Richard and Mike, we all flew to Barbados for a long-awaited and eagerly anticipated period of leave.

Richard and Mike rented an apartment and spent their time scuba diving and fantasizing about the girls that they saw on the beaches. Louie and I were extremely fortunate to have an open invitation from her godmother and her husband to stay in their house. It was wonderful to be together and for the first time since I could remember I was able to relax and leave the expedition to its own devices.

We swam in the sea, sunbathed, explored the island in the car which had been kindly lent to us and gorged ourselves on fresh food and good drink. The Grahame's were wonderful hosts: kind, generous and amusing and allowed us our own space. If there is a heaven, it was not far away.

I returned to Guyana much refreshed and ready to get back to the fray. The recce team had been busy in my absence. Andrew had tracked down our sea freight container, cleared it though Customs, moved it to a safe storage area which he had found and begun unpacking the kit. He had talked to all the air charter companies and negotiated the best possible deal to cover our outload to the jungle. He had flown out to look at two of the Amerindian villages and had prepared a report on their comparative suitability as our Forward Operating Base. He had also spent a considerable amount of time sorting out the logistics to support our training camp and finding suppliers to source the food that we needed. Provisions of all kinds, with the exception of staple foods, were in extremely short supply in the shops and orders had to be placed well in advance.

David and James had chartered a light aircraft and conducted an aerial recce of the route. This had revealed a number of interesting pieces of information. From the air, the top end of the Mazaruni had looked relatively smooth and broad and they thought that we could use boats to get most of the way to the source. They had also spotted a number of savannah areas which they thought would give us good going and enable us to make up any time that we lost fighting our way through the jungle. Lower down the river, they had flown over the chutes. They showed me video footage that they had shot of the waterfalls.

David was sure that we could shoot the falls in our boats. Looking at the video, I was far from convinced. The river was channelled into a powerful white torrent that plummeted down long, steep rapids. Looking at the rapids and falls from above it was difficult to estimate just how severe this water would be, but I was sure that the aerial perspective made it appear easier than it really was. Added to that, once in the gorge, there would be no escape.

All the local advice was against attempting to raft through the Chutes but David was adamant that we should. As he had done the majority of planning for the phase, I thought it only fair to give him the chance to test his theory, but before I was prepared to risk the lives of the team I insisted that he should use the time whilst the rest of us were training to go and do a ground recce.

There were many details to tie up, but with each of us working to sort out our respective areas of responsibility we were ready to receive the team when they arrived at the beginning of September. The day before they arrived we moved out to Timehri to occupy our temporary training base in Camp Stephenson. We were allocated the top half of the Special Forces Squadron's barrack block for accommodation and another deserted barrack block to use as a classroom.

The accommodation was extremely spartan with old iron beds, lockers that were infested with cockroaches, rats the size of cats running around the rafters and ablutions that were dangerously insanitary. However it was to be our home for a week of acclimatisation, training and logistic preparation and being both dry and secure, we were grateful for it.

For the next week we had a full programme as we tried to cram in as much knowledge and skills training as we could. This concentrated on orientation to the environment and familiarisation with all the specialist equipment that we would be using. James Geddes took everyone through the correct assembly and loading of workboats, inflatable canoes and the catamaran. Sergeant Nigel Nettlefield and Corporal John Pozzi, our two mechanics, covered the handling and maintenance of outboard engines. We then conducted boat handling training on the Demerara River. Sergeant Pete Griffith taught lessons in the use of our High Frequency radios, Global Positioning System and then the techniques of crossing rivers. I took groups through rope handling, belays, pulley systems and abseiling, in anticipation of any major waterfalls that we might need to negotiate. Mike conducted classes in First Aid, personal hygiene in a jungle environment and recognition of dangerous snakes, scorpions, poisonous plants and likely illnesses.

The jungle is an inherently unhealthy environment. Mike's research had revealed a whole variety of potential problems that we needed to be aware of, ranging from dehydration and fungal infections, to four types of venomous snake, a large collection of insect-borne diseases such as malaria, dengue fever and leishmaniasis, not to mention wild pigs, piranha, electric eels and vampire bats that carry rabies.

Sergeant Griffith was our jungle instructor. As fellow Welsh Guardsmen, we had met several times in the past although we had never worked together. I was well aware of his considerable jungle experience and reputation for prodigious strength. For his size, he was a surprisingly quiet, soft-spoken man. I quickly found him easy and enjoyable to work with. He had a most unassuming manner but underneath this a wealth of sound, well thought out, constructive advice which helped me in the final stages of the planning and leant confidence to everyone on the team.

Towards the end of the training week he split the team into two groups and took each half out into the nearby jungle on a 24-hour orientation exercise. For the first time we packed our rucksacks with hammocks, mosquito nets, ponchos, spare clothing, mosquito repellant, machetes, water bottles, cookers and various survival items and then set off on a route selected from the map.

The Guyanese jungle rapidly dispelled any illusions about the ease of movement that we were going to find. We found ourselves forcing our way through dense undergrowth, clambering over deadfall and wading through swamps and along rivers. We were perpetually soaked either from sweat or downpours.

Having reached a dry patch of land towards the end of the day, we set up camp. This involved each person selecting two strong trees, roughly eight feet apart and clearing the undergrowth from between them with their machete. We then slung our hammocks and suspended mosquito nets and ponchos over the top. This all had to be arranged so that when you climbed gingerly into your hammock and it sank down under your weight, they all worked in harmony to keep you off the ground, free of insects and dry.

We turned on the radio and having erected an antenna by hauling a carefully calculated length of electrical wire up into a nearby tree and angling it towards the receiving station, we made the evening radio check. Our safety in the jungle relied on high frequency signalling which, due to inconsistent atmospheric conditions, can be a most uncertain science, regarded as a black art and avoided like the plague by the majority of soldiers. It was vital that we should not only overcome this prejudice but that we should become proficient regardless of the local difficulties or the amount of time that it took to establish communications. Having made contact with the GDF Operations Room, we cooked up our supper. It was pitch dark by 6.30 p.m.

While the second group underwent their orientation exercise, I worked on the final details of the plan. A signals plan including radio schedules, frequencies, call signs, distress signals and routine to be adopted if you failed to make communication, had to be written as did a CASEVAC Plan detailing the actions to be taken by each link in the chain.

We had done our best to cover every eventuality and had even purchased specialist Ground to Air radios with which we would be able to alert any aircraft flying overhead if the need arose. Flares, personal-locater beacons, signalling mirrors, helicopter marker panels and personal survival kits completed our safety equipment inventory.

Andrew had been working flat out to prepare all the equipment for outload. Each individual item had been weighed and manifested. He had calculated that we needed five Skyvan flights, each capable of carrying 3,200 lb of passengers and cargo, to get us out to our Forward Operating Base. As on so many occasions, I was deeply grateful for his calm efficiency and ability to think through practical situations and spot potential problems in the making.

The plan had been refined, certainly as far as the initial deployment and quest for the source of the Mazaruni were concerned. We had decided to use Imbaimadai, the furthest upstream Amerindian village as our Forward Operating Base. We would maintain a small admin party there to man the radio, guard the equipment and supplies and be in position to react to any emergencies. The remainder of us would move upstream by boat, portage around the Chi Chi Falls and then split into two groups. I was to lead a walking party of twelve men to follow the Orekang River towards its headwaters and then cut across the high feature that separated the Orekang from the Mazaruni River. Richard was to continue with eight men and the four inflatable canoes, using the catamaran as far up the Mazaruni as he could get and then continue either by paddling the canoes, or on foot, as he saw best at the time, to meet us at a pre-arranged rendezvous point. They were to carry a ration re-supply for us up to the RV. It was vital that we maintained communications so that we could monitor each other's progress and react if either group found themselves unable to make it across the terrain. We expected to take roughly a week to walk to the source and thus, constrained by the amount of rations that we could physically carry, there was a key cut-off point for us to turn back if Richard and his group could not get there to meet us.

I had given the composition of these various groups some careful thought. Each one had its vital role to play. Andrew would run the base at Imbaimadai assisted by Sergeant Jordan but he needed two others to help him, at least one of whom needed to be a competent boat handler and mechanic in case we needed to call for help from the workboats that were to remain there. The other two groups needed a fair and sensible distribution of signallers, medics, boat handlers and jungle specialists. I reckoned that the walking party's lot would be considerably harder and so selected the more robust members of the team for that. Sergeant Griffith would come with me, as would Colour Sergeant McKeown. When the

going gets tough there is nothing like a bit of age and experience to provide the motivation and stamina required to get a team through. Two members of the GDF would go with each group. The remainder were split between the two groups according to their strengths and weaknesses.

The Skyvan turned out to be an ugly, rectangular-bodied flying beast capable of carrying up to twelve of us with our personal equipment or a substantial amount of our freight. We took off after a very short distance and wheeled away from Georgetown. I craned to see the ground beneath us through a small porthole. Neat rectangular fields of sugar cane stretched for miles either side of the roads emanating from the capital. From the air I could see that they were far more extensive than I had previously realised.

Further from Georgetown the sugar cane fields gave way to jungle: miles and miles of it and all dead flat. We flew over the Essequibo and got a feel for the scale of this massive river which was eighteen miles across at its mouth. Following the river upstream, we flew over Bartica and the confluence with the Mazaruni River. The Mazaruni snaked its way back into the jungle, the black water of the river and its tributaries, some of them substantial rivers in their own right, cutting distinct trails through the green carpet of vegetation. Patches of cloud obscured my view but later I could see great fortresses of sheer-sided rock rising out of the jungle canopy. Cliffs of bare rock towered over the surrounding lowlands, guarding access to high plateaus. It was both spectacular and daunting scenery. After an hour or so Imbaimadai hove into view: a small collection of huts atop a bare knoll on a bend in the Mazaruni.

We dropped quickly and almost before we knew it, we were taxiing up the dirt runway. Those members of the expedition who had flown ahead on earlier flights were waiting for us and willing hands grabbed all the kit. No sooner were we off the plane, than it turned around, taxied up the runway and took off once again to go back for the next load of equipment. We carried our kit to a brightly painted corrugated iron hut surrounded by a small fenced garden. Andrew Phasey had negotiated the use of this hut as our base from its characterful owner, a grey-haired negro called Robert Alfred. It had been gaudily painted inside for its intended role as a disco but it had long since ceased to be used as such.

Having stowed my kit inside the hut I set off to look around the village. The tour did not take long. There were three or four very small stores selling basic necessities, most of which doubled as bars in the evening; a rustic disco; a number of humble wooden or corrugated iron dwellings and a miners' compound. In the centre of the village, a flagpole stood outside the police post. A track lead through the village down to the edge of the Mazaruni. The river was about an hundred yards across, flowing fast between jungle-covered banks. The water was so black that when you swam in it, any part of your body that dropped below the surface was totally hidden.

The occupants of Imbaimadai were a curious mixture of Amerindians and negroes. The Amerindians largely kept themselves to themselves and lived by hunting in the jungle or running the stores. The negroes were almost all miners who either worked for the mining company which owned the village's compound or joined the teams of pork knockers. They were 'coastlanders' who came into the interior for months at a time to earn whatever money they could to send back to their families.

The second industry of the village was reputed to be prostitution. What the girls lacked in looks, they certainly made up for in their raucous and uncompromising language. No doubt with each month in the jungle and a belly full of high wine they became more attractive! Night and day loud reggae music blared out from one or more of the stores or bars and no matter that most of the inhabitants were living a life of abject poverty, somehow alcohol and women were always available. It was an odd place, an isolated pocket of semi-civilisation tucked away in the jungle.

We sent two of the boats down river to collect Richard and David Avis who had completed their ground reconnaissance of the Chutes. When they returned they confirmed that it would be totally unfeasible to try and shoot the huge waterfalls that lay concealed in the gorge. Anyone trying to do so, from what they had seen, would surely kill themselves. They had tried to follow the course of the river within the gorge but rapidly found that the terrain was almost impossible to move through with vertical rock walls and constricting steep slopes covered in impenetrable jungle. They

had however, made contact with various of the mining camps along the way who had all offered help either with accommodation or boats to move us along sections of the river when we did not plan to have our own boats.

The proximity of our departure certainly concentrated all our minds as we co-ordinated the last details of the plan: What should we do in case of a total communications breakdown? How long should the boat party wait if the walking party did not turn up? What should the walking party do if they arrived at the RV to find that the boat party had been unable to get that far up the river and thus there was no food and no transport downstream? These and an hundred other equally vital questions all had to be considered and a clear plan established to cope with all contingencies in case we found that we could not talk to each other.

On the morning of our departure we got up at 4.30 a.m., packed the last items of our equipment into our rucksacks, bolted a quick breakfast and headed down to the river bank. The boats were already in the water. We loaded eight men into each of the two workboats, the other eight men onto the catamaran, and all of the kit onto the remaining two inflatable canoes which were towed by the workboats. With little ceremony, watched only by Andrew Phasey, we set off up river as dawn was breaking.

We had to go about twenty miles upstream to reach the bottom of the Chi Chi Falls. Heavily laden as we were, we made slow but steady progress. The jungle formed a seemingly solid wall either side of the river. We passed a couple of pork knockers' camps; tattered plastic sheeting was stretched over a framework of sticks to provide some cover over the meanest sleeping quarters and, more importantly, some form of sluice powered by a portable generator. We had to manoeuvre the boats under the securing lines of a large dredge that was tethered in the centre of the stream. Further on we passed a few small Amerindian settlements. Barefooted children ran out from grass-roofed huts to wave at us as we motored by. But for the most part, the jungle was deserted.

About halfway to our destination we entered a deep gorge with sheer cliffs rising several hundred feet up on both sides a short way back from the river's edge. The river continued to twist and turn, snaking its way back into the rainforest. A rich yellow light suffused the scene giving it a gentle, welcoming aspect, relieving the otherwise rather oppressive feel of the jungle. After three and a half hours of motoring we pulled into a tiny side creek. The falls were still hidden round the next bend but we could hear them thundering in the background.

The Chi Chi Falls were not a single waterfall but a sequence of major rapids and waterfalls spread over several miles. From the creek where we had stopped, a barely distinguishable trail led off into the jungle towards the top of the falls. The two workboats were to head back to Imbaimadai, but everything else, our rucksacks, the four inflatable canoes, catamaran frame and outboard engine, radios, fuel and ration re-supply all had to be portaged around to the top landing.

Having listened to the descriptions of this trail from some of the Amerindians at Imbaimadai and looked at my map, I had decided to split the portage into two halves. Leaving a couple of people behind to dissemble the catamaran and pack away the canoes, the remainder of us set off with our first load. With all of our kit and nine days rations, our rucksacks weighed around eighty pounds. Whilst we remained in the jungle it was hot and humid and we sweated freely.

After a brief relatively easy-angled stage, the track led up a long and extremely steep hill for an hour. We hauled ourselves up using tree trunks and protruding roots. It was hot, hard work. Above, we emerged into an area of sparse scrub and largely bare rock. Without the cover of the canopy, the sun's direct rays bore into us. The heat was debilitating. We stopped at a small stream to refill our water bottles and soak our bush hats to help us cool down. Far below us, in the gorge, we could see a number of major rapids and a beautiful, tiered waterfall coming in from a side valley. We pressed on.

After three hours we came to a small wood where I had decided that we would make our camp. We slung our hammocks, relinquished our loads and after a short break, turned around and headed back down the trail to collect our second loads. These were, on the whole, even heavier than the first loads and a great deal more uncomfortable to carry: boxes of rations for ten men, jerrycans of fuel, four inflatable canoes each weighing eighty-six pounds and, worst of all, the outboard engine borne

on the catamaran frame which weighed around one hundred and forty pounds.

With little enthusiasm, we hauled these loads on and set off again. It was clearly going to take a great effort to get the heavy loads and particularly the catamaran and outboard engine up the long, steep slope. Sergeant Griffith rushed up and down the line urging, cajoling, encouraging and throwing his considerable strength at the heaviest tasks. The remainder of us were swept up in this indomitable barrage and the catamaran frame moved up the slope, pushed on by relays of hands already bearing large loads, as if in a stretcher race from our basic training days.

Despite the intense effort and pouring sweat, it was great to see everyone in the team putting everything that they had into the task. We drank water bottle after water bottle, careful to add Puritabs to each fresh lot, in an attempt to keep ourselves adequately hydrated. Even so the heat and physical strain left most people tired and light-headed by the end of the day.

With a couple of exceptions, everyone on the team had acquitted themselves well and so it was with a certain amount of satisfaction at a job well done that in the evening people sat around chatting and drinking cups of tea before the insects drove us to seek the refuge of our hammocks and mosquito nets. I lay awake listening to the chorus of frogs and crickets chirruping away.

We got up as it became light. Heavy mist sat in pockets over the surrounding country. I had woken at one point in the night to find myself really quite cold and had pulled my thin blanket tight around me. As the mist slowly began to clear, we had commanding views over the river valley and away to the mountains in the distance. The first part of the day was spent shuttling all the equipment on to the top landing. The route was not as steep as it had been the day before, although there were some awkward sections where we had to negotiate the catamaran frame over a log that bridged a broad stream or through some tight undergrowth.

Once we had completed the double shuttle, we inflated the boats and made up the catamaran. We launched them into the water just sixty yards above the top fall and then began the process of ferrying those of us on the walking party across the river. There was the usual joshing and ribaldry as the two parties split. Richard and I wished each other luck and I took my turn on the catamaran ferry to the other side of the river. As we motored out into the stream I called back over my shoulder, 'Be there!'

We both knew the importance of the boat party making it up to the RV at the top of the Mazaruni to meet those of us who were walking.

Having got our kit sorted out and seen the boat party take off upstream, the twelve of us in the walking party shouldered our loads and turned our backs to the Mazaruni. We took the first of many compass bearings from the map and headed north to join up with the Orekang River. A short distance from the river we came to a cleared bush airstrip. We knew from the aerial recce that there was an old abandoned miners' camp a little further ahead at the lower end of the Orekang and I presumed that this airstrip had been cut out to service it in its day. It was still in reasonable condition and I made a mental note that it would do if we needed to call in an aircraft for any reason.

We picked our way through the scrub and bushes to the north of the airstrip until we came to the miners' camp. It had long since been abandoned, there was no covering on the huts and the poles which made up the frames of them were blanched and rotting. We found a wild pineapple bush which provided some welcome, if rather stringy fruit. After pressing on a bit further we stopped beside a small stream. Having set up camp we established radio communication with Andrew at Imbaimadai.

The following day we continued along the faintest of tracks that took us through the jungle, roughly parallel to the east bank of the Orekang, and in the right general direction. I presumed that it was an old Amerindian hunting trail. In places it was barely discernible and we had to cast around to find it. You tended to feel the path rather than see it in the gloom of the jungle as you followed the line of least resistance through the undergrowth.

After a while the path disappeared and with it our last trace of the outside world. From then on it was map and compass work all the way. In places we had to physically push our way through the jungle to bludgeon a path through the dense undergrowth. We emerged at an area marked 'savannah' on the map. It was covered in low bushes whose waxy rosettes and sharp pointed leaves looked not unlike a form of yucca plant.

In the jungle it had been dark and relatively cool but out on the savannah it was mercilessly hot.

We took a bearing, crossed the savannah and piled through the next section of jungle beyond. It was very tight and densely vegetated. We had to literally fight our way through, scrambling over and under deadfall, between bushes and avoiding holes and bogs. There were traps everywhere: roots, concealed holes, razor-sharp leaves and trees covered in long, savage thorns that we generically named Bastard Trees. Every few minutes you would hear a loud curse as someone tripped and grabbed a Bastard Tree by accident to steady themselves.

We came out of the jungle into a much larger area of savannah. Clearly identifiable from the air and generally accurately marked on the maps, we had assumed that these savannahs would offer us much better going than we would find in the jungle. That myth was quickly shattered when we found that in many cases the yucca plants formed a thin carpet over a deep bog. Beneath the undulating surface there was thick glutinous mud up to thigh or even waist depth. With heavy rucksacks on it was absolutely exhausting.

Nerves became strained as you did not know whether the next step was going to see you sink up to your waist, driven down by the weight of your pack. When this happened it took all of your strength to force your other leg out in front of you and to haul yourself up again, only to repeat the whole process a couple of steps later. In the worst areas it was almost impossible to make any progress.

For Mike, who was carrying his medical equipment and supplies on top of his normal load, and whoever was carrying the radio, it was shattering. At times they became so completely stuck that it took several others to haul them out. There was a great temptation to lose your temper but as this just increased the annoyance, not least when everyone else laughed at some outburst of frustration, most people treated it as a joke in bad taste and laughed at their own helplessness.

When we eventually reached the far side of the clearing we stopped for a brew. Once we had collected our thoughts, we took another bearing and ploughed on. Now, the jungle too became a nightmare. It was as tight as anything we had encountered so far but was underlain with swamp which only added to the difficulties of moving through it. We waded along up to our thighs in murky, stinking water, clambering over, round and through deadfall. Wherever one of the larger trees had fallen over, it brought all of the surrounding canopy and undergrowth down with it, forming an impenetrable barrier of up to one hundred feet in diameter.

I took my turn carrying the radio. The extra weight made a most noticeable and unwelcome addition to what were already huge and awkward loads. I found myself terribly unsteady and had to take very measured paces. For the remainder of the day we alternated between swamped savannah and dense jungle. By 4 p.m. everyone was bushed so we found the first available dry patch of ground and made camp. As had become routine, Sergeant Griffith, Corporal of Horse Gallagher, Corporal Bullock and I went off to find an opening in the jungle where we could set up the radio and try and get a GPS reading. We had to cut down a lot of bush to clear an unobstructed path for the antenna. We could not raise either the boat party or Imbaimadai on the radio but managed to reach the GDF Operations Room in Georgetown to whom, after several attempts, we managed to pass our location. It had been a hard day and everyone was tired but we had made some ground and anyway, no one had ever said that it would be easy!

For the next two days we continued to shadow the Orekang River, moving roughly eastwards towards its source. We left the 'savannahs' behind us and carried on pressing our way through extremely dense jungle. Visibility was often little more than ten yards and navigation was a slow, deliberate affair as we were continually forced off our compass bearing by deadfall. The limitations of our maps made themselves rapidly apparent. Streams materialised where none appeared on the maps and other features that we selected from the maps as confirmatory points to which we navigated, were not there when we reached the given map reference.

Corporal Bob Bullock was our long-suffering GPS operator and was frequently to be seen wading out into the middle of wide stretches of the river or clambering up to the top branches of trees to try and get a clear view of the sky. A big, strong man, with a generally easy-going disposition, he took everything in his stride. He was older than

most of his peers which served only to confirm the hint of roguishness in his eyes. Despite this, I noticed that he would often offer to help the younger or weaker members of the team if he saw that they were struggling with a heavy load and frequently carried the radio for much longer than his due time. He came from the East End of London and had a cockney's quick wit which made him excellent company.

Mid-morning on the first day we stopped for the morning radio schedule. We boomed through both to Imbaimadai and the boat party. Richard told me that they too were finding the conditions a lot more difficult than the recce had suggested. Ever since we had first arrived at Imbaimadai, the level of the river had been dropping steadily; it was now down by about twelve feet. The result of this was to reveal many more rapids, small waterfalls and sunken obstacles. They had already had to abandon the catamaran due to the narrowness of the river. They had cached the frame and the outboard and were now paddling up stream in the four inflatable canoes.

They still had at least twenty miles to go to the RV and he had been told by some Amerindians that there were larger falls ahead. His news brought two reactions from our group, firstly general amusement at the thought that they were having to graft too and secondly, a genuine concern that they might not be able to make it to the RV with our rations.

We pushed on all day but by the time we stopped to camp for the evening, we had only made a little over two miles progress as the crow flies. Each short distance gained on the map was earned at the cost of a great deal of effort and sweat. Our twelve-man group was working well together and despite the rigours of the journey and the privations of living in the jungle, I never heard anyone complain.

Our daily routine was well established. Sergeant Griffith woke us as the very first rays of light penetrated the canopy and we were off, having breakfasted and packed up camp, within an hour. We worked hard throughout the day, maintaining as good a pace as we could, stopping for ten minutes in every hour to rest, with a longer stop to brew up at lunchtime. He was careful not to overface individuals and never to force the pace beyond the ability of those whose turn it was to carry the heavy loads.

Once we had stopped for the night and the GPS reading had been taken and radio calls made, we each set to our personal administration. I had learnt to my cost the implications of taking any short cuts when setting up my hammock; if it was not pitched exactly level, either you spent the entire night trying to deny the laws of gravity, or you were invaded by insects, or worse still rained on.

The relief from the heavy loads was something that we all looked forward to, as was the chance for a hot cup of tea and the chance to put on dry clothing. Wetness was a perpetual state either through rain, wading through rivers, or sweat, so much so that after a while you barely noticed it. But by evening the skin of our feet would be white and puckered and it was important to wash carefully whenever we could, dry off and powder our bodies before putting on dry clothes for the night to prevent skin infections setting in. The wet clothes were secured in a plastic bag overnight to keep them away from ants and other insects. Damp and soaked in sweat and grime, they festered and fermented.

Having got as comfortable as possible, we cooked up our boil-in-the-bag rations, savouring every bit of the reduced ration packs that we had been able to carry. I would then sit on a plastic sheet on the ground writing my diary by the light of a sputtering candle. It was dark by 6 p.m., an intense blackness enhanced by the canopy which cut out any light from the moon or the stars. Sometimes we would hear the mooing of a tapir or the wolf whistle of a particularly cheeky jungle fowl but for the most part there was just the whining of mosquitos, the clicking of crickets and the croaking of frogs.

Getting back into wet clothes each morning became increasingly unpleasant as with each passing day they became progressively more rank. Each item stank but somehow it was the clamminess of pulling on wet socks that was the absolute worst.

The further up the Orekang River we went, the thicker the jungle became. Near to the river it was almost impenetrable with deadfall everywhere. When the river flowed in the direction that we were trying to move, it was often easier to wade up the river clambering over or under all of the fallen trees up to our waists in water rather than try to battle through the thickets either side.

However, as the river took a tortuous route, twisting and turning around many long sweeping bends, at times we had no choice but to break away from it and march on a bearing through the jungle. Everything on the jungle floor was rotting and there were deep holes concealed beneath the leaf detritus and roots. Most aggravating of all were the vines, many of them no more than an eighth of an inch thick, but which snagged your feet or worse the top of your rucksack. If you had just fought your way over a rough patch of fallen branches, there was nothing more irritating or energy sapping than being hauled backwards by the top of your pack.

When the deadfall was at its thickest our progress was more a succession of gymnastics than a trek. Balancing along the trunk of a fallen tree for the umpteenth time that day, desperately trying not to be overbalanced by his huge rucksack, Mike suddenly exploded: 'If I had wanted to be an acrobat I would have joined a fucking circus!'

Sergeant Griffith's dry rejoinder echoed up the line. 'The sooner they cut the South American rain forest down the better. England used to be covered in forest and cutting it down hasn't done us any harm!' It was not not exactly the most ecologically friendly of sentiments but typical soldiers humour.

At the radio call that morning, Richard told me that they had made four portages so far and with more rapids ahead he was not sure if they could take the boats much further. He was still confident that they could make it to the RV even if they had to complete the last stage on foot.

We shut down the radio and marched on again another 500 yards to a stream junction. It was my turn to carry the radio and by the time that I got there I was pouring sweat from every pore. Under normal circumstances you would not give that short a distance a second thought and would expect to walk it in six minutes. In the jungle it could take an hour of concentrated and determined effort.

We existed in a world of shades of green and brown with glimpses of blue sky and white clouds. Working in camouflaged jungle clothing we blended into the background and it was very easy even at short distances to lose sight of the person in front. The only change in this curiously dichromatic environment were occasional small red, yellow or blue flowers or the variegated leaves of some plants.

By the sixth day we were nearing the headwaters of the Orekang River and, more importantly, the high plateau which separated the Orekang from the Mazaruni. We began to climb steadily, following its various tributaries up towards the steep, jungle-covered hillside ahead of us. As the streams dwindled, their rock bottoms, coated in a mat of bright green weed, became lethally slippery and we turned back into the jungle.

Climbing upwards we tried to keep to the less heavily vegetated ridge lines leading to the plateau. The slope rose gradually and then more steeply until near the top we were pulling on roots, branches, vines or whatever came to hand to propel ourselves upwards. We were determined to make it onto the plateau that day to make up for some of the short distances that we had covered in the first few days. We took only brief stops each hour to have a drink and swap over the radio. Each of us were drenched in our own sweat by the time that we reached the top.

On the edge of the plateau we could see through a window in the canopy out over the plain below and away to the Mazaruni and the folds of the Chi Chi Valley in the distance. I had imagined that the top of the plateau would be relatively clear of jungle but I could not have been more wrong. Instead of the open forest that I had envisaged we found tight, dirty jungle. We were persecuted by mosquitos and some particularly vicious horseflies which would land unseen and sting straight through our thin cotton clothes without warning. Aggravating and painful though these were, the result was nothing like as spectacular as when one of the men breaking trail disturbed a bees nest and a swarm of angry bees descended on those behind stinging and pursuing everyone within range.

We camped beside a small stream in a patch of dank, rotting jungle roughly in the centre of the plateau. We had covered around four miles, one of our best days to date. Establishing communications on the radio took a considerable amount of effort moving the antenna around and re-tuning the set. I managed to pass on our position and that we hoped to make it to the RV the next day. We still had three days rations but were running low on fuel and as we had already found, lighting a fire from the damp rotting wood in the jungle was not at all easy.

As I retired to the little area under my hammock to sew up a large hole that I had torn in my trousers, I wondered where the boat party were. Other than them and the voice on the end of the radio no one

else existed for us. More than at any other time on the expedition, I felt that we were totally cut off from the outside world.

Like everyone else, I had a bad night's sleep. I lay awake for hours listening to the others shifting around in their hammocks. High up on the plateau the temperature dropped right down and the jungle was embraced by a pervading damp cold. Our thin blankets provided inadequate insulation against the chill. Dawn came as a relief, and hot bacon and beans eaten direct from a foil packet rarely tasted better.

We now had to find a way down the far side of the plateau. This had been a nagging concern throughout the approach march. The recce party had reported vertical cliffs on the Mazaruni side when they flew over the area. I had seen the scale of some of these cliffs when I had looked out across the jungle from Imbaimadai. In places they dropped for hundreds of feet and would defeat all but an extreme rock climber. Without adequate ropes and laden down with all our equipment we hardly came into that category.

I was relying on us being able to find a less steep section or a stream bed that we could follow. Once again the recce party had reported seeing a point which they thought would give us a feasible descent route but, as we had already discovered, an aerial view could be very misleading. If we could not find a way down we were faced with either a very long detour or turning back, neither of which was an appealing prospect.

We marched on a bearing to the edge of the cliff line and then sent out parties in each direction to try and locate a way down. They returned having located one of the three streams marked on our maps that ran down from the plateau to form the Mazaruni. It descended in a series of fairly sharp drops but although steep, it offered a viable route. Where we joined it, at the top, it was just the merest trickle pattering down over a rock stream bed a yard wide. We clambered down from rock to rock using the trees as brakes and then broke out onto a ridge when the deadfall became too thick.

Many more streams joined the one that we were following, none of them marked on our maps, each one swelling the little tributary until by the time that we got down to the lower ground it was ten feet wide. We came to one confluence where a bowl had formed providing an inviting swimming pool. We could see various small fishes swimming about in it which provided a healthy debate as to whether they were piranha or not. Piranha were prevalent in Guyana and we had all watched a film in which a capybara had been reduced from a live animal to just a pile of bones in a matter of minutes of frenzied feeding by these carnivorous fish. The lure of the cool water overrode our concerns and we plunged in. Having cooled off and laughed at the spectacle of Corporal Bullock wading around with a fag hanging out of the corner of his mouth trying to catch the fish in his mosquito net, we pushed on.

We followed the stream down until, in the middle of the afternoon, we reached the junction with the third of the main tributaries which marked the start of the Mazaruni. We had reached the RV. The true source could be defined as any one of a myriad of small streams coming down from the mountains. We had followed one of the three largest from its very beginning up on the plateau, but at this point it became the Mazaruni. By reaching the start of the Mazaruni we had achieved our first objective, now we had to follow it all the way to the ocean.

A large tree lay across both streams. There was deadfall everywhere, both upstream and down. Trees lay across the stream every few yards. There was no way that the boats could get here and I wondered how far down we would have to walk to reach them. The tiredness showed in people's faces. Both Guardsman Lundy and Sergeant Griffiths looked drawn and unwell, Mike had twisted his knee and was struggling under the weight of his pack and Colour Sergeant McKeown had twisted his ankle.

We set up the radio and having established communications with Imbaimadai passed them our position. Before I could say more, Andrew cut in and asked if he could update me on the boat party's progress. He said that they had abandoned the boats and were making their way towards us on foot when one of the team, Sergeant Nettlefield, had fractured his foot. They were a couple of miles south of us. He had radioed to Georgetown to try and get a helicopter; one was coming from the Caribbean and should be with us the next day. The major problem was that it did not have a winch and so somehow we had to find or prepare a landing site.

Most of our group were around me listening to

this conversation. The news of the casualty brought the usual black humour from the soldiers: 'He won't need his rations now', 'Can I have his boots', 'Let's float him down the river tied to a cross like in *The Missionary*' and 'We could just eat him' were a selection of the suggestions.

Richard came up on the net and confirmed that there was no way that Sergeant Nettlefield could walk out of the jungle. We both knew how difficult it would be to try and carry someone through the jungle, squeezing between trees, climbing over deadfall and passing under fallen tree trunks. He said that it was over a day's walk with a fit party to the boats, another day including several portages down to the catamaran and another day at least to the top of Chi Chi, with the long portage still to be made back down to the lower Mazaruni from there. Somehow we had to create a helicopter landing site. He had scouted the area carefully. There were no openings in the canopy of anything like an adequate size so we were faced with finding as big a space as we could and then enlarging it. He had identified a possible spot at a bend in the river but they needed to drop two big trees and the machetes and handsaws that we carried with us were proving inadequate for tackling full-blown hardwood trees. Andrew suggested using the helicopter to drop a chain saw to us wrapped up in life jackets.

I said that we would camp where we were and set out first thing in the morning. I wished that I was on site to assess the situation for myself but although they were only a little over two miles away that could take up to a day's march if the conditions were bad and anyway darkness was approaching. We set up camp and had our evening meal: pre-cooked beef stew and dumplings washed down by a large mug of tea followed by fruit salad and a rather nasty packet of fruit pastilles that I found lurking in a corner of my rucksack. Mike had a look at Colour Sergeant McKeown's ankle which he said was chronically twisted and in other circumstances would have warranted fourteen days rest. All that he could do was to strap it up in the morning and give Colour Sergeant McKeown some painkillers.

There was a loud thunderstorm during the night which brought intermittent rain from midnight through to dawn. Having packed up and strapped the Colour Sergeant's ankle, we took a bearing inland to try and get away from the deadfall beside the river. The going was little better and to compound matters we found ourselves cutting across the grain of the country, climbing up and down steep ridges, working hard for little gain. This was exactly what we did not want to do as Colour Sergeant McKeown was in considerable pain and I wanted to try and make the going easier for him.

It is amazing how pain ages someone. He looked grey and old and the hurt was etched into the lines on his face but greatly to his credit he did not complain at all, just kept plodding along leaning heavily on his stick. I felt for him but there was not much that I could do or say to make his lot any easier and he would not have liked anyone fussing over him in any event. At the same time I desperately wanted to get to the boat party as fast as possible so that we could help them prepare the HLS and to see if we could get Colour Sergeant McKeown lifted out as well.

The going was horrendous, both inland and by the river. The river had deadfall across it every few paces and in places the fallen trees had become an impenetrable mesh. We waded in parts, climbed, scrambled, crawled and pushed our way through. It took us a little over four hours to cover the distance. We came across them at a bend in the river, working to enhance the clearing. There was a fair amount of barracking between the two parties.

Mike went to examine Sergeant Nettlefield. He was chatty and not in unbearable pain but his foot was badly swollen and he was grateful for the stronger painkillers which Mike carried. He had broken the same ankle twice in the past and so in all likelihood it was a re-break on the old site.

The clearing looked impossibly tight and was ringed by trees up to one hundred feet tall. I could not see how a helicopter could come down into it without a substantial amount of work to enlarge the gap. The river bed was covered in uneven deadfall, so in any event it would not be able to land and would have to hover whilst we loaded the casualties aboard. A general lethargy seemed to have descended on everyone, imbued by the opinion that the task was impossible. I was determined that we should get the two casualties lifted out by helicopter, both for their sakes and ours. With Colour Sergeant McKeown's assistance I managed to galvanise people into action instructing them to cut down as many of the trees that either constricted the opening or which risked falling into it from the down draught of the rotor blades.

I raised Andrew Phasey on the radio. He told me that the helicopter was due to take off from Georgetown shortly and would fly direct to Imbaimadai where he would brief the pilot and then they would overfly the site to see if it was workable and if not to drop us the chain saw. This gave a fresh urgency to our efforts and everyone set to with machetes and hand saws.

With the full team working together we achieved a considerable amount in the hour that we had before Andrew came back on the net to say that they were about to take off from Imbaimadai and would be overhead in another half hour. We could not risk cutting any more in case we did not have time to finish the job and only served to weaken trees and thereby create a hazard to the aircraft. There was some frenzied last minute activity as we tried to clear away as much of the deadfall as possible, set out helicopter marker panels, tune in both of our VHF Ground-to-Air radio sets and put out a man with a signalling mirror.

The wait seemed interminable, then we heard the rotor blades. The helicopter overflew us once, spotted us and then wheeled around for a closer look.

The pilot's rich Caribbean accent came over the radio, 'Just give me thirty seconds for a look around and then let me see if I can work a little magic.'

I held my breath as he began to put the helicopter into a hover and then inched slowly down into the clearing. Both of the cargo doors of the helicopter were open and Andrew was moving from side to side, stepping out onto the skids passing directions by intercom to the pilot.

It seemed an impossible fit. They lifted up once, gently turned around and then like a hen settling on its clutch of eggs, softly inched down again. The blades were within feet of the closest trees. My heart was in my mouth as I watched them drop below the canopy and ease down bit by bit until they stopped in a hover just above the deadfall. As they had dropped down, Sergeant Griffith threw Sergeant Nettlefield over his shoulder and with Staff Sergeant Sanmoogan helping, carried him out into the clearing. In the tight gap the downdraught was like a cyclone; leaves and small branches were being blasted in all directions and it was impossible to shout loud enough to make yourself heard.

Andrew beckoned them forward. They covered the last few feet to the aircraft, bundled Nettlefield aboard and slowly and ever so delicately it lifted back out of the trees and flew off. It had been an incredibly gutsy bit of flying. A short while later they returned and repeated the performance lifting Colour Sergeant McKeown and their two rucksacks out of the jungle. Once again it was a tense few minutes as they brought the helicopter into the trees. As the extra weight was loaded on board, the helicopter lurched unsteadily and then, once again, slowly and carefully lifted out of the trees and flew away.

Once the thudding beat of the rotor blades had died away, there was a tremendous anticlimax. For the first time ever the jungle seemed oppressively quiet. We spent what was left of the day sorting out our kit, washing in the river and comparing our experiences. It felt strange to have our twelve man group split up and integrated with the others. We had become a strong, mutually-reliant team.

That night we had not been in our hammocks for more than a couple of hours when a massive storm broke. Claps of thunder made the air reverberate and brought with them torrential rain. I lay in my hammock with my blanket wrapped tight around me, wondering whether my poncho would keep the rain out. It quickly became apparent that it would not. Water dripped through the seams with a relentless persistence. I tried ignoring it but it became obvious that if I didn't do something to try and staunch the flow I would soon be soaked. I draped my blanket cover over the poncho and then, when that didn't work, I emptied my rations out of the plastic bag that I carried them in and cut it open and spread that over the outside. It was all to no avail as the rain continued to find its way through my meagre defences. Each time I got out of my hammock to try and improve my shelter I was exposed to the direct rain until my supposedly dry clothes were soaked.

I lay shivering miserably, fantasizing about being back in my flat in London where the bed was warm and comfortable, electricity appeared at the flick of a switch, hot water came out of the taps and I could wander down the carpeted corridor without fear of stubbing my toe on a vine or being bitten by a scorpion. After a while I must have dropped off to sleep and then unconsciously shifted my weight in my hammock, because the next thing I knew was that I was plummeting through the air and landed with a splash in the large puddle that had formed

beneath my hammock. I clambered soggily back into my hammock and lay waiting for the relief of dawn. The rain fell without break for the next eight hours.

When the first grey light filtered through the dripping jungle each person emerged from their separate cocoons. Most had spent an equally bad night with the only incident to raise their morale having been the sound of me falling out of my hammock and the accompanying burst of cursing. I changed back into my wet clothes, which were marginally drier than my dry clothes and packed my kit away. A hot brew and a bag of bacon and beans helped restore body and soul and put life back into perspective.

Richard led the whole group up onto a high ridge line and then along a series of further ridges parallelling the river. The jungle was notably easier than we were used to, in places not unlike a British oak wood, and so we made good progress. Having projected that it would take all day to reach the boats we actually reached them by midday. We stopped for a brew and a rest and then set to inflating the four canoes.

The river had swollen greatly since the previous night's rain and was flying past at an alarming speed. It was still no more than fifteen to twenty feet wide and the water dashed through rapids and under deadfall. I was concerned whether we would be able to control the boats in this powerful current. There was little room for manoeuvre and it would be easy to be swept over a waterfall or become trapped under a fallen tree. There was fresh deadfall everywhere, brought down by the storm. Once we had inflated the boats, loaded on our rucksacks and equipped ourselves with life jackets and paddles, I called everyone together and gave a stern safety brief. Then in our four and five man crews we set off downstream.

We had only gone a few yards when we hit our first obstacle: a set of rapids with shallows halfway through and fallen trees blocking part of the way. For the rest of the day we spent as much of the time out of the boats, wading along up to our waists in water, as we did paddling them. We were constantly dragging them through shallows, lifting them over submerged trees and ducking under logs before leaping on as they sped through rapids. It was hard physical graft but at the same time fun and

Mark Scruton and Mark Lundy inflate one of the workboats during training on the Demerara River.

David Stephens, Andrew Harburn and Derek Mann ferry an 'injured' Charlie McKeown during jungle training.

'Pork knockers' on the Mazaruni River at Imbaimadai.

Opposite: Wearing camouflaged clothing
we blended into the jungle.

All of our equipment including the
inflatable canoes, catamaran frame and
engine had to be portaged seven miles
around the Chi Chi Falls.

The Doctor leads the way across the 'savannah' as we make our way towards the top of the Orekang River.

The Doctor examines Colour Sergeant McKeown's chronically twisted ankle.

Lance-Corporal of Horse Richard Gallagher, experiencing the practical difficulties of crossing the savannah which we had thought from the aerial recce would provide good going.

Lieutenant Duane Jervis and Sergeant Johnson relax at a rest stop on the Orekang River.

Guardsman Mark Lundy leads the way over the mesh of deadfall that covers the early stages of the Mazaruni River.

In the early stages of the Mazaruni we spent most of the time in the water dragging our boats.

Pete Griffiths and Staff Sergeant Sanmoogan lift Nigel Nettlefield up to Andrew Phasey in the hovering helicopter.

Hayden Gonzales drives his freight boat
with all of our equipment from the bottom
of the Chutes to Peaima Camp.

When we came to waterfalls we would lower the boats
over them on ropes and then carry the kit around
through the jungle.

The catamaran heads down the Mazaruni from Kamarang.

At the end of our journey, the expedition's boats motoring past the ocean-going cargo ships anchored outside Georgetown harbour.

exhilarating and a welcome break from carrying a heavy pack through the jungle.

Midway through the afternoon we came to a large series of rapids which ended in a fifteen foot waterfall that cut right across the river. It made a most impressive sight as the river dropped down in a sudden step and we could see out across the jungle canopy further down the valley. Having guided them carefully through the approach rapids, we emptied the canoes and then lowered them down the waterfall on ropes before portaging the kit around through the jungle.

I had hoped to stop early so that we could lay out our kit to dry in the sun but, as we portaged the falls, towering black cumulus clouds built up and thunder roared out again. We stopped to set up camp before the storm broke. We carried the boats well up the bank from the side of the river and tied them securely to some of the larger trees in case of flash floods coming down from the mountains. As for ourselves, we were careful to move even further from the river and to choose sturdy trees from which to sling our hammocks away from any other trees that looked weak or were leaning over. The frequent crashes as trees fell through the undergrowth the previous night had left its mark on us. The heavens opened and we spent another wet and stormy night.

By morning the jungle floor had become a quagmire and the river level had risen up yet further. We had camped above another large rapid so there was no gentle start to the morning. It was a case of getting straight into the water as we hauled the boats over rocks and trees and around other obstacles, although as our clothes were already soaked it did not make a lot of difference. It was another energetic morning as we manhandled the boats down the narrow channels.

With the exception of frequent trees in the river, this second waterfall signalled the end of the major obstacles. We were now able to concentrate on paddling downstream. The inflatable boats paddled surprisingly well and we made good going with the current in our favour. We stopped at an abandoned hut to carry out the morning radio schedule. The sun had broken through and for the first time in two days it was gloriously hot. For some reason, probably due to the stormy weather, there was a lot of interference and we had trouble raising either Imbaimadai or Georgetown.

Once everyone had had a chance to have a brew and dry off at least some of their clothes, I sent the other crews on ahead to go to the cached outboard and catamaran frame and reconstruct the catamaran whilst my crew persevered with the radio. We kept trying for another half hour, adjusting the antenna and re-tuning the set before giving it up as a bad job.

We set off down river in pursuit of the others and caught up with them forty minutes later. As we approached I could hear them calling to each other through the trees. The level of the river had risen so far that it had completely flooded the area where they had cached the engine to a depth of up to six feet. It had also totally altered the look of the place. A major search was underway with those who had been in the walking party jeering at the boat party as they waded around up to their necks in water trying to find the missing engine. This was not exactly helping their efforts so I decided that we would paddle on down towards the top of the Chi Chi Falls and leave the others to find the engine and come on when they had done so. We left them chuntering to themselves as they waded about foraging amongst the submerged undergrowth at the base of each tree.

Chi Chi Falls were still a considerable distance downstream so we set to our paddles. The river twisted and turned vigorously; one moment we would be paddling south and then we would follow a great long sweeping curve and find ourselves paddling due north. It was amazing to watch it as it grew from the tiniest trickle that we had seen at the top of the plateau to a stream and now a fully fledged river broadening, deepening and strengthening with every mile that we paddled. The gleaming black surface of the river was flecked with froth from the spate, constricted by high river banks and enclosed by tight jungle walls. Just occasionally we had a view of some distant hills.

We paddled on for several hours, determined to make it to the top of Chi Chi by nightfall. Late in the afternoon, with the sun already low over the horizon, we heard the unmistakable chug of the catamaran engine behind us. They had finally found the engine, dried it out and got it going. As they came past they threw lines to each of our canoes and towed us on down river. It was dark by the time that we pulled into the side of the small clearing above the falls.

One more long day of shuttling loads around Chi Chi Falls and another late finish saw us back to Imbaimadai with the first part of our river journey complete.

Having re-established ourselves in our old camp, we were woken up at 5 a.m. next morning by the strident tones of powerful hymns played at top volume on an old and not very complimentary cassette player. This was part of Robert Alfred's morning routine. Unfortunately he insisted on getting up before dawn and always playing the same rather stretched tape which, not being a morning person, nor particularly religiously inclined, I found somewhat wearing. I got up feeling like an old man. Every bone in my body seemed to ache. I wandered down to the river to wash and shave. It was wonderful to bathe in the cool water and better still to get rid of my beard.

After breakfast we emptied our rucksacks, repaired all the equipment, serviced our cookers and reissued rations ready for the next leg of the journey. Of all the domestic chores, clothes washing must surely rank as the most tedious. On that morning I found myself stood in the Mazaruni attacking my stinking jungle clothes with a scrubbing brush and bar of carbolic soap alongside a pork knocker scrubbing his equally filthy clothes whilst singing Bob Marley songs at the top of his voice, totally out of key.

We were expecting a visit from Brigadier Jo Singh and the Deputy British High Commissioner, Bob Webb, and so did our best to spruce ourselves up. They landed in an Islander bringing with them a Guyanese television crew. It was good to see them and to be able to recount our adventures but most exciting of all was the mail that they brought with them.

In the afternoon we organised a football match against the villagers. Goal posts were hastily built on the airstrip which provided a sort of pitch with a patch of flat even ground in the middle and scrub either side. Practically the whole village turned out to watch. The game provoked much hilarity and a lot of ribald barracking from the sidelines led by a couple of the more vociferous prostitutes. Half time was called early when a supply plane came in to land and the game then recommenced once the plane had taken off again and the goal posts

had been re-erected. The match ended in an honourable draw to the satisfaction of both sides.

That evening Mike held a medical clinic. Corporal Williams went in first with a badly infected cut on his hand which had swollen up. It had to be opened up and cleaned which produced howls of pain from Corporal Williams and a rapid shortening of the Sick Parade queue! The poison had spread a considerable way up his arm and was in danger of developing into a serious condition. Mike was fairly concerned and said that Williams would be unable to take part in the next part of the expedition until the infection cleared up and if it did not then we might have to fly him to hospital. He also said that Colour Sergeant McKeown should not walk on his ankle.

Corporal of Horse Gallagher had a badly ingrowing toenail but after some fast bush surgery which further reduced the queue he was pronounced fit to continue. Corporal Pozzi had been wrestling with a viral infection for the previous few days and looked grey and haggard but he seemed to be recovering and having spent the first part of the phase with the Rear Party at Imbaimadai he was determined to take his place with the team out on the ground. Various other people needed bits of Bastard Trees to be dug out. Jungles are inherently unhealthy places and this one was proving no exception.

Later I gave a briefing for the next stage of the journey and then settled down to enjoy my mail. Each letter would be kept, cherished and read many times.

Next day we set off downstream of Imbaimadai for the first time. Despite using all our boats, we were heavily laden and travelled slowly down river. For the majority of the day our view was limited to the velvet black water of the Mazaruni and the mosaic of green vegetation which combined to form the jungle walls either side of the river. Dark foreboding storm clouds boiled across the sky and we regularly received cold and unwelcome dousings. In the open boats, we cowered under our ponchos unable to escape from the rain.

We passed Amerindians fishing in long dugout canoes near several small settlements. These canoes are so small and flimsy and with such shallow freeboard that it is amazing that they keep afloat. Perching, crouched at one end of the canoe, paddling with rough-hewn wooden paddles which looked more like carpet beaters, whilst bobbing up and down on the river, the tiny Amerindians seemed to defy gravity. They waved as we motored past and I envied them the umbrellas which many used as shades against both sun and rain.

We also passed a surprising number of mining dredges. Areas of land had been cleared of trees either side of the river and the dredges had literally eaten away great chunks of the river bank leaving behind beaches of pure white sand. In places the course of the river was being significantly changed but of much more concern to the local Amerindians was the claimed pollution of the river by mercury and other heavy metals used in the process of extracting the gold.

As darkness was approaching we pulled in to the left bank beside the village of Kamarang. Two Amerindians came down to greet us saying that they had been sent by Father Stephen Doorman, the Roman Catholic priest, to lead us to him. Having secured the boats we shouldered our loads and followed them along a series of narrow muddy paths across the village airstrip, past a line of wooden stores, through an area of scrub and up to the tall, whitewashed Mission Church. There we found Father Stephen inside watching a video with a number of his Amerindian congregation. A tall, thin man with a hawkish nose, he welcomed us warmly and showed us to two small but clean and reassuringly waterproof wooden buildings where he said that we could spend the night. He had been expecting us and made what provision he could to make us comfortable.

Kamarang is one of the larger villages on the Mazaruni, like Imbaimadai based around negro gold miners and their supporting services with a smaller population of indigenous Amerindians. Father Peter had been there for over thirty years having come out with the Missionary Service from England. He is known the length of the Mazaruni as a man of integrity and a friend of the Amerindians.

It is a telling reflection on the manner in which he is regarded by the Amerindians that they have elected him one of the village elders and he spoke to us from the carved wooden stool that they had given him to mark his office. He spoke with care and feeling for the simple village people to whom he has dedicated his life. He has fought a lonely crusade to protect the Amerindians from some of the more destructive outside influences that have brought alcohol, disease and moral corruption to this remote jungle community.

Having taken our leave of the kind Father Peter the next morning, a couple more hours of driving down river took us to the top of the first waterfall that marked the beginning of the Chutes. We got out on the right bank at a small pork knockers' camp. Three men were living in a makeshift hut whilst they worked their sluice and dug for gold.

We dismantled the catamaran and collapsed all the inflatable canoes, loading them onto the two workboats. We had arranged that Colour Sergeant McKeown and Guardsman Turner would drive the boats all the way back to Imbaimadai where they would be loaded onto a Skyvan and flown to Correia's Mining Camp at Arawai, where we would collect them from the far side of the Chutes.

We followed a trail that led into the jungle skirting the first falls. A couple of miles further on we rejoined the river at another pork knockers' camp above the second set of falls, Tuwaima. We needed to cross over to the left bank to join the Amerindian trail that would lead us through the jungle around the main gorge that the river now entered. Somewhat inevitably, the small boat that the pork knockers used to cross the river was lodged on the far bank. I got one of the GDF soldiers to fire a shot into the air and we managed to alert the attention of some pork knockers working on the far side.

The river was more than 100 yards across and flowing extremely fast towards the rapids below. Watching them paddle the boat across did little for our confidence as they flailed furiously with sections of broken planking that served as paddles and fought to stop themselves being swept downstream. There was a marked lack of enthusiasm amongst the team to be in the first boatload to cross the river but three journeys later everyone was safely across. The miners showed us the way through their camp and across an area of trees that they had felled to join up with the trail that we sought.

For the next two days we followed the trail around the great gorge, avoiding the series of waterfalls and the dense jungle within it. In places the trail was broad and pronounced passing through fairly open jungle and at other times less obvious as we crossed open ground or traced a series of ridges. At regular intervals we could hear the roar of the river as it tumbled down falls far below us but for the most part it was out of sight and out of reach.

On the second day, having climbed up and down a number of steep-sided ridges, we dropped back down to the river level, joining it just below the Chitigokeng Falls. A central stream of fast flowing, boiling white water came charging downstream from these, the last of the falls that make up the Chutes, which were just out of sight upstream. There were some massive standing waves and boils far more powerful than anything we had seen on the Colorado and totally unnavigable.

Next morning, as promised, two boats turned up from Correia's Camp to carry us down river from the trail head to the camp. Out in the centre of the river we had a better view up the gorge to the tiered falls of Chitigokeng and further downstream we were rewarded with views of the outer escarpment. Waterfalls tumbled off the high cliffs on either side and in the distance we could see the impressive sheer-sided tepui, Ayangaik, which for reasons that were not difficult to see had still to be climbed.

Arawai Camp was quite unlike any of the other mining camps that we had seen. It was a large-scale commercial operation involving several hundred workers operating under a bewildering array of yellow T-shirted managers. On the approach to the camp we had passed a cluster of seven dredges working in a bay carved out of the jungle. Another large area of land had been cleared and bore signs and poles that marked the registered mining claims. At the end of this cleared area was a large, well-constructed runway which led up to a group of substantial wooden warehouses, workshops, stores, mess halls and accommodation buildings.

We were offered a variety of places to sling our hammocks. I selected a spot under cover in the workshop. As we waited for the Skyvan to arrive with our equipment, we watched boats moving up and down river carrying the relief crews to take their shift on the dredges. This camp was reputed to produce around 25,000 ounces of gold each year.

When the plane arrived we unloaded all the boats and equipment that we needed for the remainder of our river journey.

As torrential rain drummed on the corrugated iron roof of the workshop for most of the night I was grateful for being under cover. Some of the others had not been so lucky and appeared sadly bedraggled and sodden in the morning. Although we were past the Chutes, there were still two major waterfalls to be negotiated. The first of these, Arawai Falls, was a couple of miles downstream.

Two of Correia's boats carried us downstream a short distance to land just above Arawai Falls. A trail led down through the jungle for a couple of kilometres, rejoining the Mazaruni below the falls. Before Correia's built their airstrip, all the fuel to support their mining operation was brought up river by boat in forty-five gallon drums and then carried by porters up this jungle trail to meet other boats from the camp. We had to portage not just the inflatable canoes and catamaran, but the two workboats and their outboard engines as well, on top of all our other kit. As we struggled along through the jungle weighed down with our first loads, I felt sorry for the 'druggers' who had to carry the huge fuel drums up the slippery trail.

Halfway down the trail we met Hayden Gonzales and a team of his druggers from Peaima camp coming up to meet us. We had first met Hayden in Georgetown on one of his regular forays to town. Apart from owning a mining operation at Peaima, he also ran a fleet of open boats carrying freight up to the villages and mining concerns along the Mazaruni. He had instantly offered to support the expedition by having us to stay at Peaima Camp, carrying our supplies up river and providing one of his boat captains to guide us through the channels on the lower section of the river. At the bottom of the trail Hayden had more boats waiting to carry us down to the camp. We still had to portage around the top half of Peaima Falls so it was not worth inflating our boats.

The camp was basic and compact. Hayden had built a small wooden cottage for himself. In front of the cottage was an open building which served as kitchen and accommodation for the few miners that worked at the camp. That aside, there was a small shed housing machinery and another storehouse. He had one dredger and a land mining operation although this was temporarily closed down as the miners were taking their leave at the end of their three month stint in the jungle. A short distance from the camp he had cleared an area of jungle in which he grew vegetables for those in camp. He employed an Amerindian hunter to go out into the forest and shoot game for meat.

Their life was simple and hard working. Hayden loved living in the jungle and particularly travelling up and down river on the freight boats. He was a highly successful businessman and extremely wealthy by Guyanese standards but although he maintained a Georgetown house where he had every comfort and amenity, it was here that he truly felt at home. He was very much master of his own domain and loved to dispense hospitality freely and readily.

He was soon at the centre of the action in the kitchen doling out cups of a sweet gruel that he called porridge and shots of a clear spirit that he gleefully claimed were 69 per cent alcohol and made your eyes water. As soon as that was despatched, he insisted on making hot chocolate or coffee for everyone whilst barking out orders to the old cook who was preparing 'cook-up', a stew of rice, maize and some indistinguishable meat.

Just downstream from Peaima Camp was Peaima Falls. Although not a vertical drop, the concentrated force of the river cascading over a narrow section of tiered rock produced an exceedingly violent rapid with massive standing waves, deep holes and powerful spouts of water. We had to portage all the equipment around this menacing chute of water to the landing below.

Although not as intimidating, there were still further rapids to come. One of Hayden's boat captains took us down them in his freight boat. Powered by three seventy-five horsepower outboard engines, the streamlined wooden boat flew down the rapids, barely seeming to touch the water. The rapids were large with some big stoppers and standing waves and plenty of rocks that if broached could rip the bottom out of any of our rubber boats. The alternative was another long portage. I decided to go for it.

James Geddes and I went first in one of the workboats. Being essentially flat bottomed the workboat had little steerage and was thrown around roughly by the larger waves. We both gripped on tight to the safety line as we hurtled down the rapid but still it was a fast and exhilarating run. I was thrown off my crouched stance and bounced off the metal floor and then we were through.

We walked back up to join those who were going to take the canoes down. We had shot a number of rapids on the Upper Mazaruni, but nothing of this size. The canoes went down in pairs with Hayden's boat showing them the way. The first two had a fairly wild ride with one man being thrown overboard. In the second pair I had Hayden, whom I kept in the back with me grinning with delight at the thought of the action to come and Corporal Bullock and Corporal Mann. My instructions to them were simple: paddle when I told them to, provide the forward momentum, leave the steering to me and make every stroke count. We got our line exactly right as we rounded the first corner but then got caught by a strong eddy. At that point everything began to go wrong and no matter what I did, I could not get the boat back on line. We drifted inexorably downstream until it was clear that we could not avoid the worst of the rapid.

I straightened the boat up and with Hayden somewhat unnecessarily yelling at us to hang on we plummeted over the lip of the pour-over. I could see what was about to happen and grabbed one of the safety handles. As I did so, the boat folded and the back kicked up sending me sailing over my outstretched arm in a cartwheel, crunching down onto Corporal Bullock's head. I ended up in the water but still holding on. Hayden grabbed my paddle and hauled me back on board. Bullock was rather dazed by the whole proceedings.

The other canoe under Colour Sergeant McKeown fared even worse, submerging completely and casting all the crew into the water. The safety boat leapt into action and began mopping up boats, paddles and bodies. Once everyone was reunited with their canoe, we carried on down the line of rapids. It was a constant battle to keep them on line. They responded sluggishly initially until after great efforts, paddling continuously on one side, they would then suddenly whip around. I was not helped by Hayden, who, in his enthusiasm to assist with the steering was throwing in bow rudder strokes as often at the wrong time as the right. Still it was great fun and by the time we all got back to camp all the boats were in place ready to begin the journey on down river next day and there was a general buzz of excitement from the day's events.

For the next three days we motored slowly down river. The Mazaruni grew steadily. It was already two hundred yards across and developing into a grand river, a far cry from its humble beginnings.

Each morning thick mist cast a cool, grey cloak over the water. It gave the river a soft, mysterious appearance but the sun's rays soon burned this off. By mid-morning we were sweltering, unable to escape the sun in our open boats. Later in the day storm clouds would mass, the temperature would drop and the air become still and then we would drive round a corner to be confronted by a wall of rain. It came down in torrents, with such a defined start and finish that it was as if someone had pulled curtains of water across a particular part of the river.

At night we slung our hammocks under cover in miners' camps or the abandoned buildings of two river staging posts. They had once been proud outposts and centres of trading along the river, with smart wooden buildings raised up on stilts, managed by efficient government agencies. Now they were sadly dilapidated. Many of the buildings stood empty, left to the ravages of the weather and boring insects. At Enachu the hanging mist only added to the general air of decay. The largest of the buildings, the police post, is identified by a fading sign and a crooked flagpole.

Wherever we went, Hayden was known to the people alongside the river and doors were opened for us. Many people relied on his goodwill to allow them to travel on his river boats, carrying their produce down to sell in Bartica or Georgetown, or supplies back to their jungle villages. He was like a father figure, with a greeting or a good word for everyone, taking the time to listen to individuals' problems and often providing a loan of money or promise to help in some way.

At Issano we were expecting to meet up with another of Hayden's riverboats bearing some of the rear party and a much needed fuel re-supply. The largest of the villages on the river and the only one accessible by road, albeit only the most execrable of mud tracks leading a hundred miles through the jungle to Bartica, Issano was recognised as the most important of the river trading posts. If anything, it was in an even more pitiable state than Enachu but it was certainly more bustling and our arrival provoked a fair amount of local interest.

We pulled up at a small landing beneath the Government Rest House where Hayden had arranged for us to spend the night. Like all the other buildings in the village it was gradually falling apart. Raised on pillars, a rickety flight of stairs led up to three bedrooms. I made a mental note to avoid the mattress that lay on one of the beds in case of resident insects. The night before, ants had got onto my feet and travelled all the way up my legs to my crotch leaving a trail of itching red lumps in their wake.

Hayden had a wooden hut opposite the main landing where his guard, Coal-in, watched over his boats and cargoes. Having checked over his domain, he retired to a small store-cum-bar run by an old negro who he introduced as Mister Baptist and began dispensing largesse in the form of high wine and beer to all comers at a furious rate.

We spent what was left of the day radioing to Andrew in Georgetown, washing ourselves and our clothes in the river, fishing and exploring the village. I found the GDF soldiers embroiled in a heated game of dominoes with the village policeman. They were all shouting at once and there was much theatrical gesturing and slamming down of the counters as each person took their turn. The thickness of their accents and extent of their patois rendered their conversation almost unintelligible but their brightly shining eyes, howls of protest or cries of triumph and extravagant gesticulations conveyed more meaning than words ever could.

Down at the landing Corporal Williams and some of the others were hauling out more of the curious looking Mazaruni fish. In the evening people drifted between Hayden's hut where his Amerindian maid was doling out rice, stew and some delicious dough cakes and Mister Baptist's store where a substantial number of the village had gathered telling jokes, debating politics and 'gaffing' about life in general.

We got up next morning having escaped the attentions of the vampire bats that the locals had warned us about with such relish. Some of the team looked rather the worse for wear having over-indulged in the native rum, however none looked as bad as Lion, Hayden's boat captain, whose eyes were sunken far back in his great bear-like head. Fortunately for him another boat captain appeared, with the equally unlikely name of Piggy, so Lion was able to spend the morning asleep under a tarpaulin. With the Guyanese predilection for nicknames, I was convinced that we would have a menagerie by the time that we reached Georgetown.

We set off down river once again. Although we had precious little fuel left to run the outboards I was not overly concerned as Hayden had heard on the jungle telegraph that his boat was on its way. We entered the intricate web of channels that run between the many islands of the lower Mazaruni. The nature of the river now changed once again.

We broke the catamaran down and paddled several rapids. None provided too much difficulty. Once beyond Itaki Falls, we motored on. As we were heading through our last can of fuel the other boat hove into sight. Corporal-Major Tate, Sergeant Nettlefield and Corporal of Horse Stephens were perched on top of some huge fuel drums in a large freight boat. An Amerindian family who were travelling in the front of the boat had festooned their washing along a drying line like so many Admiralty flags. There was much hailing between Lion and Piggy and the other boat's captain, Cai-Coochi.

Sergeant Nettlefield was eager to regale us with his experiences in hospital. His foot had not been broken but he had been put into plaster and kept in for several days. By all account it had been fairly rough. There had been chickens and dogs roaming about the wards and two people had died whilst he was there. Corporal-Major Tate quickly filled me in on their progress up river and the state of logistic planning back in Georgetown.

Late in the afternoon, we stopped in front of three huts on a small island isolated in the middle of the river. Loud music blared out from the central hut. This, according to Lion, was Benny Choo's Place, a bar and cat-house serving the miners moving up and down river. He looked at home and took every opportunity to grapple with the girls as they scurried about giggling. As with everywhere else that we had been, Hayden was treated deferentially by the owner and he and I were invited to sling our hammocks in one of the huts.

It seemed strange that there should be loud music, garish coloured lights and whores stuck out in the jungle but sitting out on the sand, drinking a beer and chatting or watching the stars was infinitely preferable to the long silent nights spent trying to make ourselves comfortable in the jungle above Imbaimadai.

For two miles below Benny Choo's Place there were a series of rapids that steadily increased in size. Towards the lower end they were at the limit of volume of water that our inflatable canoes could handle. Several of the team were apprehensive of white water and the GDF soldiers were extremely reluctant to paddle the canoes. We sorted ourselves out between the various craft and set off in line down river. The canoes gave an exciting ride. There was a fair amount of nervous laughter in my canoe but as we went through progressively larger rapids our confidence as a crew built up and everyone began to enjoy themselves.

The last rapid was significantly steeper and more powerful than any of the others. Each boat dropped out of sight only reappearing as they burst over the crest of each wave. I saw a body fly off the second boat and get lost in the white water. Then it was our turn. There was a tangible sense of anticipation as we paddled out into the main stream. I steadied the crew and straightened the canoe up. We dropped down sharply into the trough of the first wave and were then submerged in the whiteness. The two guys in front were knocked backwards off their seat and the canoe reared up. I yelled at them to get back up and continue paddling. It was fast and furious and then we were through. We pulled in a short way below.

The casualty from the second boat had been Duane Jervis, the GDF officer. He had been taken down under the water three times and given a fair trouncing. The other GDF soldiers were hooting with laughter and ragging him mercilessly but it was taken in good heart. After all, as the only one amongst them who had the courage to paddle in one of the canoes, there was no doubting who held the moral high ground!

With the exception of one last rapid section, the remainder of the Mazaruni was flat. By the time that we reached Bartica at the mouth of the Mazaruni, it had grown into a grand river almost a mile wide. It seemed a world apart from the tiny trickle that we had first traced up in the highlands and the large waterside town of Bartica similarly removed from the metal shacks of Imbaimadai. Cars drove up streets lined by stores, hotels and a school.

Bartica was not particularly smart or sophisticated, the cars had nowhere to go and even in the town they competed for road space with goats and cows. The buildings were relatively spartan and the stores carried only a limited range of goods. But our arrival there brought with it the sense of re-entering the civilised world. It also signalled the completion of our mission to locate the source of the Mazaruni and trace it all the way to its mouth.

We had not yet come to the end of our journey and by no means to the end of our experiences in Guyana: a further three days on the boats took us down the Essequibo River to the Atlantic Ocean and around the coast to Georgetown.

Where the Mazaruni had been small enough to be personal and show us its character, the Essequibo was huge, over thirteen miles wide at the confluence and increasing all the way. We motored down the mirror-flat surface, stopping at the Dutch colonial fort and court building on Fort Island and the modern 4,000 strong East Indian community on Leguan Island, a river island larger than Barbados.

The sea was kind to us and calm when we rounded the coast. For hours on end the faint skyline of Georgetown with its distinctive landmarks, the clock tower on top of Stabroek market, the wooden cathedral and the Pegasus Hotel tower, grew on the horizon. Entering the main shipping lane and motoring past anchored lines of huge ocean-going cargo ships our little fleet must have looked comically small and as we pulled up to the main wharf a few bemused dock workers peered down at these strange men in their puny craft proudly flying the Union Jack, Household Division and Explorers Club Flags.

We unloaded our equipment and hauled the boats up onto the wooden deck of the wharf alongside mounds of wicker baskets containing screeching scarlet macaws, green parrots, mangoes and pineapples. Stevedores watched with the idle curiosity of people accustomed to observing life go by, as we carried the kit out of the confines of the dock area to where the Admin Party with the Pinzgauer was waiting for us. We drove out into the bustling mayhem of Stabroek market, through the colourful mêlée of hustling Rastafarians, street stallholders, boys driving horse-drawn carts and women clutching their plastic shopping bags. We were back where we had started.

Chapter Six

Andean Exploits from Ecuador to Aconcagua

Within forty-eight hours of getting out of the jungle I was on an aeroplane back to England. We had been walking a financial tightrope since the outset, having left for Alaska far short of the total sponsorship target that would provide the budget that we needed to complete all six phases. By the time that we had reached Panama, Richard and I had been forced to conclude that our finances could only support us for another two phases even when working from our most optimistic predictions. This dire situation had been partly relieved by the arrival on the scene of our major sponsor, British American Tobacco, who provided a large financial boost to the expedition but we still faced a cash flow crisis.

Finance aside, we had problems in other areas. Midway through the year we had been told that due to a territorial dispute between Chile and Argentina we would not be permitted to attempt our last proposed challenge, the crossing of the Southern Patagonian ice cap. This meant finding a fresh aim for Phase Six and completely re-starting the operational and logistic planning. On a much more immediate note, political clearance had still not been granted by several of the host countries on our planned route south through South America from Ecuador.

There was a gap of just three weeks between emerging from the Guyanese jungle and the new team flying out to Ecuador. During this time our operation needed to be closed down in Guyana and all of the equipment sent back to England, the central cadre had to fly to Ecuador to meet up with a recce party who had gone out from England, and between them they needed to negotiate the passage of the containers holding our vehicles and camping equipment which had been shipped down from Panama through Customs. Everyone was busy.

In England, I dashed from meeting to meeting begging extra support from our existing sponsors and trying to generate new financial support. I went to give a presentation to BAT mindful that their sponsorship was being given in three tranches

and that each one was reliant on the success of the last phase and none were guaranteed. I had several meetings with the Household Division hierarchy to brief them on the expedition's progress to date and to plead for a £25,000 bridging loan to keep us afloat. On the planning side, I decided that we would transfer our attention for the last phase to the Northern Patagonian ice cap. It was significantly smaller than the southern ice cap but crossing it would still pose a major challenge and it had the distinct advantage of being totally within Chile and therefore uncontentious. It also had the added advantage of requiring similar equipment and logistic support and therefore all of the procurement and advance planning that Andrew Phasey had done would not be wasted. Still there was a great deal of research to be done to hone the plan into a workable state.

In amongst all of this hectic crisis planning I caught up with as many friends as time allowed, held an impromptu party for my thirty-first birthday and snatched two wonderful weekends with Louie at her home in Lincolnshire. All too quickly I became far too used to comfortable warm beds, hot baths and plentiful good food and drink. Before I knew it the time was up and I was back on an aeroplane with the new team bound for Guayaquil in southern Ecuador. It had been a successful visit. BAT's sponsorship was assured, several other sponsors had pledged further support, a couple of new ones had joined us, the bridging loan had been approved and the Phase Six planning was up and running and taking shape in the way that I wanted.

Arriving in Guayaquil was a welcome return to the realities of expedition life and a relief from the claustrophobic bustle of London. It was good to see Richard and the others on the advance party and to hear their news. They had arrived in time to watch our containers being offloaded from the ship. To their horror, they had witnessed the crane operator dropping a container on top of the one of ours that had

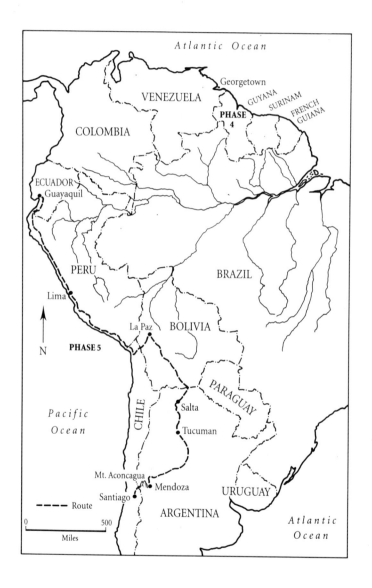

Phase 5 Vehicle Journey

our vehicles inside. Luckily no major damage had been done.

It had taken them a week to get the vehicles through Customs. They had hired guards to protect them from robbers whilst they were at the docks and then found a secure compound in which they were able to safeguard them until we arrived. They were now looking forward to getting out of this dingy and decidedly unsafe coastal city and onto the road once again.

We got up at 6 a.m., washed, shaved and showered, packed up the vehicles and having briefed the team on the plan for the phase, took the road south. The road took us alternately through flat scrubland and cultivated banana plantations until we arrived at the border town of Huayquillas which was in full swing with All Saints Day Festival. The Customs post was located in the centre of the town. The roads were blocked with jostling crowds moving between market stalls and bands playing from makeshift platforms. Moneylenders, ominous looking men with their eyes hidden behind dark glasses and black briefcases full of currency at their feet, sat in rows underneath umbrellas at the roadside.

Having located the correct office and managed to get the requisite stamps and signatures on our papers, we found a local boy to guide us through the dusty backstreets and across the municipal rubbish dump towards a small bridge over the dried up river which marked the border with Peru. After extensive formalities in a variety of shacks on both sides of the border we were finally clear to proceed.

A short distance into Peru we joined the Pacific coastline. Miles of desolate wasteland with rugged cliffs and windswept shores were interspersed with long, sweeping beaches lined with fishermen's shacks outside which hung brightly coloured nets. We chose an empty stretch of beach outside a small village on which to camp for our first night on the road. We had around four thousand miles to travel through Peru, Chile, Bolivia and Argentina to reach our objective for the phase, Mount Aconcagua and although our schedule was tight, we had for once built in time to do some exploring along the way.

Next morning we were up early. Lines of pelicans flew past in formation, searching for shoals of fish. By 7 am some of the fishermen were already swimming out through the freezing waves clutching their nets to set them in the calm water beyond the surf. A

haze hung over the surrounding country obscuring clear views but lending a soft, flattering glow to the arid hills. Clusters of open fishing boats and trawlers were anchored in the bays outside each village that we passed. The country alternated between rolling hills and dead flatness. The inland towns were based around artificial oases created by irrigation ditches bringing water piped down from the mountains or across from the nearest river to plantations of palms, bananas and sparse ground crops.

Further south we crossed the desert of Sechura. We entered a great arid plain with no vegetation save straggly nutritionless desert grass. The wind blew constantly. Beside the road were huddles of low mud buildings with donkeys tethered outside. Miles from any other population and with no obvious form of sustenance it was hard to see how either man or animal lived there or what drew them to such a barren spot.

As we drove further into the desert, the sand drifted in mini dunes around each tussock of grass and then, where the grass finally receded, bigger dunes had formed; great sweeping crescent-shaped formations thirty feet high and a couple of hundred feet long. With every grain of sand blown into place as the dune slowly crept forwards, their impossibly smooth faces dominated the country. Occasionally we came across one that was far more grandiose, towering above the desert. In other parts, the road was raised up on a causeway over a flat, featureless pan of white sand.

The emptiness of the desert contrasted sharply with the bustle of the oasis towns. The monotony of narrow dusty streets lined by low mudbrick buildings was relieved by markets which were a riot of sights, sounds and smells. Each was a maze of tightly packed avenues of stalls stacked with clothing, jewellery, haberdashery, and the necessities of everyday life. Fishmongers slabs were piled high with mounds of squid, octopus, clams and a great number of often huge fish. Butchers' stalls were festooned with meat cuts and plucked chickens, fruiterers appeared behind mountains of oranges, bananas and pineapples and flower sellers beamed from amongst a blaze of colour. I was afraid that they would be camera shy but when I rather tentatively produced my camera, I was practically mobbed and led from stall to stall by a great throng of children. The older women posed with an endearing coyness encouraged by gales of laughter from all those watching.

As we continued our journey south, the country-side was constantly changing but almost always desert of one type or another. The road conditions varied from being excellent to diabolical with deep, closely packed potholes and encroaching sand dunes. Tall, dark mountains rose up in the distance, their mystique heightened by the haze that obscured them.

At sunset we rejoined the ocean at Huanchaco where fishermen were paddling out through the surf in reed rafts fishing with circular, weighted nets for small sea fish. It was a highly skilled operation. The rafts were 10ft long tubes of reeds bound together, cut off square at the back and rising up in the front in a sharp, up-turned prow. They were solid save for a small compartment cut into the back where the fish were carried. The fishermen sat with their legs dangling in the water, astride their raft, paddling with half of a split bamboo. The rafts were extremely heavy and not at all easy to balance and yet they were paddling out through 5ft surf where they sat casting their nets. It made a fine sight against the golden rays of the setting sun.

We continued on our way through the desert, bound initially for Lima. We drove through great flat sandy plains passing increasingly frequent and large dunes and high bare earth mountains. It was inspiring and rapidly changing scenery. At one moment we were in classical desert with pastel-coloured sand dunes contrasting pleasantly against the dark mountains and the next we were passing through irrigated fields of orange flowers. The people seemed to become even more distinctive: both men and women wore a version of Panama hats. The women had their hair braided into two long plaits and wore voluminous skirts and blouses in the brightest possible colours.

One evening we turned off the road to the village of Puerto Calabras in search of somewhere to camp. At the end of the narrow dirt road we came to a barrier in front of a high wall bearing some rather warlike slogans where a guard armed with a pump-action shotgun made it clear that we were not welcome. Fifteen miles further down the Pan American Highway we turned off again, this time only to find that the side road led into a dirty village full of rather hostile locals and at the water's edge two evil smelling factories belching out smoke.

Darkness was upon us and with nowhere to camp we retreated back up the track and pulled off into what looked like a disused quarry in a cold and windy spot overlooking the village. As it grew light next morning and we were able to look around us, we began to notice the area was strewn with bones. On closer inspection it became quickly apparent that they were the scattered remains of human skeletons.

One of the soldiers called me over to look at a skull with some hair still attached to it, elsewhere skulls, jaw bones, femurs and vertebrae lay in the open. Some of the bones were blanched white whilst others had merely yellowed which I took to mean that they were more recent. Just to complete this rather macabre scene, a skull with two crossed bones had been suspended from a nearby telegraph pole. It was impossible to tell how old the bones were or how they had come to be there. Whether it was an ancient burial site that had been accidentally ploughed up by the road builders or a mass grave either of victims of disease or something more sinister was not apparent.

Although more settled now, Peru has a troubled history including the very recent past. Throughout the majority of the country's roughly 4000-year human history, competing tribes had been locked into battles with each other for control of the sizeable kingdoms which they ruled. The Spanish conquistadors brought a new dimension to the previously native conflicts and the start of the wars between the Conquistadors and the Incas. Subsequently there were wars with Bolivia and Chile but much more recently, throughout the 1980s and 1990s the country had been locked into a particularly vicious internal struggle between the right wing government forces and the Maoist terror-ist organisation, the Sendero Luminoso, or Shining Path. Both sides had resorted to some fairly ruthless methods and although since the capture of the movement's leaders in 1992 the government was more in control, the position was not totally secure.

We were told that an overcrowding problem in Lima's prisons had been resolved on one occasion by transporting the inmates to the national stadium where they were machine-gunned, and on another occasion by taking them up in military aircraft and throwing them out over the jungle. Were it not for the reliability of the source, it would be hard to credit such an action but now looking at the bones lying around me I had a distinctly uneasy feeling. Camp was packed up in record time and we got on our way.

The situation within Peru had not been improved by the spread of narcotics production and there were still areas of the country under the control of both guerrillas and narcotic warlords. I had noticed a heavy military presence in most of the main towns that we had passed through. The soldiers appeared alert and businesslike peering out from heavily protected barracks.

Political clearance for us to enter the country had been in the balance until the very last minute and even now there were strict restrictions placed upon us by the British Embassy. Essentially we were limited to the coastal desert and were to avoid all routes into the interior. This meant that when we reached the south we would be unable to drive to the famous sites of Machu Picchu and Cusco but much more sad to me was not being allowed to branch off into the mountains and valleys of the Andes. Just to our west a mountain road led up into the Cordillera Blanca, Cordillera Negro and Huayhuash right past the base of such famous mountains as Yerapuja and Huascaran about which I had read so much. I would have dearly loved just to be able to look at them and to visit the tight valleys and remote villages surrounding them but there was no choice but to press on south.

Seemingly in recompense for this disappointment, a short while after passing the turn off towards the mountains, we entered an area of grandiose desert with fantastic vistas across miles of dunes. Looking towards the coastline I could see lines of what appeared to be people on the beach a couple of miles away. For want of a distraction from driving, we found a tight, sand track and drove down to see what was going on. All along the beach fishermen were working in teams. They loaded great long nets into brightly painted, open fishing boats and rowed out through the surf laying the net in a huge arc. Then two lines of men took hold of either end of the net and hauled it up onto the beach full of squid, crabs, the odd fish and star fish. All but the squid were rejected and these were scooped into barrels and then loaded onto trucks waiting behind each team. At the back of the trucks the womenfolk had set up small open air kitchens

and were cooking up fish on braziers, surrounded by pans, plates and clutter. We moved from group to group watching them work the nets or chatting as they ate or relaxed lying on reed mats on the sand. They all wore balaclavas or scarves wrapped around their heads and faces to protect them from the wind and the blasting sand.

At the back of one truck I came to the pitiful sight of a tethered seal. It had been caught in one of the nets and battered about the head until it was now nearly dead. Looking out to sea, I could see seals diving in and out of the nets robbing the catch. They reared and leapt through the surf with a wonderful exuberance, a marked contrast to the sorry state of their captured comrade. At times they congregated in schools and burst out of the water together until the water seemed to erupt with seals. Gulls hovered overhead and dived, taking their share of the spoils. The fishermen worked hard. No sooner were the nets emptied than they were loaded back into the boats and rowed out through the surf again. Set against the backdrop of the dunes and the distant mountains, it was a fabulous sight.

We carried on south spending the night on another remote, windswept beach savouring the isolation and watching the prolific birdlife. Tall, white egrets were spread along the beach, tiptoeing out behind the receding waves to catch the crabs that each wave brought in and then scurrying back to safety as the next breaker rolled in. Lines of pelicans flew low along the surf scouting for shoals of fish and a tightly grouped flock of oyster catchers wheeled about us in a flash of black and white wings.

All the way down the coast there had been unlimited space which brought with it a great feeling of freedom and wildness. That ended abruptly as, just south of Ancon, we encountered the first of the dusty mudbrick shanty towns that line the mountains and dunes which flank Lima. For the next twenty miles these shanty towns grew bigger and more tightly compacted until they swelled into the suburbs of the capital. It is a suburbia of an almost unsurpassed squalidness with dirt, grime and pollution on an overwhelming scale. The centre of the city with its elaborate Spanish colonial architecture, palaces, cathedral, ornate houses and statues comes as a strong contrast to the environs but even here the buildings are blackened and filthy from the all pervasive smog.

The people too seem hard faced and aggressive compared to the welcoming, homely smiles of the country folk.

Within this oppressive façade there are undoubtedly gems to be found. We roamed around the city's streets and squares, watching the goose-stepping Presidential Guard in their splendid eighteenth century uniforms, grimacing at the ghoulish instruments of torture in the Museum of the Inquisition and trying to avoid the attentions of the ever-present police. Policemen stood at every street corner and outside every public building, some in standard uniform, some in riot gear with the full complement of body armour, visored helmets and shields, all armed and some overtly carrying CS grenades and machine-guns alongside their batons. Their presence in such numbers only served to emphasise the tenuousness of the security situation giving one the feeling that the magnificence of the Plaza de Armas and the many surrounding broad avenues could come crumbling down at any time.

Amongst the most impressive of Lima's sights is the Gold Museum which provides a fascinating insight into the ancient Peruvian lifestyle and customs and their infatuation with killing, sex, death and preparation for the afterlife. Rooms were filled with gold ornaments, artefacts and implements collected from all the archeological sites in Peru. There was every form of earring, necklace, amulet and body adornment through to weapons, wall hangings, death robes and mummified corpses. Several mummified heads had loops through the crania so that the warrior who had killed them could display them around his belt at ceremonies. Other skulls had been exhumed years after burial, wounds repaired, teeth replaced by gems and the skull then covered in bright feathers or semi-precious stones.

Another area was dedicated to pottery depicting the ancients' way of life from medicine to agriculture, models of heads emphasising moods and racial characteristics and demonstrating every imaginable form of sexual activity. The museum enabled one to appreciate the scale and sophistication of the cultures of such ancient cities as Chan Chan where an estimated 10,000 people had lived in a walled adobe city of palaces, temples, dwellings, storehouses, workshops and gardens linked by an intricate system of roads, streets and irrigation channels.

Continuing on our journey south, we pressed on through the grape-growing region around Ica, before re-entering the desert. For two more days the desert flashed past as we made our way ever southwards, past Nazca and the mysterious lines etched into the desert, and on to Arequipa. Nestling at the foot of the 19,000-foot El Misti volcano, Arequipa must surely be one of the most beautiful cities on earth. Open and airy, yet at the same time small and intimate, the city and its people exude a cosy welcoming sophistication missing in most other South American cities.

The colonial buildings are constructed from pale volcanic stone that is flattered by crystal clear air and bright blue skies. The Plaza de Armas is dominated by the twin-towered cathedral which runs along the whole of one side with the mystical snow cone of El Misti looming above everything.

The Santa Catalina Convent is a city within the city. Walking around you enter an enclosed world of floral alleyways, cloisters and buttressed buildings full of variously apportioned chapels and tiny chambers where up to 450 nuns, the daughters of rich families, lived a comfortable but secluded life of prayer for the wellbeing of their families. I wandered around the intricate web of twisting, sky blue and terracotta alleys, photographing the tranquil scenes of ornate carved doorways, hanging floral displays, gurgling fountains, neat gardens and the views across the tiled roofs to the real world outside.

The one major deviation from the Pan America Highway for which we had gained permission, was to branch off into the hinterland from Arequipa to the Colca Canyon. The mellow mood imbued by Arequipa had been somewhat shattered by the news from England that firstly we still did not have clearance to enter Chile, which we needed to do in three days time if we were to stay on schedule, and secondly and far more fundamentally our proposal to cross the Northern Patagonian ice cap had just been turned down.

The international commission set up to adjudicate in the territorial dispute over the southern ice cap had just published its findings in favour of Argentina's claim. This had provoked an outbreak of nationalist fervour in both Argentina and Chile with a great furore in the press. The governor of the appropriate Argentine region had had to be restrained by the authorities in Buenos Aires from deploying an occupying force of troops direct to the 'new' territory. The Argentinians had however promptly laid claim to the northern ice cap which now became the focus of the two countries' ongoing territorial dispute and hence the denial of our application.

It was very disappointing news. We had done a great deal of research and planning and a 40ft sea container holding all the skis, pulks and specialist tents and clothing which we had procured for this particularly hostile wet-cold environment were already on their way to Chile. As we drove out of Arequipa past El Misti I pondered this new turn of events. I was determined that by hook or by crook we would complete the journey and get to Cape Horn.

We climbed along a rough dirt road up to a high bleak plateau at around 12,000 feet which left the vehicles struggling for power and us gasping for breath. For several hours we drove on across the plateau. There were few settlements; those that we did encounter were mean outposts of low, stone buildings out of which peeked ruddy-cheeked children and traditionally dressed women in heavy layers of skirts, jerseys and shawls topped off with elongated bowler hats decorated with silk rosettes of a matching colour on one side.

On the far side of the plateau we entered the mountains and followed a series of dirt roads up narrow valleys as we climbed up towards the canyon. Every available inch of ground was claimed in a patchwork of tiny terraced fields enclosed by drystone walls. Men tilled the fields with ox-drawn ploughs; women worked the ground with hoes whilst children watched over herds of cattle, alpacas and sheep. With the exception of some of the alpaca herds, none were very large, rarely running to more than twenty beasts.

The alpacas looked like outsized cuddly sheep with long legs and necks and rather cheeky faces. Many of them had red ribbons through their ears that looked like earrings and did nothing to make them appear any less cartoon-like. The people were small in stature and had long faces which in the older people where tanned and deeply lined. Many had terribly blackened teeth from constantly chewing coca leaf.

Darkness fell and the temperature plummeted as we made our way on up the valley system.

Frequent earthquakes had reduced the roads to narrow broken trails along which we picked our way gingerly. At 10.30 p.m. we finally reached a windswept promontory overlooking the canyon where we could make camp.

We woke to a dramatic dawn with the rich, low-angled light exaggerating the shadows in the vertical rock walls. For two hours we peered up and down the canyon for a sight of the condors which we had travelled so far to see and were eventually rewarded with rather distant views of one of these huge birds. With this token success, we turned back.

We stopped in Maca, one of the villages that we had passed through in darkness. Now in daylight, we could see the ravages of the earthquake that had destroyed many of the buildings four years previously. Families were still living in tents outside the ruins of collapsed stone dwellings. The village church was curiously misshapen: one of the two original towers that had stood either side of the main façade had disintegrated and the huge wooden doors hung limply in the centre of heavily cracked walls. All around were the engaging scenes of village life: children playing in the dusty road, a woman selling dried beans by the roadside, other women chatting at street corners whilst spinning wool and men riding by on donkeys or driving flocks of sheep. One man came out to see us with two eagles which he said had been injured.

We made our way back towards Arequipa, this time crossing the plateau to the east of the mountains surrounding the city on even rougher and more remote roads. Isolated herds of alpacas browsed the coarse tussock grass whilst flocks of Andean ducks and flamingos appeared on the upland lakes. Passing through one village, we came upon a wedding procession making its way across the Plaza de Armas from the church. The bride was in an European-style frilled white wedding dress and the groom was wearing a suit. All around them thronged Indian women in traditional dress showering them with rice. Children ran around throwing fire crackers and at the back of the procession was an eight-piece brass band playing loud Andean music.

Back on the highway we kept on south through more fabulous desert scenery. Flat plains covered in curious horn-shaped dunes alternated with rolling hills, a gentle blending collage of pastel colours.

The border crossing into Chile was blessedly calm compared to those that we had experienced before. Our clearance to enter the country had been notified at the last moment. We flitted through northern Chile, spending one night camped outside Arica, before turning east and heading up into the Andes and Bolivia. We had only taken this rather unusual route as a result of the more usual route via Puno and Lake Titicaca having been judged by the embassy as still being liable to terrorist attacks.

We heard that ahead of us the wet season had begun in Bolivia and that the rough road that ran over the altiplano passed through thigh-deep rivers in places. Our battered fleet of vehicles were feeling the pressure of their long life and the rigours of our journey. We were beginning to experience an alarming quantity and frequency of problems. I embarked on each day's travel with a sinking doubt as to whether we would reach the evening with all vehicles still intact.

A good tarred road wound its way steadily up into the dry hills at the foot of the Andes. We climbed direct from sea level to over 15,000 feet in the space of just a few hours as we entered the Lauca National Park. Great snow-capped volcanos towered all around us overlooking lakes thick with wildfowl and flamingos.

At the Chilean frontier the good road simply ended. The dirt track running across the several miles of no man's land to the Bolivian frontier post was an execrable trail of deep potholes, savage rocks and mud. We queued behind lines of lorries to get to the formalities and then made our way from office to office with our paperwork, huddled into our fleece jackets against the biting cold.

Once the formalities were completed we set off once again on more rough dirt roads. We bounced through deep sand, heavy ruts and mud, at one point fording a river that came up to the bonnets of the vehicles. Mercifully they all kept going. The altiplano is a grey, bleak area. The mountains stand like sentinels over the flat, windswept plain with the volcano, Sajama rising up highest. At times we saw herds of llamas but for the most part the country was devoid of life.

It was dark by the time that we pulled in to the rather nondescript dusty town of Carahuara

de Carangas. We drove along a narrow, dimly lit street flanked by drab stone and mud houses until we came to the Plaza de Armas where Bolivian soldiers in greatcoats and balaclavas mooched about outside their barracks with their rifles over their shoulders.

We had arranged through an agreement between our office in London, the Embassy in La Paz and the Bolivian Army to spend the night here but not altogether surprisingly, word had not reached this isolated outpost. Nevertheless, they showed us a place to camp on a patch of open ground behind the barracks. We spent a subdued night trying to stay warm and ignore the pounding headaches that most of us had incurred. If I made any sudden movement or bent down it felt as if my head was going to explode.

The next morning we carried on across the altiplano following a succession of rough unmarked roads through mile after mile of wild and desolate country. No matter how carefully we drove it was impossible to protect the vehicles from the jolting and jarring of the ruts and rocks that lay hidden beneath a thick coat of dust and sand.

Only one of the Broncos had functioning four-wheel drive and neither the minibuses nor the trailer, with its already inverted springs, was in any way designed to cope with this sort of punishment. To my honest relief we were still in one piece when we arrived at Patacamayo, albeit shaken to the last bone and rivet. We joined the main route to La Paz and a couple of hours later we entered the grimy outskirts of El Alto before dropping down into the bowl in the altiplano within which the main part of La Paz is packed.

As a general rule, the lower you are in the bowl, the more affluent the area and buildings around you. Up the steep sides of the bowl, single-storeyed houses are piled up on top of each other climbing right up to and over the rim. Regardless of where you are in the city, your destination always appears to be up one of the steeply rising streets which, starting higher than many Alpine summits, soon have you gasping for breath. We checked into a small backstreet hotel and set about linking up with our Embassy contact.

Over the next two days we established communications with our contacts in England, Argentina and Chile, delivered an impromptu lecture to the Anglo-Bolivian Society in English and Spanish, collected our mail and a film crew who had come out to meet us and explored the city. In the business quarter smartly dressed businessmen in suits and chic ladies rub shoulders with Cholca women in their skirts, bustles, shawls and bowler hats lending the city an unexpectedly cosmopolitan feel.

Just a short way from the centre the narrow streets are choked with people shopping at the many street stalls that line them. This area is the preserve of the Indians. The Cholca Indians are short and squat with flat, often expressionless faces and the same ruddy cheeks that we had seen elsewhere. The women seemed to be constantly eating sweets or glasses full of jelly, yoghurt or ice cream as they tended their stalls. The stalls offered the usual profusion of meat, vegetables, doughy bread, household appliances, bolts of woven cloth, skirts, flowers and bowler hats. A heavy emphasis was placed on foodstuffs including potatoes, which we had rarely seen since we left the USA, flowers and spurious witchcraft items varying from dolls to dried llamas foetuses which were supposed to offer protection to the occupants if buried in the foundations of a new house.

Having panted my way up to almost the top of the city I came to the main flower market outside the high walls of the city cemetery. Although a somewhat unconventional choice of place to visit, the cemetery was quite the most remarkable feature of the city. A large acreage was given over to row upon row of family and communal mausolea. The communal mausolea were long, flat-topped constructions containing tiered rows of windows. Behind each of these windows were small statues, photographs and dedications to the deceased together with a certificate certifying that the lease on the plot had been paid for.

If the relatives of the deceased could no longer afford the rental, then the body or ashes were removed from the space behind the display and the whole of it vacated for a new tenant. Almost every window contained arrangements of fresh flowers. At the other end of the spectrum there were elaborate marble mausolea put up by wealthy families complete with statues of angels, gilt inscriptions and all manner of architectural decorative adornment. Apart from the rather surprising visual bombardment that this offered, the cemetery afforded fantastic views across the city to the crammed upper terraces and beyond to

the powerful form of Illimani, Bolivia's best known if not highest mountain, that watches guard over the city.

From La Paz we needed to keep to a tight schedule in order to reach our planned rendezvous with escorting officers from the Argentine Army at the border in five days time. After that we had allowed another five days to travel south through Argentina to reach our intended training base in the Andes where we were to acclimatise and prepare for our ascent of Aconcagua. In total it was a journey of around 1,700 miles, much of it on rough roads through remote areas.

All went according to plan for the first couple of days as we made our way across the altiplano towards the silver mining city of Potosi. We crossed endless flat plains covered in lichen and coarse, pointed tussock grass that looked as if it had been electrocuted. Further on, the country became more hilly and we drove through narrow valleys connecting broad plains ringed by distant snow-covered mountains.

Placed apparently haphazardly, many of the hillsides had stone-walled enclosures built on them; some tiny corrals and others large pastures. With no obvious connection to these enclosures were low, stone dwellings with circular earth ovens and walled courtyards to protect them from the wind.

We arrived at a remote mountain village to find the monthly market in full swing. Indians had converged from miles around and now filled the small square. Cholca women sat selling their wares or cooking strips of ominous-looking meat over braziers. Baskets of bread competed for space with pyramids of eggs, piles of various indistinguishable herbs, spices and vegetables, bolts of cloth, great stacks of bowler hats and mounds of the ubiquitous coca leaf. Minstrels strolled around plucking at rustic guitars. Goats and chickens were being bought and sold, goods traded and there was a general bustle. More than anything else, it appeared to be a major social event and opportunity to talk and exchange news for people who for the most part lived a hard, lonely existence in their austere homes on the bleak altiplano.

We climbed up into the mountains on winding dusty roads with sheer drops on one side, to reach Potosi which, at well over 13,000 feet, claims to be the highest city in the world. We found it in the throes of a fiesta. Once the bands had stopped playing and the revellers had staggered home, we spent the night in the crenellated Army fort before heading on the next day. At that point everything began to go wrong. The road wound its way further up into the mountains. After a period of reasonable driving on a corrugated, dirt track we came to a narrow defile where there was deep, soft sand. The first three vehicles got through okay but the last vehicle towing the trailer became stuck. It took about half an hour to dig and push it out. A short distance further on the trailer had a puncture and then only a couple of miles later a second. With tubeless tyres and no more spares the trailer could not be moved until we could get at least one of these punctures repaired but the nearby mountain village had no mechanic's shop. In the event I had to drive over 100 miles before I could find somewhere to repair the tyre.

This was only the first of many punctures and a succession of other more serious problems. Many of the tyres that we had were old re-treads purchased at a prohibitive premium and when they punctured as often as not the tyre totally shredded, sometimes seriously damaging the wheel rim at the same time. My vehicle suffered total power failure due to a fault in the recharging system, which meant that it cut out without warning and could only be restarted by exchanging the battery with one of the other vehicles and then keeping the vehicle running as long as possible.

Our two mechanics, Staff Sergeant Eddie Devaney and Corporal Dougie Wilson, worked ceaselessly to keep the vehicles going in the face of a whole catalogue of breakdowns. Much later, at the end of a long night of driving and recoveries in appalling conditions with heavy rain and deep mud that left the precipitous tracks lethally slippery, the fuel line in my vehicle ruptured. By this stage we had vehicles spread over a considerable distance in various states of disrepair and one that had somehow missed a turning and was now lost in the darkness out of range of our CB radios. It was 3 a.m. by the time that the remaining three vehicles limped into Tarija.

With only twenty-four hours to our rendezvous, which was still a considerable distance away over more high passes, we got up early to set about repairing the fleet and trying to locate the missing vehicle. Neither the army nor the police had heard

any news of the vehicle and I struggled to suppress the awful idea that they were not lost but might have toppled over the edge of one of the mountain roads in the dark.

Before we could be in any position to mount a search party we had to buy new tyres and wing mirrors, have the trailer welded back together, repair the broken fuel line on my vehicle and find another electrical component to fix the charging system also on my vehicle. We split those who spoke Spanish and the mechanics into search parties to go and seek the necessary parts and tools from the backstreet mechanics' shacks and the wrecks of dead vehicles around the small provincial town. Our vehicles were of a type rarely seen in Bolivia.

Somehow by early afternoon we were ready to go. Just as the last piece of equipment was being re-loaded into the trailer, the missing vehicle appeared. A ragged cheer went up from the team. Having missed the turning they had carried on towards the border until they judged the driving conditions too dangerous to continue and had camped. As soon as it was light again they had driven all the way to the border and not finding us there had turned back to find us. We now had to turn them round once again and start back.

Once on the road again the first part of the journey in daylight was not quite as hair-raising as it had been the night before when we were clawing our way along without lights. An hour of driving took us back to the turn off and with the sun going down we began to cross some spectacularly desolate stony plains. We came across occasional small herds of sheep or donkeys. The shepherds had built stone walls a few feet long and a couple of feet high to afford themselves some protection from the wind.

As darkness fell we began to climb up into the mountains again. For the next five hours we twisted and turned, hugging the tight narrow bends of the dirt road as it clung to the sheer hillsides. We were passing through the most grandiose scenery but, except when lit up by the lights of lorries passing from the other direction, the dizzying drops were only apparent as patches of more intense blackness. With the road switching constantly to left and right around hairpin bends it demanded strained concentration from each driver. There were none of the rewards of wonderful views, just tantalising shadows to hint at what we were missing and underline the dangers of a lapse in attention.

Shortly before midnight the border town of Villazon loomed out of the darkness. Having knocked up the local military unit we found a place to camp and settled down for what was left of the night. Although we were in position to cross the border on time, the state of the vehicles hardly boded well for the long journey that still remained ahead of us.

Our arrival at the Argentine border brought into focus the delicacy of the situation that we were about to enter. It had taken over two years of sensitive but concerted diplomatic effort to enable us to enter the country during which there had been numerous occasions when it had appeared that clearance would not be forthcoming.

As the first British military expedition to enter Argentina since the Falklands War we bore considerable responsibility to ensure that our visit was both successful and without any incident that could in any way be harmful to the continuing process of improving diplomatic relations between our two countries, a process that was fragile at best. Although none of our team had taken part in the Falklands War, several of the regiments who had been involved were represented. My own regiment had lost thirty-six men in the war and for the Argentinians doubtless the casualty statistics were far worse. I had no means of knowing how the Argentinians would feel about hosting their previous enemies or how we might expect to be received.

Regardless of any official policy laid down by their senior military staff, who would I was sure be as keen as I was to avoid any embarrassment, there were bound to be individuals who were bitter about the outcome of the war or who had lost friends or relatives in it. My greatest fear was that we would be split up in the various barracks in which we had been told to stay and that an argument could spring up between the soldiers of either side and in the name of national honour a fight might break out.

The following morning, once we had all got changed into the best clothes that we had with us, I called the team together. Very slowly and carefully I ran through the background to the Falklands War, our regiments' parts in it and now the subsequent process to re-establish full diplomatic relations. I explained how much effort had been put into enabling us to be there and how fortunate we were to have the opportunity to enter a country that had been closed to us for the previous twelve years. I went on to talk about the small part that our expedition played in the ongoing process and how easy it would be for us through carelessness, ill discipline or overzealousness to set the whole process back.

I described what I knew about Argentina and its people, the places that we were going to and the regime under which we would be operating. I emphasised how difficult it could be for them to accept us, the victors, in their country and the passion with which they believed that the Falkland Islands were rightfully theirs. I ran through the contentious issue of the abuse of prisoners of war which was still being played up by the British press. I stressed the need to maintain the highest personal standards of behaviour, to keep a low profile and to avoid at all costs discussions about the Falklands War and particularly being drawn into any argument over it.

Once I had finished I handed over to Colour Sergeant McKeown who reiterated the underlying message. He spoke clearly, earthily and from the heart. His talk was extremely well delivered and had a clear impact on the soldiers. Before driving down to the frontier post we removed the Union Jacks that were flying from our vehicle antennas.

A Bolivian Army Lieutenant guided us through the town to the frontier and helped shepherd us through Customs and Immigration. Neither presented any problem and were little more than formalities. We piled back into the vehicles and, with a mounting sense of both excitement and nervous anticipation, drove the 100 yards across the border. There was no sign of any of the escorting officers so we began the formalities. I kept thinking that something would go wrong but we were processed quickly, efficiently and in a friendly manner, our British passports not raising so much as an eyebrow.

Once details of all of the electrical appliances, camera, computers, radios and the like had been entered into our passports and the passports duly stamped we were free to continue. We drove slowly out of the controlled area past a large sign showing a map of the Falkland Islands bearing the logo 'LAS MALVINAS

SON ARGENTINAS' which did little to reassure me.

Our escorting officers never materialised, but as we stopped to fix yet another puncture just beyond the border, one of the team came up to me with an Argentine Army officer in tow. He had directions for us to reach the 5th Regiment of the Argentine Army at Salta, 250 miles to the south, with whom we were due to stay the next two nights. As we left the Argentine border town of La Quiaca, we dropped down from the mountains onto broad, flat plains below. Large paddocks of rough grass were fenced, enclosing herds of sheep, donkeys and llamas. The few villages that we passed through contained simple whitewashed mudbrick buildings and, from the implements lying around, were clearly agricultural communities.

The roads were far better than those in Bolivia, broader and flatter, but dirt all the same and heavily corrugated in places. I kept up a fairly relentless place and then stopped at the beginning of the asphalt. Surely now our problems were over. Not so. The CB radio crackled into life, over it, Mike said that his vehicle had a puncture and that they had not seen the vehicle behind them for some time. I turned around and drove back to them.

The tyre was not so much punctured as totally shredded. Leaving them to change the wheel, I headed on back until I met the Colour Sergeant approaching in his vehicle. As he drew up I could see that he was not towing the trailer as normal. He said that the axle had snapped but that if we unloaded the equipment from the trailer into the other vehicles there was just a chance that we might be able to tow it to the nearest village.

We tried this but it did not work. The wheels were splayed outwards and despite all of the mechanics' best efforts with crow bars and sledge-hammers they were unable to create free tracking for the wheels. The only option was to strip the axle, take it to a town or village with welding facilities, repair it and refit it. This was obviously going to take quite some time. There did not seem any point in keeping the whole team waiting whilst this happened so I left a small team behind to deal with it and the remainder of us pressed on.

It was midnight by the time that we reached Salta along a road that turned so frequently and sharply that it became mesmerising for the drivers. We pulled up outside the first military installation that

we saw. The sentry recognised us immediately and said that the whole garrison had been told about us. He gave us directions to the 5th Regiment's barracks. There, a Captain came out to greet us and led us into a closely guarded inner courtyard. He showed us barrack accommodation for the soldiers and rooms in the officers mess for the officers. At that point a Lieutenant appeared who had been appointed to be our host and guide during our stay with the regiment. He spoke basic English and was very pleasant and keen to help. Having settled us into our accommodation he offered to show us to a restaurant where we had some of the largest steaks I had ever seen. Over dinner he told us a little about the area and his regiment, stressing several times that he would do anything that he could to help us and that his Commanding Officer had pledged every possible assistance. Back at the barracks I sank into bed between fresh sheets for the first time in several weeks but not before revelling in a hot bath. I was beginning to like Argentina already.

In the warm, sunlit morning the barracks looked open and pleasant. Large low buildings were surrounded by well tended lawns. The 5th Regiment is a cavalry regiment and there was a definite cavalry air to the place. The Second-in-Command of the regiment, a Lieutenant-Colonel, came into breakfast in riding breeches and knee-length brown leather riding boots. Breakfast was a comparatively meagre affair of coffee and rolls with butter and jam after the carnivorous feast of the night before.

When we had finished, our guide, Lieutenant Luis Maria Cabanillas, took me to 'salute' the Commanding Officer. We found Colonel Santos Maria schooling his horse in the indoor riding school, every inch the cavalry officer. He greeted me from the saddle, offered us every hospitality and went back to riding his horse. I might as well have been visiting the Household Cavalry at Windsor or Knightsbridge.

The day was spent sorting out our administration after the upheavals of the previous few days, re-provisioning and having a look around the beautiful colonial city of Salta. Late in the day the mechanics turned up with the trailer once again more or less intact. That evening the regiment laid on a traditional barbecue, or asado, for us. Apart from a few token side dishes of salad and highly spiced potatoes, it was a meat-eating frenzy with large hunks of barbecued meat, blood sausage, chorizo, ribs and steak all cooked to perfection. Great cuts of meat kept coming around, deliciously salty and washed down with beer and red wine. Argentina is not a country for a vegetarian.

For the next few days we made our way steadily southwards via Army bases in the cities of Tucuman, Catamarca, La Rioja and Mendoza. Any concerns that I had about our reception were swiftly dispelled as at each barracks we were received with the utmost hospitality. Our hosts could not have been more welcoming or have done more to assist us. Brigade Commanders and Commanding Officers greeted us personally and we were entertained at a succession of asados in our honour by the officers of the regiments with whom we stayed.

Far from being a contentious subject, they were keen to discuss the Falklands War and the experiences of both sides. I had a fascinating conversation with a Captain who as a trainee officer had been taken out of his basic training to go and command a platoon in the Falklands after the Argentinians had invaded and prior to the British Task Force's arrival. He told me that the Argentinians had been deeply concerned that if there was a fight with the British, there was every likelihood that the Chileans would take advantage of the moment to invade the south of Argentina. Later on I was to hear from many Chileans that they believed conversely that if the Argentinians had not invaded the Falkland Islands in 1982 then they would have tried to take Chilean-held territory in Patagonia and Tierra del Fuego. There was certainly no mistaking the deeply rooted enmity between the two countries.

Marcel told me that in the infantry company that he had joined, none of the non-commissioned officers or officers had worked together before they deployed and all of the soldiers were conscripts, many of whom had only been in the Army for two weeks when they left for the islands and some of whom had never even fired their rifles before. Thus they went to the Falklands poorly trained and with little unit cohesion or *esprit de corps*. Conditions during the two and a half months that they spent on the islands before the British Task Force arrived had been uncomfortable and difficult. They had been poorly equipped and supplied. There was little food, they had no rucksacks and during all that time he had one shower. When the fighting

had started his platoon had been involved in three battles including those on Mount Tumbledown and Twin Sisters and they had fought against 45 Commando, 1st Battalion Scots Guards and 1st Battalion Welsh Guards.

A large number of his men had been killed: only one by mortar fire and the rest by small-arms fire which emphasised the extent of the action that they had been involved in. He had been taken prisoner and said that on the whole his treatment had been good, certainly better than he had expected, and that he felt he had been handled with respect. He was not at all emotional when discussing the war and certainly appeared to harbour no bitterness. He believed that taking all considerations into account they had given a good account of themselves and had done a good job in extremely difficult circumstances.

He had recently returned from a United Nations tour in Kuwait where he said that the British officers had been amongst his best friends. On the way back he had travelled around Europe with his family. He said that London was by far the nicest and most friendly city. By pure coincidence they had bumped into a Household Cavalry officer in Regents Park who had invited them to his house and on another occasion he had talked to a Chelsea pensioner who had invited them to the Chelsea Hospital for tea.

He had a great sense of humour telling many stories and his sense of proportion given all that he had gone through was most impressive. His underlying attitude, reflecting many previous occasions in history, was that at the end of the day we were all soldiers doing a difficult and unpleasant job and regardless of which side we were on we had much in common with each other, certainly more so than with the politicians who had committed us to battle.

Our conversation left me disquieted. It underlined what I had begun to notice – just how similar our two Armies were in many of the ways that we did things, although by no means in all things. With sovereignty of the Falklands still not fully resolved I found myself fervently hoping that the conflict would never break out again as I had no desire to fight people so similar to us and who I found myself liking more and more.

We drove south through rich, open country with huge estancias, luxuriant crops and all the trappings of large-scale agriculture. In many ways the space and terrain reminded me of parts of East Africa. All the while, high mountains bordered our view to the west. Further on we passed through vineyards and fruit groves until we emerged on the arid plains to the east of the Atacama desert. Our journey was only marred by continuing vehicle problems. First it was more punctures, then blowing gaskets and finally the armature supporting the fan in one of the minibuses sheared. The fan had flown off, bending all its wings and slicing its way through the radio as it did so. We limped into Mendoza under tow.

We found our way through the streets of the regional capital to the barracks of the Signal Regiment of the 8th Mountain Brigade who controlled all the military within the area and had co-ordinated the support for our climb. There to greet us was a Brigade staff officer and with him another officer, Lieutenant Javier Salgado who spoke excellent English and announced that he was to be our liaison officer for the remainder of our time in Argentina. His black velvet beret and cap badge of a tank gave him away as a cavalry officer. He told me that his regiment were stationed 200 miles further south and patrolled the border region on horseback.

Javier cut an unlikely figure for someone planning to make the arduous climb to the highest point in the Americas: his ill-fitting uniform failed to conceal that he was somewhat overweight. This was emphasised by him walking with his feet facing outwards. He wore a perpetual grin on the sort of face that was made for laughing and instantly came over as being relaxed and easygoing. I took to him immediately.

The Argentinians had laid on a bus tour of the city with Javier as our guide. Due to an average of two serious earthquakes annually, most of the buildings are modern and none allowed to be more than eight storeys high. The city centre is a grid of broad tree-lined avenues and pedestrian precincts filled with expensive well-stocked boutiques and open air street cafes. The pride of the city is its park; a huge lush oasis of grass, shrubs and palms. On this Saturday afternoon it was full of families having picnics, people playing football or tennis, jogging, rollerblading or sunbathing in a warm and safe environment.

Looking over the whole city, on top of Cerro de la Gloria, is a magnificent monument to Argentina's most revered hero, General Jose de San Martin, who liberated Argentina from the Spanish and then marched his army across the Andes from Mendoza to do the same for Chile and on north to Peru. San Martin sits astride his horse flanked by infantry and cavalry soldiers in front of the main plinth, on top of which leaping horses carry sword-brandishing men into battle complete with buglers, men carrying the colours and a great swooping eagle.

Statues honouring El Libertador can be found in most cities in the southern countries of South America, but few are as dramatic as this huge tiered monument with its stepped plinth, friezes and bronze figures. Javier had a house in the city with his wife and small child and showed us around, pointing out the main features and describing the history with obvious pride.

Once more leaving the mechanics to deal with a stricken vehicle, we set off next morning on the last leg of our journey to reach our objective. We drove west out of the city and across dry plains up into the foothills of the Andes. The road followed a steep river valley that carved a course between high snow-capped peaks. The lower slopes of these mountains looked barren and unwelcoming, a sensation that was heightened as we moved further into the Andes and the cloud descended, putting a gloomy grey ceiling and dull light on the scene.

After three hours of driving we pulled up at the arched gateway of a small army outpost. High in the Andes and within a few miles of the Chilean border, this was the permanent base of the Compania de Cazadores, the Argentine Army's special forces or Hunters, and in this case their specialist mountaineers.

A stiff, icy wind carried sleet across the parade ground as we disembarked from the vehicles. The Company Commander sent out his Second-in-Command to instruct Javier that we should line up ready for him to come out and meet us. The Brigade Officer in Mendoza had been at pains to stress that the Company Commander, Major Jose Hernandez, was highly experienced and respected as a mountaineer, had planned everything for our training and the climb and heavily implied that he would not only take all the decisions but would, in effect, be in command of us. I was not altogether comfortable with this assumption and wanted it understood that, whilst delighted to co-operate in a joint venture, I would be in command of the British element.

I had no intention of standing in line and so went forward to meet him when he came out and then shook his hand before accompanying him down the line introducing each of the members of the expedition in turn. He was a small, dark, fit-looking moustachioed man. Neither he nor his deputy, Captain Riccardo Juarez, spoke any English and so everything had to be done through interpreters.

I was fortunate in that one of the soldiers, Guardsman Mickey Purtell, had lived in Central America for much of his early life and spoke good conversational Spanish. Purtell was a medic in the Irish Guards and in keeping with the reputation cultivated by 'the Micks' had more than a touch of the rogue in him. He had translated for me during our presentation to the Anglo Bolivian Society which had been fairly hysterical as we hadn't had the chance to rehearse and I kept coming out with phrases that he did not know or accidentally mis-translated with, at times, devastating effect.

Having completed the introductions we were shown into the Officer's Mess which was to be our base for the next three weeks. Having stowed our gear in our rooms we went downstairs for lunch. The Major and I talked through our intermediaries over the meal. He remained cool and dour. At one point I heard him chide Javier for referring to the Falkland Islands rather than Las Malvinas and on another occasion he made a curious comment about trying the War again. This was said with a deadpan expression.

Afterwards we ran through the plans. He had designed a very thorough and detailed acclimatisation programme including climbs of two subsidiary peaks before attempting Aconcagua. He emphasised that it was not a technical climb and required little technical equipment but was a dangerous mountain and regularly claimed lives. We were attempting the climb in December at the very beginning of the climbing season and as we could see merely by looking out of the window and listening to the wind howling around the building, the weather was not yet settled enough to attempt the summit.

Looking at his plan, it was certainly comprehensive and there was no doubting that the barracks

offered an excellent training base but I was slightly concerned that we seemed to be spending too much time acclimatising at relatively low altitudes and not enough as we went up the main mountain. However he had programmed-in training climbs and I bowed to his greater experience of the region. I certainly did not want to provoke any disagreement at this early stage.

At dinner that evening he thawed out a little but I was still very conscious that we had entered a very different atmosphere to that which we had experienced in the other barracks that we had been to. I was not sure whether we might have been foisted upon his unit or whether there was some other issue in the background, but put it down to a natural suspicion between two groups who were thrown together and had to face a serious mutual challenge.

I had experienced similar situations when working with other British regiments for the first time and so dismissed my misgivings as unnecessary oversensitivity. He might merely have been trying to establish a formal chain of command. Not only was he technically my senior, but he was considerably older than me and in British terms he would almost certainly have been ranked a Lieutenant-Colonel. He decreed that there was to be no alcohol drunk until we had climbed the mountain: his camp, his rules. There was certainly no mistaking his professionalism, sense of purpose or determination that nothing should go wrong with this expedition.

One of the soldiers came to speak to me having been to the Second-in-Command's office to pick up some paperwork. On the wall of the office was a photograph of the Second-in-Command, together with some other Argentine soldiers standing over the prostrate bodies of Royal Marines who were part of the tiny British Garrison captured during the initial invasion of the Falklands.

Next day I left the team to begin their training and together with Javier headed back to Mendoza to try and purchase the requisite spare parts for the broken-down vehicle. Having left at dawn, the mountains looked fantastic in the early morning light. We spent a frustrating day flogging around Mendoza's spares shops, garages and scrap dealers trying to locate fans, fan belts, water pumps and a number of other minor items. We suffered disappointment after disappointment as Ford minibuses were almost unheard of in Argentina, but finally we found a man living in a back street who repaired water pumps. We totally failed in our search for a new fan as, for some reason that I could not fathom, fans in Argentina turn in the opposite direction to those that we needed, so the mechanics had to try and beat what was left of ours back into shape. My patience with technical matters is extremely limited, in line with my knowledge of such things, but Javier seemed totally at ease and unperturbed and kept at the quest all day with commendable determination. It was not until 8 p.m. that we had purchased the last widget and dropped the mechanics back at the Signals Barracks where they could fit the spare parts the next day.

Throughout the day I had been quizzing Javier about a suitable Christmas present for Louie. She was arriving to join me in Chile on the same day that the soldiers were departing so I would not have much time to get anything there. Never happier than when discussing women, Javier tackled the subject with enthusiasm. He now led me off towards the better shops. I had it in mind that as Argentina was famous for its leather, a jacket would be a good present but I was not at all sure how to go about buying such a thing in English let alone Spanish and in any event carried the usual English reserve that made clothes shopping for women a painfully embarrassing proposition. Javier had no such qualms and leapt to the task with characteristic Latin flair.

The enterprise was made considerably more complicated by first of all me not knowing Louie's sizes until we stopped to ring her from a roadside kiosk, at which point she roundly accused me of being a pervert for wanting to know the details of such things, and Javier refusing to go into any shop in which he did not think the shop assistant attractive enough to be worth flirting with.

We made our way from shop to shop with me trying to cover my confusion and Javier giving me a rundown of his opinion of every woman that he saw which, with the streets coming alive with late-night shoppers and promenading couples, was considerable. Whenever I pointed out an article that I liked he would dash out into the street and accost some passer-by until he found one that he could persuade to come in and model for us. Eventually we found a jacket which I liked and he approved, so I bought it, but in doing so

I spotted a matching miniskirt which I thought would suit Louie and do no end of good for my morale. Unfortunately they did not have one to fit which provoked an even more hilarious and outrageous race around the shops until we finally ran out of time and the shops closed.

We drove back to Puente del Inca in the dark after a long but ultimately successful day and with me clutching my prize. Little did I realise what a beneficial effect that this shopping trip was going to have. The next day when Javier relayed our experiences to the Major and his Deputy a complete transformation of attitude overcame them. With much mimicking of women's figures, extravagant gestures and howls of laughter there was great discussion about what Louie looked like and a furious debate on the length of skirt that I should buy for her. As she is relatively tall and most Argentine women are tiny, the conversation was in danger of getting totally out of hand.

The ice was well and truly broken and over the next two weeks almost as much time went into further conjecture about this now famous skirt and the logistics behind purchasing it as did into the planning of our climb. Whenever the Major introduced me to anyone he would clap me around the shoulder and grin in a very knowing way and then introduce me as Captain John before embarking into another of his theatrical performances which inevitably reduced all of the Argentinians to convulsions.

Our days were filled with walks in the local areas, our training climbs and making the logistic preparations for Aconcagua. Somewhat inevitably, our sea container of mountaineering equipment, which had been shipped first to Valparaiso in Chile and then trucked overland to Argentina, had gone adrift and was located locked into Customs bond in Mendoza from which it had to be extricated. The Cazadores took us to see the various local sights: the ski resort which currently stood empty beneath bare earth slopes, the Inca bridge which gave the mountain village its name, the old hot-spring baths set into the cliff under the bridge and more soberingly the graveyard for mountaineers who had died on Aconcagua. There were the graves of Spaniards, Germans, Italians and Argentinians and one inscription to a British Captain of Hussars called Mardon who had died on the mountain in 1928.

Our first training climb was up Banderita Norte, a peak of around 13,500 feet. Having filled our flasks with *mate*, (pronounced ma-tay) a concoction of heavily sweetened herbal tea that the Argentinians drank throughout the day claiming that it had restorative qualities, we packed windproof clothing, put on dark glasses and sunblock and arming ourselves with ski sticks, set off after our guides. Captain Juarez, the Second-in-Command, led the climb with a corporal out in front of him searching for the best route. Immediately outside the company base we began climbing steeply up the valley side. To begin with the valley was enclosed in a solid, unbroken wall but after an hour and a half of climbing it became broken into a jagged line of peaks. The summit that we were heading for was perched on top of a rock pyramid and did not look to be far away but it took a couple more hours of concerted effort scrambling up steep but awkward screes to reach it. It was hard physical graft and a relief to stop when we arrived at the top, but it was not difficult and I was pleased to see that none of our team had experienced any problems.

We sat on top in the brilliant sunshine drinking *mate*, eating chocolate and taking in the spectacular views all around. In every direction there were fantastic mountain vistas, but the one that held our attention was to the north-west where Aconcagua stood thirty miles away. It rose up in a massive, broad-based block. We were looking at the daunting aspect of the South Face, the sheerest of its sweeping faces, broken only by ice cliffs and near vertical couloirs. We would be climbing from the far side.

Having spent some time admiring the view, chatting and filling our names into the book attached to the summit cross, we set off down the mountain. The Cazadores took the line of the steepest scree slopes and we flew down, running the screes at full tilt. Regardless of the dangers of twisting or breaking an ankle the soldiers were really enjoying themselves. At last we were getting on with what we had come to do and there was both hard work and excitement to be had.

During the long hours of travelling south from Ecuador and nights spent around the camp fire, we had all got to know each other reasonably well but now the characters really began to emerge. There was a gang of Irish Guardsmen: Guardsmen Mickey Purtell and Paul Curran who both played up to the Mick image; Lance-Sergeant Paul Moffett who I knew well from the past, having climbed and canoed together; and Lance-Sergeant Steve Hill who joined the Army relatively late, having worked first as a farmer and had subsequently transferred to the Irish Guards from the Household Cavalry. He was rather more reserved than the others, a pleasant easy-going man who looked as though he would be steady in a crisis. These were joined by Staff Sergeant Eddie Devaney our irascible and, in military terms, aged chief mechanic who was also Irish and shared their affinity for tall stories and hard liquor.

Trooper Bob Amos had travelled most of the way in my vehicle and we had spent happy hours talking about the British countryside as his father had worked as a gamekeeper. There were two Scots Guardsmen, Johnny Lynn and Neil Lawrie, who both looked fit and strong. The Coldstream Guards were represented by Guardsman David Bowness, known as 'Bones' to the team on account of his lack of physique, who talked of leaving the army to go to university and played the harmonica, and Corporal Spencer Wright from the West Country. The second REME mechanic, Corporal Dougie Wilson, was more intelligent than most. At times a bit prickly and disconcertingly body conscious, he was a fit, self-confident man with clear determination and ambition. Besides the permanent cadre, which Corporal Steggles had rejoined at the beginning of this phase, that left Corporal Steve Vickers who had come out as a last minute replacement joining us in La Paz and Lieutenant Bruce MacInnes from the Welsh Guards. Son of a clergyman, Bruce was an extremely laid-back, verging on horizontal, Oxford graduate. He had enthusiasm in spades and filled a vital role by being one of the few Spanish speakers on the team but often drove me mad by taking so long being charming to people and generally dilettanteing around the place, that we were often in danger of getting nowhere.

He was extremely bright but in many ways very naive to the ways of the world, a fact which the soldiers were quick to take advantage of. If I had reason to admonish or chivvy him, which I frequently did, or the soldiers started mobbing him up, he would look at me with a sort of quizzical puppyish indignation. That said, he put a great deal of effort into the day-to-day running of the team and bore the brunt of many of the most mundane and tedious chores and there was no doubting that he was extremely amiable and good for the general morale of the team.

During the days of training and evenings around the dining room table, the soldiers had done a great deal to further relations with the Argentinians and none more so than Colour Sergeant McKeown. Initially his rather flamboyant manner and broad Glaswegian accent had left them looking bewildered and perplexed but although they continued to suspect that he was quite mad, they soon came to recognise his strength and larger than life character.

I would often hear the Major yell out across the room 'Charleey' and then they would both throw their arms around each other with furious clapping of shoulders, an habit that we were rapidly picking up from the Argentinians as it generally seemed to foster good relations. They would then gabble away furiously to each other with much excited shouting and posturing regardless of the fact that neither one of them understood one solitary word that the other was saying.

On the evening of our first training climb, the General in command of the 8th Mountain Brigade, Brigadier-General Llavar, arrived in Puente del Inca and came to have dinner with us and the Cazadores officers in the mess. He had the look of a soldier's soldier and was clearly at ease with his Mountain Troops. He had served in the Cazadores as a junior officer and had climbed Aconcagua three times as well as taking part in some Argentine expeditions to the Himalayas. Through Javier we talked of many things over dinner but mainly of a common love for mountains. Apart from the interest of talking about the Argentine Army with one of its senior generals, his presence had the added merit of getting the Major to lift his embargo on alcohol and produce beer and good Argentinian wine to accompany the meal.

After dinner the General made a short speech. As he welcomed us to Argentina and wished us well as we worked alongside his Mountain Troops, he said that he did so, not as any diplomatic gesture, but simply as soldier to soldier. He bade us good luck and a safe climb on Aconcagua. It was a simple but well-made speech which struck a chord with the soldiers and helped underline the importance and momentousness of working together.

I later learnt that just before we had entered Argentina, the Government had slashed the Defence budget and the Army High Command in Buenos Aires had ordered that support to the expedition should be reduced to a bare minimum. Brigadier-General Llavar had taken a personal decision to go against this and continue to provide every assistance that he could from the 8th Mountain Brigade. I was indebted to him.

While we waited for our equipment to arrive, we went to visit the border town of Las Cuerras just a few miles up the valley, at the head of the pass leading across the Andes into Chile. The old village had been destroyed in a landslide in the 1960s. The abandoned Customs house straddled a disused road. A few modern Alpine-style chalets and cafes had been built on either side of the new highway.

Back at the barracks the container had finally arrived and Colour Sergeant McKeown set to sorting out the equipment. We went through every item with the Cazadores before deciding what would be carried on the mountain. They rejected every item of technical equipment including, to my surprise, ropes and crampons. Later, each man was issued rucksacks, boots, down clothing, Goretex oversuits, socks, gloves, thermal underwear, tents, headtorches, rollmats, bivi bags, candles, compasses and the plethora of other small items of equipment that we would take with us.

Another day was spent issuing the rations for the climb, allocating tent groups, discussing conditions that we could expect to encounter and talking to the team about the routine and tactics that we would employ on the mountain. Again to reduce weight, Major Hernandez wanted to keep the rations to an absolute minimum. I argued against this, not wanting a lack of rations to halt us if we got held up by bad weather. We were receiving reports of high winds and deep snow at 14,000 feet and cases of frostbite being incurred by the few groups who tried to go any higher.

This time for administration and discussion periods was also useful both to make our preparations and to lay the ground rules for the climb in the minds of everyone on the team, but I felt frustrated that we were not out training harder and getting better acclimatised. Working at 10,000 feet was all very well but we were intending to climb to 22,850 feet on a very fast schedule and only time would tell if we would be adequately acclimatised at the higher levels.

Our relations with the Argentinians were improving all the time: both the Major and his deputy had started calling me by my Christian name although they did not invite me to do the same to them, and they began asking more questions about England, our history, the Royal Family and the British people's impression of Argentina. These conversations were light-hearted with a lot of banter, but I was always conscious of treading on delicate ground. When they laughingly accused all English of being pirates, as they often did, there was no doubting that they were referring to recent as well as Elizabethan history.

Our second training climb came as a welcome escape from the barracks. This time the Major led as we set off early in the morning once again and made our way across the Inca bridge and up the far wall of the valley towards Banderita Sur. We climbed up the steep grassy lower slopes and then up a narrow defile that cut through the rock band that formed the natural ceiling to the immediate valley wall. Above, we emerged onto an open grassy plateau that led gently up to the base of some perilously steep screes which climbed over a thousand feet straight up to another rock band and finally a last section of screes to the summit.

The main scree slope had only the faintest covering of shale over a base of earth and shattered rock that offered little purchase. It was so steep that the slightest slip risked a fall of hundreds of feet down the slope. The greatest hazard however was the constant bombardment of rocks dislodged by those climbing at the front of the team. Those at the back had to duck and dodge these missiles without losing their footing. The incessant calls of 'Below!' and the fizzing of stones past our heads began to cause ragged nerves. Where the scree was channelled into a narrow couloir we had to take it in turns to climb with those below sheltering behind a rock buttress as two or three people at a time scrabbled their way slowly up.

As we reached the top of the second rock band Guardsman Purtell began to throw up. He had spent most of the climb with his eyes clenched tightly shut holding onto the back of the person in front. He had no head for heights and was at various points totally incapacitated by an overwhelming fear, but even more seriously and not in any way

his fault, he seemed incapable of acclimatising to altitude. He had remained behind when we made our first training climb to interpret for Richard as he tried to negotiate the release of our container from Customs. One of the Cazadores had taken him up on his own the next day but he had returned ashen-faced having been unable to make it to the summit. Even at the Colca Canyon he had suffered from nausea and now it was clear that he could not safely climb any further. His chances of getting up Aconcagua were slight.

Leaving him to rest where he was, the remainder of us pressed on for the summit up the last 500 feet of steep scree, still packed with the remnants of the previous winter's snow. I was feeling the altitude and had to stop several times to catch my breath. I was almost blown off my feet by a gust of wind as I clambered up onto the exposed summit. All around there were fantastic vistas of snow-covered peaks but once again it was Aconcagua which drew our gaze. It stood proud, far higher than all the peaks around it. Looking at its summit in the distance, it was difficult to estimate its height in relation to our present position; it did not look to be another 10,000 feet above us. How deceptive appearances could be.

Having paused for a rather draughty brew from our flasks and posed for a photograph of the summitteers clutching both Argentine and British flags, we set off down. The descent was made amidst a flurry of skidding feet, scrabbling fingers and flying rocks. By early afternoon, having climbed and then descended over 5,000 feet, we were back in the Officers Mess enjoying a large lunch. It had been another good day for all but the unfortunate Guardsman Purtell and to complement the party atmosphere the Major authorised beer for everyone.

It was two further days before the weather had cleared up sufficiently and we were ready to start making our way up to the mountain. In the intervening period we sorted ourselves out into tent groups, allocated the last items of equipment and prepared the loads for the mules who were to carry the bulk of our heavy supplies up the Horcones valley to our base camp. It had been snowing on the mountain and the weather was still extremely unsettled. It was clear that once we were in place we must be ready to climb fast and take advantage of any window in the bad weather.

The delay and hanging about were irksome. Having completed the first stages of our acclimatisation and made our preparations, we were all keen to get onto the mountain and tackle the matter in hand.

On the morning of our departure we were up well before dawn. Breakfast was a rather desultory affair. Most people were still sleepy and the Cazadores' breakfast of rock hard bread with a smear of jam and a cup of coffee held little appeal. We loaded ourselves and the equipment that we were to carry onto the back of an old lorry which then carried us up the valley. The first rays of sunlight were tinting the mountain tops a bright orange but down in the dark shadows of the valley it was bitterly cold. We turned off the road onto a rough dirt track and then bumped along it for a couple of miles until we came to a barrier signalling the boundary of the National Park around the mountain. By 7 a.m. we had shouldered our packs and were making our way in Indian file up the Horcones Valley.

As soon as the sun's direct rays crept down the mountainsides and over the valley floor, the day warmed up dramatically and we gradually peeled off several layers of clothing as we made our way on over the dry earth and shale. After a couple of hours a shout went up from the back of the line to stop. Guardsman Purtell was bent over throwing up. For whatever reason his body had totally failed to acclimatise. Major Hernandez and I looked at each other in accord; there was no question of him climbing the mountain, he could walk on to our night stop but must then go down with the mules.

For four hours we walked on up the broad valley. Initially it was covered in tough tussock grass. The trail followed the rolling valley floor climbing in and out of steep side re-entrants, over streams, crossing and re-crossing the main river. Further on, it flattened out into a plain of bare stones. Hares loped off into the distance as we approached and flocks of duck floated unconcerned on small ponds that had been left by the river when it was last in spate. The scenery was spectacular with Aconcagua a solid white block at the head of the valley and on either side ridges of towering white peaks contrasting brightly with the clear blue sky.

From having been extremely cold when we started, the valley became fiercely hot, the bare stones reflecting much of the heat and offering no cover. We halted, hot and tired after about twelve miles and put up our tents beneath some large boulders. For the remainder of the afternoon we lay out in the sun or baked in our tents drinking brew after brew to rehydrate ourselves.

Towards evening two groups of laden mules came cantering by driven by their muleteers. The second lot were the Army mules carrying our kit. They pressed on past us heading up for base camp at Plaza de Mulas. Trailing behind them and in excessively poor humour came Javier. He had been adjusting the video player in the Officers Mess a couple of days earlier when somehow he had knocked the television off the table that it had been resting on. It had fallen on his foot inflicting a deep gash and severe bruising. By this rather inglorious accident he had rendered himself *hors de combat* and now had to suffer the ignominy of riding up to Plaza de Mulas on the back of a mule. Only further enhancing his accident prone reputation, he had selected a particularly recalcitrant animal which refused to go forward regardless of constant urging and latterly some energetic use of the savage spurs which he had strapped onto his boots.

Man and beast were far from being in harmony and were regarding each other with mutual malevolence. Javier was hot and tired and no doubt in considerable discomfort from his injured foot and the constant bouncing up and down on the hard Argentinian saddle but as usual he wore his broad smile. Now to add to a generally disagreeable day he had to suffer a barrage of abuse from Cazadores and British alike, all of whom took advantage of the moment to rib him about cavalry officers being unable to hack the pace and needing a steed to carry them up the mountain. He bore it well and having stopped for a brief chat, bounced off into the sunset cursing his mount all the while.

The following day dawned bright again. It was clear and crisp in the rarefied air but just above freezing as we set off up the valley once more. The track followed the undulating right side of the valley clinging to the steep scree and rock slope. We seemed very small, like ants on a jungle path, as we clambered along totally overwhelmed by the scale of the mountains around us. The deep red of the rock set off the snow-clad upper faces and the flawless blue sky above. After a few more miles the track dropped back down to the valley floor which was brought to a sudden halt by a steep face of moraine that climbed directly up to Plaza de Mulas. We stopped for a drink and some chocolate beside the ruins of a military hut. It was of a fairly elaborate design with solid stone walls and heavy beams but it had been destroyed by an avalanche a few years previously.

The slope above was a long steady pull for several hundred feet. The trail zigzagged as it wound its way up the steep scree. We took our time taking slow measured paces until we walked over the top of a mound to see another much smaller hut in front of us with a tall radio antenna attached to it from which was flying the Argentinian flag and that of a Spanish expedition. Javier emerged along with the Cazadores muleteers and the military signallers who were manning the mountain post. We set up our tents around the hut.

We were now at 14,000 feet. There was another 9,000 feet of climbing above us to reach the summit. Several of the team were feeling the effects of the altitude and a number were light-headed and breathless. I was concerned about Guardsmen Curran and Bowness in particular who had made hard work of the climb up the last steep slope. Bowness's pulse was racing by the time that we reached the camp site and took a long time to settle down. He was a small man anyway and must have found the loads proportionately much heavier than the rest of us. I felt sorry for him. He was a genuinely pleasant and helpful man but the other soldiers ragged him fairly mercilessly for his lack of physique and slightly offbeat sense of humour and I knew that he wanted to prove himself to them on the mountain.

The forecast was for another good day the following day but changeable thereafter. The Major's plan was for us to press on to Nido de Condores at around 18,000 feet the next day and then go for the summit the following day. Normally I would have said that this was dangerously fast and would have insisted on a slower rate of ascent.

3,000 feet per day is the standard maximum recommended rate of ascent and at higher altitudes that is normally split up by rest days after every couple of days climbing to acclimatise at the next level. Somewhere between eight and eleven days was the usual time taken to reach the summit and we were intending to do it in four, but few groups spent the amount of time training and acclimatising that we had at Puente del Inca. It was impossible to evaluate how much acclimatisation benefit our

training climbs would have now we were on the mountain.

I felt very trapped by the diplomatic connotations of our situation. Our Defence Attaché had stressed that the Argentinians would be in command and Major Hernandez was adamant that we should stick to his programme but at the same time all of my own experience as a mountaineer was flashing warning bells. I decided to let things ride for the moment but to re-assess the condition of the group at each stage with Mike, the Doctor.

We woke up next morning to be confronted by a large lenticular cloud enveloping the summit of the mountain, a classic sign of bad weather to come, which provided a welcome rest day. Instead of moving up to Nido de Condores we went for a long walk, climbing 1,500 feet up the slope behind us to help build our acclimatisation. We were rewarded with fantastic views of the mountain massif and out over the surrounding subsidiary peaks.

Back down at Plaza de Mulas we crossed the uneven plateau of moraine to visit the mountaineering hotel that some optimistic speculator had built. As it was still some time before the main climbing season, it was not yet open. Back at the camp site I found most of the Cazadores huddled inside the hut brewing up endless mugs of *mate*. The single, horn mug was passed from hand to hand never stopping. As soon as it was empty, a Major Domo figure produced a small skin pouch of *mate* leaves from which he re-charged the mug adding sugar and boiling water. I sat listening to them telling stories, either with Javier occasionally translating or just absorbing the meaning from the small amount of Spanish that I understood and their very theatrical way of speaking.

Next day it was clear again. Bowness had decided wisely and unselfishly not to try and go any further so we left him with a tent and set off upwards. Most of us had had a poor night's sleep and were not feeling our strongest. Major Hernandez led setting a slow but deliberate pace. The route climbed up in a series of long steep sections which had us all feeling the weight of our packs. After an hour or so Guardsman Curran stopped. He had a blinding headache, his chest was tight and he was having trouble breathing. Corporal Vickers did not feel much better and so they turned back together. Another long, steep and equally relentless slope led up to a col at 17,000 feet. I felt as though

I was walking in treacle and trying to breathe oxygen-less air. Every step seemed to require a great effort. From the col the angle eased and it was a long, heavy plod over the snow up to the plateau at 18,000 feet.

The Eagles Nest is an apt name for the plateau that we found ourselves on. Totally exposed to the wind and bitterly cold, our eyrie had sweeping views out across the Andes. At that height everything seemed to take on a blueness; the air, the ground and the distant peaks all blending together into a hazy pastiche. Over half the team had strong headaches so the first priority was to rehydrate and try and get some food into us, fighting back the natural nausea that altitude brings on. Once that was done we settled in as best we could, erecting our tents, tying them down securely and creating a limited windbreak from the loose rocks that were lying around. For most of us the remainder of the day was spent either drinking as much fluid as we could melt and force down or lying still to try and minimise pounding headaches. The plan was to check the weather at 3 a.m. and, if conditions allowed, push on for the summit next day.

Having eventually managed to drift off to sleep I woke up roughly each hour on the hour until the appointed time. Crawling out of my down sleeping bag and straight into duvet jacket, thick gloves and hat, I looked out of the tent. The whole sky was a carpet of brightly shining stars piercing the inky blackness with not even a wisp of cloud overhead. I wandered over to Major Hernandez's tent to confirm his assessment of the conditions. He said that although it was clear overhead there was cloud building to the north and east which threatened to bring storms with them so we should wait another day.

I walked around each of the tents telling the team to stand down. There was a general air of relief at the prospect of a day of rest and a chance to gather some strength. Most people climbing the mountain make another camp 1,500 feet higher up at the shell of the abandoned Berlin hut and mount their summit bid from there. The Cazadores argued that it was impossible to sleep or even rest at that height. Your body was only deteriorating up there so it was better to go for a longer summit day from Nido de Condores, added to which you avoided the requirement to haul heavy tents and camping gear up the extra distance. It was hard to know which

option would be better but there was no doubting that a summit day requiring 5,000 feet of ascent was going to require a very great deal of energy.

I got up again at 8 a.m. unable to resist the call of nature any longer. It was a beautiful clear day with no sign of the prophesied storm. I had a splitting headache and wandered over to the doctor's tent to get a paracetamol. Mike handed me a pill saying that he felt absolutely ghastly and did not think that he would be up to going any higher. Over the next two hours the other members of the team appeared out of their tents. Several of them looked pretty rough. Trooper Amos was grey and haggard and Corporal-Major Tate said that he could not keep any food down and felt dizzy every time that he sat up. Two of the Cazadores were also suffering so the three of them packed up their kit and headed down together. The team was thinning down.

With plenty of drinks and fresh air, those remaining began to pick up as the day warmed. We spent the time lazing in the sunshine, dozing, chatting, reading and playing cards. When I could summon up the energy, I wandered around taking photographs of the mountain.

A couple of teams came down either from the summit or the Berlin hut. Most of them looked pretty deadbeat and some appeared to be in the advanced stages of Acute Mountain Sickness. No one had attempted to reach the top from where we were but what conclusion should we draw from their dishevelled state? I had some serious reservations that we might be biting off more than we could chew by not making a higher camp but to the Cazadores the condition of those coming down only supported their theory. As the day wore on, clouds began boiling up to the west. By evening there was a mass of thick grey cumulus towers arrayed across the sky. We could but hope for a clear day and the strength to get to the top and so settled down for the night.

I turned over and over but could not sleep. Corporal Wilson, with whom I was sharing a tent, was having the same problem and eventually we gave up and had something to drink and chatted for a while. We tried to sleep again but with little result. The clock crept frustratingly slowly around to 3 a.m. as each of us tried to con our bodies into relaxing and getting some much needed rest in preparation for the climb ahead. I heard Bruce get up and call the Major. He shouted through the wall of my tent that the sky was clear and the climb was on. Having crawled out of my bag and into my pile and Pertex shirt and salopettes, with a down jacket thrown on top, I made my way over to the doctor's tent to get some headache pills. The water was so cold that the Dispirin which he gave me would not dissolve.

Corporal Wilson put a brew on for the two of us as I went round checking on the remainder of the team. Trooper Amos still felt rough and withdrew himself from the climbing party. We were now down to two teams of five with a handful of Cazadores split between the two groups. I was surprised to find that none of them had head torches and the Major had to borrow one of ours to lead the way. At 4 a.m. we set off into the darkness. There was a strong wind blowing in gusts and it was bitterly cold as we made our way over a short, relatively flat section of boulder-strewn ground towards the steep slope that led up into the blackness towards the Berlin hut.

The Major set a spanking pace which made it hard for the Cazadores without head torches to pick their way over the rocks and for those at the back to keep up. Regardless of this he pressed on, pausing occasionally and only briefly to check that we were following and chide us to keep up. We had not gone very far when there was the sound of violent retching from behind me. Colour Sergeant McKeown had fallen victim to the altitude and had to turn back. As it was not far to the tents he was able to go back alone but from that point on, anyone turning back would have to be accompanied by at least one other.

We pressed on, concentrating on keeping up. Bruce MacInnes dropped off the back of our group and joined those behind with Captain Juarez. We came upon the dim shadow of the Berlin hut with almost no warning. Derelict, it offered little protection from the fierce cold. Our group had now pulled well ahead. Major Hernandez announced that we would stop for just five minutes.

Although I longed for a proper rest I knew that he was right. It was so cold that we would have begun to freeze had we stopped for longer but at the same time I worried that we were in danger of blowing up if we maintained this killing pace for much farther. The tea that we poured from our flasks was tepid as soon as it landed in our mugs.

No sooner had we stopped than we were on the move again, continuing steeply upwards. Looking back I could see the head torches of the second group approaching the hut and Bruce's distinctive purple duvet jacket. The pace continued to be savage but the biggest problem now became the cold. We moved out of the gully that we had been climbing and onto a more open slope. There was no protection from the wind at all which knifed through our protective clothing and was gusting strong enough to blow us over.

At almost exactly the same moment Guardsman Lynn and I lost the feeling in our hands. Lieutenant Oprandi, the youngest of the Cazadores officers was straight in to help. He took my gloves off and massaged my hands while another of the Cazadores rooted through my pack for my overmitts. Such had been the rate of our climb that I had not had time to put them on. Someone else did the same for Lynn. The return of feeling to my fingers was painful but reassuring. Under control once again, we all put on balaclavas and goggles and pulled up our hoods.

While we were sorting ourselves out the remnants of the second group caught up with us. Apart from two of the Cazadores, there was only Richard and Guardsman Lawrie left, both of whom seemed to be going well. Sergeant Hill, Corporal Steggles, Staff Sergeant Devaney and Captain Juarez had all turned back.

We struggled on up relentlessly steep slopes in the face of buffeting winds. To our left the north face dropped away to the Polish Glacier. Dawn was breaking but there was no sign of the wind dropping. It became a constant battle against cold and breathlessness.

I was beginning to feel weaker and weaker and I was having to work hard to keep up with the Major in front. Louie's words, written on the back of the photograph of her that I carried in my diary, kept whirling around in my head: 'Be strong, be careful and be yourself. Remember that I love you and that I will be with you every step of the way.' At one moment I felt strong and confident and the next despairing through total lack of energy. I tried to shut out any negative thoughts, attempting to dismiss them as temporary weaknesses and concentrating solely on keeping going.

The summit still seemed impossibly far away. Why did I not have more strength? I wanted to reach the summit of this mountain so badly. Not only had I not reached the summit of McKinley, which still rankled, but with the fate of the last phase still unclear this might be the last major challenge of the expedition. Regardless of that, my place as an officer and expedition leader was at the front of the team not caving in like some weak recruit. I focussed on the Major's boots, matching him pace for pace.

There was a long, steep slope of loose scree ahead of us leading up and over a ridge to the Independencia Refuge at 21,000 feet. There we planned to drop our packs and continue with just ski poles and ice axes. There was still several hours climbing including the infamous Canaletta to reach the summit. A cry went up from the back to wait. Guardsman Lynn was having trouble keeping up. He said that he could not get enough oxygen in.

As we paused for him to get his breath, I looked around the group. Richard was going well, as was Corporal Wilson. Lawrie did not appear to be in any particular difficulty. Of the five of us, aside of Lynn, I assessed myself to be the weakest and resolved that if he had to go down I would be the one to escort him. We pushed on.

Some distance before the top of the slope, the cry went up from the back again. Lynn had reached his limit. All the Cazadores looked around to see who would go down with him. I stepped forward. Lieutenant Oprandi tried to stop me. The two of us got on well and had enjoyed climbing together. I was touched by his human concern but, loathsome as it was, I knew that it was the correct decision. It would have been quite wrong to have made one of the others turn back when they stood a better chance of reaching the top than I did.

I did not want to prolong any discussion and so having wished good luck to the three remaining members of my team and the Cazadores, I turned downhill. I was extremely choked up inside and had to blink away the tears from my eyes as I trudged slowly downwards. I felt an overwhelming disappointment that my summit bid was over and not a little ashamed that I had not had greater strength to continue.

I fervently hoped that the other three would finish the job and do so safely. Surely all of the planning, fund raising and diplomatic effort had not been in vain. All three had looked fit and well, particularly Richard. If anyone could get up, I was sure that he could. I, better than most people, knew the single-mindedness, resolve and

sheer physical grit that he held within him and as I had turned away I had seen that familiar look of set determination come over him.

I stopped to look back. The others had already turned once more to the slope and were making their way slowly upwards. I glanced at my altimeter. We were at 20,500 feet, higher than I had ever been before, but that was scant compensation. Neither of us felt particularly strong but Lynn was swaying and having trouble clearing his head. I led slowly, picking the safest possible path and stopping frequently wherever I could find shelter to give him time to rest and collect himself. With the sun up, the views were sensational down the sheer north face and out to the surrounding peaks. All lay well below us.

Once we got back to Nido de Condores I went around the team to see that everyone was alright and to hear their stories. Colour Sergeant McKeown had stopped throwing up, but his blood oxygen level was still very low and Mike wanted him to go on down to the richer air at Plaza de Mulas. Lynn also needed to go down as soon as he had a chance to rehydrate. Captain Juarez had been throwing up during the ascent but seemed to be back to his normal chipper self.

Bruce had stopped to help a Spaniard who he had thought in the darkness was one of the Cazadores and had helped the man back down to camp. Now, having realised that it had not been one of the team, he felt cheated and asked if there would be a chance of making a second summit bid the next day. We had adequate rations and I was keen to give it another go myself but when we put it to Captain Juarez we got a categoric no. The Argentinians clearly saw this as our one chance and intended to evacuate the mountain as soon as the summit party returned.

For the next couple of hours I tried to relax and get my energy back with hot drinks and food. I kept going over my decision to turn back in my mind, cursing myself for not keeping going. There was no sign of the climbers high on the mountain but then I saw two figures descending the slope below the Berlin hut. As they got closer I could make them out as Major Hernandez and Guardsman Lawrie.

Lawrie had run out of steam after Independencia. Corporal Wilson had offered to take him down but the Major had intervened and sent Corporal Wilson and Richard on towards the summit. He said that they were both doing very well. He himself looked

Reed boat
fisherman,
Huanchaco,
Peru.

A woman watches over her herd of llamas on the Bolivian altiplano.

Opposite: Fishermen haul in their catch of squid. Peru.

A man holds up an eagle that he has saved in front of the earthquake damaged church at Maca, Colca Canyon, Peru.

Major Jose Hernandez leads the team up our second training climb, Banderita Sur, with Aconcagua in the background. Argentina.

Paul Curran and Dougie Wilson scramble down a rock section on Banderita Sur.

Paul Moffet scree running.

Making for the summit of
Banderita Sur, 14,100 feet.

Mount Aconcagua, 22,850 feet, the highest mountain in South America.

Walking up the Horcones Valley on the way to climb Aconcagua.

Lieutenant Javier Salgado discusses the finer points of riding recalcitrant mules with Major Jose Hernandez and Captain Riccardo Juarez.

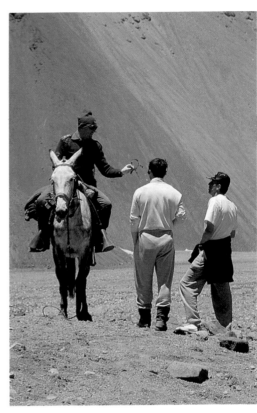

Our joint Anglo-Argentine team at Plaza de Mulas, 14,000 feet, Mount Aconcagua.

Paul Curran, Paul Moffat, John Steggles, Bob Amos and Johnny Lynn relax at 14,000 feet, Mount Aconcagua.

Richard Gaffney and Dougie MacDonald with four of the Cazadores on the summit of Anconcagua. *(Richard Gaffney)*

shattered. It had been an extremely magnanimous gesture to stand down for one of our team and I was hugely grateful to him. He also said that it had not been as cold as it was now on the mountain when he had previously attempted to make a winter ascent.

For the next few hours we waited. At one point earlier on we had just been able to make out a number of tiny figures ascending the traverse towards the Canaletta. Clouds had been flying over the mountain so it must have been savagely cold near the top. It was down to Richard and Corporal Wilson now. I prayed that they were okay, hating the feeling of powerlessness to help. Midway through the afternoon Captain Juarez ran over to where I was sitting watching the mountain. He had just received a radio call from Oprandi. Seven people including Richard and Dougie Wilson had made it to the summit at 1.30 p.m. and were on their way down. I was enormously relieved that they were alright and that we had achieved the aim. Whatever the post mortem as to how we might have got more to the top, at least the objective was achieved and British and Argentinians had stood on the summit together. They had been on the way down for three hours by the time that they were able to get through on the radio.

They finally staggered into camp at around 5 p.m. looking absolutely shattered. Having left their packs at Independencia they had climbed on up another slope until they came to the ridge that led to the base of the Canaletta. When the Cazadore who was leading had stepped out onto the ridge he was blown straight back into the arms of the man behind. It had taken them an hour to cross the ridge, bent double against the wind and then another four hours to climb the steep scree of the Canaletta up to the summit cross.

The Canaletta had been totally exhausting, a sheer battle of determination and stamina against the unending scree, taking a few steps at a time, scrabbling for any available grip and then pausing to rest before taking the next few steps. Corporal Wilson had suffered frostnip to his fingers and toes and had been in considerable discomfort but had carried on without complaint. Richard also praised Major Hernandez for his extremely selfless action in helping Lawrie down and Lieutenant Oprandi who he said had been a tower of strength and support throughout. I felt extremely proud of them. The

highest peak in the Americas was added to our trophies.

I asked if they wanted to stay the night where we were and go down the next day; they had certainly earned the rest, but after several hot drinks and some food they said that they would rather get down to a lower level where we could all sleep better. We packed up the camp and with heavy packs and tired bodies made our way slowly and unsteadily down the steep screes back to Plaza de Mulas. There, there was a rousing reception from all of the Argentinians and the remainder of the team with much cheering, hand shaking and hugging and beers for all. That night, despite being at the bottom corner of a tent packed with four men, I slept better than on any other night on the mountain.

We marched out the next day all the way back to the road head. The river had swollen considerably in the short time that we had been on the mountain. We had to use our ski poles at their fullest extension to vault between islands of rocks in order that we could cross it down on the valley floor. We maintained a fairly furious pace to cover the distance in a single day but our reward was well worth the effort. The Cazadores laid on an enormous feast for all those, Argentinian and British, who had been on the mountain. Everyone dressed up for the occasion and the Colour Sergeant brought out his now well-travelled kilt.

A massive barbecue grill groaned under the weight of steak, blood sausage, chorizo and all manner of oddly-shaped entrails. We were fed plateful after plateful of the rich, strongly spiced meat washed down by bottles of full-bodied Argentine wine and beer. After our mountain diet of freeze-packed rations we gorged ourselves. Major Hernandez was playing host and letting out ever more elaborate cries of 'Charleey', 'Bruce' or 'Doggie' down the table. He gave a speech of congratulations to those who reached the summit and proposed a toast to Argentine and British soldiers working together.

Once all the food had been cleared away I replied, concentrating on the help and hospitality of the Argentine Army, the professionalism of the Cazadores and the honour that it was to work and climb with them. Afterwards we presented them all with certificates, plaques and gifts to commemorate the occasion.

The evening degenerated into a good-natured

singing and drinking event. Sergeant Moffat led with some good Irish ballads, a number of the soldiers produced some rather off-key rugby songs and Bruce was howled down when he tried a rather serious operatic number. The Argentinians countered by sending for a guitarist and a number of the other men from their company who sang wonderful traditional ballads. Javier challenged Colour Sergeant McKeown to a drinking competition which I thought a little ill-advised but he was old enough to look after himself so I left him to it.

Our transition the remaining few miles across the border and then south to Santiago was rather more time-consuming and problematic than I had envisaged. It took several days to negotiate the passage of our equipment back through Customs and even longer to secure final clearance to enter Chile.

The Cazadores could not have done more to help us. On the first morning after the party, the Major drove Richard, Javier and I down to Mendoza to call on the General and obtain a letter from him seeking the assistance of the Head of Customs. I felt like grim death as I got up at 6 a.m. The only consolation was seeing Javier who looked much worse and was shaking in a cold sweat from the night's excesses.

The General received us in his office which was hung with pictures of himself on expedition in Argentina and Nepal. He presented Richard and I with a china sculpture of an old boot each bearing the emblem of the 8th Mountain Brigade. We talked of the climb and the possibility of future British military expeditions to Argentina and then he bade us good luck and farewell.

The Major was in flying form. Taking us up the mountain had been his last task while in command of the Cazadores and all had gone well. Now walking around his home town on a hot spring day he was extending bonhomie to all of the many people who recognised him. There was a lot of joking about the stunning, scantily-clad Argentine girls that we passed in the street. When we reached the Customs office it took some time to get to see the Customs chief so he went around each room kissing every girl in the place to the accompaniment of a fair amount of heckling.

When presented with the General's letter, the Customs Chief duly signed a paper authorising us to clear Customs in Puente del Inca rather than bringing all the kit back to Mendoza. Clutching this victoriously, we moved on. We continued with television and radio interviews that the Argentinians had organised and lunch in the Officer's Club before a rather unsatisfying and disturbing meeting with our appointed Customs agent during which a furious argument broke out in Spanish between him and our Argentine guides which did not bode well for our border crossing.

Later, amid much general amusement, we went to buy the mini-skirt for Louie. Having accomplished that, my courage ran out when the Major, amidst howls of laughter, began discussing 'interior ropas' and trying to steer me towards a lingerie shop.

It took several more days to iron out the various problems that beset us both sides of the border. It was a period of intense frustration as I desperately wanted to get to Santiago as quickly as possible to start trying to sort out the planning and clearance for the last phase. As it was we were already looking at a delay of a month.

In the end all was settled but not without considerable assistance from the Cazadores; the turning of a blind eye to some of the paperwork by the local Customs chief, who just happened to be invited to the Cazadores Officers Mess for an asado the night before we left and went away bearing gifts of camping rations for his son; and a large number of telephone calls to England and Santiago to try and ease the bureaucratic and political difficulties the other side of the border.

The morning that we left, having said goodbye to Javier and all the Cazadores who had helped us, we set off for the Customs Hall a few miles up the road from the base, escorted by the Major. We were travelling in our own vehicles with the bulk of our mountaineering equipment being carried in an Argentine Army truck as far as the Chilean border, courtesy of the Cazadores.

The Major assumed his normal proprietorial role and with his assistance and the usual round of backslapping and hugging, our papers were processed without delay and we were free to proceed. When it was time for us to leave, he went down the line of the team hugging each man in turn and exhorting us to return soon and climb with them again. As we drove away I looked back to see him waving frantically, a small man with a big heart who had become a true friend.

Chapter Seven
South to Cape Horn

Even by the time we reached Santiago, political clearance had still not been confirmed for the last phase and I could not tell the other members of the permanent cadre, who were flying home to spend Christmas with their families, either whether it would be able to take place or when it might start.

Richard and I had opted to spend Christmas in Chile. I had arranged for Louie, my sister Jenny, and a couple of friends, to come and join us. By a series of coincidences and the greatest of good fortune, we had been adopted by a Chilean businessman, Jorge Sarquis, who had kindly arranged all our Christmas plans for us.

He and his brother Sergio, ran a large family fishing and canning business. He was passionate about Chile, espousing it as the most civilised, secure and beautiful country in South America. His political perspective was particularly interesting as he had gone into self-imposed exile in Venezuela during the period of social and economic chaos caused by the Marxist coalition government of President Salvador Allende in the early 1970s. With the assumption of power in a military coup by the head of the Army, General Augusto Pinochet, and the rule of his right wing military government, Jorge had returned to Chile. He was desperately proud of all that Chile had achieved and was determined that we should see the best of it.

After a few days in Santiago, he arranged an apartment for us in Renaga overlooking the ocean. Normally I do not care for beach holidays but after a year of being constantly on the move it was great to just relax, read and not worry about the day ahead.

We moved on for a second week to the Chilean Lake District. Surrounded by wild ranch-style farm land, the clearest of lakes and rivers, forests, mountains and snow-capped volcanos, we walked, fished and explored. It was country to revel in. I drank in the scenery and got high on the pure air and sense of freedom. The time flew past all too quickly.

The girls flew home and Richard and I returned to Santiago to try and knock the last phase into some semblance of shape. We had eventually received clearance to start our journey down to our final objective, Cape Horn, at the beginning of February. We had until then to put some flesh on the bones of our outline plan. Richard took off on a recce to the south, charged with tying up the various ferries that we needed and chartering a boat to carry us from Punta Arenas down to Cape Horn.

The permanent cadre, together with Andrew Phasey, came back out in mid-January and spent most of their time preparing the equipment for the phase. Andrew, Mike and Corporal Steggles set off in one vehicle a week before the arrival of the team, to establish a base camp in Torres del Paine National Park in the far south of the country where we were to spend almost three weeks trekking.

Having picked up the team we set off once more in our battered fleet of vehicles. With the Andes forming an unbroken barrier in the distance to our east, we drove through miles of vineyards, orchards and fields of flowers before entering fabulous unspoilt pastures and wild countryside. We spent our first night camped beside Salto del Laja, a magnificent waterfall that cuts across the Laja River. An island splits a huge curtain of water 150 feet high and several hundred yards across that then plunges down into a series of narrow, twisting canyons.

Next morning, we drove on into Los Angeles to link up with the rafting guides who were to take us to the Bio Bio River. Along with the Zambesi and Colorado Rivers, the Bio Bio is considered to be one of the world's three highest grade white-water rivers that can be commercially rafted. Having done the other two, we did not want to miss the opportunity to add the Bio Bio to our list, particularly as it was in the process of being dammed and would soon be ruined for rafting.

Having collected the guides, rafts and all the gear, and bought provisions for the next few days, we turned east and headed towards the Andes. Fifty

Phase Six Route

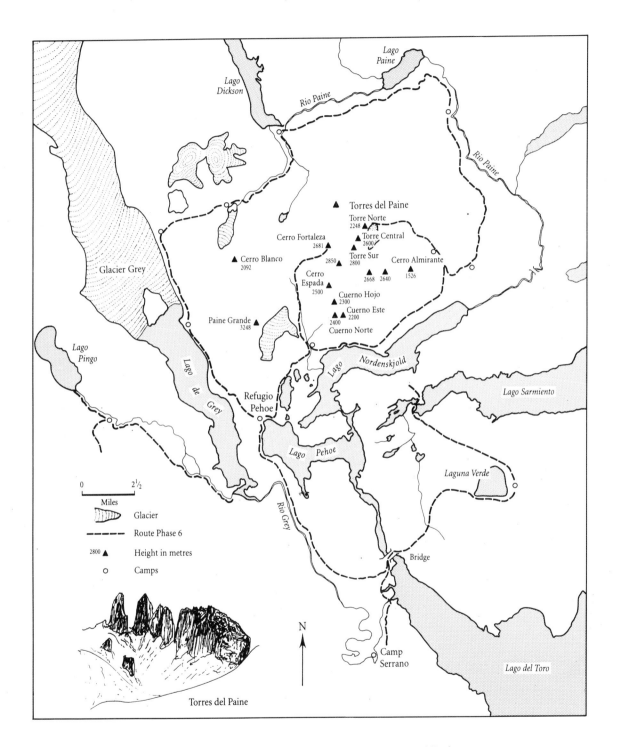

Route of Exploration in Torres del Paine National Park

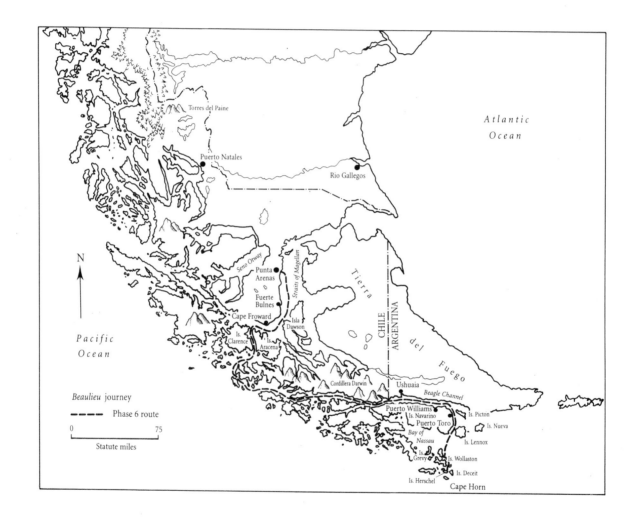

Route taken on board the *Beaulieu*

miles later, we came to a small village and the end of the tarred road. We carried on along a rough dirt track bouncing over protruding rocks and sending out billowing clouds of dust behind us. Below us, the Bio Bio glittered in the afternoon sunshine. The river was enclosed in a narrow steep-sided valley whose walls, when not cliffs, were clad in dense forest.

Away in the distance we had views across to towering volcanos: to our north the great pyramid of Antuco with a large glacier running down the middle of it and to our south the lofty cones of Tolhuaca and Lonquimay. Immediately above us, tree-covered ridges led up first to scree and then the snow-covered slopes of Volcan Callaqui.

We passed the dam site, a swarming mass of men, lorries and earth movers. Work was well advanced and substantial sections of the dam wall were in place. Water had begun to back up in the lower gorges which had held some of the best of the rafting. Of much more concern is the fate of an area of outstanding natural beauty and the livelihood of the Araucanian Indians who inhabit this remote valley. Many of their small farms and homesteads on which they pursue subsistence farming will be flooded when the dam is complete.

The dam company controlled access to the whole region and it had already been made illegal to take a boat into the lower gorges. Driving up the valley, we had to stop frequently to wait for drilling and blasting operations on the valley wall above us and then for the rockfall to be cleared. Engineers were blasting a new road across the valley several hundred feet above the river. The current road, whilst raised well up from the river, was below the predicted flood level.

As we drove along the soldiers chattered excitedly. In my vehicle I had Lieutenant Charlie Andrews, Corporal Wayne Bell and Guardsman Alan Hangar who was, somewhat predictably, nicknamed Cliff, along with a couple of the American raft guides. I knew Corporal Bell very well. He had come on 'Roof of Africa' and we had stayed in touch ever since. Although he was only twenty-four years old, he had seen an impressive amount of service during two tours in Northern Ireland, the Gulf War and having recently returned from Bosnia. Being naturally both garrulous and extrovert, he was taking full advantage of a captive audience and enjoying shocking the Americans with an unbroken

stream of war stories. He was in fact one of the older members of this team but by no means untypical. Most were still in their early twenties but, with the exception of Guardsman Shaun Nelson, who at nineteen was the baby of the group, they had all seen active service in one theatre or another.

We established camp in an open paddock below a small farmstead midway along the stretch of river that we were to raft. The late afternoon sun was still burning hot. Having set up tents, we washed off the journey's dust and grime in the river. Running down from the Andean snowline, the water was bracingly cold, but at the same time wonderfully refreshing.

The following morning was bright and clear. Having had a hearty breakfast, we drove several miles further on up the rough valley track to a point where the road dropped down close to the river. There we sorted ourselves into two raft crews, inflated the boats, equipped ourselves with life jackets, helmets and paddles and took to the water.

The guides ran over the safety points and then drilled each of the crews in the paddling techniques and reactions to commands. Below us, the river entered a high tree-lined gorge. The colours were turning from all shades of green to autumnal russets and golden yellows. We gripped our paddles and powered forwards.

The Bio Bio is quite different from the other two rivers with which it is associated. The country through which it passes is far more lush and green, the water is far colder and the volume of the river is significantly less. But of the three it is much the most serious and committing. As it drops down the valley, the river enters a series of sheer-sided gorges within the overall main gorge. These areas of hard rock constrict the flow of the water making it pick up speed. As it does so it charges through narrow boulder-strewn channels and over some savage drops.

The rafting is fast and furious, requiring quick reactions and technical moves to follow the safe channels. Without the volume of water to create cushions of water over the large rocks sticking up in the centre of the river, there is a severe danger of a raft or swimmer being dashed against them or grated along the bottom of the river where it passes over shallows.

We were quickly into the action as we tackled

one rapid after another. Each of the large rapids required careful scouting after which the guides would get their crews together and talk us through the intricate series of moves that they planned to make. Once we were dashing along in the current, bounced around by waves, cannoning off rocks and dropping over ledges, these plans frequently came to naught and we simply reacted to the way that the water took us.

In the bigger rapids the commands came thick and fast with, at times, mere urgency verging on panic. Milky Way came and went in a blur of white water as we hurtled down the rapid with the rock walls flashing past on either side. Lost Yak claimed three swimmers, and Lava South, namesake of the largest rapid on the Colorado, took three more including one of the guides. They all had fairly violent swims, a couple of them being taken underwater, bashed off rocks and having their shoes ripped off them by the force of the water.

In between the rapids the views were sensational. High waterfalls poured down the side walls from streams running off the mountains. One of these poured over a lip of rock a couple of hundred feet above us and descended in a great thundering cascade. At various points on the river, where the valley broadened or the side walls dropped away, we could see the snow-covered summit of Volcan Callaqui set high against the azure sky. The rock walls were predominantly lava which had flowed and then set in psychedelic rock trails or vertical hexagonal columns and in places appeared scalloped as if chiselled into a regular pattern.

We stopped for a break at the mouth of a small tributary. A couple of us followed it upstream, scrambling over rocks and swimming through the short, deep pools. We came across a pair of torrent ducks which shot off upstream ahead of us leaping into pools and hurling themselves up the small waterfalls.

Almost the last rapid of the day and by no means the largest of those that we had negotiated produced one of the most awesome displays of power that I had experienced rafting anywhere. As we powered through Last Laugh, crunching through successive standing waves, we dropped into a massive hole created by a huge reversing wave and then stopped dead in our tracks as though held by some giant hand. I had been caught in stoppers when kayaking

before, but now the entire raft was dragged backwards.

Despite facing downstream with the whole crew paddling for all we were worth, the large rubber raft remained motionless, surfing on the wave. Gradually the back of the boat was drawn down into the water and we began to submerge. The boat turned broadside to the current. We high-sided once and by paddling with all the strength we could muster we managed to get one end out of the stopper, but then we were suddenly swung around broadsides in the other direction. We high-sided again, more desperately, but this time with people floundering in the bottom of the semi-submerged boat and water pouring in all the time, the downstream side reared up and we nearly capsized.

We were totally powerless to escape the grip of the water. The other raft came charging past. With the guide yelling instructions and the rest of us grabbing each other whenever it looked like someone was about to be tipped out, we paddled this way and that until finally we popped out. We tried to regain control but with the weight of the boat totally full of water it was almost impossible. We ploughed on through the wave train dropping into the final hole broadsides. Again we nearly flipped but somehow we got away with it and drifted down to the flat water up to our waists in water, panting with the effort and excitement.

It was early evening and shadows were filling the valley by the time that we pulled the rafts into the bank beside our camp. We arrived to find Tito, the Araucania farmer on whose land we were camped, standing by a wood fire over which he was barbecuing an entire lamb's carcass. Accompanied by delicious hot fritters dipped into a fiery sauce, potatoes and a tomato salad all produced by his wife and washed down by beers chilled in the river it was a feast beyond praise. We spent a contented evening stood around the camp fire, gnawing on hunks of meat and telling ever taller stories.

The following day the majority of the team took back to the water to complete the second half of the Bio Bio's rapids. I, together with a couple of others including Craftsman Lee Smith, our new mechanic, set off in the opposite direction to rescue one of the vehicles which had broken down at the top of the river. We tried towing the stricken minibus with a Bronco but despite four-wheel drive and a V8 engine it could not cope with the weight on the steep, rough track.

I decided to try and find a lorry or tractor to tow the vehicle. I knew that up in the mountains this was a bit of a long shot but the alternative was to remove the faulty part, which Craftsman Smith thought was a fuel cut-off switch, take it to Los Angeles to be repaired and then bring it back and re-fit it. The danger was that we could do a seven-hour round trip in vain if he was wrong. Fortunately we found a farmer with an old rusty tractor who agreed to drag the minibus to the road head. The two-hour journey back to the main road was fairly eventful as we bounced and jolted back along the rocky track.

At one point the road was blocked by a massive boulder that had come down as a result of blasting on the new road above. Little seemed to be happening to clear the route and as we waited other vehicles began to pile up either side of the blockage. Finally, unable to stand it any longer, I grabbed the heavy-duty tow rope that we carried and approached the driver of a local bus that was parked on the far side to see if he would try and tow it clear. With a great deal of shunting, the enthusiastic levering and pushing of the assembled crowd of drivers and much shouting and miming, we managed to clear the route all the while watched impassively by the officials of the engineering company.

The rafters had a great day. First thing in the morning they had practised capsize drills and righting a raft if it flipped and then went looking for the wildest runs down the rapids. We met them at the end of the day, below the last rapid, charged up with adrenalin and totally euphoric.

The tractor had eventually made it out of the mountains to the main road and so having dropped off the tents and camping gear with the rafters, we hooked up the broken down minibus to one of the Broncos and towed it all the way to Los Angeles. The evening sun glinted off the mountain tops. Either side of the road each field was enclosed by roughly carved post and rail fences. The low-angled light picked out the knots and character in the weathered wood and highlighted the crops.

After a considerable amount of sucking of teeth and head shaking at several garages, the minibus was coaxed back into life. The rather reluctant and uncertain manner in which this was achieved left me far from convinced that it would work for long but having returned to the river, collected the rafters and deposited the guides and their equipment once more in Los Angeles, we continued on our way.

Another 180 miles further south it broke down once again. For the remaining 200 miles to Puerto Montt Craftsman Smith tussled with fuel blockages, faulty electrical systems and mysterious gremlins that appeared to be wreaking unaccountable havoc under the vehicle's bonnet.

The further south we travelled, the greener and more lush the country became. Either side of the road were pastures with sleek dairy cows and swaying fields of wheat and oats. The verges were a jumbled profusion of wild flowers and blackberry bushes heavy with ripe fruit. For much of the journey the skyline was dominated by one or more volcanos.

As we dropped down into Puerto Montt the roofs of the town glittered in the sunlight against a backdrop of distant volcanos and jagged Andean peaks, framed by the Gulf of Ancud. White horses danced on the surface of the cobalt blue water and old wooden buildings with decorated façades lined the streets which inclined steeply down towards the waterfront.

Puerto Montt had been established in 1852 by German settlers as part of a determined policy by the government of the day to open up the land in the south of Chile. Originally the territory of the Mapuche Indians, early attempts by the Spanish to settle the area had met with determined resistance and an uprising in 1598 had forced the Spanish to abandon the cities that they had established. These were re-established during the following century and further toeholds were gained by missionaries and pioneer settlers. The arrival of the Germans signalled a concerted attempt to accelerate this colonisation process. The Germans successfully carved homesteads out of the dense rainforest that covered the region.

Today the area is well developed and effectively farmed but much of the German character remains. Lutheran churches, wooden houses built with Alerce shingles and farms and towns strongly reminiscent of rural Germany abound. Cafes offer kuchen and schnapps.

On the day before our ferry sailed Richard and I drove up to Lago Llanquihue, the third largest inland lake in South America and an important link in the settlers' chain of supplies and communications. From the pretty German lakeside village of Frutillar we looked across the lake to the sweeping lines of the perfect cone of Volcan Osorno. We followed the network of farm tracks that link all the farms alongside the lake to another of the early settlers' towns, Puerto Varas.

Old clapboard farmhouses and tall barns were surrounded by orchards of apples and crab apples. Milk churns stood at each farm's gate. Many of the farmhouses had colourful window boxes and troughs filled with geraniums. Ducks, chickens and pigs waddled about in cluttered farmyards amongst antiquated machinery and lush pastures were grazed by fine dairy cows and thoroughbred horses. At the lake's edge we passed a number of small fish farms.

Turning back towards Puerto Montt, we followed the old dirt road through more desolate country. The only population was the small village of Alerce, a collection of ramshackle wooden houses and shacks. The otherwise drab nature of the dusty village was startlingly relieved by its church. One of the few buildings in a decent state of repair, it was built from shingles in the traditional style and had a narrow-tiered tower. It had been painted a vivid turquoise with pink facing.

From Puerto Montt we branched out again, this time eastwards on the Carretera Austral. It is not possible to drive to the southern regions of Chile without going into Argentina. Chile is cut into two by the 230 mile long Southern Patagonian ice cap which totally cuts off the Magallanes Region to the south. The Carretera Austral runs south from Puerto Montt almost as far as the northern end of the ice cap, joining the remote communities and farms that have been settled alongside the large number of fjords that cut into the country. It makes many ferry crossings over the fjords and has the reputation for being both spectacularly beautiful but time-consuming and cruel to vehicles.

I longed to drive it, but without permission to enter southern Argentina it did not offer us a viable route. We drove a short way along the route, juddering our way over the corrugated surface. We crossed the Rio Chico on a wooden bridge and stopped in the hamlet of Chamiza, a loose collection of farmhouses and houses set amongst orchards and plantations of poplars.

Down a side track we located another Lutheran church. It looked very fine surrounded by the open farm land, with a magnificent Araucania tree standing beside the carved gate and Volcan Osorno looming in the background. Every headstone in the small cemetery beside the church bore a German name, many written in old Gothic script.

The following day we boarded a Navimag ferry, the MV *Eden*, for the 900 mile journey to Puerto Natales at the southern end of the ice cap. Having seen our vehicles safely aboard we went to locate our cabins and settle in for the three-day voyage. We drew out of Puerto Montt in bright sunshine which lit up the distant volcanos and mountains.

For the first twenty-four hours we cruised down the Gulf of Ancud between the mainland and the protective bulk of the island of Chiloe. The scenery became increasingly impressive as we wended our way between the smaller islands lying off Chiloe. The islands were of all shapes and sizes: some tiny, some large, some rounded, some steep, most unpopulated and all tree covered. To our east, fjords cut regularly into the mainland where forested slopes led up to bare snow-covered tops. We passed occasional fishing boats working nets or lines of crab pots, otherwise the only signs of life were the plentiful marine birdlife.

Dinner on the second evening was a fairly spartan affair as the boat prepared to break out onto the open sea before cutting back into the inner passage that leads through the myriad of offshore islands beside the southern ice cap all the way down to Puerto Natales. The eight-hour crossing was often extremely rough but aside of some fairly gentle rolling we spent a peaceful night.

One of the soldiers had been ill in the night but two of the others appeared with badly swollen faces and streaming, half-closed eyes in the morning. We had been warned about the strength of the sun and in particular the dangers of a hole in the ozone layer which sat above southern Chile. Having ignored these warnings and not bothered with sunblock, they were both in considerable discomfort.

It was a cold grey morning with no views in the broad channels so I spent the time reading. By midday the hanging mist had dissipated and the sun had reappeared. The islands and mainland still bore the same rounded hills but the slopes were bare save for low scrub. There was a dusting of snow even on the low tops and as we got further south we began to see permanent snow and mantles of fissured ice cloaking the mountain peaks.

Midway through the systems of channels we branched off into Paso del Indio. We rounded the end of an island and then turned back towards another island on which we could see a collection of about forty wooden dwellings scattered along the waterfront. This was the village of Puerto Eden, home to the last few Alacaluf Indians. It is totally cut off from the outside world except for the ferry's fortnightly visits.

As we pulled into the harbour a small fleet of fishing boats of all sizes and descriptions motored out to meet us. They clustered around the stern of the ferry, taking it in turn to come up to the side of the loading ramp and off-load goods and villagers to be carried to Puerto Natales. There was a good deal of excited shouting and jeering as they jostled for position. The people were dark with swarthy faces, high cheekbones and narrow eyes. Imposing snow-capped peaks rose up from the green wooded slopes behind the village.

We set off again. It was a mild afternoon and I stood on deck watching the mountains and the islands drift by. The water was of the deepest blue, perfectly still save for the wake of the boat or the splash of a diving gull. Towards evening we entered some much narrower channels. Waterfalls tumbled down ravines on the hillsides. Shortly before dark we had a fabulous view up one of the fjords to the southern ice cap, a huge carpet of ice broken only by the mountain peaks. Even from the safety of the boat it looked cold and foreboding. Not for the last time I felt a secret relief that we were not trying to battle our way across it as we had originally planned. The sun ducked down behind the seaward islands leaving the hillsides opposite glowing a softening pink.

I had been worried that the soldiers might become bored and restless during such a long period of enforced inactivity. Quite to the contrary, they were enjoying the scenery and had started an active card school in the saloon and if the attractions of those wore off, then there was a captive group of female passengers to be chatted up. Adopting a rather unconventional tack, Charlie Andrews was playing games of draughts with a German girl in an attempt to evade the overzealous chaperoning of her father.

The following day started with a beautifully sunny morning. The channels were flanked by tall mountains; imposing broad-based massifs culminating in rock towers with cascades of blue glacial ice trailing down their sides to snow-covered ice fields below. Where the channel narrowed, the mountains seemed even more dominating, they were like impassive watchmen observing our progress. They formed the Cordillera Sarmiento, an extension of the Andes to the south of the southern ice cap. A cold wind blew up the channel sending us burrowing into our rucksacks for fleece jackets. I stood on deck talking to a charismatic British postman who had taken unpaid leave from delivering mail to the citizens of Coventry to travel around South America. Later I talked to some Dutchmen who had been to climb Aconcagua after us. They had sat out two major storms and said that the mountain had experienced its worst weather for forty years. The week after they had left, three people had died having succumbed to the cold.

At around 4 p.m. we swung east through the Kirke Pass and into the Gulf of Almirante Montt. The mountains dropped back from the water's edge leaving a flat plain surrounding the wide bay. At the far end lay Puerto Natales, a huddle of brightly painted buildings on the shore beneath a long, flat-topped mountain.

As we waited for the pilot to come aboard and guide the boat to its berth, the wind increased steadily. The pilot duly came aboard but still we waited. Finally an announcement was given out over the ship's tannoy saying that the wind was too strong for the ferry to berth safely and we would have to spend the night at anchor and hope that it had died down by morning. I was not particularly concerned as we had allowed extra time for just such eventualities. There were times when the ferry could not berth for several days on end.

This announcement caused general uproar amongst many of the passengers who only had a very limited time to spend in Patagonia. However, once they saw that there was little to be achieved by ranting, a sort of survivors' spirit gripped everyone and there was a spontaneous party in the dining room. I found myself wedged between a buxom, red-haired Norwegian woman called Pia and a beautiful blond girl from Dresden called Annette. She had deep blue eyes, a musical laugh and wore a spotted handkerchief tied around her hair. She described her life as a primary school teacher in Dresden under the communist regime. Despite the restrictive lifestyle, she held a deep love for her homeland. When the Berlin Wall came down and the Soviet Union crumbled, she had been the youngest of a glut of teachers and was forced out of teaching. She was now studying sociology and revelling in her new found freedom and the ability to travel. Her optimism for the future and the positive way that she spoke about everything that she did and saw was totally uplifting. She was like a little bird flitting about and bringing a ray of happiness wherever she went.

I woke to find that we had docked. It was a crisp, clear morning with strong, low light that brought out the full colours of the bay and the mountain ranges beyond. The passengers were able to disembark quickly but it was some time before the vehicles were unloaded. While I waited I took my cameras and wandered along the sea shore. The water's edge was a teeming mass of gulls, tufted ducks and black-necked swans all feeding and preening themselves. I came to an old pier entirely covered by a colony of cormorants. Wherever I pointed the camera there were sensational views.

Once the vehicles had been unloaded and we had linked up with Andrew Phasey and his Advance Party, we drove up to the small town centre to collect some supplies before setting off into the country. The streets were lined with low buildings, many in a poor state of repair with the wood rotting and paint flaking off. Puerto Natales mirrored the declining meat industry of the area which it had serviced.

Driving north out of the town, we crossed a huge, open plain. Low trees and scrub filled any unfenced land and were resplendent in autumnal gold, auburn and russet and every shade of green. We turned west on a dirt track, towards Ultima Esperanza Sound and the towering form of Cerro Balmaceda on the horizon with the Balmaceda Glacier pouring down its flanks. We stopped to camp in a sheltered spot beneath a high rock outcrop known as the Devil's Chair.

A short distance away, there was a large cave leading back into the hillside. Here in 1895, Captain Eberhard, one of the first German settlers in the region, discovered the remains of a prehistoric giant tree sloth called a Milodon. The cave had a commanding view over the Sound and mountains to the west and a life-size model of the Milodon standing on its hind legs at the entrance. When viewed in silhouette from the back of the cave it provided a strangely prehistoric impression. As soon as the sun slid below the horizon, the temperature dropped sharply sending us hunting for thick jerseys and pile jackets. People huddled around the camp fire.

Cold fingers took down wet tents after a heavy dew. Having had breakfast, we continued on our way north towards Torres del Paine National Park. We drove through broad valleys of fenced ranch land bounded by the all encompassing mountains. Estancia houses stood isolated, islands in a sea of swaying grass, each protected from the wind by a screen of tall trees. We came to a huge open paddock containing several hundred head of prime cattle. Elsewhere we saw healthy, heavily fleeced sheep.

With each passing mile the amount of vegetation decreased, even the scrub diminished, giving a feeling of immense space on the huge plains. Occasional copses of dark conifers provided pockets of shelter but elsewhere, all appeared windswept and bare. As we drove past, a herd of horses galloped across the steppes leaping and throwing their heads in wild exuberance, an exhilarating display of freedom against the backdrop of snowy peaks. A large brown eagle crouched over a hare that it had killed. Elsewhere falcons and buzzards hovered and swooped. Coots, ducks and flamingos clustered around the edges of the many lakes and great flocks of upland geese, buffnecked ibis and lapwing congregated on the plains to feed.

We stopped at Cerro Castillo. There was a barrier across the road outside a small Carabineros post. Another road bore away east into Argentina. The Corporal on duty was expecting us. Having telephoned his superior to let him know that we had arrived, he offered us any assistance and then waved us on our way. The scenery became increasingly spectacular and desolate as we approached the Southern Patagonian ice cap. After several tantalising glimpses we crested a rise to be confronted by the fantastic spectacle of the full range: on the left, the solid block of Cerro Paine Grande, its great summit heavy with cornices and fluted snow faces; in the centre, the chocolate-coloured spires of the Cuernos; and on the right, the sheer rock walls and perfect lines of the Torres, the alluring towers that gave their name to the region.

We drove on into the park with the mountains growing steadily in size before us. The wind that had been blowing strongly all morning dropped and the surface of the lakes became still, revealing their strong turquoise colour and reflecting the mountains and glaciers. Herds of guanacos, another member of the llama family, browsed on the rough tundra alongside rheas, the South American ostriches. A magnificent grey fox with a huge bushy tail loped off into the distance as we approached.

We continued, stopping regularly to take photographs and gaze up at the majestic peaks, until we reached our camp site on the bank of the Rio Serrano. This was to be our base for the next two and a half weeks. It was a warm afternoon as we set up our tents and sorted out food, wood and the storage of equipment. A pair of eagles looked down on us from their eyrie on top of a high ridge the far side of the river. Buzzards swooped between the trees around the camp and a condor soared overhead for much of the afternoon.

Later, I went for a walk alongside the river. Duck, geese and herons were all swimming or wading in the water. I watched as two gauchos chased some wild horses over the plain and then drove them through the river. Further on, I crossed the river on an old warped wooden bridge and climbed up the ridge the far side to look out over the river and its flood plain and away to where the tendrils of the ice cap were curling around the edge of the massif.

Using the camp as our base we made a couple of treks to the outlying lakes and glaciers at the south of the park and then a six-day circuit of the massif. The country in the south was glorious; wild rolling uplands carpeted in spiky moss-covered gorse and low scrub, and wooded valleys filled with tall deciduous trees. On the first walk we camped beside a remote estancia on a windswept plateau at the edge of Laguna Verde.

Patagonia is subject to violent mood swings. At one moment it can be warm and invigorating, a canvas of rich natural colours alive with the sounds of honking geese, the cries of raptors and the hammering of woodpeckers, and the next moment it can be wild, comfortless and austere.

Oppressive grey clouds would descend over the mountain tops and spread over the whole region. As the light diminished, gale-force winds would spring up, whipping the surface of the lakes into a frenzy of white-capped waves and then blowing the crests off the waves into a moving haze of spray. Faced with this onslaught, every animal and bird sought shelter.

On our second foray into the southern region, we followed a trail that led us alongside Rio Pingo, crossing side streams on felled logs and clambering up and down steep forested re-entrants as we made our way towards Lago Pingo. Within the forest the views were limited to brief glimpses of the mountains but in their place we found ourselves in a rich world of ferns, mosses and lichens.

It began to drizzle and the wind picked up. By the time we reached the plain beyond, a heavy layer of slate-grey cloud had settled overhead and a storm had set in. We took shelter in a tiny hut beside the trail. The old refuges were basic wood and tin constructions with crude wooden benches and platforms to sleep on. Some were little more than a shell with a bare earth floor but when Patagonia showed its less benevolent side, with the wind howling and the rain beating down, they afforded more secure and restful shelter than the manically flapping fabric of a tent.

The next day we followed the trail on to Lago Pingo. On the far side of the lake, great swathes of ice spilled down from the glacier above to the lake's edge. This was one of the many fingers of the Southern Patagonian ice cap that ended in the lakes around Torres del Paine. It was as if the great 240-mile field of moving ice had finally run out of energy when it reached the immovable mass of the Paine massif. Low cloud obscured the mountain peaks and cast a dull light over the country deadening the vibrant colours. A few icebergs floated far out in the lake. From where we stood they looked almost magical, weird sculptures that seemed to emanate a light of their own from within the blue glacial ice.

For our circuit of the massif we split into two teams; Richard took one group in a clockwise direction and I started with the remainder heading anticlockwise. The first morning was beautifully clear, one of the rare perfect Patagonian days, with unblemished azure skies and burning hot sunshine. We set off from the foot of the Torres Valley, contouring around the lower slopes at the base of the massif towards the lakes and plains beyond.

As we made our way gradually around the trail, we got increasingly impressive views of the Torres and the surrounding peaks, many of which we had been unable to see from the other side of the massif. Different layers of rock produced amazing and marked changes in colour: cream or grey suddenly gave way to strong chocolate or even purple zones. The views were equally captivating on either side. The trail squeezed between the towering profusion of peaks, ridges and spires of rock that comprised the mountain range and the huge sweeping ice cap to our north.

The higher mountains were cloaked in mantles of snow and ice with glaciers perched in the hanging valleys between them as if suspended by invisible cords from the summits. But increasingly, it was the great expanse of ice cap to our northeast that drew our gaze. From our second camp on the shore of Lago Dickson we could see one of the subsidiary glaciers dropping down to the far end of the lake in a great tortured mass of seracs and crevasses.

At the north-eastern extremity of the massif, the trail climbed up to an high pass which overlooked the ice cap. We began the long ascent through the lower forests which gradually steepened as we hopped between tussocks and old stumps through a deep mire.

Incessant banter passed up and down the line. Corporal Colin Pote, one of the younger members of the team was leading. Rarely at a loss for words, his south-coast chirp maintained a constant white noise in the background. Larger than life in character, he was small in stature and from behind looked like a rucksack with legs. With his short stride he was having difficulty bridging the gaps between the islands of hard ground. He reached out for one log, the only stepping stone in a large circle of bog, only to see his foot slide straight off it. Driven on by the weight of his pack he plunged headlong into the mud. He dragged himself out soaked to the waist, with thick black mud dripping down his trousers. This rather pathetic cartoon character brought a chorus of abuse from the others, each one secretively relieved that it was not them.

We climbed on using the gnarled branches and roots of the stunted trees for support until we emerged on the bare scree and shale slopes that led up to John Garner Pass. An hour of concerted effort, climbing into the face of biting winds, brought us to the crest. Looking back along the line of the valley that we had ascended we could see all the way into Argentina. The peaks of the Paine massif appeared as tightly packed turrets in some fairyland castle. But in front, the vast expanse of the Southern Patagonian ice cap was almost too much to take in. The Grey Glacier, one of the subsidiary glaciers, stretched as far as the eye could see as it filled the valley in front of us in an immense sweep of ice punctuated only by a line of bare rock peaks that separated it from the main bulk of the ice cap.

On the far side of the pass, the ground fell away 1,800 feet down sheer screes and through more stunted forest to another trail that had been carved into the mountainside. The gradient was such that it required total concentration and, swinging down from the twisted morass of trunks and roots, was every bit as energetic as climbing the far side had been. Having gained the path we followed it along the hillside crawling under low branches and climbing over fallen trees. The closer that we got to the surface of the ice cap, the better we were able to appreciate the full scale of it. For much of the way it was screened by trees but in places we broke out of the forest and could see right over the ice plateau. As we approached we could see that it was impossibly broken by closely packed and intertwined crevasses.

We continued along the slope, shadowing the edge of the glacier until we came to its snout overlooking Lago Grey. The end of the glacier was a wall of ice up to 50ft high above water level and split by cracks, fissures and caves. Every so often a massive block of ice would calve into the lake with a boom that would resonate around the wide bay. Two vast icebergs, both over a 100 yards in length and the same in width, floated free in the lake.

Looking down the lake I could see other icebergs that had been blown for several miles before being washed up against the shore of one of the bays. Watching the edge of the ice, it appeared animated as if with its own life-force as the massive pressures created by its relentless progress along the valley caused it to strain against itself. The constant creaking and cracking as it slowly shifted was most eerie.

Having camped at the lake's edge we continued on our way next morning. Overnight the upper slopes of the mountain that had lain below the snowline had become coated in fresh snow. Looking upwards to where the mountain disappeared in the cloud and hugging my pile and Pertex jacket around me against the wind and sleet, I was glad that we were not trying to cross the Pass. We followed the trail, once more keeping to the side of the massif, climbing and dropping and climbing again, in and out of the valleys that ran down from it. We crossed back to the more familiar south-east face of the massif where we came to a refuge on the shores of Lago Pehoe. Regardless of the overcast day, the lake was a brilliant turquoise. Wooden screens had been erected in the campsite to provide some protection for the tents.

I wandered across to the refuge and spent what was left of the day writing my diary and chatting to a Chilean mountaineer. He was a great bear of a man with a head of wild, frizzy hair but for all his outlandish appearance he was very friendly and extremely amusing. He was passionate about Chile, the mountains which he said were a part of his soul, and the pretty blonde Swedish girl who was running the refuge who he said was his girlfriend.

In his rather stilted English he told me, 'I have found my woman. She is a very good woman.'

He said that in the past girlfriends had made him choose between them and the mountains but he had not found that a difficult choice to make. Now he was in considerable angst having totally fallen in love with this girl, over whom he continued to wax eloquent like some old bard, but yet having come to Torres del Paine intent on making a solo attempt on Cumbre Principal, the highest peak in the massif. All of the peaks in the massif required technical ascents.

Going up alone into these remote and inaccessible mountains was a serious and committing undertaking. Looking up at the peak, shrouded in mist and cloud, it looked cold and inhospitable. The Swedish girl clearly was not happy but was putting on a brave face. The Chilean and I chatted about mountaineering in general, the opportunities in Southern Chile and the implications of trying to force a crossing of the ice cap but each time the conversation drifted back to his girlfriend.

As this was the most accessible part of the Park, the refuge was of a much higher standard. I longed to get stuck into one of the sizzling steaks that were

appearing from the kitchen but I did not think that it would look very good in front of the soldiers and so stole myself away from the enticing smells, back to my tent where in the midst of a minor gale I heated up another of the Army's foil-wrapped gourmet extravaganzas.

Everyone in the camp site debunked for the evening into the refuge. I found myself talking to a fascinating American who had just retired as a fire-fighter in Alaska. He had spent his summers in one of the fire teams parachuting into the smoke ahead of fires and cutting firebreaks with chain saws. In the winter he taught skiing in the lower United States. Now at fifty-seven years of age and just retired, he was taking two years to travel before returning to write a book about his years as a fire-fighter. When he left to go to bed his space was more than amply filled by the Chilean mountaineer. I had a re-run of his twin love affairs with the mountains and the Swedish girl.

Five hours at a fast pace took us alongside Lago Pehoe, over some high ground to Rio Grey and then across flat, expansive plains to the Park Headquarters where we had left a vehicle. Late in the afternoon, Andrew returned with the other group from the far end of the park and, of more interest to our thoroughly whetted appetites, a huge pile of groceries that he had collected from Puerto Natales. That night we had a huge feast of steaks, fresh vegetables and potatoes enough for an Irishman, cooked over an open fire as we celebrated Craftsman Smith's twenty-fourth birthday.

After a day to sort ourselves out, our final foray in the area was up the two valleys that led high into the massif. Not wishing to spend time trekking over the same ground twice, we had planned to take the ferry boat across Lago Pehoe to the refuge and set off from there. We woke to a windy morning. As we drove to the jetty we could see that the lake was covered in rolling white-capped waves. The ferry was a small diesel-powered motor launch. We found the old man who ran it who said that conditions were marginal but he would attempt to make the crossing.

The jetty was tucked into a cove in the lee of some high ground and thus fairly well protected but as soon as we rounded the headland we were exposed to the full force of the wind. Our rucksacks had been lowered into a hold below the short forward deck whilst all the passengers were packed tightly into a covered cabin. A constant barrage of spray swept across the little boat as it pitched and corkscrewed its way through the waves. Out in the middle of the lake it rolled to a most alarming angle. I looked up at a sign in English and Spanish headed 'Safety Instructions'. It read:

If there is a fire at the front of the boat
1. Go to the rear
2. Stay calm
3. Await the instructions of the Captain

If there is a fire at the rear of the boat
1. Go to the front
2. Stay calm
3. Await the instructions of the Captain

One only hoped that the Captain did not get burnt first or washed overboard.

I kept thinking that it would only take one wave just a fraction larger than the rest and it would roll us over. From their expressions, so did several of the others. Some sat bolt upright, whilst others like Corporal Pote who had an innate fear of water lay down with their eyes clenched tightly shut and pretended that it was not happening. The little boat battled gamely on and as we came into the lee of the mountains on the far side of the lake, the waves began to diminish. It was something of a relief to step onto the reassuringly stable pier. Having given everyone a few minutes to collect themselves before we headed up the first valley, I went to see if I could track down my Chilean friend and get any route tips from him. I found the Swedish girl who said that he had gone up to Cumbre Principal for a few days to have a look at the route but that he was not planning to climb it.

As we set off towards the Frances Valley little of the massif was visible beneath the cloud. It began to rain, not heavily but persistently enough to make us thoroughly wet by the time that we crossed the Rio del Frances and reached our campsite at the mouth of the valley. We set up our tents in a wood perched well up the side of the mountain. The trees blocked the view which our position deserved and dripped soggily.

I retreated into my tent for a while until the worst of the rain died down but then, unable to stand the inactivity, put on waterproofs and headed on up the valley. Richard came with me. We left the others standing around a fire that they had built to dry their clothes out. We climbed fast, scrambling up the side of the fast flowing river. After a short distance we passed the snout of the Frances Glacier on the far side of the valley. We kept going along a narrow twisting path which wound its way through further forest, across an area of open marsh and up onto a pinnacle of rock from where we could survey the entire cirque.

Our situation was spectacular. It was as if we were in a giant's mouth with rows of teeth encircling us. The bowl of the cirque was covered by forest above which bare scree slopes and sheer rock faces led up to a jagged crescent of spires and pyramids linked by sharp ridges. Most of the peaks were hidden by cloud although, despite us being blasted by wind, rain and hail, somehow the three peaks immediately to our right, Cerro Espada, Cerro Hoja and Cerro Mascara, were intermittently bathed in sunshine. We sheltered behind some rocks and shared a packet of sweets as we waited to see if the headwall of the cirque would clear.

The cloud billowed in and out, never completely clearing, but allowing us to snatch photographs. We were on the point of turning back when Corporal Bell appeared. Several of the others had climbed up as far as the end of the glacier but he had come on alone. He was all for climbing higher up to the pass that led up and around the back of the Torres and ultimately to the Ascensio Valley.

There was no path up the extremely steep valley side and it was already late in the afternoon. Richard said that we were mad and he was heading down, but curiosity got the better of me. Now we had come so far I desperately wanted to see over the back of the pass. Corporal Bell led off at a furious pace. We climbed quickly above the tree line and up a steep moss-covered slope to a grassy platform. Although we had gained a good deal of height we could still see little more of the main towers whose summits were peeking over the skyline.

We carried on up a long boulder-strewn slope for another 1,000 feet until we reached the shoulder of Cerro Forteleza. We could now see that the top of the pass was a further mile away across a steadily rising field of large boulders. Beyond, the last of the sunlight was playing across the west face of Torre Sur. Although we longed to go on to the head of

Ranch land in the Magallanes region of Chile with the backdrop of Cerro Balmaceda.

The expedition's vehicles cross the Rio Pehoe with the Cuernos behind.

Looking over Rio Serrano to the full Paine Massif; Paine Grande on the left, the Cuernos in the centre and the Torres on the right.

Crossing a suspension bridge on the Paine circuit.

Lee Smith crosses a natural bridge en route for Lago Pingo.

Glacial icebergs in Lago Los Perros.

A rainbow over Glacier Grey, one of the major off-shoots of the Southern Patagonian ice-cap.

The snout of Glacier Grey from which icebergs over 100 yards in length break off.

Opposite: Colin Pote and Wayne Bell pause on the Paine circuit overlooking Glacier Grey.

The west face of Torre Central.

Looking out from Fuerte Bulnes across the Straits of Magellan.

Opposite: The team with the Household Division flag in front of the Towers of Paine.

Puerto Williams, the southernmost permanent habitation, on the Beagle Channel.

The *Beaulieu* tied up to the left of the pier in Puerto Toro. Tierra del Fuego in the distance.

On board the *Beaulieu* at the southernmost point that we reached, within sight of Cape Horn.

the pass and look directly up at the great walls of the Towers, there was no way that we could make it back before nightfall and re-crossing this boulder field in the dark without head torches was not a pleasant or sensible prospect. There was also no guarantee that what appeared from our present vantage point to be the head of the pass was not another false crest and that there would be more difficult ground to cover beyond. We turned back.

The next day we dropped back down out of the Frances Valley and contoured eastwards around the massif. We passed underneath the Cuernos, dropping in and out of the ravines that ran down the sides of the mountains. Open moorland with some patches of scrub filled the ground below us between the mountainside and Lago Nordenskjold. Above, waterfalls tumbled into ravines and glaciers hung over the lips of high cols.

As we rounded the side of the slope into the Ascensio Valley we were hit by gusts of wind that almost blasted us off our feet. We had to lean forward with our full weight to make any progress as we made our way along the left wall of the valley. Our camp that night was a draughty affair. The tents flapped and bent under the onslaught as if possessed by spirits and our candle lanterns whirled crazily on their hanging chains. Corporal Holmes had to get up in the middle of the night to save his tent from total collapse. I could hear his booming Bradford accent relaying his experiences of grappling with the frenzied flysheet to the others as we cooked our breakfast.

Leaving our tents in place, we followed the side of the valley staying below the tree line for an hour until we branched directly uphill towards the cirque of the Torres. A stiff pull up steep screes, hopping from boulder to boulder, brought us over the lip of the rise to the most amazing vista. We had purposefully saved this moment until the end. Before us lay a broad but deep, boulder-strewn depression with a lake in its base. On the far side, above a high wall plastered over with old, stone-encrusted glacial ice, rose the three soaring monoliths of the Towers of Paine. Their fine lines and sheer east faces swept up to imperious summits high in the sky.

In an area totally undeveloped except by sheep ranchers, it was not until the sixties that these imposing peaks came to the attention of mountaineers around the World. When they did, the race was on amongst the leading mountaineers of the day to be the first to scale them. In 1963 Chris Bonnington and Don Whillans were the first to reach the summit of Torre Central from the west just beating an Italian team by a day. The same British expedition made the first ascent of the North Tower. However, it was not until 1974, with the advent of more advanced technical climbing equipment, that a South African expedition was able to ascend the apparently flawless east face of Torre Central. An ascent of any of the Towers demanded sustained technical rock climbing of the highest standard. We could only look in wonder.

With our exploration of Torres del Paine complete, it was time to continue our southerly journey towards Cape Horn. On the morning after we descended from the massif we got up before dawn for the final stage of our road journey. The sky was still black and clear with the southern constellations shining brightly. We packed away camp and grabbed a quick breakfast of cold, rather stale buns filled with the last of the bacon and hard-boiled eggs and mugs of tea. The darkness began to seep out of the sky and the stars gently faded from prominence.

As we started the vehicles, the first oblique rays of light from a sun still far below the horizon painted the undersides of the clouds a gentle pink which strengthened as each minute passed. The great faces of the Torres changed from a ghostly white, barely discernible in the dark, through shades of primrose yellow to an equally soft pink. With time, the clouds became fiery red, heralding a dramatic dawn. They were arrayed, great sheets of cirrus, to our south leaving the mountain massif standing clear and proud. We drove slowly along the rough track towards Laguna Amarga and squeezed over the narrow suspension bridge across Rio Ascensio, gazing behind us all the while.

As the day was gradually born, we headed back through the expansive estancias and grandiose scenery along the way to Puerto Natales. We disturbed a couple of large foxes prowling around the outbuildings of an estancia in search of an unguarded chicken. A gale-force tailwind chased us across the pampas, buffeting the vehicles and forcing all the livestock and wildlife to seek shelter. A couple of hours later, looking across the plains to Puerto Natales, I was struck by just how small and remote the little town was. We paused to repair a couple of punctures before pressing on again. The road now led for 160 miles to Punta Arenas.

The landscape was desolate. I stared out of the window for signs of life but there were just endless miles of long golden grass rippling in waves. It was neither lush nor nutritious but, with banks of moss, was all the forage on offer. We passed through a large forest and then thousands of acres of dead trees with no obvious clues to their demise. There was no charring to indicate a forest fire. Some areas had been cleared and the trunks piled up in mounds.

For land so famous for its ranching there was amazingly little livestock in view. The stock levels increased as we grew nearer to Punta Arenas but if anything, the land was even more barren and windswept. Whole flocks of sheep lay down in the lee of whatever cover they could find. Their grey fleeces made them look like tussocks of grass at a distance. In the entire 160 miles, I saw just one field of cut grass with men collecting bales of hay that was still green. Buildings were few and far between. They varied from humble huts to substantial estancia houses with outbuildings for staff quarters and large shearing sheds. Condors wheeled overhead.

I did not want the journey to end. Although not particularly momentous in any one spot, the feeling of space and sense of travelling to somewhere unimaginable was exciting. For the last twenty miles we dropped down alongside the western shore of the Straits of Magellan.

We drove through another in the regular chain of Carabineros posts. There were a couple of wrecked boat hulls sticking out of the water and some other fishing boats anchored nearby. Closer to the city, the road was flanked by sprawling industrial sites, oil refineries, sawmills and scrapyards. It had a dirty feel to it after the unblemished country. We drove through the outskirts and found our way to the small backstreet residencial where we had booked rooms. Our hosts Roxanne and Claudio Paredes made us more than welcome.

For the next few days, whilst we waited to board the boat to carry us to our final objective, we explored Punta Arenas and the surrounding area. Settlement of the area had suffered shaky beginnings. Originally it had been occupied by four native tribes: the Tehuelches, Onas, Yahgans and Alcalufes. After the discovery of Chile in 1520 by the Portuguese sailor Ferdinand Magellan, operating in the service of Spain, the Spanish sought to protect their interests by establishing a series of forts along the safe passage used by traders and pirates alike that linked the Atlantic with the Pacific Ocean.

This first attempt at settling the Straits of Magellan in 1584 ended disastrously. Out of the fifteen ships and 4,000 men who set sail from Spain, only three ships and 300 settlers reached their destination. Three years later, an English pirate, Thomas Cavendish, landed at Puerto Hambre, to find barely any survivors. The remainder had starved.

The next concerted attempt to colonise the area was not made for almost 250 years once Chile had wrested its independence. In 1843, at the direction of President Bulnes, a small group of largely military settlers built a fort overlooking the Straits. This proved unsuitable for expansion and the settlement was moved in 1848 to the present site of Punta Arenas.

Its early development was far from smooth. Originally created as a penal town to which military insurgents and criminals were exiled, it was only when sheep ranching thrived after the introduction of sheep from the Falkland Islands that the city took off. The success of the sheep ranching led to the development of massive corporations who between them opened up and farmed over a million acres. Latterly, the oil industry has overtaken sheep farming in financial terms but along with coal mining and fishing it remains a key industry.

Modern suburbs lead in towards a fine cedar-lined Plaza surrounded by ornate colonial mansions and the cathedral. In the middle of the Plaza, a statue of a bearded Ferdinand Magellan standing with cap in hand is raised up on a pedestal above two bronze statues of native Indians.

A visit to the Museum of the Salesian Missions that had been established at Rio Gallegos to the north and Isla Dawson in the Straits helped put a few more pieces of the jigsaw of history, discovery and settlement into place. Alongside a large quantity of religious artefacts; books, sacramental garments and photographs depicting life at the missions; were shelf upon shelf of stuffed mammals and birds, collections of eggs and fossils, and specimen jars containing all manner of fish, lizards, frogs and berries.

More captivating even than the great range of mothballed fauna and flora on display, rows of puma, chinchilla, fox, armadillo, beaver and alligator skins and every imaginable bird from penguins to albatrosses, was the tragic story of the Indian tribes. Woven baskets, skin canoes, bows, stone arrowheads, fishing spears, capes of guanaco skins and sealskin mukluks unveiled their lives as hunter-gatherers. However it was old sepia photographs that told the depressing story of their discovery, enforced conversion to Christianity by the missionaries and ultimate eradication by disease and ruthless settlers who shot them down like animals for hunting on the land that the settlers had claimed. The demise of the Indians made sorry reading and had close parallels to the Eskimos with whom they shared a very similar lifestyle.

Elsewhere in the museum maps showed the routes and discoveries of the early explorers and sailors: Magellan, Drake and much later Darwin. On the way out I saw a heavily weathered wooden cross on which was carved 'In memory of Commander Pringle Stokes RN, HMS Beagle, who died from the anxieties and hardship incurred while surveying the Western shores of Tierra del Fuego 12.8.1826'.

From the Plaza the streets run down hill to the busy port. Fishing boats, container ships and Chilean Naval vessels were tied alongside the main pier. I wandered along watching fishermen with weather-beaten faces unloading cargos of sea urchins into plastic trays to go to the refrigeration plant. Japanese and Korean seamen were washing down the decks of their factory ships and smart uniformed sailors of the Chilean Armada stood guard at the foot of the companionways leading off their ships. I noticed civilian cars and some Indians stood on the deck of the largest of the Naval vessels. The Navy provide the only means of communication and supply to some of the most remote farms on the islands and up the isolated fjords.

Walking back through the centre of the city, the main road leads out past statues of President Bulnes and General Bernardo O'Higgins. O'Higgins was the illegitimate son of an Irishman, Ambrosio O'Higgins, who had risen in the Service of Spain to become Viceroy of Peru. In 1810, Bernardo led a revolt to oust the Spanish colonialists, joining forces with the army of General San Martin when it marched across the Andes from Argentina. On independence, O'Higgins was created Head of State and although subsequently deposed by the landed classes for his liberal views he is still regarded as Chile's Liberator. Alongside the statue of O'Higgins is a bust of Jose Menendez the largest of the original sheep barons and then further along the road, a more evocative statue of a sheep farmer in the manner of a Voortrekker, leading his horse into the face of the wind with his cape flying out behind him, his dog at his side and a flock of sheep in front. Just beyond, is the large, walled city cemetery where on the headstones and inscriptions of the uniform lines of graves and mausolea, the spectrum of nationalities who have taken part in the development of Patagonia is reflected.

Although predominantly Spanish, there are a large number of Germans and Slavs and a sprinkling of British; mainly Scots brought in for their expertise with sheep. Every now and then I would come to a grave bearing the name MacDonald, Sutherland, Scott Campbell, Richards or Williams. The position that an individual had reached in the social order was reflected in the lavishness of their memorial, from the humble Service gravestone of a Stoker 2nd Class killed in the course of his duties to the elaborate mausolea of the great ranching families complete with statuettes of trumpeting angels, flaming torches and ornate urns. Second in prestige to these, were the mausolea of many of the financial and civic institutions all packed around the smartly preserved central area with its topiary cypress trees. At the far end of the graveyard, beyond the individual graves, were the mass mausolea with the same windows that I had seen in La Paz for those who could not afford anything more elaborate. In a shaded spot under an old tree, I found a small but striking memorial to Admiral Graf Spee and the other men lost from the ships of his fleet in a victory and then subsequent defeat during battles for the Falkland Islands in November and December 1914.

One day we drove out to Fuerte Bulnes. A dirt road took us for forty miles south along the shore of the Straits. We sped past isolated shacks, two-room tin or wood shanties, all peeling and fusty. On the seaward side, most of the shacks had fishing boats of varying sizes and condition laid up beside them. Those inland were mostly small holdings with sheep sheds and outhouses. Over the years, as the early leases acquired by the ranching corporations expired, large tracts of the land were split down and re-allocated to individual settlers. Flocks of gulls, terns and pure white kelp geese fed along the shoreline whilst out in the water we could see dolphins diving through the waves.

The Chilean Army have reconstructed the fort on its original site. Perched on a rocky knoll and with commanding views over the Straits of Magellan, palisades made from the trunks of pine trees enclose a collection of accommodation buildings, store rooms, a church and some stables. The fort looks directly across the Straits to the top of Isla Dawson, another place with stories to tell.

Long after Fuerte Bulnes had been abandoned, the Salesian missionaries had brought in Indians and 'civilised them' in the mission that they established there. Later, a prison was built on the island which in its time had housed amongst others the ousted cabinet of Allende's Marxist government. Looking across at the bleak, wind-scoured island, I shuddered at the thought of being incarcerated there for several years as they had been. The long, low shoreline of Tierra del Fuego appeared as a grey smudge on the horizon.

We had reached the end of the road. Only farm tracks lay across the pampas beyond. Twenty-five miles further down the coast a huge cross at Cape Froward marks the southernmost point of the continental landmass. We turned back towards Punta Arenas.

On another day we went out to a Magellanic penguin colony on the shore of Otway Sound. As was becoming all too familiar, we arrived in a howling gale to find squalls of rain sweeping along the shoreline. There were no rocks or cliffs, just flat peaty ground and a shingle beach. I wandered along with my camera at the ready, itching to take classic portraits of penguins. In the face of the winds there were no penguins in sight save for trails of white belly feathers outside their burrows.

Having ascertained that there were no penguins above ground level and with rapidly mounting disappointment I began peering into the burrows. After gazing into a large number of empty holes and despairing of ever seeing so much as a glimpse of a penguin, I found myself looking at four webbed feet below two white feathered and rather stout bodies. Had they been human, the rolls of flesh

and looseness about the stomach would have been called corpulent. A short stubby beak followed by a head appeared under the confined and insufficient height of the burrow. The head turned continuously left and right studying me carefully. And thus we remained for a considerable time with me cold and getting wetter by the moment, willing the penguins to come out so I could get a better look at them and the penguins warm, comfortable and quite sensibly having no intention of moving.

I finally admitted to myself that we had reached an impasse and if I did not move soon I would freeze to the spot. I trudged soggily on to where I could see other clusters of burrows dug into the side of the peat hags. At last my persistence was rewarded by two groups of penguins who emerged to feed and groom each other at the edge of their burrows.

As penguins go, the Magellanic variety are small and plain, nothing like the splendid Emperor penguins of Antarctica. That said, they epitomise the comic image of the penguin with their fat white tummies, giant spectacle-shaped rings around their eyes and stubby black wings which wave around as they waddle along in their curious rolling gait. I took as many photographs as my cold fingers and the limited poses of a group of miserably huddled penguins would allow before returning to the vehicle soaked but happy.

We found the *Beaulieu* tied up alongside the main pier in the harbour. Dwarfed by the naval vessel in the next berth, I had almost missed it amongst the much larger ships and the myriad of fishing boats but then I spotted the name *Beaulieu* on its old orange life preservers. Looking down from the pier it seemed disconcertingly small for a boat that was to carry us into some of the most notorious waters known to sailors. While I waited for the crew to appear, I paced out its length on the pier, 70 feet. That sounded quite a lot but most of the other boats rose far above the pier's wooden decking whilst you had to peer down at the *Beaulieu*.

A head appeared out of a hatchway and after a brief exchange of identities I climbed down a set of wooden steps and onto the steel deck. The engineer showed me around. It did not take long. Every part of the little ship was crowded and cramped. There was a galley that could sit six people at a squash. Next to that a connecting door led through to the wheelhouse in which three people could stand side by side so long as they did not try to move about. These two rooms constituted the only covered area above decks.

At the back, a steel hatch was opened to reveal a steep companionway leading down to the officer's cabin. There were five berths; bare leather banquettes, some of them hinged against the bulkhead, crammed into a space little bigger than their length with a cupboard containing a loo, washbasin and shower. The lockers under each of the bottom bunks were crammed with life jackets and other safety equipment.

Moving forward of the wheelhouse, hatches secured a small hold half-full of 45-gallon drums and two other cabins, one for the remaining members of the crew and one with eight even more microscopic bunks. Access to the engine room remained a mystery but it was somewhere under the galley. Three of us were put into the available spaces in the officer's cabin and the remainder into the eight-man cabin. Given the cramped conditions, I hoped that the weather would be fine enough to enable us to spend much of our time on deck.

With the crew of six, we made a total ship's complement of seventeen. Richard, together with the remaining four members of our team, Andrew having already flown home, would fly down to Puerto Williams. On arrival we would have to apply to the port authorities there for permission for the *Beaulieu* to carry all of us together on the final ten-hour journey to Cape Horn. This would exceed the boat's approved safety limit. If this was not forthcoming, we would have to make the trip in relays. Richard's group would remain with the *Beaulieu* for the sail back to Punta Arenas whilst I, with four others, would fly back from Puerto Williams.

We settled into the little space that we could find. We had been warned to bring minimal equipment over and above sleeping bags and some warm and waterproof clothing. I laid my sleeping bag out on an unoccupied bunk in the officer's cabin which had room for my feet to dangle over the end and was shielded from the bright overhead light by the bunk above.

The remaining members of the crew drifted on board throughout the afternoon and then shortly before our planned departure, the Captain and the boat's owner turned up. After the appropriate introductions and once I had handed over the substantial charter fee, the Captain quickly prepared to get underway.

We cast off and pulled away from the pier at 4 p.m. With a strong tailwind we headed fast down the Straits of Magellan staying close to the mainland shore. We stood on deck watching the land pass by. A variety of sea birds flew by and a school of dolphins congregated just in front of the boat, chasing each other through the waves. They would explode out of a wave in a shower of spray, leaping totally clear of the water and then arc over onto their backs in a flash of black and white before lunging back in again. Underneath the water they flitted about like shadows, changing direction with an amazing speed and adeptness. It appeared a wonderfully carefree and joyous existence.

We passed between the top of Isla Dawson and Fuerte Bulnes as the light was fading. Sadly we would miss Cape Froward in the darkness. In the galley, the ship's cook, a round-faced cheerful soul, produced an excellent spaghetti bolognese and soup, which tasted suspiciously of seaweed, for relays of people. Having taken my turn at the table I went below to find that my bedding had been moved aside and one of the crew had settled into the bunk. The only remaining space was on one of the much smaller top bunks directly under the glaring overhead light and a cold air vent. When I went to sleep, the boat was pitching but not excessively so.

During the night we passed through a narrow channel between Isla Clarence and Isla Capitan Aracena and from there through a series of further channels to Desolation Bay. There had been a fair amount of movement in the water without being anything dramatic. Throughout the morning we crossed the bay and passed through a further series of channels until we reached the western end of the Beagle Channel. A solitary red house sat overlooking the channel. The Captain told us that it was a Chilean naval post for monitoring the shipping, manned by two men at a time on a thirty-day rotation.

To our south, the bare hillsides of the islands were covered with a dusting of snow. To our north, a long peninsula extending westwards from Tierra del Fuego formed a solid barrier. A range of mountains, the Cordillera Darwin, ran the length of the peninsula. Many of the summits rose straight up from the shore to 6,000 feet with the tallest at over 8,000 feet. Much of the range is covered in permanent ice and as we progressed further down the Beagle Channel we could see glaciers spilling down to the water's edge.

During the fine parts of the day I stood on deck watching the islands and mountains slide by. Patches of sunlight and rain chased each other in a never-ending game of cat and mouse. At those times when the storm enveloped us, I retreated to the galley to read my book.

The various members of the team dealt with our incarceration on the boat in their different ways. A couple lay on their bunks willing the pitching to cease when we were in open water. Most moved between the deck, the galley and their bunks depending on the weather. As soon as he had got on board, Corporal Pote had put on a life jacket which he refused to remove wherever he was in the boat. Guardsman McManus maintained a constant vigil from the roof of the wheelhouse. He seemed oblivious to the cold and rain in his determination to spot dolphins, seals and albatrosses.

The Beagle Channel is well sheltered and so our passage was fairly smooth. We passed the lights of the Argentine town of Ushaia at midnight and docked at Puerto Williams in the early hours. After breakfast I went with the Captain of the *Beaulieu* to the Port Captain's office to register and seek clearance to take on the extra men. A naval rating went to fetch the Captain. Our details were taken down and I answered some basic questions about who we were and what we wanted to do.

Looking over the harbour, I could see that there were two jetties. The first, to which we were moored along with a number of fishing vessels, and a second to which was moored what looked to be a World War One battleship which they said that the Chilean Navy had bought from the British. It no longer moved and was itself used as a mooring but the rating told me gleefully that the guns still functioned and could be trained across the Beagle Channel to fire into Argentine territory. Tied up to it were three sleek black patrol boats. A much larger patrol boat was also moored to the second pier.

Having completed our business at the Port Captain's office, we set off in search of Richard and his group. Puerto Williams stretched out in a long line of low buildings. With a population of 1854 according to a sign at the harbour, and a

thousand of those naval personnel on posting, it claims to be the southernmost town in the World. It is a curious place; half modernised for the military and the remainder depressed and dilapidated.

We tried a couple of hosterias with no result and made our way on to the Plaza. It barely warranted the name, a small triangular scrap of ground with a bust of El Libertador bearing the motto 'Live with honour, die with glory', a wooden sign and some garishly painted anchor chain attached to a number of wooden posts. We continued to the rather grandly named Commercial Centre, a square of grass similarly protected by painted chain surrounded by a boardwalk and wooden shops. We located the DAP air charter office and ascertained that they had arrived the previous night and then headed back towards the boat.

On the way we passed the mounted prow of the *Yelcho*, the Chilean naval vessel that had rescued Sir Earnest Shackleton's crew of the *Endurance* in August 1916 from Elephant Island. The story of their rescue was a remarkable one. After the *Endurance* had been caught in the Antarctic pack ice and then crushed until it was totally destroyed, Shackleton and his crew set about making their way, first over the ice and then in boats that they built from the wreckage, towards safety.

Finally, exhausted, after several weeks of terrible effort in appalling conditions battling against winds and tides that carried them in the wrong direction, Shackleton ordered the majority of his men to remain where they had become marooned on Elephant Island. Selecting the fittest, he then made a remarkable journey in an open boat which they sailed and rowed 800 miles across the perilous waters of the southern Atlantic to land on South Georgia. Then in another remarkable feat of determination and fortitude they crossed the heavily glaciated mountain range to reach the whaling station of Grytviken on the far side of the island. From there they were taken to Chile and after several failed attempts by other ships, finally the Chilean cutter *Yelcho* was able to reach and rescue the stranded men on Elephant Island several months after Shackleton had left them.

We found Richard waiting at the dockside. They had arrived late in the evening after a very rough flight and had stayed at a hosteria beside the airport. He had not expected us to arrive so early. As they went to collect their kit, I completed my exploration of the town. Lines of bones lay assembled on the grass in almost complete whale skeletons outside a small wooden chalet. A sign on the door announced that it was the Martin Gusinde Museum.

Inside, along with the inevitable displays of stuffed birds and animals, were a series of early photographs of the indigenous Yahgan Indians. One picture, taken in 1907, showed a group of Yahgans crossing a stretch of tidal river barefooted and dressed only in guanaco skins. It was difficult to comprehend people living in so primitive a manner and in such hostile conditions in modern times. I found it even harder to reconcile the physical evidence of their recent existence with their extinction. The crudely fenced cemetery at the far end of the town contained the grave of the last of the Indians, Rosa Yahgan, who had died in 1983.

Captain Robert Fitzroy of the British ship *Beagle* discovered the nomadic Yahgans in 1830 and had taken four of them to London where they had been educated for two years and were even presented at the Court of King William IV, before being returned to Isla Navarino, on which Puerto Williams is now sited. Unfortunately this attempt at 'civilisation' did not imbue them with a love of Europeans for some years later one of their number, who had been nicknamed Jemmy Buttons by the crew of the *Beagle*, led two attacks against Anglican missionaries killing seven at Banner Cove on Picton Island in 1851 and another four at Wulaia Cove on Isla Navarino in 1859.

As soon as Richard and his group had returned to the boat and installed themselves in the only available space that remained, amongst the fuel drums in the hold, we got under way once again. As we pulled out into the main channel we could appreciate Puerto Williams' position. It was perched on the shore beneath tall forest-clad hills with bare snow-covered summits. Between a gap in these coastal hills, a serrated line of high rock peaks were visible rising up in the centre of the island.

With Puerto Williams dwindling behind us we continued along the Beagle Channel for another two hours. Seals basked on rocks close to the shore of Isla Navarino beside flocks of gulls. Penguins swam in the current and cormorants dived for fish. Just before the conical rock outcrop that was Isla Snipe, we turned south away from the

Beagle Channel and between Isla Navarino and Isla Picton.

The three tiny islands in the mouth of the Beagle Channel, Isla Picton, Isla Lennox and Isla Nueva were the unlikely venue for a gold rush starting in 1890 which brought over 800 prospectors from Europe and the Americas. Later, in common with much of the remainder of the region, the emphasis switched to sheep farming. For over 100 years the delineation of the border between Chile and Argentina had been the subject of passionate dispute between the two countries and nowhere was it more sensitive than in Tierra del Fuego and the surrounding islands. In 1984 Pope John Paul II had to act as mediator to prevent the two countries from going to war over the issue of sovereignty of these three tiny, inhospitable islands.

We turned into Puerto Toro, a sheltered cove at the eastern extremity of Isla Navarino. There were a couple of fishing boats already moored alongside a short jetty. As we motored in, I could see fishermen repairing crab pots and some uniformed men strolling about. Near the waterfront there were a couple of buildings which looked like warehouses and offices for the 100 strong naval detachment, a Carabineros post and a number of huts scattered up the hill behind, which were used seasonally by the fishermen. The long-legged, spiny, pink carapaces of king crabs decorated many of the doorways.

Our plan was to spend a few hours here and then start out after dark, cross the open water of the Bay of Nassau to another safe harbour in the Wollaston Islands and from there make a dash to Cape Horn when the weather allowed. With a few hours to kill I got off the boat and went for a walk. The warm afternoon sun cast a rich yellow light over the island.

I wandered around to the far side of the inlet to photograph the *Beaulieu* berthed against the pier. I crossed a tiny shingle beach and then followed a faint but discernible track onto an equally tiny peninsula, no more than a bump of land with a few trees and bushes on it. It was only 20 yards across at its widest point. I was surprised by a heron which flew out from beneath a rock at my feet. The ground was carpeted in a springy plant coated in minute red berries. As I bent down to photograph it, I noticed that turfs had been freshly cut and moved. Looking closer, they had been draped over a mound to conceal it. Being naturally inquisitive,

I went to investigate, and found myself looking at a shallow trench with a corrugated iron roof which had been camouflaged. Scouting around I found several more. They had been recently prepared which suggested that the Chileans still took the threat to their sovereignty seriously.

Continuing my walk, I made my way up between the huts to the Carabineros Post at the top of the settlement. It had a fantastic view across the bay and for several miles along the coastline. Sergeant Alan Bissett came up to join me and we stood taking our photographs and chatting. With plenty of daylight left we decided to try and explore a bit more of the island and so took off up a track that we had seen leading into the country from the back of one of the huts. It was not much of a path, narrow and muddy, but we followed it up the hill behind the village as much for the exercise as anything else. As we arrived at the top we came upon a camouflage net and then fifty yards beyond another. Concealed beneath the nets were artillery guns. They were far from modern but they were properly dug in, reinforced with sandbags and greased up ready for action. Behind, there were locked metal sea containers, also camouflaged, which presumably held the ammunition. We walked on past the end of the track. The country alternated between open bog and woodland. A beaver's dam formed a pool in one of the streams. I longed to explore further but somewhat concerned by what we had seen and with the nagging question in our minds whether there might be protective mines sown in the area, we made our way back to the boat.

The harbour was a picture of tranquillity. After supper, the navigator came into the galley where I was reading and said that the weather around Cape Horn was bad with 60mph winds and waves 12-15 feet high in the open water. It promised to be an eventful night.

The *Beaulieu* pulled out at midnight. The first couple of hours were smooth as we motored through Paso Goree between Isla Navarino and Isla Lennox but as we moved out into the unprotected waters of the Bay of Nassau we were exposed to the full effects of the weather. For the next two hours, as we ran for the cover of the Wollaston Islands, I could feel the boat pitching through the waves, raising up and slamming back down onto the water with a jar that ran right through the vessel. Having reached Cape Ross at the top end of the main island, we crept south in the lee of the landmass. By 6 a.m. we were crossing the southern end of the island. The wind was fierce, shrieking around the little boat but still the Captain continued south along Paso al Mar del Sur, the Pass to the Southern Sea. We moved down the side of Herschel Island and then anchored in a sheltered bay to take stock of the situation. The Captain radioed to the Chilean Naval Mission on Isla Hornos for a local weather check. Back from what must be the loneliest of outposts came the reply; 40 knot winds from the west equivalent to Force 8 on the Beaufort Scale. Both Captain and navigator were adamant that we should not attempt to go around the Horn in those conditions. It was not so much the wind as the size of the waves that it was creating that they were worried about. We settled down to wait.

Even in the lee of Herschel Island strong winds were blowing up waves around us. I watched a cormorant desperately battling its way towards the coastline. Despite beating its wings as fast as it could, it was making precious little headway. The sun rose over the long low lozenge of Deceit Island immediately to our east and a school of dolphins gambolled around the boat. As the morning went on, the weather conditions deteriorated.

We had hoped to either sail around the Horn or, better still, to anchor in one of the bays of Isla Hornos and land using the *Beaulieu*'s dinghy. There was a low hill at the southern end which I wanted to climb so that we could look out towards Antarctica from the true southernmost point of the Americas. From our safe anchorage behind Herschel Island it was no more than six miles away but with the prevailing weather conditions pinning us down it might have been on the other side of the Moon.

We ate lunch having still not moved. Shortly afterwards I went with Charlie Andrews to talk to the Captain. Having got a fresh weather report he reiterated that it was impossible to try and reach the Horn. Even if we could have got there, the swell would have made a landing out of the question. The wind might blow for two more hours or two more days before it died down but with the barometer dropping steadily the prognosis was not good.

There was one compromise option if all else failed and that was to use the dinghy to land on Herschel Island from our present position and walk the couple of miles across to the South side of the island from where we could at least see Cape Horn.

As Charlie and I discussed this idea the Captain and navigator started conferring between themselves. Just as we were about to go and round up the team and start implementing this plan, they said that they would take the ship as far down Paso al Mar del Sur as they safely could from where we would be able to see the Horn. I gratefully accepted this suggestion and with the decision taken, they began to get the ship underway.

I dashed down to my bunk to grab my camera and pull on some protective clothing and then went to the hold and forward cabin to rouse the others. Looking out into the passage, we could see much larger waves amidst a haze of spray. The *Beaulieu* edged out of the bay and down the side of Herschel Island. We passed another bay and then one more. There was a large rock, almost a small island, splitting the channel at its mouth. Past the end of the two islands we could see huge green, white-capped waves out in the open water and beyond that the outline of Isla Hornos against the grey sky. Part of the island was shielded from us by the two islands either side of us, but what we could see started low in the east and climbed up gradually to a high point. With the wind gathering speed all the time, I had to brace myself against the guard rail to steady my camera.

I called everyone together for a final team photo, having to yell to make myself heard above the wind. As everyone huddled around the bow with the Union Jack and Household Division flags a massive squall hit us sending waves crashing across the deck. There was water flying in every direction. The centre of the boat was being swept by waves and the air was white with spray. The front of the boat was pitching up and down, rearing high above the waves before plummeting back down into the next.

We must have looked insane to the crew watching from the glassed protection of the wheelhouse, as we clung to the rail, lashed by spray, riding the storm. With Isla Hornos now totally obliterated from sight we seized the moment, timing the break in the waves and dashed back to the safety of the galley. I felt totally exhilarated. Our bodies, cameras and clothes were soaked and our hands and faces frozen but we had seen the Horn. The *Beaulieu* hauled around and turned back north. We had reached Latitude 55 53'South and Longitude 67 11'30" West. It was as far as we could get from Point Barrow.

We kept in the lee of the Wollaston Islands as far as it was possible and then broke back out into open water in the Bay of Nassau. Struck by the full force of the westerly wind, which was increasing in ferocity all the time, the boat corkscrewed and slewed through the waves. Lying on my bunk watching the water sloshing across the porthole and the lights swaying around with the motion of the boat, I began to feel decidedly queasy. The storm continued to increase in ferocity and I had to cling on tight to my bunk to stop myself being hurled against the bulkhead.

After a couple of hours I had to get up to have a pee and was ricocheted off the four walls of the tiny lavatory for my trouble. I returned to the relative safety of my bunk and lay listening to the noises of the boat as it fought its way on towards the sheltered water ahead: the insistent droning of the engine, the crash of each wave as it resonated through the steel hull and the continual creaking and banging of the superstructure.

Some time later, around 10 p.m., we berthed at Puerto Toro. The quiet and cessation of bouncing and lurching came as a blessed relief. People began to emerge from all quarters of the boat. Guardsman McManus and a couple of the others claimed to have remained above decks throughout and were describing the size of the waves and the boat's more extreme movements. Charlie Andrews had spent most of the time in the wheelhouse where he said that the Captain had been taking photographs as the boat listed thirty degrees to either side. He and the navigator had worked hard at the wheel to counter the action of the 15-foot waves and winds of 50-60 knots, Force 11 on the Beaufort scale. Richard had stayed in the galley where Charlie said that he had stared fixedly out of the same window, keeping his eyes on the horizon, for two hours. A couple of soldiers had been sick, as had the cook.

After a good night's rest we had an uneventful passage west along the Beagle Channel to Puerto Williams. It was a grey, heavily overcast day which reflected my rather melancholic mood. The journey was over. I thanked the captain and crew and disembarked with my group leaving the remainder to carry on to Punta Arenas on board the *Beaulieu*.

The twin-engined aircraft lifted off, taking us on

the first leg of our journey back to England. As we flew over the spiders web of peaks, glaciers and snow-covered ridges that make up the Cordillera Darwin, Point Barrow and Mt McKinley seemed very far away both in time and distance; yet culturally and climatically, although at the other end of two continents, they were not that far removed.

How far had we come? Each one of us had made our common but different journeys and undoubtedly bore the indelible marks of them within us. Exposing oneself to a challenge where there is no guarantee of success and every likelihood of the embarrassment of failure is ultimately an enriching experience. The lessons can be hard learnt and the futility of one's best efforts humiliating but the knowledge and self esteem gained from merely trying, from putting oneself on the line and taking the knocks along the way, leave you stronger and more capable to meet the challenges of the future.

The value of an expedition is not just in the travel or the exhilarating adventures that you encounter but the trials and tribulations, the moral and physical dilemmas, the triumphs and disasters and the path that it leads into your own soul. Returning to the so-called real world, I felt like a bird who had flown free but was now to be put back in my gilded cage.

Epilogue

It is impossible to quantify the value of the expedition. We achieved all of the goals that we set ourselves which we were able to attempt. We reached the northernmost, westernmost and southernmost points in North and South America; climbed the highest summits in each continent; kayaked and rafted the wildest rivers and ventured deep into the jungle. Mercifully, no serious casualties were sustained in the pursuit of these goals.

As each team returned to England at the end of their phase, the soldiers dispersed to their regiments to resume their normal military lives. Many of the 92 people who took part in the expedition have moved on to new posts and been promoted. Once again it is not possible to evaluate to what extent the experiences gained on the expedition contribute to an individual's future performance or enhance their chances of early promotion.

Since the expedition, members of the team have served in a variety of trouble spots around the World. At times it goes against every natural instinct to stand up and confront the situations that you encounter in such places and we expect soldiers and commanders as young as eighteen years old to do so. Whilst the British Army remains committed to active service tasks, the character development and leadership training inherent to Adventure Training and expeditions of this kind will continue to have a direct relevance.

We visited many countries and areas that in recent times had been closed to British military expeditions and forged links, albeit at a low level, with the foreign militarys of several of our host countries. In the case of Argentina, it was particularly satisfying to establish friendships amongst people we had previously regarded as enemies.

Amazingly, given our precarious finances during the expedition, we not only returned in funds but went on through the generous offices of our sponsors to raise over £30,000 for our charitable beneficiary, The Midlands Centre for Spinal Injuries.

Once the Post Expedition Report was written, the accounts audited and all the equipment returned to Army stores, the permanent cadre also dispersed. Richard Gaffney reverted to his original plan and left the Army to read law. Mike Charlson also left the Army and headed to New Zealand to take up a doctoring post. Andrew Phasey returned to his regiment in the post of Quartermaster, a well deserved promotion following his huge logistic effort. Corporal Mark Jordan was delighted to be posted back to a Cavalry Regiment. He recently wrote to me from Mrkonjic Grad where he is working as Squadron Clerk. Corporal John Steggles is working as a clerk within a large headquarters. Having married his fiancée, he is now attempting to gain an attachment to the Army Air Corps as a trainee helicopter pilot.

I decided that after fourteen years extremely happy service in the Army it was time to move on and hope to pursue photography and writing full-time. A year after returning from Chile, on top of a hill in Wales, Louie accepted my proposal of marriage.

Appendix

Team Members

PHASE 1 TEAM

In Alaska:
Permanent Cadre:
Captain John Warburton-Lee	Welsh Guards
Captain Richard Gaffney	Welsh Guards
Captain Mike Charlson	Royal Army Medical Corps
Colour Sergeant Charlie McKeown	Scots Guards
Lance-Corporal John Steggles	Adjutant-General's Corps

Quartermaster:
Captain Andrew Phasey	Grenadier Guards

Phase Team:
Major Dougie MacDonald	Royal Army Veterinary Corps
Lieutenant Andrew Holman	Blues & Royals
Lance-Sergeant John Dyer	Irish Guards
Lance-Sergeant Wayne Scully	Grenadier Guards
Lance-Corporal Paul Martin	Royal Electrical & Mechanical Engineers
Lance-Corporal Glyn Painter	Coldstream Guards
Lance-Corporal Timothy Pearse	Household Cavalry Mounted Regiment
Lance-Corporal Kevin Shaw	Scots Guards
Lance-Corporal Alan Ordish	Welsh Guards
Guardsman Nicholas Perry	Irish Guards
Guardsman Thomas Miller	Scots Guards
Guardsman Ceri Thomas	Welsh Guards
Guardsman Jason Manassie	Scots Guards
Guardsman Justin Owen	Welsh Guards
Trooper Kieron Canning	Household Cavalry Regiment

Dog sledding instructor:
Mr Roy Monk

In England:
Major George Doughty	Territorial Army
Lance-Sergeant Mark Jordan	Adjutant-General's Corps

PHASE 2 TEAM

In North America:
Permanent Cadre:
Captain John Warburton-Lee	Welsh Guards
Captain Richard Gaffney	Welsh Guards
Captain Mike Charlson	Royal Army Medical Corps
Colour Sergeant Charlie McKeown	Scots Guards
Lance-Corporal John Steggles	Adjutant-General's Corps

Phase Team:
Lieutenant Sandy Carrick-Buchanan	Scots Guards
Second Lieutenant Charlie Morgan	Welsh Guards
Colour Sergeant Pete Richardson	Coldstream Guards
Colour Sergeant Craig Offless	Parachute Regiment
Corporal of Horse Andy Wells	Household Cavalry Mounted Regiment
Lance-Sergeant Andrew Brown	Welsh Guards
Lance-Sergeant Anthony Brown	Welsh Guards
Corporal Taff Mason	Parachute Regiment
Lance-Corporal Andy Howard	Royal Electrical & Mechanical Engineers
Lance-Corporal Jason McCauley	Household Cavalry Mounted Regiment
Lance-Corporal Paul Allison	Household Cavalry Regiment
Guardsman Nigel Davies	Welsh Guards
Guardsman Wayne Davidson	Coldstream Guards
Guardsman John Cardwell	Irish Guards
Guardsman Danny Brown	Irish Guards
Guardsman Simon Elms	Irish Guards
Trooper Paul Roskell	Household Cavalry Regiment

In England:

Major George Doughty	Territorial Army
Captain Andrew Phasey	Grenadier Guards
Lance-Sergeant Mark Jordan	Adjutant-General's Corps

PHASE 3 TEAM

In North America:
Permanent Cadre:

Captain John Warburton-Lee	Welsh Guards
Captain Richard Gaffney	Welsh Guards
Captain Mike Charlson	Royal Army Medical Corps
Colour Sergeant Charlie McKeown	Scots Guards
Lance-Corporal John Steggles	Adjutant-General's Corps

Phase Team:

Captain Simon Gammell	Grenadier Guards
Lieutenant James McBrien	Irish Guards
Sergeant Andy Everett	Royal Electrical & Mechanical Engineers
Lance-Corporal of Horse Simon Knowles	Household Cavalry Mounted Regiment
Lance-Corporal Ivan Key	Grenadier Guards
Lance-Corporal Carl Woodward	Welsh Guards
Lance-Corporal Andrew MacConnachie	Scots Guards
Lance-Corporal Alan MacDonald	Royal Electrical & Mechanical Engineers
Guardsmen Andrew Jamieson	Scots Guards
Guardsman Scott Wilson	Scots Guards
Guardsman Peter Rylands	Grenadier Guards
Guardsman James Montgomerie	Scots Guards
Guardsman James McIlvogue	Welsh Guards
Guardsman Scott Cartwright	Irish Guards
Trooper Clive Spencer	Household Cavalry Mounted Regiment

Grand Canyon Raft Guides and boatmen:
Dick McCullum
Geoff Gourley
Martha Clark
Carol Fritzinger
Doug Mallock
Dale Strout
Dirk Pratley
Fred Hopi
Robin Hopi

In England:

Major George Doughty	Territorial Army
Captain Andrew Phasey	Grenadier Guards
Lance-Sergeant Mark Jordan	Adjutant-General's Corps

PHASE 4 TEAM

In Guyana:
Permanent Cadre:

Captain John Warburton-Lee	Welsh Guards
Captain Richard Gaffney	Welsh Guards
Captain Mike Charlson	Royal Army Medical Corps
Captain Andrew Phasey	Grenadier Guards
Colour Sergeant Charlie McKeown	Scots Guards
Lance-Sergeant Mark Jordan	Adjutant-General's Corps

Phase Team:

Lieutenant James Geddes	Grenadier Guards
Lieutenant David Avis	Life Guards
Staff Corporal Anthony Tate	Household Cavalry Regiment
Sergeant Pete Griffiths	Welsh Guards
Sergeant Nigel Nettlefield	Royal Electrical & Mechanical Engineers
Lance-Corporal of Horse David Stevens	Household Cavalry Mounted Regiment
Lance-Corporal of Horse Richard Gallagher	Household Cavalry Regiment
Corporal John Pozzi	Royal Electrical & Mechanical Engineers
Lance-Corporal Bob Bullock	Grenadier Guards
Lance-Corporal Derek Mann	Coldstream Guards
Lance-Corporal Dean Williams	Welsh Guards
Guardsman Andrew Harburn	Irish Guards
Guardsman Derek Turner	Irish Guards
Guardsman Mark Scruton	Grenadier Guards
Guardsman Mark Lundy	Coldstream Guards

Guyanese Defence Force:
Lieutenant Jervis

Staff Sergeant Sanmoogan
Staff Sergeant James
Sergeant Johnson

In England:
Major George Doughty   Territorial Army
Lance-Corporal John Steggles   Adjutant-General's Corps

PHASE 5 TEAM

In South America:
Permanent Cadre:
Captain John Warburton-Lee   Welsh Guards
Captain Richard Gaffney   Welsh Guards
Captain Mike Charlson   Royal Army Medical Corps
Colour Sergeant Charlie McKeown   Scots Guards
Lance-Corporal John Steggles   Adjutant-General's Corps

Phase Team:
Second Lieutenant Bruce MacInnes   Welsh Guards
Staff Sergeant Eddie Devaney   Royal Electrical & Mechanical Engineers
Staff Corporal Anthony Tate   Household Cavalry Regiment
Lance-Sergeant Paul Moffett   Irish Guards
Lance-Sergeant Steve Hill   Irish Guards
Corporal Dougie Wilson   Royal Electrical & Mechanical Engineers
Lance-Corporal Spencer Wright   Coldstream Guards
Lance-Corporal Lee Vickers   Grenadier Guards
Guardsman David Bowness   Coldstream Guards
Guardsman Paul Curran   Irish Guards
Guardsman Neil Lawrie   Scots Guards
Guardsman Johnny Lynn   Scots Guards
Guardsman Mickey Purtell   Irish Guards
Trooper Robert Amos   Household Cavalry Mounted Regiment

Argentine Army:
Major Jose Hernandez
Captain Riccardo Juarez
Lieutenant Oprandi
Lieutenant Javier Salgado
Sergeant Rouk
Sergeant Rios
Sergeant Bulacious
Corporal Sosa

In England:
Major George Doughty   Territorial Army
Captain Andrew Phasey   Grenadier Guards
Lieutenant David Avis   Household Cavalry Regiment
Lance-Sergeant Mark Jordan   Adjustant-General's Corps

PHASE 6 TEAM

In Chile:
Permanent Cadre:
Captain John Warburton-Lee, Welsh Guards, Expedition Leader
Captain Richard Gaffney, Welsh Guards, Deputy Expedition Leader
Captain Mike Charlson, Royal Army Medical Corps, Expedition Doctor
Colour Sergeant Charlie McKeown, Scots Guards, Equipment Manager
Lance-Corporal John Steggles, Adjutant-General's Corps, Clerk & Video

Phase Team:
Lieutenant Charlie Andrews, Scots Guards
Lance-Sergeant Alan Bissett, Grenadier Guards
Lance-Corporal Christopher Gillham, Grenadier Guards
Lance-Corporal Wayne Bell, Coldstream Guards
Lance-Corporal Paul Holmes, Grenadier Guards
Lance-Corporal Colin Pote, Coldstream Guards
Lance-Corporal Nathan Allan, Coldstream Guards
Guardsman Alan Hanger, Coldstream Guards
Guardsman Stephen McManus, Scots Guards
Guardsman Shaun Nelson, Irish Guards
Craftsman Lee Smith, Royal Electrical & Mechanical Engineers

In England:
Captain Andrew Phasey, Grenadier Guards, Expedition Quartermaster
Captain Christopher Daly, Household Cavalry Regiment
Lieutenant David Avis, Household Cavalry Regiment
Lance-Sergeant Mark Jordan, Adjutant-General's Corps, Clerk

Index